Y0-BVN-946

Cross-National Research in Self-Reported Crime and Delinquency

NATO ASI Series

Advanced Science Institutes Series

A Series presenting the results of activities sponsored by the NATO Science Committee, which aims at the dissemination of advanced scientific and technological knowledge, with a view to strengthening links between scientific communities.

The Series is published by an international board of publishers in conjunction with the NATO Scientific Affairs Division

A Life Sciences	Plenum Publishing Corporation
B Physics	London and New York
C Mathematical	Kluwer Academic Publishers
and Physical Sciences	Dordrecht, Boston and London
D Behavioural and Social Sciences	
E Applied Sciences	
F Computer and Systems Sciences	Springer-Verlag
G Ecological Sciences	Berlin, Heidelberg, New York, London,
H Cell Biology	Paris and Tokyo

Series D: Behavioural and Social Sciences - Vol. 50

Cross-National Research in Self-Reported Crime and Delinquency

edited by

Malcolm W. Klein

Center for Research on Crime and Social Control,
Social Science Research Institute,
University of Southern California,
Los Angeles, U.S.A.

HV
6018
,N38
1988
West

Kluwer Academic Publishers

Dordrecht / Boston / London

Published in cooperation with NATO Scientific Affairs Division

Proceedings of the NATO Advanced Research Workshop on
Self-Report Methodology in Criminological Research
Noordwijkerhout, The Netherlands
26–30 June, 1988

Library of Congress Cataloging in Publication Data

```
NATO Advanced Research Workshop on Self-Report Methodology in
  Criminological Research (1988 : Noordwijkerhout, Netherlands)
    Cross-national research in self-reported crime and delinquency /
edited by Malcolm W. Klein.
      p.   cm. -- (NATO ASI series. Series D, Behavioural and social
sciences ; no. 50)
    "Published in cooperation with NATO Scientific Affairs Division."
    "Proceedings of the NATO Advanced Research Workshop on Self-Report
Methodology in Criminological Research, Noordwijkerhout, The
Netherlands, 26-30 June, 1988"--T.p. verso.
    ISBN 0-7923-0345-8 (U.S.)
    1. Criminal statistics--Evaluation--Congresses.   I. Klein,
Malcolm W.  II. North Atlantic Treaty Organization.  Scientific
Affairs Division.   III. Title.   IV. Series.
HV6018.N38  1988
364'.042'072--dc19                                        89-15318
```

ISBN 0–7923–0345–8

Published by Kluwer Academic Publishers,
P.O. Box 17, 3300 AA Dordrecht, The Netherlands.

Kluwer Academic Publishers incorporates the publishing programmes of
D. Reidel, Martinus Nijhoff, Dr W. Junk and MTP Press.

Sold and distributed in the U.S.A. and Canada
by Kluwer Academic Publishers,
101 Philip Drive, Norwell, MA 02061, U.S.A.

In all other countries, sold and distributed
by Kluwer Academic Publishers Group,
P.O. Box 322, 3300 AH Dordrecht, The Netherlands.

Printed on acid free paper

All Rights Reserved
© 1989 by Kluwer Academic Publishers
No part of the material protected by this copyright notice may be reproduced or
utilized in any form or by any means, electronic or mechanical, including photo-
copying, recording or by any information storage and retrieval system, without written
permission from the copyright owner.

Printed in The Netherlands

for

Margy Gatz,

Cross-National Scholar,
Colleague, and Companion

TABLE OF CONTENTS

PARTICIPANTS: NATO ADVANCED RESEARCH WORKSHOP

Professor Hans-Jorg Albrecht
Max Planck Institute
Gunterstalstrasse 73
D-7800 Freiburg im Breisgau
FEDERAL REPUBLIC OF GERMANY

Professor Anthony Bottoms
Institute of Criminology
Cambridge University
7 West Road
Cambridge CB3 9DT
UNITED KINGDOM

Dr. Amelia Diaz Martinez
Facultad de Psicologia
Depart de Personalidad
Universitat de Valencia
Valencia
SPAIN

Dr. Jan van Dijk, Director
Research and Documentation Center
Ministry of Justice
Postbox 20301
2500 EH The Hague
THE NETHERLANDS

Dr. Delbert S. Elliott
Institute of Behavioral Science
University of Colorado
Campus Box 483
Boulder   CO 80309
USA

Dr. Uberto Gatti
Institute of Criminal Anthropology
University of Genoa
Via detoni 12
16132 Genoa
ITALY

Dr. Ulla Bondeson
Kriminalistisk Institut
Kobenhavns Universitet
Sankt Peders Straede 19
DK-1453 Kobenhavn K
DENMARK

Dr. Gerben J. W. Bruinsma
Faculty of Public Administration
University of Twente
Postbox 217
7500 AE Enschede
THE NETHERLANDS

Professor Paul Dickes
Centre d'Etudes de Populations de
Pauvrete et de Politiques
   Sociales
B.P. 65
L-7201 Walferdange
LUXEMBOURG

Dr. Fokke Dijksterhuis
Criminologisch Instituut
Rijksuniversiteit Groningen
Haddingestraat 2
9711 KD Groningen
THE NETHERLANDS

Dr. David Farrington
Institute of Criminology
Cambridge University
7 West Road
Cambridge CB3 9DT
UNITED KINGDOM

Dr. Timothy Hartnagel
Department of Sociology
University of Alberta
Edmonton, Alberta T6G 2H4
CANADA

Dr. David Huizinga
Institute of Behavioral Science
University of Colorado
Campus Box 483
Boulder   CO 80309
USA

Marianne Junger
Research and Documentation Center
Postbus 20301
Ministry of Justice
2500 EH The Hague
THE NETHERLANDS

Professor Martin Killias
Faculty of Law
University of Lausanne
Place du Chateau
CH-1005 Lausanne
SWITZERLAND

Dr. Britta Kyvsgaard
Kriminalistisk Institut
Kobenhavns Universitet
Sankt Peder Straede 19
DK-1453 Kobenhavn K
DENMARK

Professor Rolf Loeber
Western Psychiatric Institute
University of Pittsburgh
3811 O'Hara Street
Pittsburgh   PA 15213
USA

Professor Anastasios Marcos
The American College of Greece
Aghin Paraskevi Atikis 153 10
GREECE

Professor Carl-Gunnar Janson
Department of Sociology
Stockholms Universitet
S-106 91 Stockholm
SWEDEN

Dr. Josine Junger-Tas
Research and Documentation Center
Postbus 20301
Ministry of Justice
2500 EH The Hague
THE NETHERLANDS

Professor Malcolm W. Klein
Center for Research on Crime and
   Social Control
Social Science Research Institute
University of Southern California
Los Angeles CA 90089-1111
USA

Dr. Marc Le Blanc
Ecole de psycho-education
Universite de Montreal
750 Blv. Gouin, est
Montreal, Quebec H2C 1A6
CANADA

Professor Friedrich Losel
Institut fur Psychologie I
Der Universitat Erlangen-Nurnberg
Bismarckstrasse 1
D-8520 Erlangen
FEDERAL REPUBLIC OF GERMANY

Dr. Terrie E. Moffitt
Department of Psychology
University of Wisconsin
1202 West Johnson Street
Madison WI 53706   USA
USA

Ms. Joy Mott
Home Office
Research and Planning Unit
Queen Anne's Gate
London SW1H 9AT
UNITED KINGDOM

Dr. Dan Olweus
Department of Personality Psychology
University of Bergen
Oysteinsgate 3
N 5000 Bergen
NORWAY

Professor Carl-Heinz Reuband
Zentralarchiv fur Empirische
   Sozialforschung
University zu Koln
Bachemer Strasse 40
5000 Koln 41
FEDERAL REPUBLIC OF GERMANY

Dr. Margaret Shaw
3425 Avenue de Vendome
Notre Dame de Grace
Montreal H4A 3M6
Quebec
CANADA

Professor Terence Thornberry
School of Criminal Justice
State University of New York
   at Albany
135 Western Avenue
Albany NY 12222
USA

Professor Bernhard Villmow
Facultat fur Rechtswissenschaften
Universitat Hamburg
Van-Melle-Park
2000 Hamburg 13
FEDERAL REPUBLIC OF GERMANY

Dr. Per-Olof Wikstrom
Brottesforebyggande radet
Atlasmuren 1, 2 tr
113 21 Stockholm
SWEDEN

Dr. Jan Nijboer
Criminologisch Instituut
Rijksuniversiteit Groningen
Haddingestraat 2
9711 KD Groningen
THE NETHERLANDS

Professor Albert J. Reiss
Department of Sociology
Yale University
Yale Station, Box 19165
New Haven   CT   06520
USA

Dr. Jerzy Sarnecki
Brottsforebyggande radet
Atlasmuren 1, 2 tr
113 21 Stockholm
SWEDEN

Professor Peter Sutterer
Max Planck Institut
Gunterstalstrasse 73
D-7800 Freiburg im Breisgau
FEDERAL REPUBLIC OF GERMANY

Professor Jacques Van Kerckvoorde
Faculteit Rechtsgeleerdheid
Katholieke Universiteit Leuven
Blijde Inkomststraat 5
3000 Leuven
BELGIUM

Mr. Elmar Weitekamp
Sellin Center for Criminology
University of Pennsylvania
3733 Spruce Street
Philadelphia PA 19104
USA

Dr. Haluk Yavuzer
Child Psychology and Education
   Department
University of Istanbul
Bayazit, Istanbul
TURKEY

INTRODUCTION

Malcolm W. Klein
Center for Research on Crime and Social Control
University of Southern California

1. BACKGROUND

In June of 1988, approximately forty scholars and researchers met
for four days in the Leeuwenhorst Congres Center in Noordwijkerhout, The
Netherlands, to participate in a workshop entitled Self-Report Methodology in Criminological Research. The participants represented 15
nations and 30 universities and research centers, a diversity that was
matched by the experiences and focal interests in self-report methods
among the participants. This volume is the result of the workshop
process and in particular of the invitations to participants to prepare
pre-conference papers for distribution prior to the workshop. The
chapters in the volume were selected from the larger set of pre-
conference papers.

As workshop convener and volume editor, it falls on me to set some
of the context for this enterprise.

Self-report crime is "admitted" crime, derived from interview and
questionnaire responses obtained from adults and juveniles (regardless
of whether or not they have been arrested) concerning their own illegal
behaviors. Growing awareness of the limitations of official crime
statistics has led to the development of self-report procedures.
Despite the lack of standardization, these procedures are coming to be
used widely, and this is an opportune time to take stock of the state
of the art and foster improvement. Self-report questions can cover a
wide variety of offending behaviors, over varying periods of time,
sometimes connecting those behaviors to peer associates or other contextual matters including official arrest and court action. Most self-
report research has been carried out with juveniles, and this fact is
reflected in many of the papers contained herein. My own concentration
on issues of delinquency over the years may also have contributed to
this balance. It certainly is responsible for the initiation of the
workshop.

In the mid-1970s, my students and I launched a rather ambitious
program to evaluate the effectiveness of police practices in diverting
juvenile offenders away from the justice system. Outcome measures
based on subsequent arrest data indicated dramatic differences in

1

M. W. Klein (ed.), Cross-National Research in Self-Reported Crime and Delinquency, 1–13.
© *1989 by Kluwer Academic Publishers.*

recidivism rates between randomly assigned (1) non-diverted offenders, (2) those diverted to treatment programs, and (3) those diverted without further action. But fortunately we also gathered self-report data over a 27-month follow-up period, and these showed no significant differences across the three randomly assigned groups. Youth behaviors were not differentially affected by the assignment conditions; police responses were affected (Klein, 1986). The presence of the self-report data saved us from drawing some very erroneous conclusions; the contrast between the self-report and arrest data allowed us to understand far better the processes of recidivism and some of their determinants. Ever since, I have lit a candle at the altar of self-report methods.

A second personal involvement was in the publication of Western Systems of Juvenile Justice (Klein, 1984) which marked something of a turning point in comparative studies of delinquency. Despite several U.N. publications (Stewart, 1978, 1982), this was the first compilation of structural depictions of juvenile justice systems, written by experts from their own nations, with each depiction speaking to common issues of system structure, discretion, cross-system connections, diversion programs, demographic characteristics of offenders, and political trends. However, the readiness with which experts could provide comparable structural descriptions highlighted the problems of achieving equally comparable cross-national compilations of the behaviors to which the juvenile justice systems respond. Preliminary conversations with these writers and other researchers in various countries underscored the need to develop data systems capable of yielding cross-national delinquency descriptions which might lead to more effective approaches to prevention and control. Three approaches are possible.

First, victimization studies have advanced to the point that comparable data are beginning to emerge (e.g., U.S., Canada, U.K.). But these are very expensive and clearly least useful for incidents involving juveniles as perpetrators (Lynch, 1986). The second and most common approach is the use of official arrest or court statistics, and the third is the use of the rapidly developing self-report methodology.

With the exception of some comparative work in the Scandinavian countries (e.g., see Greve, 1974, and Hauge, 1983 and the references therein), most of the countries represented in the Workshop, as reported by the participants themselves, have produced very few self-report studies and therefore not much progress in methodology. It may seem odd -- or arrogant -- for an American to convene a European self-report conference, but there are good reasons beyond those of personal interest.

a. The U.S. lives with the different penal codes of 50 states, the District of Columbia, and the federal government. Police and court records reflect major statutory differences which can to a considerable extent be overcome by use of a single, uniform self-report instrument. A good example is provided by the instrument developed for the National Youth Survey (Elliott and Ageton, 1980). The U.S. needs and therefore has developed relatively sophisticated approaches.

b. In comparison with some European countries and particularly the Scandinavian countries, U.S. researchers do not have available to them comprehensive and reliable data registers on U.S. residents. In the juvenile area, our records are normally sealed or purged at the point of adulthood. Self-report procedures can fill some of the resulting vacuum.

c. Our national-level records, such as the FBI's Uniform Crime Reports, merely aggregate the data, and therefore the errors and gaps, contained in local records. Self-report avoids this problem.

d. The emphasis on the protection of civil rights in the U.S. often leads to the denial of official records to researchers. Within the limits of Human Subjects confidentiality guarantees imposed upon our researchers, self-report allows access to data denied in police and court records.

e. The U.S., more perhaps than any other nation, has devoted a great deal of attention and resources to the empirical evaluation of crime prevention and control programs. Such programs run by or account-able to the justice system agencies most properly should be evaluated using data not controlled by those agencies. To evaluate a police project using the police department's own collected data raises serious questions of redundancy, tautology, and even ethics. Self-report data permit the maintainence of an independent approach to assessment.

Still, the fact that more developmental work has been necessitated by the American research context does not make the U.S. unique, nor does it suggest that American solutions will necessarily apply well to other nations or, in the case of the goals of this workshop and volume, to cross-national studies. The problems of official statistics inevita-bly reflect nation-specific histories, values, penal codes, and institu-tional needs, and are compounded in direct proportion to the number of nations involved (Bayley, 1985). Official statistics are invariably incomplete due to problems in recording procedures. Self-report instru-ments, especially as developed by Elliott and Ageton (1980), have proven their capacity to surmount at least some of the problems associ-ated with official data sources and avoid some biases often noted in official statistics. Compared to self-report, official sources greatly underestimate delinquency prevalence and incidence, greatly underesti-mate involvement in serious offenses, overstate differentials by age, race, sex, and social class, and tend to overstate the effectiveness of prevention and control programs (Elliott, Huizinga, and Morse, 1987; Elliott and Huizinga, 1984; Klein, 1986).

The most recent studies of self-report methodology (Hirschi, Hinde-lang, & Weis, 1980; Hindelang, Hirschi, and Weis, 1981) have conclud-ed that self-report advantages over official statistics from police and courts include more sensitivity to the broad spectrum of delinquent behavior, more flexibility of application to varying research needs, greater detail about the offense situation, and greater validity. The reliability and validity estimates were found to be equivalent to those of many standardized social science instruments, and "remarkably consis-tent over time, place, and procedure." However, these two extensive reviews include bibliographies in which only three of 32 and eleven of 168 references are to non-U.S. writings. Crossnational exploration requires a major initiative.

4

2. WORKSHOP FOCUS

While the newer self-report methods provide major advances over the use of police and court statistics, they raise other problems for cross-national research which require our focused attention. For example:

1. <u>Conceptual Equivalence</u>: this issue includes the questions of what behaviors are criminalized, how they are categorized, and how different criteria affect what is considered serious (e.g., traffic offenses in Scandinavia, minor drug offenses in the U.S.).

2. <u>Measurement Equivalence</u>: although non-uniform data systems are avoided via self-report, the accommodation to linquistic differences and nuances, cultural differences in survey response experience, and researcher preferences in survey formatting raise subtle issues for comparability.

3. <u>"Emic" and "Etic" Components</u> (Brislin, 1986): etic phenomena are those with common core meanings across cultures, while emic phenomena are more culture-specific. These distinctions are explicitly embodied in the penal and welfare codes of nations with institutionalized justice systems. For example, "status" offenses common to the U.S. system are excluded from criminal sanctions in most European systems. Instrumentation must take advantage of common components and yet find standardizable accommodations to inclusion of nation-specific components.

4. <u>Population Equivalence</u>: communities or groups sampled in different countries need to represent comparable populations. Lonner and Berry (1986) speak effectively to "matching" problems. The issue is more than one of technical sampling statistics. It refers as well to capturing subtle cultural variations and to sampling communities that represent national characteristics and yet are comparable in their import for generalizing within and across nations.

These four problems and similar considerations translate into some very practical issues that were the focus of deliberations in the workshop. We settled on six as being particularly important.

1. <u>Instrument Formats</u>: The Elliott and Ageton SRD, with a general scale and a set of substantive subscales, has emerged from both conceptual and methodological analyses and proven applicable over a wide variety of settings in the U.S. and Canada. A version has also been employed in Denmark (Balvig, 1984). The workshop used the SRD as a point of departure for technical discussions of question formats, response alternatives, "telescoping," independence of categories, measures of seriousness, self-reporting of arrests, and similar issues. Because the many self-report instruments of the past have yielded widely varying results, standardized instrumentation is a necessity.

2. <u>Sampling Frames</u>: Discussions concentrated on the meaning of cross-national equivalence and intra-national respresentativeness as countervailing needs. Specific proposals for community selection and national sampling were considered.

3. <u>Translation and Common Meanings</u>: Specific offense behavior and categories were discussed, looking especially for intra- and cross-national components.

4. <u>Analytic Issues</u>: Common procedures for measuring incidence, prevalence, seriousness, and peer involvement.

5. <u>Longitudinal Accommodations</u>: Major advances now taking place in longitudinal approaches to crime causation require self-report methods that are replicable over time and can distinguish between instrument, period, cohort, and maturational changes. These issues were considered by North American and European researchers currently engaged in major longitudinal delinquency projects.

6. <u>Penal Code Accommodations</u>: Self-report methods must yield data that allow one to compare the reported <u>behavior</u> to categories of <u>offenses</u> in arrest and court records. Measuring self-report behaviors that provide such behavior/report comparability across nations will greatly enhance the chances of achieving generalizable and influential findings on delinquency as it varies from nation to nation, so considerable attention was paid to this issues.

Given the above, the workshop goals were both ambiguous and ambitious. In the short term, it was designed to yield collegiality and information sharing among a diverse group of participants, with fertilization of ideas across national boundaries. Within its four-day span, it was hoped that progress could be made toward a shareable, acceptable self-report instrument available to all. As will be discussed in the concluding chapter, these two goals were more than achieved.

In the long term, the goal is to see a major expansion of comparable and cross-national studies of crime and delinquency, with common self-report instrumentation, yielding both descriptive and theory-relevant data. In that process, we would hope to see more of what McClintock and Wikstrom (1987) characterize as "cooperative" in contrast to "safari" research. At this point we don't need more brief incursions into each other's territories as much as planned and shared, long-term collaborative, cross-national journeys.

As an aside, I might mention one of the few hesitant notes to arise during the workshop. Because the goals were ambiguous and the procedures emphasized discussion rather than structured didactic activities, some participants began to suspect a hidden agenda -- the possibility that this writer and the organizing committee had a "Master Plan" in mind, presumably for a major cross-national study into which participants were being seduced as contributors. "The Master Plan" and "The Study" began to be reified, but good humor prevailed as the organizers' inability to construct such a study soon became apparent to all! Indeed, this vacuum may very well have contributed to the organizational plans for continuing work after the workshop which arose spontaneously among the participants. This is described in the last chapter of the volume.

3. THE WORKSHOP

The sessions in the workshop were designed to move from topical reviews, to didactic presentations on technical issues, to small group discussions with feedback and critiques, and then back to full plenary discussions. The program as presented in the first evening is reproduced below to illustrate this structure and also to serve as a possible model for others contemplating NATO-funded Advanced Research Workshops. The format seemed to all of us to have worked out very well.

Sunday, June 26:   Afternoon or evening arrival. Dinner served at participants' expense until 21:00 hours
21:00 Meeting of Organizing Committee

Monday, June 27:
8:30 Registration
9:15 Welcoming statements by host organizations
10:00 Introduction to workshop organization (Klein)
10:30 Break
11:00 Special presentation on self-report problems and recent solutions (Elliott)
Lunch
13:15 Brief summaries of national reports (Junger-Tas, Killias, Reuband, Shaw, Marcos, Moffitt)
14:30 Break
15:00 Summary of theme areas in pre-conference papers (Klein)
Dinner
20:00 Planning session (Director and six Group Coordinators)

Tuesday, June 28:
8:30 Technical presentations:
a) Incidence and prevalence (Olweus)
b) Penal code variations (Albrecht)
c) Longitudinal issues (Le Blanc)
10:00 Break
10:30 Workshop introductions: Group Coordinators (Farrington, Albrecht, Junger-Tas, Le Blanc, Olweus, Elliott)
11:00 Open discussion
Lunch
13:15 First work-group meetings:
a) Instrument Formats (Coordinator: Elliott)
b) Sampling Frames (Coordinator: Farrington)
c) Meanings and Translations (Coordinator; Junger-Tas)
d) Penal Codes (Coordinator: Albrecht)
e) Analytic Issues (Coordinator: Olweus)
f) Longitudinal Issues (Coordinator: Le Blanc)
Participants for this session will be assigned to work-groups by the Workshop Director. Recorders appointed by Coordinators.
Dinner

<table>
<tr><td></td><td>20:00</td><td>Planning session (Director and six Group Coordinators)</td></tr>
<tr><td>Wednesday, June 29:</td><td>9:00</td><td>Recorder reports from first work-group meetings; open discussion</td></tr>
<tr><td></td><td>10:30</td><td>Break</td></tr>
<tr><td></td><td>11:00</td><td>Critiques of reports (<u>Janson</u>, <u>Reiss</u>)</td></tr>
<tr><td></td><td>Lunch</td><td></td></tr>
<tr><td></td><td>13:15</td><td>Second work-group meetings. Topics and Coordinators remain the same. Participants will be reassigned to different groups.</td></tr>
<tr><td></td><td>17:00</td><td>Coordinating Committee</td></tr>
<tr><td></td><td>Dinner</td><td></td></tr>
<tr><td>Thursday, June 30:</td><td>9:00</td><td>Recorder reports from second work-group meetings</td></tr>
<tr><td></td><td>9:30</td><td>Critiques of reports (<u>Janson</u>, <u>Reiss</u>)</td></tr>
<tr><td></td><td>10:30</td><td>Break</td></tr>
<tr><td></td><td>11:00</td><td>Open discussion</td></tr>
<tr><td></td><td>Lunch</td><td></td></tr>
<tr><td></td><td>1:15</td><td>Final plenary session. Critique of workshop, future directions, etc.</td></tr>
<tr><td></td><td>3:00</td><td>Adjournment</td></tr>
<tr><td></td><td>3:30</td><td>Organizing Committee Meeting</td></tr>
</table>

4. COMMON THEMES IN PRE-CONFERENCE PAPERS

In the solicitation of pre-conference papers, many of which have been selected and edited for this volume, no common format was dictated nor topics assigned. The only early control exerted was to request preliminary outlines so that I could increase the relevance of the contributions to the workshop concerns. It is striking, then, that so many common themes and concerns emerged, sometimes in a few papers and sometimes in many. Because of their relevance and as a guide to the reader wishing to be selective, these are briefly summarize here with citation to the most relevant papers.

4.1. Instrument Formats

Among the many sub-topics under this heading can be found the following:

4.1.1. <u>Item specificity</u>: Elliott and Huizinga, Dickes.

4.1.2. <u>Item overlap</u>: Elliott and Huizinga.

4.1.3. <u>Time (recall) periods</u>: Elliott and Huizinga, Le Blanc.

4.1.4. <u>Methods of administration</u>: Elliott and Huizinga, Le Blanc, Junger-Tas, Moffitt, Hartnagel and Krahn.

4.1.5. <u>Response options</u>: Elliott and Huizinga, Le Blanc.

4.1.6. <u>Event descriptions</u>: Elliott and Huizinga, Albrecht.

4.2. Sampling Frames

    This was a topic that raised some notable differences of viewpoint during the workshop. Four concerns are prominent in the papers:

4.2.1. <u>At-risk populations</u>: Lösel, Le Blanc.

4.2.2. <u>Chronic offenders</u>: Weitekamp.

4.2.3. <u>Attrition and non-response biases</u>: Junger-Tas, Sarnecki, Thornberry.

4.2.4. <u>Goal-specific sampling</u>: Junger-Tas, Sarnecki.
    Study goals clearly relate to sampling frames. Descriptive studies of national delinquency prevalence call for different samples than do theory-testing goals, and both differ from the needs of program evaluation. With these differences noted in the first day of the workshop, it was agreed to concentrate discussions on descriptive studies at first, moving on to more theory-oriented operations later in the proceedings. Evaluation goals and related sampling received the least attention.

4.3. Translations/Common Meanings

    Anecdotes were used to epitomize this problem. Thornberry reports the case of the young extortionist who was given 25 cents by his victim in response to a demand for 10 cents. The offender returned 15 cents in change, and was charged with "highway robbery." I offered my own favorite police report which charged two young college students with "assault with a deadly weapon" after they used slingshots to propel miniature marshmallows of less than half a gram each at their "victims." The offenders pleaded in court to have the charges reduced to "misdemeanor battery."
    More scholarly points on this problem are made in the papers by Moffitt, Junger-Tas, Albrecht, and a non-included paper on Greek drug sales by participant Anastasios Marcos.

4.4. Analytic Issues

    In a workshop emphasizing the dependent variable in criminological research, it is not surprising that both general and crime-specific issues should command attention.

4.4.1. <u>Reliability</u>: Moffitt, Hartnagel and Krahn, Thornberry.

4.4.2. <u>Validity, especially problems of under- and over-reporting</u>: Elliott and Huizinga, Reuband, Moffitt, Junger-Tas, Sarnecki.

4.4.3. Measuring Seriousness: Weitekamp, Moffitt, Elliott and Huizinga. Participants were reminded in the workshop of several points:
4.4.3.1. Seriousness measures have consistently been shown to be less
sensitive to change than frequency of offending.
4.4.3.2. Various scales for measurement of offense seriousness (e.g.,
Sellin-Wolfgang, 1964; Rossi et al., 1974; Dunford & Elliott, 1984;
U.C.R.) have different conceptual implications and vary widely in the
variety and number of offenses to which they apply.
4.3.3.3. Unidimensional (e.g., Rossi et al., 1974) versus multidimensional measures of seriousness are not conceptually equivalent.

4.4.4. Peer involvement: Shaw and Riley. The presence of Albert Reiss
as a critic in the workshop further reminded participants of the
complexity of the "co-offending" issue. My own research in comparing
gang with non-gang offenses was invoked to emphasize the point that
peer influence in crime incidents alters other aspects of those incidents, and thus alters the meaning of the self-reports of the same
incidents.

4.4.5. Frequency: Elliott and Huizinga. Comments from Olweus alerted
participants to the inappropriate use of the term "incidence" that many
of us have adopted. "Frequency" was accepted as a preferred alternative.

4.4.6. Prevalence: Elliott and Huizinga, Loeber et al. A non-included
paper by participant Haluk Yavuzer noted differences in violence rates
in Turkey as a function of family honor and blood feuds.
    A final summary point was offered to the participants with respect
to program evaluation goals. It was suggested that different goals may
yield differences in recidivism measurement, with frequency more sensitive to short-term program effects (the case in point being a six-month
period, at the end of which prevalence differences had not yet
emerged).

4.5. Longitudinal Issues

    Major attention to these is to be found in Weitekamp, Le Blanc,
Moffitt, Hartnagel and Krahn, and Thornberry. This topic, included
among the original six issues, was considerably expanded in connection
with a companion grant from the U.S. Office of Juvenile Justice and
Delinquency Prevention. It fits well with a strong trend in U.S.
research and has spawned a sometimes acrimonious debate in the literature between Travis Hirschi and Michael Gottfredson on the one hand
and, on the other, some of our participants -- David Farrington, Delbert Elliott, David Huizinga, Terence Thornberry, Rolf Loeber, and
Albert Reiss -- among others (see the relevant articles in the 1988
issue of Criminology, volume 26, #1). In the workshop, the debate was
muffled as the implications of longitudinal designs for self-report
methods remained the issue at hand.

4.6. Penal Codes

Papers by Albrecht, Moffitt, and Junger-Tas cover many of the issues. Perhaps no concern better captures the complexity of cross-national criminological research. Age of non-responsibility and age of adulthood vary widely; crimes vary, sanctions vary, meanings of offense categories vary, and so on. Yet one of the major recent advances in self-report technology is the fitting of self-report offense descriptions to legally relevant offense categories. Albrecht's paper, in particular, anticipates much of this concern and even suggests specific offenses appropriate for both inclusion and exclusion.

The problem of handling "status offenses" -- those that can be charged against juveniles but not adults -- was discussed as a case in point. These are critical in the U.S. system, but excluded in many others from consideration in the justice system. Our analysis (as yet unpublished) of the juvenile codes in 50 U.S. states yields five principal status offense categories (runaway, incorrigibility, habitual truancy, curfew violations, and alcohol possession). These can each be handled in one of four statutory classifications (status, delinquent, dependent/neglected, no mention). In 15 of the 20 combinations, there are several variations possible in permitting or prohibiting secure detention of offenders, both before and after adjudication. There are also variations in time permitted in detention and response to offender violations of court dispositions for status offenders.

Careful cross-state and cross-national comparisons involving status offenders are thus revealed to be no simple matter. An additional anomaly is worth noting. A recent book by one of our participants (Junger-Tas & Block, 1988) has reported the utility of running away and truancy as predictors of delinquency. Stating the relationship in that way is entirely appropriate in Holland, where the research was carried out, given the exclusion of status offenses from the juvenile code. But in the U.S. the same research might well be criticized as redundant or tautological, since running away and truancy there are usually components of delinquent patterns.

All of the above refers to the themes that were built into the workshop structure. Others were raised in the pre-conference papers and, not surprisingly, emerged in some of the workshop deliberations. All are relevant to the concerns of this volume and so are reported here.

4.7. Emergent Themes

4.7.1. Ethnic differences: Elliott and Huizinga, Junger-Tas (citing Junger on Turks, Moroccans, Surinamers, and Native Dutch).

4.7.2. Triviality of juvenile offenses: Shaw and Riley (include trivial items), Moffitt (can't avoid trivial items), Elliott and Huizinga (be wary of trivial items), and Weitekamp (exclude trivial items).

4.7.3. Age: Weitekamp, Reuband, Le Blanc, Moffitt, and Loeber et al.

4.7.4. <u>Gender</u>: Junger-Tas, Shaw and Riley, and a non-included paper by
Amelia Diaz Martinez from Spain.

4.7.5. <u>Problems of scaling</u>: Elliott and Huizinga, Le Blanc, Bruinsma,
Dickes, Moffitt. A major technical question is whether one can sensi-
bly do summations over self-report items. Elliott and Huizinga, along
with Le Blanc, fear not. Others, those stressing behavioral versatility and a major underlying construct of delinquency proneness, suggest
the opposite. This seems to be a critical <u>theoretical</u> concern in doing
cross-national self-report research. The assumption of a broad underlying construct (a deviance trait, an anti-social tendency, or delinquency proneness) should be manifested behaviorally in a broad delinquency <u>factor</u> or <u>cluster</u> of offenses. Such a factor has been empirically documented (Klein, 1984) and presumably therefore should be measur-
able by a reliable, multi-item scale with summative properties. The
point is particularly well stated in the paper by Paul Dickes.

5. ACKNOWLEDGEMENTS

    In a way, it is a shame that each reader of this volume could not
have been at the workshop and must use these chapters to get some sense
of the collegiality and intellectual challenge that enthused the participants. That all went so well, and that this volume has resulted, is
in large measure a tribute to a number of people and organizations who
collaborated to bring it all about.
    The workshop was hosted by my own Center for Research in Crime and
Social Control at the University of Southern California. That none of
my Center colleagues were permitted to attend must seem a strange
approach to rewarding people, but they know they have my gratitude.
    The Dutch Ministry of Justice served as co-host. Dr. Jan van
Dijk, Director of the Research and Documentation Center (W.O.D.C.),
deserves particular credit. He offered the auspices of the Ministry,
provided additional funds to bring a number of participants to the
workshop, and -- fortunately for us -- found time to participate in
many of the sessions.
    Principal funding came from the Scientific Affairs Division of
NATO. So far as I could determine in over a year of testing various
public and private funding sources, NATO was in fact the <u>only</u> organization that would entertain this type of enterprise in a major way.
All of us who participated in the workshop have reason to be grateful
to the NATO staff and reviewers, and I recommend that like-minded
scholars seriously consider testing the supportive waters at NATO.
    As noted earlier, in order to amplify the longitudinal emphasis of
the workshop, the Office of Juvenile Justice and Delinquency Prevention
substantially supplemented the NATO grant. The OJJDP has recently
determined a need to increase its capability to foster and collect
self-report delinquency data, and this workshop was seen as one way of
approaching that goal. OJJDP Research Director Pam Swain recognized
the connection and saw to it that the right buttons were pushed. Six
Europeans, six North Americans, and this writer have reason to express

12

appreciation for her help. I should add that our publisher, Kluwer, has shown unusual flexibility in permitting OJJDP to package separately some of the papers in this volume.

On a more personal level, I need to express my full appreciation to Josine Junger-Tas, David Farrington, and Delbert Elliott who provided multiple services as members of the Organizing Committee. They were my sounding board, my critics, my supporters, and played a critical role in identifying potential participants and selecting the papers for this volume. Josine Junger-Tas, in particular, located the Congres Center, carried out with me the technical negotiations, and graciously spent more time co-chairing the sessions than either of us anticipated would be necessary.

Others playing special roles -- and important roles in the workshop process -- were Marc Le Blanc, Dan Olweus, Hans-Jorg Albrecht, CarlGunnar Janson, and Albert Reiss. They gave extra time, expended extra effort, and I hope reaped sufficient pleasure in the outcome.

Marianne Junger emerged as an unanticipated extra dividend in the workshop. Judith Webb emerged as a fully anticipated and easily documented source of support in handling the logistics at U.S.C., including a major role in preparing all the chapters in this volume.

And if any form of dedication of this book is allowable, then it certainly is dedicated to Margy Gatz. She supported the enterprise, she beat the worst of Dutch viruses, and clearly deserves another shot at a most delightful country, Holland.

REFERENCES

Balvig, F: On the social class bias in juvenile delinquency. Sociological Microjournal, 18:2-19, 1984.
Bayley, DH: Patterns of policing: A comparative international analysis. New Brunswick: Rutgers University Press, 1985.
Brislin, RW: The wording and translation of research instruments. In Lonner, WJ, & Berry, JW (Eds.), Field methods in cross-cultural research. Beverly Hills: Sage, 1986.
Dunford, F, & Elliott, DS: Identifying career offenders with self-reported data. Journal of Research in Crime and Delinquency, 21:57-86, 1984.
Elliott, DS, & Ageton, SS: Reconciling race and class differences in self-reported and official estimates of delinquency. American Sociological Review, 45:95-110, 1980.
Elliott, DS, & Huizinga, D: The relationship between delinquent behavior and ADM problems. Proceedings of the ADAMHA/OJJDP Research Conference on Juvenile Offenders with Serious Drug, Alcohol, and Mental Health Problems. Washington, D.C.: U.S. Government Printing Office, 1984.
Elliott, DS, Huizinga, D, & Morse, B: Self-reported violent offending. Journal of Interpersonal Violence, 1:472-514, 1987.
Greve, V: Our non-deviant criminals. In Scandinavian studies in criminology, volume 5, 99-106. Oslo: Universitetforlaget, 1974.

Hauge, R: Definition and scope of comparative studies in crime trends, including a review of work carried out since 1945. In Council of Europe (Ed.), _Trends in crime: Comparative studies and technical problems_, 25-49. Strasbourg: 1983.

Hindelang, MJ, Hirschi, T, & Weis, JG: _Measuring delinquency_. Beverly Hills: Sage, 1981.

Hirschi, T, Hindelang, MJ, & Weis, JG: The status of self-report measures. In Klein, MW, & Teilmann, KS (Eds.), _Handbook of criminal justice evaluation_. Beverly Hills: Sage, 1980.

Junger-Tas, J, & Block, RL: _Juvenile delinquency in the Netherlands_. Amstelveen: Kugler Publications, 1988.

Klein, MW: Labeling theory and delinquency policy: An experimental test. _Criminal Justice and Behavior_, 13:47-79, 1986.

Klein, MW: Offense specialization and versatility among juveniles, _British Journal of Criminology_, 24:185-194, 1984.

Klein, MW: _Western systems of juvenile justice_. Beverly Hills: Sage, 1984.

Lonner, WJ, & Berry, JW (Eds.): _Field methods in cross-cultural research_. Beverly Hills: Sage, 1986.

Lynch, JP: _A comparison of prison use in England, Canada, West Germany, and the United States: A limited test of the punitive hypothesis_. Washington D.C.: American University, School of Justice, 1986.

McClintock, FH, & Wikstrom, P-OH: _Violent crime in Scotland and Sweden: The rate, structure, and trends_. Stockholm: University of Stockholm, Department of Criminology, 1987.

Rossi, PH, Waite, E, Bose, CE, & Berk, RA: The seriousness of crime: Normative structure and individual differences. _American Sociological Review_, 39:224-237, 1974.

Sellin, T, & Wolfgang, M: _The measurement of delinquency_. New York: Wiley, 1964.

PART I. STUDIES IN SEVERAL NATIONS

The six papers in this section provide examples of self-report
research as affected by its national contexts. Other planned papers,
for example from Italy and Switzerland, had to be abandoned when the
authors' reviews revealed a paucity of research in those countries. As
noted in the Epilogue to this volume, these latter nations are more the
rule than the exception. The reader should note that the papers in
Part I are not "cross-national" or "comparative." It is only by seeking parallels and dissimilarities in what they report that they contribute specifically to the field of comparative criminology. They serve
this function, as well, by offering concrete instances of research to
which the issue-oriented papers of Parts II and III may be applied.
Even for the methodologically oriented reader, we urge reading of the
papers in Part I prior to those in the next two sections.

SELF-REPORT DELINQUENCY RESEARCH IN HOLLAND WITH A PERSPECTIVE ON
INTERNATIONAL COMPARISON

Josine Junger-Tas
Research and Documentation Center
Ministry of Justice, The Hague
The Netherlands

1. INTRODUCTION

The objective of this paper is twofold. In the first place I want
to discuss the way in which the self-report method is used in Dutch
criminological research. Dutch self-report delinquency studies started
in the sixties. One of the first was Buikhuisen's study among university students (1969). There were many to follow, and although the
method was applied to adults as well as juveniles, it has become an
accepted research method mainly in the field of studies among juveniles. The Dutch studies present considerable variety in sampling, in
delinquency measures, in method of administration and in measuring
validity. Moreover -- although in many ways comparable -- they differ
in some respects from American studies in the same field.

The second objective is to examine some of the issues that are
important to the construction of a common instrument, seen from a Dutch
viewpoint. In considering problems of sampling, the definition of
delinquency and its operationalization, and questions of validity, I
will present some comparisons with American self-report studies. This
will be done for essentially two reasons.

In the first place, it has to be recognized that since World War
II most of European criminology has been dominated by American sociology. Many important criminological theories have been developed by
American scholars. Moreover, Anglo-Saxon empiricism has spread all
over the world and has become the accepted way of conducting empirical
research. At first -- in the 50s and the 60s -- theories and methods
were accepted without much questioning, but later, when European criminology reached a scientifically more sophisticated level, a certain
consciousness developed on both sides of the ocean about the relativity
of theories and models designed in one specific cultural setting. Many
realized that crime and deviance are not the same phenomena all over
the world, and that the criminal justice system does not operate in the
same way in all western countries. It is therefore important to ask
ourselves at every stage to what extent research results are valid and
generalizable to more than just one country. Second, if we wish to
construct a self-report delinquency instrument for comparative

M. W. Klein (ed.), Cross-National Research in Self-Reported Crime and Delinquency, 17–41.
© *1989 by Kluwer Academic Publishers.*

research, it is absolutely essential to establish both the common ground and the differences and particularities of each country in order to achieve some consensus.

In cross-cultural research the following problems have been noticed.

1.1. Problems of Conceptualization and Operationalization

When Clinard conducted his replication study in Sweden (1960), he had to modify the word "arrest" because in Sweden the proceedings were not handled by the police and the court, but by a special youth board. The same was true for the word "gang" which had quite a different connotation in Swedish. Friday had similar problems with his research on Stockholm juveniles, when he found no equivalent term for "area" expressing the neighborhood structure and organization. The concept did not have any meaning to the boys who always referred to the entire city instead of their own restricted living area (Friday, 1974).

When researchers want to use their instruments in other cultures they meet the problem of equivalence of indicators and equivalence of meaning, and often have great difficulty in solving this problem. Levinson states (1977) that a rigorous cross-cultural study should control at least the following problems: unit definitions, sampling regional variations, data paucity, untrustworthy data, validity, reliability, and group significance.

1.2. Problems Related to Differences in Legal Procedures and Classification of Crime

Among countries in Europe and the U.S., vast differences exist in statutory frameworks concerning such things as limitation or termination of parental rights, status offense jurisdiction, institutions that process juveniles (special boards, commissions of juvenile court), initiating of proceedings, rights of parties during proceedings, and disposition of offenders (Le Poole, 1977).

It is quite clear that this situation makes it extremely difficult to use official documents as a basis for comparison. This is all the more true for the comparison of crime statistics. Not only do countries differ in police and court organization and meaning of the same legal terms, but it is impossible to control for inadequacies and lack of uniformity in the collection and presentation of crime statistics (Vetere & Newman, 1977).

Vetere and Newman cite Interpol's comparative police statistics but they note serious deficiencies: lack of reliability, discontinuity in information, and differences in definition of offenses. The fact that crime statistics may cover such different data on referrals, arrests, court proceedings, convictions, and prison population makes them hard to use by either scientists or policy makers. This situation has led to the development of other types of studies such as self-report studies, victimization surveys, surveys of fear of crime, and evaluation of the police.

1.3. Problems Related to Different Operational Definitions of Crime

Researchers have adopted a great variety of definitions of what constitutes crime. Many adopt legalistic definitions, thus making comparisons among studies very hard indeed. This problem is particularly apparent in many self-report studies. Trying to compare my own self-report findings in Belgium with those that had been reported by researchers in other countries I found to be impossible (Junger-Tas, 1977). The volume of self-report delinquency depends of course on the researcher's definition of delinquency. When Gold studied hidden delinquency in Flint (1970), he included in his definition status-offenses such as truancy, running away from home, incorrigibility, and behaviors such as physical violence against parents, sexual intercourse and alcohol use, whereas I included only acts that would have been considered offenses if committed by an adult.

Comparisons are also made difficult because of different research populations: Christie (1965) and Antilla (1966) used army recruits. Buikhuisen questioned university students (1969); Elmhorn (1965) and Gold (1970) interviewed younger children .

1.4. Problems in Executing the Research

Problems may arise when a specific methodology or instrument is used in different cultures. For example, if we use a structured instrument in order to quantify results, our ethnocentricity may blind us to differences in meaning of concepts and operational indices which will impair validity. But if we opt for open ended interviews or observations, the validity of the results is also questionable. The same is true for interviewers or observers. Should we conduct the research ourselves or should we use local interviewers? In the latter case, differential meaning of concepts and operational definitions add up to differences in perception and interpretation by interviewers, making the instrument less and less valid and the interpretation of results more and more hazardous.

The second problem arises when, having used a structured, quantifiable instrument in the first place, we are unable to use it in a different cultural setting, and as a consequence are forced to make all kinds of adaptations to the local situation in order to use it. This seems a very weak design indeed and the results of these studies seem hardly comparable.

Cross-cultural research presents many problems that are hard to solve. In the following pages I will examine the possibilities for arriving at some common denominators that will enable us to conduct comparative research. To that end I will review the ways in which Dutch researchers solved some of the methodological problems such as sampling method, method of administration, and questions of reliability and validity.

2. SAMPLING

The sampling method used is of essential importance for two reasons. First there is the question of non-response which may introduce considerable bias. Second, generalizability to the population may be endangered by the type of sample drawn. In Dutch research both of these problems are present.

As mentioned before, Buikhuisen (1969), in one of the first Dutch self-report studies, took a random sample of one out of every six students in one state university. He drew both male and female students in the age bracket of 18-30 years. He then used the split-half method to test reliability.

It is clear that such a sample has a strong middle-class bias, so that findings cannot be generalized to similar age groups of the Dutch population. (At that time, however, it came as a shock that such respectable young people as university students confessed to having committed so many offenses.)

A number of researchers, as in the U.S., have used high school samples. Sometimes this was justified by the research problem . Thus Nijboer and Dijksterhuis (1983) wanted to study the relationship between functioning in school and delinquent behavior. They selected different school types in one middle-sized city and then drew a representative sample of all classes in these schools. Although the sample is certainly not representative for the country, the researchers considered that this was not necessary in view of their objective, to examine whether processes within the formal education system could have criminogenic effects.

Parents were informed and could refuse participation for their children, which occurred in about 12% of cases. However, the rate of refusal was much higher among parents of predominantly female students in domestic science training schools, 27% versus only 7.5% in the other schools. Overall the response rate was 85.5%.

Other researchers used high school students mainly for reasons of convenience. For example, Bruinsma (1985), testing differential association theory in the version of a German scholar, K. D. Opp, approached 15 schools in one city, of which five agreed to participate. The others refused, claiming participation would be "too time consuming," being tired of "another of those sociological studies in their school," or considering it inappropriate to use the roster of students for research purposes.

Bruinsma justified this procedure by pointing out that his objective was not to reach generalizing statements about the total Dutch school population, but to test some theoretical propositions. His sample included juveniles under the age of majority, that is 12 to 17 years old. As he questioned only students in the first three classes of the five participating schools, he got primarily the younger students. Bruinsma's sample was a cluster sample which could present a problem of homogeneity in the scores of respondents, and thus of higher sampling error, because of a reduction in the number of independent observations. He controlled for homogeneity by comparing the variations in scores of some important variables between respondents of the five clusters, and in a random selection of the total sample.

Another recent example is a study of differential treatment of girls and boys within the juvenile justice and the youth protection systems (Van Schie, v.d. Houwen, Willemsen, 1987) The main hypothesis in the study is that stereotypes concerning desirable and undesirable behavior of boys and girls determine decision-making and differential treatment of the sexes. To test this, parents as well as more formal educators such as teachers, police, juvenile judges were approached, and school children were questioned both on their delinquent behavior and their opinions about that behavior.

The survey took place in two middle-sized cities, among all existing school types. The sample was restricted to third classes only, including mainly 15 year olds. This choice was made on the basis of the finding that delinquent behavior greatly increases at this age. With only 16 juveniles, or 2.2% absent, the response rate was about 98%.

There have been some efforts to try the self-report method on adults. An example of this is Veendrick's study on "Hidden and recorded crime in Groningen" (1976). In the city of Groningen, 37 (of 55) rather homogeneous neighborhoods were selected. On the basis of population data available at the municipality,[1] a random sample of 1.5% of the population aged 15 to 65 was drawn, totaling 3,367 persons. The response rate was 70%; about 10% refused to participate, another 10% returned blank questionnaires, and another 10% were impossible to find. Non-response was considerably higher (over 50%) in one old working-class neighborhood, with a majority of elder inhabitants, and it was much lower (12%) in one higher class area. Non-response was also related to age: the older the people, the more non-response or incomplete returns.

Non-response was also related to being known to the police. Analysis showed that this was especially the case for the younger age groups (15 to 27). About 5.5% of the non-response group in this age bracket had a police record compared to 2% in the general population of the same ages.

One major criticism of self-report studies is that they are generally conducted among populations that have been in little contact with the criminal justice system. It is not improbable that studies among populations who have had such contacts are much harder to achieve and will suffer from validity problems.

To test this hypothesis Angenent (1984) drew a sample of 222 men who had been arrested by the police during the five preceding years. The instrument was a questionnaire, delivered and collected by collaborators of his institute. Only 34% of the respondents completed the questionnaire; the others returned a blank one. In a comparison group of the same sex, age, SES and neighborhood, the response rate was 42%. However, this group also included a high percentage (43%) of persons having been previously arrested. Angenent concludes that in the case

----
1. Population data such as sex, place and date of birth, marital status, recent address of city inhabitants, are normally established in every municipality of the country.

of populations that have had serious contacts with the criminal justice system, the self-report method is not appropriate because of the high non-response rate.

Finally, there are some studies where efforts were made to achieve representativeness of the Dutch youth population. Junger-Tas et al. (1983) conducted a self-report study with two main objectives: first to get some insight into the nature and extent of delinquent behavior in a representative group of "ordinary" juveniles of 12 to 17 years, and second, to test social control theory. Two fairly large samples were drawn, one in a large city, the other in a small one.

In one of the cities, the random-walk method was used: the city was divided into neighborhoods and streets and on the basis of global population data a number of addresses were drawn. This method led to an under- representation of 16- and 17-year-olds due to the fact that youngsters in this age group are less often at home, and even when contacted, responded less often to the invitation to participate. This resulted in a response rate of 73%.

In the other city, the sample could be drawn on the basis of the available municipality population data, so that respondents could be approached by their name and address. This resulted in a higher response rate -- 85% -- and a better representation of 16- and 17-year-olds.

This sample of about 1,850 juveniles was used to get an indication of delinquent behavior, police contacts, and prosecutor intervention in a "normal" youth population. However, in order to test social control theory, a greater number of juveniles with recorded contacts with the juvenile justice system had to be included both at police level and at the level of the prosecutor. Therefore we conducted a number of additional interviews with apprehended juveniles at the police station and at the prosecutor's office. The procedure followed is similar to the one followed by Hindelang et al. (1981) in their Seattle study, with the same objective to represent the general adolescent population of Seattle and to maximize variance on delinquency (Hindelang et al., 1981, p. 31). There are, however, some differences: Hindelang's sample consisted of students enrolled in Seattle public schools and the age range was 15 to 18 years. Moreover, they excluded students with a known police or court record so as to achieve a pure official non-delinquent sample, where we preferred to include in the sample the 126, or 7%, juveniles with a police record and 50, or 2.5%, juveniles with prosecutor contacts.

Two years later we did a follow-up study among a stratified sample drawn from the original one (Junger-Tas et al., 1988). Of a total of 543 juveniles approached, 61% were re-interviewed. However, response rates differed by specific groups:
- those who had not reported any offense at time 1 - 60%;
- those who had reported at least one offense, but no police contacts - 55.5%;
- those who had reported offenses as well as police contacts - 43%;
- those who had recorded police contacts - 34%;
- those who had prosecutor contacts - 44.5%.

The differences in response rate clearly suggest that contacts with the juvenile justice system influence willingness of youngsters to participate in self-report studies (and maybe in social research in general). However, analysis comparing respondents and non-respondents on a number of variables, including delinquency, did not show any bias in the response group.

Another study, quite relevant to our topic, is one conducted among ethnic minority groups in Holland (Junger, 1987). The aim was twofold: to examine the validity of the self-report method for ethnic minority groups and to test social control theory with respect to these groups. Three different ethnic groups were included in the study: Turkish, Moroccan, and Surinam boys, aged 12 to 17 years. Girls were excluded for practical and financial reasons. The Turks and Moroccans in Holland are foreigners. They had been recruited by industry in the '60s and '70s to perform mainly unskilled jobs, so they are unevenly spread throughout the country. Therefore a selection was made of those munici- palities where they represented a least 10% of the population. Once selected, the local police force was contacted because they keep the records of all foreigners living in that municipality. On the basis of their registration, a random sample was drawn of Moroccan and Turkish boys. A sample of Surinam boys, most of whom have Dutch nationality and cannot be easily traced, was drawn with the assistance of the Cen- tral Statistical Bureau on the basis of population data.

The size of the samples drawn was three times as large as the number of desired respondents because considerable non-response was expected. In fact, this turned out not to be the case. Comparing respondents with non-respondents, there were minor differences in age and city size (respondents were slightly younger and came somewhat more often from smaller cities), but no differences in the nature and fre- quency of officially recorded offenses.

A control group was designed of Dutch boys of the same age, living in the same neighborhood or street as the minority boys, so as to match as much as possible on SES. This group clearly differed from the repre- sentative sample described in the The Hague-Venlo study mentioned (Junger-Tas et al., 1983): SES and educational level are both lower and more youngsters had official judicial contacts.

However, although the researcher tried to match the control group on SES, differences were huge: 73% of the Moroccan fathers and 62% of the Turkish fathers had unskilled jobs, versus only 25% of the Dutch and Surinam fathers. In addition, 40% of Moroccan fathers and one third of Turkish and Surinam fathers were unemployed compared to only 17% of Dutch fathers. Finally, educational level of Dutch and Surinam boys was much higher than that of Moroccan and Turkish boys.

The last study I want to mention is one in which a national sample of the Dutch juvenile population of 12 to 17 years was taken (Junger- Tas & Kruissink, 1987). The sample was drawn by selecting 119 munici- palities representative of the national distribution in regions and degree of urbanization and then a random selection of addresses in each municipality from the postal codes register. The sample included 1,120 juveniles of both sexes.

Controls were introduced for age distribution, sex, area, degree of urbanization, and family size. The sample appeared to be reasonably representative of the Dutch youth population, except for the representation of ethnic minorities. Because of the concentration of these groups in the four largest cities and somewhat more difficulties in approaching them, they are underrepresented. Of the total number of juveniles approached, 23.5% refused to participate and 6% could not be reached, which results in a response rate of 70%.

We may conclude that Dutch self-report studies are confronted with the same sampling problems as those elsewhere:

- High-school samples suffer from various drawbacks. If the instrument is administered at one specific moment in time there will be a number of absentees. An unknown number of these will be truants.[2] There is reason to think that this group differs from non-truants in important aspects, including delinquent behavior (Baerveldt, 1987; Mutsaers, 1988). Moreover, the sample will not include an unknown but growing proportion of school dropouts, especially among the 16- and 17-year-olds. This group, too, differs in important ways from those who stay on and get a certificate or diploma (Junger-Tas, 1977). This issue is all the more important in countries where going to school up to 18 years of age is not universal. The conclusion must be that generalization on the basis of this type of sample is often hazardous. Self-report studies that include adults have shown essentially that the method is less easily applicable to older persons because of the lower response rate.

- When questionnaires are administered to persons with a police record, the response rate is very low indeed. Response rate in this case may vary with the situation: in an institutional setting, people may well be willing to answer such a questionnaire, but may not wish to do so when they are living in the community. This was shown in a study with adult respondents, but similar problems arose in a follow-up study where a number of juvenile respondents were selected on the basis of police or prosecutor contacts: the response rate was considerably lower than in the group of juveniles not so identified (Junger-Tas et al., 1985).

- Representative samples are not without bias: they do not locate the more serious offenders because the latter are difficult to reach and less likely to participate (Cerkonvich, Giordano, & Pugh, 1985; Junger-Tas, 1986). Thus if one uses self-report measures as "social indicators" (Hindelang et al., 1981, p. 89) the results will probably underestimate the prevalence and incidence of delinquency in the youth population. The solution proposed by Cernkovich et al. (1985) to include institutionalized delinquents can only be used when one wishes to test theory. Adding a certain number of these delinquents to a representative youth sample results in an overrepresentation of

---

2. Recent information from two large vocational training schools showed that more than half of all cases of absenteeism in a period of three months is caused by unjustified absences.

serious delinquents to an unknown extent.

My main conclusion would be that in comparative research one should be all the more cautious because the various biases, the extent of which probably differs among countries, would add up in unknown ways and would seriously impair the validity of the study. Therefore, all things considered, the best guarantee for comparable results, I believe, is to have a representative youth sample, drawn on the basis of reliable population data, in each participating country.

3. FACE VALIDITY

By face validity we mean the relation between the definition of delinquency and its operationalizations. Most Dutch researchers define delinquency as violations of penal law, referring to juveniles and adults alike.

Reviewing the operationalization of delinquency in various Dutch studies shows that the first studies included a great number of offenses. Buikhuisen (1969) conducted a pilot study inquiring about 52 offenses which he then reduced by half, finally including six theft offenses, three offenses concerning fraud, four aggressive offenses, five traffic offenses, three offenses related to joy-riding, three drug and two sex offenses.

Veendrick (1976) wanted to have a representative sample of all possible offenses in penal law. This proved to be impossible. He finally decided not to include: rarely committed offenses, economic offenses which had an extremely complex formulation, offenses that almost always lead to discovery or that are related to specific professional categories, and sexual offenses. He ended up with 26 offenses, including such "white collar" crimes as tax fraud, bribery, illegal withdrawal of goods from a bankrupt firm, blackmail, and illegal dumping of dangerous chemicals. Later researchers reduced the number of offenses still more (Nijboer & Dijksterhuis, 1983; Van Schie et al., 1987; Junger-Tas et al., 1983, 1985). Some took only property offenses (Bruinsma, 1985), but most of them made a selection including at least property and aggressive offenses. There have been attempts to introduce some standardization in the operational definition of delinquency. The self-report study conducted by the WODC[3] on a national youth sample (Junger-Tas & Kruissink, 1987) included ten offenses, most of which had been used in other WODC studies (Baerveldt, 1987; Mutsaers, 1988) and in a study at Leiden University (Van Schie, 1987).

One important question is what criteria are used to specify the operational definition of delinquency. It has to be admitted that with the exception of Veendrick (see above) and Bruinsma, who asked nine boys of 13 to 15 years of age to judge the questionnaire, and some pilot studies, the basis of the operational definition is rather vague.

Although many claim that the definition is based on the research literature, I think it is fair to say that offenses selected are those that frequently appear in the police statistics as juvenile crime, as

----
3. Research and Documentation Center, Dutch Ministry of Justice.

well as those known to be frequently committed by juveniles, such as vandalism or using the public transport system without paying. For purposes of illustration the items used in the national survey are listed in Appendix I.

This means that, except for the earlier ones, a number of studies have an overrepresentation of non-serious offenses, that is, offenses that would, if discovered, probably not lead to official intervention. The most that can happen if discovered by the police is that they would lead to a warning followed by a dismissal. The reason for this approach is that the more serious offenses figuring in a questionnaire addressed to a "general, normal" youth population, might frighten them and thus invalidate the instrument. In fact, one of the later studies reintroduced some very serious offenses such as rape, assault and robbery. However, this study ran into serious validity problems which will be explained later (Junger, 1987).

Despite similarities, there is one overriding difference between Dutch and American studies: all items included in Dutch instruments are offenses as defined by penal law, whether committed by juveniles or by adults. So-called status offenses in the U.S. are not considered offenses in France, Germany, or The Netherlands. Although, for example, juveniles are not allowed to smoke in public in Germany, the parents are held responsible (Le Poole, 1977). The same is true with respect to truancy in The Netherlands. In these three countries child protection measures for non-criminal "problem" behavior are authorized on the basis of criteria comparable to the U.S. proceedings in dependency and neglect cases. The criteria used refer to the juvenile being in a "state of danger."

In The Netherlands the juvenile court may order a civil measure of supervision when a child's "moral or physical integrity is threatened." In France "educational assistance" is ordered when a minor's health, security or morality are endangered or when the conditions necessary to receive a proper upbringing are seriously jeopardized. The German code speaks about "dangers to the mental or physical welfare of the child." The English and Swedish statutes are different in that they make a distinction between children who are victims of misbehaving parents and children who themselves misbehave. Sweden's legislation is most comparable to the U.S. with respect to status offenders: children processed for non-criminal "problem" behavior are treated in the same way as children having committed offenses. What is alike in all countries discussed, however, is the vagueness of the criteria applied. The authorities have considerable discretion in deciding whether the facts indicate a "state of physical or moral danger" of the child, or whether he should be labeled a delinquent.

The problem is apparent in most American instruments. They include items such as alcohol use, getting drunk, cheating on exams, cutting school and even measures of parental defiance. It is true that some more recent American studies (Elliott and Ageton, 1980; Hindelang et al., 1981) used instruments including both minor delinquency and serious crime. But the Seattle self-report instrument also comprises a drug index including 11 items of which six are either no crimes in Dutch law (alcohol use or purchase) or are classified as misdemeanors (public drunkenness) or are not prosecuted (marijuana use). Another index, "School and Family Offenses," includes seven items, none of which is an offense in Dutch juvenile penal law.

In my studies I also found that truancy and running away are good predictors of both unofficial and official delinquency (Hindelang et al., 1981, p. 37; Junger-Tas et al., 1983, 1985, 1987). Moreover, in our national survey we found a relationship between truancy, alcohol use, soft drug use, and promiscuity, and this cluster was also related to delinquency. So apparently, a rather "deviant" lifestyle among adolescents is positively related to delinquency (Junger-Tas & Kruissink, 1987). This is not the same however, as considering these behaviors as delinquent. Therefore, I would suggest that in a comparative study these items should be included under a different definition, such as, for example, "problem," "deviant," or "risky" behavior, and that they should not be taken as operational elements of the delinquency definition.

With respect to Dutch self-report research, it can be concluded that although the definition of delinquency as penal law violations is generally respected, most instruments include a number of non-serious offenses which, if discovered by the police, would almost certainly be dealt with unofficially.

4. METHODS OF ADMINISTRATION

A major question is whether one specific method of administration can be demonstrated to be superior to others, in terms of response rate and validity.

In Holland, as in the U.S., different methods have been used. Buikhuisen (1964) sent an introductory letter, explaining the purpose and relevance of the study, and then sent the questionnaire. Half of them were collected by a collaborator of the institute at a time announced beforehand. The other half of the respondents were asked to send back the questionnaires in an envelope addressed to the institute. Both procedures yielded high response rates (94% and 92%). Some years later female students were approached in the same way, asking them to send back the completed questionnaire, resulting in a response rate of 80%.

The same method was used with adult populations. Veendrick (1976) had a response rate of 70%, but 10% returned blank questionnaires.

Those who approach high school populations do of course get high response rates: they miss only those whose parents do not agree to the study and the absentees (Nijboer & Dijksterhuis, 1983; Bruinsma, 1985; Van Schie et al., 1987). The response rate in this case depends in the first place on the sampling method: sampling on the basis of known names and addresses yields a higher response rate than the random walk method. This was especially the case when interviews were held among ethnic minorities, where it was thought to be very difficult to get in touch with these groups. In fact, the response was higher than expected -- 66% -- with only 11% refusals and 12% repeatedly not at home (10% could not be found).

In one of the last studies (Junger-Tas & Kruissink, 1987), a mixed method was used: the juveniles were interviewed but the self-report list was completed by the youngsters themselves. As this study was completely anonymous, no checks on validity could be performed. We used the method in order to avoid validity problems related to the presence of parents or other persons at the interview.

As appears from this selection, the method of administration chosen is in most cases a matter of convenience for the researcher rather than anything else. Studies testing the merits of one method as compared to another are rare. Buikhuisen et al. (1969) first tried out a postal survey among all 21 year old male citizens of a northern city. Getting a very low response -- 47.5% -- they then decided to collect the questionnaires themselves. However, their research population differed from the one in the postal survey: it included only male university students and this might be part of the explanation for the higher response rate under the second condition.

In Angenent's study on adult men with a police record (1984), data collection was based on a postal survey. Angenent attributed his very low response rate to the inadequacy of the self-report method with adult samples. Unfortunately, he did not try out the interview method, which might have yielded a higher response rate.

So as far as Dutch research is concerned, we can't say whether one or the other method would give more valid results, as this type of comparison has not been made. However, Hindelang et al. (1981) have tested different methods of administration under anonymous and non-anonymous conditions. They found that no one method was generally superior to any other method, perhaps because "respondents do not find efforts to measure their delinquent behavior particularly threatening" (p. 124), a finding that is confirmed in Dutch research. Their conclusion is that results of self-report delinquency studies are independent of method of data collection, although they observe that the results of interview or questionnaire are similar only under optimal conditions.

5. RELIABILITY

Reliability is defined here as "the level of precision of an instrument; it refers to the extent to which the measuring instrument would produce identical scores if it were used to make multiple measures of the same object" (Huizinga & Elliott, 1986).

Huizinga and Elliott argue that the best method to test the reliability of an instrument is the test-retest estimate of reliability. They state that in fact the majority of researchers have used a test-retest procedure, commonly using the product-moment correlation between test and retest scores as the reliability coefficient.

Most Dutch researchers have not gone so far. Some of them have presented the items chosen to different judges; for instance, Nijboer and Dijksterhuis (1983) asked educational experts and criminologists to examine the delinquency items for relevance and formulation. Others saw to it that offense definitions closely approximated penal law definitions or that items were unequivocal and clear. Many took care that the self-report part of the survey gave careful instructions either to respondents or to interviewers. Van Schie et al. (1987) introduced questions on "being detected" or "being punished," to control for consistency in the answers. Moreover, they changed the order of the questions and of the pre-coded answers in such a way that neighbors in the classrooms could not check each other's questionnaire.

Buikhuisen et al. did two pilot studies: one to construct the list of self-report items and one to try out the method of administration and response rate. In addition they used the split-half method.

It has to be admitted that the problem of reliability does not seem to have worried Dutch researchers a great deal. This lack of concern surely is not justified. It is one of the reasons Dutch self-report studies, even when based on instruments of colleagues, are hardly comparable, because, as Hindelang et al. (1981) state, slightly different wording has a direct impact on answers given.

An example of a reliability problem in our last self-report survey among a national youth sample and in two high school studies, is the measurement of arson, one of the offenses included in the instrument (Junger-Tas & Kruissink, 1987; Baerveldt, 1987; Mutsaers, 1988).

The item was "Have you, during the last school year, set fire in a cave, a cellar, a bicycle shed, a wooden barrack, or somewhere else?" Some 10% admitted to what we defined as arson. However, contrary to our expectations, these percentages were much higher among the youngest age groups and among boys (12 to 14 years), i.e., 18% and 15.5%.

The explanation probably lies in the circumstance that for several years the traditional burning of Christmas trees on New Year's Eve has become a massive happening, organized and supervised by the police, and in which many youths -- especially the younger ones --participate. There are indications that the time of data collection -- in one study this was shortly after the new year -- also had an impact on the number of positive answers to this question.

These and similar problems threaten the reliability as well as the validity of Dutch studies. It is clear that such problems would multiply in the case of comparative research unless great care is taken to overcome them.

6. CONCURRENT VALIDITY

Concurrent validity refers to methods checking whether self-report delinquency results are consistent with the results of other sources of knowledge about delinquent behavior. These sources can be official statistics, or persons who know the juvenile, such as teachers, friends or family.

Most Dutch researchers have taken at least some elementary steps to increase the validity of the instrument. In order to reduce memory problems, distinction is generally made between questions asking whether a youngster has ever committed a particular offense or whether the offense has been committed in a limited period preceding the survey.

For example, in the national youth survey (Junger-Tas & Kruissink, 1987) we found the period of the preceding school year the most relevant limitation in time, considering that the majority of Dutch juveniles go to school up to 18 years (94% of the sample went to school regularly). The two studies among university students (Buikhuisen, 1969; Jongman & Smale, 1972) included questions about police contacts for specific offenses, but this was more of a consistency measure because no external criterion was used to measure validity.

6.1. Self-Reported Delinquency and Official Delinquency

Only a limited number of researchers have tried to attack this problem. Veendrick (1976), who took a random sample of all 15 to 65 year old males of the city of Groningen, compared his data to the city's police records. He found four offenses that showed greater frequencies in police records than in the self-report data: burglary, assault, joy riding and hit-and-run offenses. More than eight times as many burglaries figured in police records than might be expected on the basis of the self-report data.

In the case of assault the proportion was four times as much and in the case of hit-and-run offenses and joy riding it was twice as much. Offenses with equal numbers in the self-report survey as in police records were driving without a license, receiving stolen goods, and extortion.

With respect to most of the other offenses (17 of 24) the frequency of the self-report data was vastly greater than the police data. If we assume that police data refer to offenses that have really been committed, these results suggest that in a random adult male sample there is clear underreporting of some specific offenses. Comparing the nature of criminality between recorded and self-report offenders for the ten most frequently committed offenses, Veendrick notes the greater frequency of burglary, assault, drunken driving and receiving among recorded offenders.

This study raises the question whether the self-report method is adequate in the case of adult samples, a question that has also been examined by Angenent (1984). His sample was composed of 222 males, of average age 46, with a court conviction. He found that 49% of the respondents who had completed the questionnaire, mentioned offenses that were recorded by the police. Despite the weakness of the methodology, the study did show that the validity of the self-report method is questionable in the case of adults living in the community, with either a police record or a court conviction.

On the basis of these results, it might be concluded that the self-report method is more appropriate for juveniles than for adults. This does not mean there are no problems in this respect. In one rather large scale self-report study (Junger-Tas et al., 1983) a validity check was performed on the group of youngsters with recorded police contacts. Of a total of 307 juveniles with recorded police contacts, about 19% did not mention an offense figuring in the record. This group included 130 juveniles who had been interviewed at the police station or at the prosecutor's office in order to have an additional sample of juveniles with official contacts, so the interview situation may have increased the number of invalid answers.

All in all the results suggest reasonable validity and in this respect they are no different from American studies (Hindelang et al., 1981). In the follow-up study conducted two years later, the answers with respect to delinquent behavior and police contacts were compared with those of the first study. They showed a proportion of about 12% inconsistent answers: 11.5% of those having reported at time 1 to have committed at least one offense did not report so at time 2; two-thirds of them had reported only one offense, and one-third, two offenses. The discrepancy is not too large and these results may simply be due to memory effects, either forgetting certain events or telescoping them (Kalton & Schumann, 1982).

Quite a different picture emerges when one looks at the answers with respect to contacts with the police and prosecutor. One-third of those with earlier police contacts did not report them, while 41% of those with earlier prosecutor contacts did not report them. These results indicate that juveniles are more willing to report offending behavior than they are to admit involvement in the juvenile justice system. There apparently is more shame and stigma attached to police and judicial intervention than there is to delinquent behavior.

Junger (1987) did a substantial validity study, testing the self-report method on juveniles from ethnic minority groups. There were four self-report measures: offenses committed "ever" and "last year," police contacts "ever" and "last year." The same measures were designed with respect to official delinquency. Because it is very difficult to match self-report and official data exactly, the validity criterion was rather crude: juveniles known by the police had to admit at least one offense and one police contact; if not, the answer was considered to be response error.

Expectations were that answers on delinquency would be more valid than those on police contacts and that validity would be higher for respondents with greater involvement in delinquency. Similar to the self-report studies mentioned earlier, it appeared that admitting delinquent behavior does not present too many problems for juveniles: among those with police contacts, 71% declared having "ever" committed offenses and 61% reported this with respect to "last year." In contrast, the validity of self-report police contacts is weak: only 30% (ever) and 23% (last year) admitted to such contacts. The more official police contacts juveniles have had, the more they tend to report delinquent behavior as well as the police contacts. The number of offical police contacts is only weakly correlated with response error of self-reported delinquency ("ever:" $r = -.10$; "last year:" $r = -.16$). The association of official police contacts with response error of self-report police contacts is stronger ("ever:" $= r -.35$; "last year:" $r = -.31$).

In addition, there are large differences in validity among the ethnic groups, especially on the "ever" question.

These results are similar to what has been found by Hindelang et al. (1981) and Elliott and Ageton (1980) with respect to differences between blacks and whites. One of the explanations for the discrepancy is, according to Elliott and Ageton, a racial bias in the police handling of juveniles. Junger remarks that this explanation is not valid

for The Netherlands because validity is practically the same for Dutch
and Surinam boys. It is highly improbable that police bias would operate only in the case of Turkish and Moroccan boys and not in the case
of Surinam boys.

Response error and ethnic group (boys, 12 - 18 years)[4]

	Delinquency "ever"	Police contacts "ever"
Dutch (N = 30)	13%	57%
Surinam (N = 47)	13%	64%
Turkish (N = 46)	44%	87%
Moroccan (N = 65)	37%	68%
	$x^2 = 16.3$; p = <.01	$x^2 = 9.8$; p = .02

The table clearly shows that the answers of Dutch and Surinam
boys, most of whom are of Dutch nationality, have the same high level
of validity. The Turkish and Moroccan boys have comparable low levels
of validity. Moreover, this study raises the question of whether the
self-report method should be used to study delinquent behavior in ethnic minority groups. Junger's conclusion is that when comparing different ethnic groups, analysis of official data should be preferred to the
self-report method as they have the same degree of validity for all
ethnic groups.

6.2. Known Group Comparisons

Comparisons between known groups, in order to establish the validity of the self-report method, require that data collection include both
official and self-report data. As we have seen, only a small number of
Dutch studies have collected data from these two sources. In some
studies, juveniles were asked whether they had had contact with the
police (Buikhuisen et al., 1969; Jongman & Smale, 1972; Van Schie et
al., 1987), and invariably those who admitted to police contacts reported more delinquent behavior than the other juveniles.

Veendrick (1976) and Agenent (1984) did collect self-report and
official data. However, Veendrick's official data are city-wide police
statistics which are not strictly comparable to his sample of the Groningen adult population. His conclusion is that despite heavy under-
reporting of four specific offenses, the self-report method seems on
the whole adequate even in the case of adults.

Angenent did not compare delinquent behavior between those without
and those with a police record. Moreover, the methodological drawbacks
of his study do not permit any firm conclusions in this respect.

----

4.   Junger, M., 1987; some elements from Table 9.2.

Junger (1987) also collected both types of data, but on the basis of her findings in the validity study, she decided to use official data

Contacts with police and prosecutor and delinquent self-reports (%)[5]

	Only self-report	Self-report police contacts	Recorded contacts	Prosecutor contacts
Number of different offenses	N = 504	N = 224	N= 104	N = 113
1	64	44	36	26
2	25	27	30	26.5
3	8	18	18	21
4 or >	3	11	16	26.5
	100	100	100	100

$p \leq 0.001$

for further analysis. Some relevant data came from the panel study (Junger-Tas et al., 1983, 1985) because one of its purposes was to distinguish groups with differential involvement in the juvenile justice system. The preceding table shows clear differences.

Of those who did not have any police contacts, two-thirds reported only one offense versus one-fourth of those with prosecutor contacts. Only 3% of the former reported four or more offenses, versus 26.5% of the latter. The table clearly demonstrates that juveniles known to be different on official delinquency also differ in the number of self-reported offenses.

The conclusion of this section on Dutch self-report studies confirms what we know from self-report studies all over the world: they have moderate to high validity and enable the researcher to order his respondents on a continuum from least involvement to frequent involvement in delinquency.

7. SPECIAL PROBLEMS

There is considerable diversity among the western countries in juvenile justice and protection systems, in legal and penal procedures, and in many social and cultural aspects. For example, the age of penal majority varies over countries. The same is true for the participation of girls in delinquency. Also, each country has its own ethnic minorities and these present different problems.

A certain degree of consensus should be reached on the way some elementary variables will be included in the study or will be measured

----
5. Junger-Tas et al., 1983, Table 13.

34

in cross-cultural research.

7.1. Age

In some countries penal majority is at 16 years, in others 17 or 18 years. Insofar as the respective researchers want to compare self-report data with their national statistics the issue is of relevance. One solution is to select the upper limit in order to satisfy all concerned.

There is another reason to opt for a large age range, for instance 12 to 18 or 20 years, and that is the established relationship of delinquency with age. Comparative research would enable us to examine differences in this respect among countries. Moreover, if the studies are repeated over time, changes in the relationship could be observed; it would also be possible to test the Hirschi and Gottfredson hypothesis (1983) of a constant relationship between delinquency and age, independent of time, place, sex, ethnic background and other social conditions.

7.2. Sex

There are still large differences in extent and nature of delinquent behavior between boys and girls, although in our country the differences are diminishing. In our national survey (Junger-Tas & Kruissink, 1987), 56.1% of boys and 38.6% of girls reported having committed at least one out of ten included offenses, a ratio of 1.5:1.

A much greater proportion of girls than boys commit offenses with low frequency. The turning point is five offenses, many more boys than girls reporting six or more offenses. Average number of offenses reported by boys is 14.4 and by girls, 8.2 (t = 2.66; p < 0.01).

Differences are small with respect to using public transport without paying, graffiti, and shoplifting. Differences are considerable for vandalism, arson, receiving stolen goods, bicycle theft, and burglary. Boys continue to report more serious offenses than girls. A review of official statistics since 1980 shows an increase of girls known to the police by 30%. The ratio boys to girls at the police level was 9:1 in 1980, and was 7.5:1 in 1986. However, we found that girls start offending at a later age than boys and they stop offending at an earlier age.

In conclusion, there are very good reasons to include girls in comparative self-report research: both differences among countries in this respect and the changing role of girls could be followed.

7.3. Social Class

Like many American researchers (Hirschi, 1969; Gold, 1970; Hinde-lang et al., 1981), we did not find any relationship between social class and delinquency (Junger-Tas et al., 1982, 1985). The absence of relationship has been taken as proof of social class bias in the processing of juveniles by the juvenile justice system.

Self-reported offenses by frequency and sex (%)

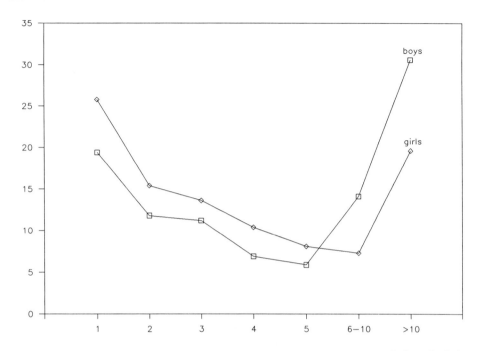

Since we had collected self-report data as well as official data, we were able to examine the interrelations. We found indeed that children of skilled and unskilled workers ran a higher risk of having official police and prosecutor contacts than middle class juveniles. However, more analysis showed that the relation between SES and official intervention was apparent primarily at low offending frequency: when frequency increases the relationship disappears.

We checked this again by considering some other variables indicating SES, such as father's employment status, level of education and dropping out of school, controlling for age and for frequency of offending behavior. All these variables showed a relationship to official intervention. However, the relationship was not very strong. Our conclusion is that there certainly is some class bias in the way the system is working. Class-related factors do influence decision making of the police and other officials to a certain extent, but the overriding factors determining official intervention are the nature and the frequency of the offending behavior.

There is, however, some inherent flaw in the measurement of social class by father's profession. I would like to plead for a different conceptualization of social class by taking into account the position of juveniles in a status system that is of vital importance to them: the school system.

We found quite a strong relationship between the level of education and delinquency: "low stream" schools (vocational training/

technical schools) had higher proportions of offenders than "high
stream" schools (preparing for university). The relationship holds
even when controlling for age and SES. Moreover, poor performance in
school, in terms of achievement and social behavior, is a strong predictor of delinquency.

In this view the class position of a juvenile is essentially determined by his school status, defined by the type and level of the
school, and by his cognitive and social functioning therein. It does
seem worthwhile to try to construct a number of variables measuring
this concept for comparative purposes.

7.4. Ethnic Groups

As mentioned earlier, every country has its own ethnic minorities,
which means different cultural backgrounds and different problems.
Some have the same nationality as the white population such as the
Blacks in the United States, the West Indians in Great Britain, and the
Surinamers in Holland. Others are foreigners and they have an even
more precarious social and economic position. There are a certain
number of difficulties related to the use of the self-report method
with these groups. Some of these difficulties are rather technical.

It is possible that in very deprived and irregular life situations, offenses of the kind measured by self-reports have low salience
or are more quickly forgotten. On the other hand, it may be expected
that the interview method will yield better results than the simple
questionnaire. Hindelang et al. (1981), trying to establish the validity of independent variables such as school performance among different
ethnic groups, used an "everyday knowledge" scale as an external standard. They found equally low validity of the independent variables as
for the dependent variable for black males.

Junger (1987) examined the relationship between validity and some
background variables. She found that boys with very conventional attitudes about delinquency were more reluctant to admit having committed
offenses than boys who did not feel so strongly about it (p < .01).
The same is true for "traditionalism": a traditional outlook on life
operationalized by opinions on women's role in society, went together
with lower validity.

As was expected, the less knowledge there was of the Dutch language, the lower the validity of responses. Contrary to expectations,
there was no relationship between fear of expulsion and low validity.

The interesting point here is that validity among Surinam boys is
no different from that among Dutch boys. In this respect it is worthwhile to note that the Surinam population as a whole is far better
integrated in Dutch society than the Turkish and Moroccan population;
Surinam juveniles speak the Dutch language, have higher SES, and have a
higher level of education.

The conclusion seems to be that the less well integrated the
minority groups are into the host society and culture, the greater the
distance between the traditional cultural values and those of the dominant culture, the more deprived and marginalized they are, then the
lower the validity of their responses on a self-report instrument. The

question then becomes: should we, for purposes of comparative research, exclude all ethnic minority groups from participation in an international study based on the self-report method? Or, should we exclude certain specific groups and include others, for instance those who have the nationality of the host country?

8. CONCLUSIONS

Recalling the three possible goals for self-report researchers as suggested by Hindelang et al. (1981, p. 88-89):
1) the construction of a measure of delinquency identical to the official measure but without its shortcomings;
2) the testing of theories of delinquency;
3) the construction of a social indicator reflecting incidence and prevalence of delinquent behavior in the population, it seems to me that in comparative research we should try primarily to realize the first goal. This would constitute a first step leading perhaps to the second goal at a later stage. The third goal still appears out of reach for some time to be. To conclude, some suggestions will be presented with respect to several elementary requirements for an instrument that might be used in comparative research.

8.1. The Sample

Dutch self-report research presents a great variety in sampling populations and sampling procedures: samples were drawn of university students, high school students, adults with or without a police record, and the general youth population.

The evidence suggests that the self-report method is not very adequate in the case of adults; results show low response and questionable validity. On the other hand, most sampling procedures have their drawbacks and biases; high school samples miss the dropouts and truants, while really troublesome youth are generally not included in representative samples.

Considering the risk of multiplying bias in comparative research, the best option seems to me to draw a representative sample from the national youth population.

Taking into account the relationship of delinquency to age, I would suggest a relatively large age range, for example 12 to 18 or 20 years of age. Considering the changing role of girls and women in society, girls should be included. As for ethnic minorities, I would suggest including juveniles who have the nationality of the participating country, but excluding young foreigners.

8.2. The Definition of Delinquency

Large differences in operational definitions exist among the various western countries. One problem is that in the United States, so-called status offenses are part of that definition, while in many western countries these behaviors are defined only as problematic or deviant and thus cannot lead to prosecution.

Which items should be included in the delinquency definition?

We know that there is a relationship between self-report delinquency and officially recorded delinquency; the risk of official registration and intervention is related to seriousness and frequency of delinquent behavior (Gold, 1970; Junger-Tas et al., 1983; Hirschi, 1969; Hindelang et al., 1981).

The research literature also teaches us that some offenses such as graffiti, vandalism and shoplifting -- though not always prosecuted -- are typical juvenile offenses. Although not very serious they have a great nuisance value and they contribute to deteriorated neighborhoods and housing estates. Given these considerations and the wish to get some insight into the nature and extent of juvenile delinquency in the respective countries, I would suggest combining a certain number of rather serious offenses figuring in the police statistics, along with a number of non-serious nuisance delinquency items. Behavior related to adolescent status (status offenses) should not be part of the definition of delinquency.

8.3. The Method of Administration

Hindelang et al. (1981) have tried out different methods of administration: questionnaires and interviews in anonymous and non-anonymous situations. They found that no one method was superior to the other, although the non-anonymous interview gave slightly better results in the case of young black males. This may have resulted from a somewhat better understanding of the study's questions in the interview situation. This assumption was at the basis of Junger's decision to interview ethnic minority respondents in her study. In Holland, questionnaires are almost always administered in an anonymous situation, while in the case of interviews the condition is frequently non-anonymous. Unfortunately no tests have been done to compare the different conditions.

The most important outcome of Hindelang's study therefore is that no condition gave a higher reliability or validity than the other. In conclusion, given some uncertainties about participation of different ethnic groups in the various countries as well as the generally higher response rate in the case of the interview method, I would have some preference for the non-anonymous interview.

8.4. Reliability

Problems of reliability of the instrument that confront every isolated study are multiplied in cross-cultural research where differences in wording, in meaning, and in interpretation accumulate. Therefore, it does seem necessary -- once the instrument has taken a more definite form -- to conduct one or even two pilot studies to test it out and to calculate test-retest estimates of reliability.

To reduce difficulties I would opt for a very structured interview-schedule which allows for non-problematic quantification. Moreover,

careful attention should be paid to the <u>selection of interviewers</u>, to
their instruction and to <u>the control of their work</u>.

8.5. Validity

Deciding to make the data collection non-anonymous would allow
introduction of adquate validity controls. The question is whether
access to police or the prosecutor's office is possible in all participating countries.

Assuming that this could be realized in most of the countries,
there are great advantages to performing a validity control. Not only
would it give more insight into differential validity between countries, but it would also give more information on the relations between
official delinquency and self-report delinquency.

In other words: <u>validity control</u> appears all the more <u>necessary</u>
in <u>comparative research</u> and it would considerably enhance the significance of a cross-national study's results.

REFERENCES

Angenent, M: Medewerking aan enquetes over niet-geregistreerde criminaliteit. <u>Tiljkschrift voor criminologie</u>, 1984, nr. 6.

Antilla, I, & Jaakhola, R: <u>Unrecorded criminality in Finland</u>. Helsinki: Kriminologiness Tutkimuslaitos, 1966.

Baerveldt, C: <u>School en delinquentie</u>. The Hague: WODC (Ministerie of
Justitie), 1987.

Bruinsma, GJN: <u>Criminaliteit als sociaal leerproces</u>. Arnhem: Gouda
Quint, 1985.

Buikhuisen, W, Jongman, RW, & Oving, W: Ongeregistreerde criminaliteit
onder studenten. <u>Nederlands Tijdschrift voor Criminologie</u>,
11:69-89, 1969.

Cernkovich, SA, Giordano, PC, & Pugh, MD: Chronic offenders. The
missing cases in self-report delinquency research. <u>Journal of
Criminal Law and Criminology</u>, 76(3):705-732, 1985.

Christie, N, Andeneas, J, & Skirbekke, S: A study in self-reported
crime. <u>Scandinavian studies in criminology</u>, Vol 1. London: Tavistock Publications, 1965.

Clinard, MB: A cross-cultural replication of the relation of urbanism
to criminal behavior. <u>American Sociological Review</u>, 25:2, 1960.

Elliott, DS, & Ageton, SS: Reconciling race and class differences in
self-reported and official estimates of delinquency. <u>American
Sociological Review</u>, 45, 1980.

Elmhorn, K: A study in self-reported delinquency among school children
in Stockholm. <u>Scandinavian studies in criminology</u>, vol 1. London:
Tavistock Publications, 1965.

Friday, PC: Research on youth crime in Sweden: Some problems in methodology. <u>Scandinavian studies in criminology</u>, vol. 46. London:
Tavistock Publications, 1974.

Gold, M: <u>Delinquent behavior in an American city</u>. Belmont, California: Brooks Cole, 1970.

40

Hindelang, M, Hirschi, T, & Weis, J: <u>Measuring delinquency</u>. Beverly Hills: Sage Publications, 1981.
Hirschi, T, & Gottfredson, M: Age and the explanation of crime. <u>American Journal of Sociology</u>, 89:3, 1983.
Hirschi, T: <u>Causes of delinquency</u>. Berkeley: University of California Press, 1969.
Huizinga, D, & Elliott, DS: Reassessing the reliability and validity of self-report delinquency measures. <u>Journal of Quantitative Criminology</u>, 2:4, 1986.
Jongman, RW, & Smale, GJA: Ongeregistreerde criminaliteit onder vrouwelijke studenten. <u>Nederlands Tijdschrift voor Criminologie</u>, 14:1, 1972.
Junger, M: Slachtofferschap en deviant gedrag onder jongeren uit etnische minderheden. Unpublished interim report. The Hague: WODC, 1987.
Junger, M: Validiteit van zelfrapportage van delinquentie bij jongeren uit etnische minderheden. In de Jong Gierveld, J, & van de Zouwen, J (Eds.), <u>De vragenlijst in het sociaal onderzoek</u>. Deventer: Van Loghem Slaterus, 1987.
Junger-Tas, J: Patterns in delinquent behavior. In Junger-Tas, J, & Block, RL (Eds.), <u>Juvenile delinquency in the Netherlands</u>. Berkeley: Kugler Publications, 1988.
Junger-Tas, J: Hidden delinquency and judicial selection in Belgium. In Friday, PC, & Stewart, V. Lorne (Eds.), <u>Youth crime and juvenile justice</u>. New York: Praeger, 1977.
Junger-Tas, J, Junger, M, & Barendse, E: <u>Jeugddelinguentie II - De invloed van justitices ingrypen</u>. The Hague: WODC, Ministerie van Justitite, 1985.
Junger-Tas, J, Junger, M, & Barendse, E: <u>Jeugddelinquentie-achtergronden en justitiële reactie</u>. The Hague: WODC, Ministerie van Justitie, 1983.
Junger-Tas, J, & Krinssink, M: Ontwikkelinf van de jeugdcriminaliteit. The Hague: WODC, Ministerie van Justitite, 1987.
Kalton, G, & Schumann, H: The effect of the question on survey response: A review. <u>Journal of the Royal Statistical Society</u>, series A, vol. 145.
Le Poole, F: Law and practice concerning the counterparts of "persons in need of supervision" in some European countries with a particular emphasis on The Netherlands. In Teitelbaum, LE: <u>Beyond control: Status offenders in the juvenile court</u>. Cambridge, MA: Ballinger Publications Company, 1977.
Levinson, D: What have we learned from cross-cultural surveys? <u>American Behavioral Scientist</u>, 20:5, 1977.
Mutsaers, M: Experiment criminaliteitspreventie in het LBO. <u>Justitiële erkenningen</u>, juni 1987.
Nijboer, JA, & Dijksterhuis, FPH: <u>Onderwijs en delinquentie</u>. Rijksuniversiteit Groningen: Criminologisch Instituut, 1983.
Schie, ECM van, van der Houwen, G, & Willemsen, TW: <u>Wat halen meisjes en jongens uit en wat vinden we daarvan?</u> Leiden University: Department of Psychology, 1987.

Veendrick, L: <u>Verborgen en geregistreerde criminaliteit in Groningen</u>.
Rijksuniversiteit Groningen: Criminologisch Instituut, 1976.
Vetere, E, Newman, G: International Crime Statistics: An overview
from a comparative perspective. <u>Abstracts on Criminology and
Penology</u>, 17:3, 1977.

APPENDIX: National Survey Items (Junger-Tas & Kruissink, 1987).

Have you, during the past school year:

1. taken the bus, tramway, or underground without paying;
2. taken something from a shop without paying;
3. damaged or destroyed on purpose:
   - a telephone box;
   - a streetlight;
   - windows (crashing);
   - a car;
   - a bicycle;
   - objects within bus/tram/underground.
4. vandalized or plastered walls, abris, or buses/trams with sprays or
   other material;
5. taken a bicycle;
6. threatened someone with a knife or other weapon;
7. set fire in a cave, bicycle shed, wooden barrack, or somewhere
   else;
8. beaten up and kicked purposely someone in the street, in school, in
   a disco, or in a cafe;
9. broken in and entered someplace without permission and with the
   objective of stealing something;
10. sold or bought something which you knew had been stolen?

ACCOMMODATING SELF-REPORT METHODS TO A LOW-DELINQUENCY CULTURE:
A LONGITUDINAL STUDY FROM NEW ZEALAND

Terrie E. Moffitt
Department of Psychology
University of Wisconsin
Madison, Wisconsin

1. INTRODUCTION

In 1984 I had the opportunity to travel to New Zealand for two
years to collect data for a program of research into predictors of
delinquent behavior. I had proposed to investigate in particular the
relationship between self-report delinquency and neuro-psychological
variables, and had identified an ongoing longitudinal study of the
health and social development of a birth cohort of 1037 New Zealand
children that would be the ideal context for my investigation. Prospective data were to be made available to me concerning the subjects'
perinatal, medical and neurological health, their educational achievement, and childhood behavior disorders. The subjects would become 13
years old soon after I arrived, a suitable age to measure both emerging
delinquency and neuropsychological status.

I had read, but apparently not internalized, Hirschi's (1980)
caution that items from established self-report delinquency instruments
will likely not be uniformly appropriate to particular age, sex, or
cultural groups with varying expected levels of delinquent involvement.
Armed with the excellent self-report instrument from the U.S. National
Youth Survey (Elliott, Huizinga, Ageton, Knowles & Canter, 1983), I
left inner-city Los Angeles for Dunedin, New Zealand, a university town
and agricultural trading center of approximately 120,000 citizens. One
of my first cross-cultural shocks came when I noticed my Kiwi neighbors
placing coins on their steps at sundown, in complete faith that the
coins would remain in plain view on a dark city street until the milk
was delivered hours later. I believed at that moment that I had made a
terrible mistake.

At least, I thought, the subjects and I do speak the same language. That was my second mistake.

In truth, I had not been entirely ignorant of the fact that New
Zealand had a crime rate much lower than that of the United States or
Great Britain. I knew that in 1983 the murder charge rate was 1.4 per
100,000 (44 cases nationwide), and that in 1984 94.2% of arrests were
for nonviolent offenses. In 1981 the conviction rate between the ages
of 15 and 24 was 7.7% for males and 1.1% for females. Only about 3% of

43

M. W. Klein (ed.), Cross-National Research in Self-Reported Crime and Delinquency, 43–66.
© 1989 by Kluwer Academic Publishers.

New Zealand's juveniles 10 to 16 years old (2,857 per 100,000) had appeared before Children and Young Person's court in 1982, although fully one third (32,820 per 100,000) had come to the attention of the juvenile justice system, but were processed at lesser levels by Youth Aid constables or in Children's Board hearings. Traditionally, New Zealand has enjoyed a popular reputation as a low crime country. That may be changing. A recent report from Interpol and the World Health Organization, based on 1984 statistics, ranked New Zealand among Denmark, Sweden, Canada, Australia, West Germany and The Netherlands on prevalence of most types of offenses. The report showed that New Zealand's crime rate is now growing at a rate among the fastest in the western world, equivalent to Canada's growth rate. Since 1978, rape increased by 63%, robbery by 13%, burglary by 21%, and car theft rates in New Zealand and Australia now exceed those in the U.S. as a whole. Nevertheless, crime density and offense types are milder than the severe problems seen in large cities in Britain and the United States. The "low-crime" reputation remains true especially in New Zealand's south island, where my research was conducted, because its population is more rural and more racially homogeneous than that of the north island.

There were possible advantages to New Zealand's low crime rate. I had argued, based on the writings of Thorsten Sellin (1938), that investigations of individual difference factors in the etiology of deviance are most profitably undertaken in societies with high group resistance to crime, and thus low crime rates. Sellin noted, "Offenders who have overcome the greatest and most comprehensive group resistance probably disclose more clearly than others the type of personalities which are important to our aims of research." In other words, individual difference signals may be most clearly detected against a background of low social variation "noise." The aim of the research was to test for the existence of neuropsychological correlates of antisocial behavior. The hypothesized correlations were not likely to be of astonishing strength. A low-delinquency setting might maximize the chances of detecting such weak associations.

2. AIMS FOR THE RESEARCH, AND IMPLICATIONS FOR DATA COLLECTION

Nevertheless, the low-delinquency cultural setting, as well as several broad objectives of the research, presented certain measurement problems. The first objective was to tap individual variation in antisocial behavior in a group of subjects who could be expected to report little serious delinquent behavior, that is, behavior likely to result in arrest if detected. The subjects were residents of a small city (and its rural surroundings) in a low-delinquency nation; half of them were girls and only two percent were minority group members. They were to be interviewed within one month of their thirteenth birthdays, making the reporting period age 12 and younger.

The second objective was to collect data that would enable viewing delinquent behavior longitudinally as a development process. Much research in criminology has tacitly assumed that delinquency is a new behavior pattern that spontaneously emerges about the time of puberty. This assumption was natural when delinquency researchers relied solely upon official record data for making designations of delinquent versus nondelinquent. Age of onset was legally defined (e.g., Gottfredson & Hirschi, 1986). Now that child psychiatry and criminology have begun to converse (however gingerly) it is becoming generally acknowledged that antisocial behavior patterns are remarkably stable across childhood, adolescence, and early adulthood (Loeber, 1982; Olweus, 1979; Robins, 1966). In the New Zealand study, excellent prospective data had been collected regarding childhood behavior problems and conduct disorder between age 3 and age 11. It was hoped that the delinquency instrument selected for administration at age 13 could provide continuity of measurement and capture differing rates of transition from childhood manifestations of antisocial behavior to illegal forms of antisocial behavior.

The third objective was also dictated by the longitudinal nature of the study. Follow-up waves of data collection were planned to continue at least through age 17, and possibly beyond. It was planned to test the capacity of neuropsychological (and other) variables to discriminate prospectively youths who develop lengthy, recidivistic, serious offense patterns from those who engage in only mild or brief delinquency, or who refrain from delinquency altogether. Delinquency data spanning at least the juvenile career would be needed for these analyses.

The first two objectives, assessing limited variation and ensuring continuity with childhood behavior problems, suggested including in the instrument not only items describing illegal behavior, but a sample of items from the universe of "norm-violating" pre-delinquent behaviors as well. On the other hand, flexibility in age-appropriateness was desirable in light of the longitudinal follow-ups planned. Items should remain relevant across ages 12 to 17, and should effectively tap the more serious illegal acts expected at older ages. Self-report instruments have frequently been criticized for overemphasis on relatively trivial items (Hindelang, Hirschi, & Weis, 1979; 1981), and much admirable work has been done (e.g., Elliott et al., 1983) to design measures that maximize the semantic match between legal definitions and subjects' own meanings of the serious acts they report. It was important that the instrument selected be able to capture quality data from the serious/illegal end of the continuum of antisocial acts, as well as from the "trivial" end.

3. SOME PRACTICAL CONSIDERATIONS FOR DEVELOPING A SITE-SPECIFIC INSTRUMENT

Pilot work with the American instrument originally proposed for the research proved that instrument to be unsuitable for a number of reasons; it contained few norm violation items, the interview protocol was unwieldy given our small resources in time and personnel, certain of the instrument's items violated community sensitivities, and many items would require substantial rewording. Indeed, needed alterations were so substantial that it became apparent that I would no longer be able to claim to be using the original instrument. The instrument ultimately used in the research evolved through a process of successive accommodations, and it is the steps in that process that this chapter describes. In addition to the broad measurement objectives outlined above, several other issues required attention in order to accommodate a self-report instrument to idiosyncrasies of the setting, enhance measurement validity, and maximize limited project resources. Since these issues are likely to be germane to other researchers who employ the self-report method in a novel setting, they are outlined below.

3.1. Data Uses

Hindelang et al. (1981) have differentiated two goals of self-report research: (1) providing epidemiological data about incidence and prevalence of delinquency in the population, and (2) describing the delinquent characteristics of subjects for testing theory about the development of delinquent behavior. The researcher should be clear about the use to which the data will be put, because the two goals have somewhat differing implications for instrument design. For example, if the goal is providing epidemiological data for a new setting, then representative sampling from the domain of acts that are illicit in the local culture, reporting period length, consensus between legal and subjective definitions of acts, and act-specific validity checks will all be crucial characteristics of data collection. The second goal, measurement of a (presumably) continuously distributed delinquent "behavioral state" in individuals, was more pertinent to the present research. Therefore concerns about test-retest stability of scale scores, systematic contributors to error variance (such as reading disability), normative New Zealand opinions of the relative seriousness of acts, and general corroboration of self-report by other sources (parent, peer or teacher report) were relatively more salient.

3.2. Sensitivity to Local Mores

Local views on delinquency had impact upon the self-report study in two ways. Specifically, research into sexual behavior is taboo in New Zealand. Although I was distressed by this institutionalized restriction of scientific inquiry, I was willing to omit items referring to sexual behavior from the self-report instrument in the interest of professional rapport. The second influence of local mores was more insidious. There was strong feeling among the members of the local research unit that "our children wouldn't possibly do that!" Having followed the subjects since birth, the staff viewed them somewhat protectively and, understandably, were reluctant to expose the children to any shocking material that might produce high attrition rates. Dr. Phil Silva, unit director, had kindly agreed to pilot candidate instruments with local children, and after a few administrations of the Elliott et al. (1983) interview wrote, "I dropped some items that I believed were likely to be offensive (mainly to do with sex, drugs, and violence)...On tryout it took about ten minutes but left the young people somewhat upset, bewildered, or thinking the whole thing must be a joke!" Much negotiation was required before a few drug use and violence items were reinstated. Overcoming the trepidations held by local staff in a low-delinquency country may be nearly as difficult as overcoming cultural eccentricities of foreign-designed instruments.

3.3. Interviewer Considerations

My research budget was small and did not provide adequate funding for the recruitment and training of interviewers, so the New Zealand Alchoholic Liquor Advisory Board had generously agreed to provide the time of an interviewer already on Dr. Silva's staff who might be trained to collect the delinquency data. The interviewer was a wonderful woman, but she was a prim and proper piano teacher, and looked it. I found her intimidating myself; no 13-year-old could be expected to confess unspeakable acts to her. The data collection protocol had to be accommodated further to incorporate the semi-anonymous private card sorting procedure previously employed by West and Farrington (1973). The advantages and disadvantages of self-administered questionnaires versus personal interviews have often been debated (Farrington, 1973; Krohn, Waldo & Chiricos, 1975; Warner, 1982). The protocol we finally followed included each, eliminating disadvantages of reliance upon one method. An initial self-administered card sort session maximized subjects' comfort with reporting, and a brief follow-up interview (conducted by myself) captured more detailed information and provided a validity check. In this way excellent data were obtained on a small budget. However, this accommodation should certainly be avoided by securing enough funding and a ready local supply of appropriate interviewers before attempting to collect data in a foreign setting.

Very little attention has been paid to desirable characteristics of delinquency interviewers, but social psychology research has shown that parameters such as age, gender, race, expertise and attitudes can yield demonstrable effects upon data obtained by interviewers (Sudman & Bradburn, 1974). Teilmann (1977) has shown that a race and gender match between interviewer and subject can enhance the validity of delinquency reporting. A personable but professional interviewer may actually elicit more valid reporting by putting subjects at ease. One New Zealand boy said in the follow-up interview, "Oh, if it's you that wants to know, I have smoked pot then, but I wasn't gonna tell that to just anybody." Interviewer considerations are especially crucial for cross-national research because data quality depends upon the cultural and language match between interviewers and subjects, and because a ready supply of suitable native interviewers may not be available in some settings.

3.4. Subject Literacy

Many authors have noted the futility of using written questionnaires to obtain data from a population likely to be relatively poor in reading skills (e.g., Hirschi, Hindelang & Weis, 1980). In fact, the question of whether delinquency _is_ differentially associated with

disability in reading or written language remains controversial (see
Murray, 1976, versus Sturge, 1982). Nevertheless, although not frankly
illiterate, many delinquents do have some difficulty with reading and
writing, and any self-report data collection protocol employed should
be able to capture valid reports from even the poorest of readers. An
interview procedure accomplishes this goal most effectively. The New
Zealand study used a card sort procedure to obviate written responses,
but known poor readers (detected in a learning disabilities examination from an earlier wave of the longitudinal study) automatically
received an oral administration of the cards. All words used on the
item cards were selected to be at or below the fourth grade reading
level. Researchers wishing to collect self-report data from countries
with high rates of illiteracy or low national educational attainment
levels will need to consider carefully the difficulty level of words
used by interviewers as well.

3.5. Accommodation to Local Dialect and Opportunity

    There is a trade-off between the extent to which an instrument is
tailored to the local culture and the extent to which we can generalize
its results outside the culture. Again, it is well to consider the use
to which the data are to be put. If the goal is solely the measurement
of "delinquentness" in individual subjects, then items should be tailored to fit locally unique opportunities for illicit behavior as well
as translated to fit language or dialect. Likewise, if the goal is to
describe the epidemiology of delinquent acts within a single nation,
for example for policy planning by that nation, tailoring can be extensive. However, if <u>cross-cultural</u> comparisons are to be attempted,
items reflecting unique local opportunity will impede generalization.
For example, the New Zealand instrument includes "Stealing money from
milk bottles." That item would spuriously inflate New Zealand's incidence score in comparison to the scores from countries where people buy
milk in shops. Another consideration, especially in low-delinquency
settings, is whether to retain items very low in local opportunity for
the sake of cross-cultural generalizability. High school cocaine use
is epidemic in the United States, but the fact that New Zealand is an
island nation, off the Latin American shipping lanes, with diligent
customs inspection at its two international airports, means that there
is virtually no cocaine to be abused there. Nevertheless, if an item
inquiring about cocaine abuse were not included in the instrument,
there would be no empirical documentation that cocaine abuse is rarer
in New Zealand than in the United States. If one wishes to compare
automobile theft rates across nations, then automobile theft must be
included as a "key item" in the multinational instrument, regardless of
the availablity of automobiles in the countries studied. Information
about differential local opportunities for "key" delinquent acts must
be sought out and used when cross-cultural data are interpreted.
    One answer to this problem is to include both items of local oppor-
tunity and items necessary for cross-cultural comparison, and to tag
items for separate data analysis procedures. For the New Zealand
study, comparability with the item content of established instruments

of high quality was desirable, and we also wished to be able to pursue cross-cultural comparisons with previously published data from other countries. To that end, items most frequently duplicated from four previously published instruments (Elliott et al., 1983; Hindelang et al., 1981; Magnusson, Anders & Zetterblom, 1975; and West & Farrington, 1973) were selected for inclusion in the instrument and tagged in the codebook for "instrument of origin". Many of these items required rewording to match New Zealand dialect or slang. For example, an American billy club, a British cosh and a New Zealand baton are similar instruments of assault. No American boy would be caught dead with a baton, and New Zealanders make tea in their billys.

To sample adequately from items of local opportunity, assistance was sought from criminologists Michael Stace and Professor Warren Young of the Victoria University of Wellington's Department of Criminology, and from constables in the Youth Aid Section of the Dunedin Police Department. These gentlemen were invaluable in reviewing items from foreign instruments for local meaning, dialect, and slang usage. They also nominated numerous items of local opportunity and many norm violation items they knew to be typical of New Zealand "louts." These items can be excluded from analysis when cross-cultural comparisons are made.

3.6. Social Meanings of Items

A single delinquent act may have quite different meanings for the subjects in one culture from those it holds for the researcher from another culture. No two countries exhibit identical definitions of illegal behavior in their penal codes, a fact resulting in difficulty for cross-cultural studies using official data. The use of self-report avoids many of the validity problems to be expected from discrepant definitions, policies, and procedures of recording criminal behavior used by foreign law enforcement agencies. Nevertheless, a problem remains because juveniles everywhere form their subjective notions of what behaviors are "delinquent" partly by knowing what behaviors are defined as illegal (and how seriously illegal) by their national judicial systems. For example, we have learned from previous research in Denmark that theft of a bicycle carries substantially greater meaning of crime severity for Danes than for Americans. This is because bicycles are a major form of adult transportation in Denmark, and are not considered mere recreational possessions. In Los Angeles, gang-perpetrated wall graffiti has become a serious public policy problem, with property owners demanding severe sanctions. In New Zealand, graffiti remains at the level of scratching a sweetheart's name on toilet walls, and is not viewed as worthy of much attention. Glue sniffing had not yet been given any official status in New Zealand at the time first wave data were collected, yet children sniffed fumes from paper bags of glue in streets and shopping malls, in open defiance of powerless constables. National attitudes about glue sniffing were being formed in the daily press. New Zealanders gave drinking alcohol in a public place a lower seriousness rating for 13-year-olds than trespassing, a social meaning opposite that likely held in the southern United States.

The approach we followed to address differing social meanings of
items reduced the social meaning discrepancies to a single dimension,
relative seriousness. A survey was conducted in which samples of New
Zealand university students and juvenile justice professionals were
asked to rate their notions of the seriousness of each act included in
the self-report instrument. Individual items were subsequently weighted by these seriousness scores, giving each subject a score reflecting
not only the variety of acts reported, but some indication of how deviant the reporter's acts would be perceived within the local community.
A multinational comparison project might collect locally-derived seriousness weights to allow direct empirical investigation of cross-
cultural discrepancies in social meanings of delinquent acts. Newman's
(1976) study of seriousness ratings from six countries showed that,
although there was generally good agreement across cultures regarding
the severity of "traditionally criminal" acts (e.g., robbery), disagreement emerged regarding the social meanings of "traditionally deviant"
acts (e.g., homosexuality, marijuana use). Newman's findings imply
that obtaining local seriousness ratings may be most important if "norm
violation" items are assessed, as may be done in low-delinquency
settings.

4. DEVELOPMENT AND APPLICATION OF THE SELF-REPORT EARLY DELINQUENCY (SRED) INSTRUMENT

4.1. The Subjects

Subjects were adolescents from a complete cohort of consecutive
births between 1 April, 1972 and 31 March, 1973 in Dunedin, New Zealand. The cohort's history has been described by McGee and Silva
(1982). Briefly, perinatal data were obtained, and when the children
were traced for follow-up at three years of age 1139 children were
deemed eligible for inclusion in the longitudinal study by residence in
the province of Otago. Of these, 1037 (91%) were assessed. Since
then, follow-ups have been conducted every two years, with 850 subjects
(82% of the three-year-olds) available for study at age 13. McGee
(1985) has compared children who were lost to the study at each age
with those remaining by age 11 and found no notable differences in
social class, IQ, or a variety of behavioral variables. When compared
to the New Zealand general population the cohort is slightly biased
toward higher social class levels. It is predominantly of European
ancestry (less than 2% Maori/Polynesian).

Many self-report delinquency studies have relied upon school-based
samples (e.g., Farrington, 1973; Hardt & Peterson-Hardt, 1977; Hirschi,
1969; Short & Nye, 1958; Warner, 1982). Farrington (1973) has pointed
out that these studies exclude truants, drop-outs, suspended children,
and institutionalized children, and are therefore not likely to be
representative of the children who are most at risk for delinquency in
the community. It is also possible that administration of a questionnaire about delinquent acts in the authoritarian school setting will
reduce subjects' willingness to self-disclose, even though they are

assured of confidentiality. The present study utilized a true birth cohort, participation was independent of school attendence, and assessment was conducted in a neutral research unit setting. The subjects had voluntarily participated in comprehensive assessments biannually since age three, and their confidentiality had never been violated by the research unit staff. It is believed that these research setting factors contributed distinct advantages to the study.

4.2. Representativeness

Of the 850 subjects who participated at age 13, 108 lived too far away to come into the unit for delinquency assessment. Of the 742 who were available for testing, three subjects were unable to understand the self-report instrument because of severe mental retardation, three subjects did not complete the instrument because of restricted time, and 12 subjects' responses to the instrument were judged invalid by the examiners (the subject sorted the cards randomly, appeared not to take the task seriously, or stated his/her reluctance to respond honestly). Data considered valid were therefore obtained from 724 subjects from the original 1037. The 313 missing subjects did not differ from studied subjects on a measure of family social class that was taken at the child's birth (Elley & Irving, 1972), t = 0.59.

The cohort subjects proved to be representative of their community age peers in official delinquency. The most recent (1981) New Zealand census recorded 1,683 13-year-olds living in the Dunedin police district. Youth Aid Section police files held records for 105 13-year-olds, establishing a population official delinquency rate for 13-year-olds of 6.2%. Of the 659 cohort subjects who lived inside the police district, 40 were known to the Youth Aid constables; a cohort rate of 6.1%. Shoplifting accounted for 32% of the police contacts for all 13-year-olds in Dunedin, burglary and other thefts for 45%, assault for 4%, willful destruction of property for 8%, and other various offenses for the remainder. Percentages of arrest types were very similar for the cohort subjects: shoplifting, 43%; burglary and other theft, 41%; assault, 5%; property destruction, 8%.

4.3. Procedure

Approximating the method of West and Farrington (1973), each subject was presented with a deck of 58 randomly sorted index cards, on each of which was printed a delinquent act. Confidentiality was explained, and the subjects were instructed to sort the cards first into a postbox apparatus according to their knowledge that "my friends or other people my age that I know" had engaged in the act "never," "once or twice," or "three or more times." This card sort obtained data about peer delinquency and ensured that the subjects understood the task before their own self-reports began. The subjects were given a second identical deck of cards and asked to repeat the task, now reporting for themselves. Unless the subject was a poor reader (in which case the cards were automatically read aloud to the subject) the examiner withdrew to engage in other activity elsewhere in the room, thereby remaining available to respond to questions, but allowing the subject privacy.

Later the same day, I conducted a follow-up interview based upon each subject's responses from the card sorting session. The interview sought detailed descriptions of the circumstances of each act (to detect inconsistencies of over- or under-reporting), whether any act had brought the subject to the attention of the police, and whether or not the subject was able to be honest in reporting. The subject's estimate of his/her age at the time of the act was queried, and acts occurring before age seven were excluded. Well-defined reporting periods (e.g., six months, one year) have been recommended when estimating incidence and prevalence of delinquent acts is the research goal (Elliott et al., 1983). However, the research objective was etiological rather than epidemiological, and an open-ended reporting period was used in the present study for two reasons. First, the density of delinquent behavior was not expected to be great, given the youth of the subjects. An unrestricted reporting period allowed reporting of a potentially greater number of acts. Second, past experience with the cohort suggested that very young adolescents, although able retrospectively to report incidents (e.g., injuries) validly, often were uncertain about temporal aspects of the incidents, sometimes erring by more than a year. Where inconsistencies were found between interview and card sort data, interview data were used. Finally the card sort examiner and the interviewer scored their own estimates of the validity of each subject's responses to the SRED.

4.4. Psychometric Properties of the SRED

4.4.1. Items. The 58 items of the SRED are listed in Table 1. Few subjects endorsed the "three or more times" frequency category for the items (mean number of subjects endorsing per item = 13.5). The category was judged to be somewhat less reliable than a simple "at least once" criterion, so the two frequency response categories ("once or twice" and "three or more times") were collapsed for this report. (Questionable reliability of frequency reporting was also noted by Erickson & Empey, 1963.) More boys than girls reported every act except smoking cannabis, taking hard drugs, getting drunk, hitting a parent, and graffiti. Thefts (especially shoplifting) accounted for 41.2% of acts reported by the subjects, minor assault for 24.7%, and vandalism and substance abuse for 10.7% and 9.9%, respectively.

4.4.2. Seriousness weights. Cultural-context-appropriate seriousness weights for the items were obtained from a survey of 30 local respondents whose professional roles involved them in the problem of juvenile delinquency. These were two Young Persons' Court judges, a principal of a youth detention home, three Youth Aid constables, six youth social workers of the Department of Social Welfare, and a sample of 18 teachers from local secondry schools. Survey responses were also obtained from a class of 30 psychology undergraduates at the University of Otago. Respondents rated each of the 58 SRED items on a Lykken scale from 0: "harmless prank", to 20: "extremely serious, requiring

TABLE 1. Self-report early delinquency items: Frequencies of endorsement by 13-year-old subjects, and seriousness weights.

Item	% Reporting boys (n=376)	girls (n=348)	Seriousness weight
29-item illegal scale			
1.Running away from home and staying away overnight	6.8	4.5	1.25
2.Carrying a weapon in case it is needed in a fight (like a knife, chain or piece of wood)	10.1	1.5	1.67
3.Going around with a group of 3 or more damaging property or getting into fights	12.4	4.8	1.70
4.Damaging something in a public place (such as streets, movie theatres, buses, toilets)	8.7	3.9	1.46
5.Purposely damaging or destroying something belonging to your parents	4.2	2.7	1.36
6.Starting a fire where you should not burn anything	11.0	2.1	1.43
7.Damaging a parked car (like breaking an aerial, slashing tyres, scratching paint)	2.0	1.2	1.66
8.Raising a false alarm (such as dialling 111 or setting off a false fire alarm)	2.5	0.9	1.40
9.Stealing a thing or money worth between $2 & $40	7.9	5.7	1.36
10.Stealing a thing or money worth over $40	2.0	0.3	1.55
11.Breaking into a house, flat, or vehicle (to try to steal something or just look around)	3.4	0.6	1.57
12.Stealing something from an open shop or store (shoplifting)	15.2	13.8	1.53
13.Stealing something out of a parked car	2.0	0.3	1.57
14.Stealing goods or money from a video machine, public telephone or vending machine	5.1	2.1	1.44
15.Stealing a bicycle	3.1	0.9	1.32
16.Taking a car or motorcycle for a drive without permission	0.8	0.0	1.44
17.Sniffing glue, petrol or other things in order to feel "high"	2.5	1.2	1.60
18.Smoking cannabis (pot, marijuana, hashish)	0.8	1.2	1.36
19.Using any illegal drugs other than cannabis (heroin, cocaine, speed)	0.3	0.3	1.73
20.Buying or drinking alcoholic drinks (beer, wine, or spirits) in hotels or any other public place	6.2	3.3	1.03
21.Drinking alcoholic drinks during school hours or at lunchtime on a school day	3.1	2.4	1.46
22.Getting suspended or expelled from school	1.1	0.3	1.56
23.Playing truant from school (skipping school)	12.4	6.9	0.90
24.Hitting one of your parents	3.9	7.2	1.41
25.Fighting in the street or other place (not fighting at school)	12.5	3.7	1.42

54

TABLE 1 (continued)

26.Struggling to get away from a policeman	1.4	0.0	1.31
27.Using force or threats to get money from someone about your age or younger	2.5	1.2	1.68
28.Using force or threats to get money from someone older than yourself	0.8	0.6	1.65
29.Using any kind of weapon in a fight (like a knife, chain, broken bottle, or rock)	4.8	0.3	1.89

Norm violation items

30.Cheating in school tests or exams	18.3	14.1	1.15
31.Going to R-rated films without parent's permission	10.4	6.6	0.54
32.Driving a car, motorcycle, or motorscooter on a public road without a license	12.4	6.6	1.25
33.Trespassing anywhere you are not supposed to go (like railway yards, private property, empty houses, or building sites)	47.9	23.4	1.00
34.Spending $2 or more on gambling (betting), without your parent's permission	14.9	6.0	0.63
35.Making rude telephone calls, such as ringing someone and saying dirty or threatening things	5.9	5.1	1.25
36.Swearing loudly in a public place	26.8	21.9	0.83
37.Purposely littering the street or footpath by smashing bottles or tipping rubbish bins	8.2	3.6	1.41
38.Purposely damaging property that belongs to a school	9.3	7.5	1.41
39.Painting or writing graffiti words on a wall in a public place	14.1	14.1	1.11
40.Doing damage in a park or public garden	9.6	3.3	1.43
41.Breaking the windows of an empty building	18.6	4.8	1.17
42.Letting off a fire extinguisher when there is no fire	7.3	1.5	0.98
43.Placing something that may damage a train on railway tracks	4.5	0.6	1.69
44.Moving or damaging a traffic sign or road works equipment	7.9	1.8	1.35
45.Letting down tyres of a car, truck, or motorcycle	13.0	2.1	1.19
46.Stealing a thing or money worth less than $2	22.5	16.8	1.08
47.Taking money from home without permission	21.4	15.3	1.33
48.Stealing something from another pupil at school	5.9	2.7	1.49
49.Stealing school property (like books or sports gear)	10.4	9.0	1.31
50.Travelling on bus or going to the movies without paying	10.7	3.6	0.87
51.Taking a badge or hubcap from a car or truck	4.8	0.6	1.24
52.Stealing money from milk bottles	14.9	4.8	1.23

TABLE 1 (continued)

53.Getting drunk on alcoholic drinks	3.4	4.2	1.13
54.Stealing beer, wine, or spirits from a shop, your parents home, or other place	3.1	2.7	1.45
55.Getting into trouble with your friends, family, or school because you were drinking alcohol	3.1	1.5	0.84
56.Throwing objects, such as rocks or bottles, at people or moving cars	9.9	3.3	1.49
57.Hitting another young person in a serious effort to hurt them (not a brother or sister)	17.7	7.5	1.66
58.Being cruel to an animal so as to injure the animal	3.1	0.3	1.72

police intervention." Item ratings for the student and professional groups did not differ significantly, so the responses were combined. This similarity of ratings across survey groups is consistent with the findings of Rossi, Waite, Bose & Berk (1974) and Sellin & Wolfgang (1964). The mean rating thus obtained for each item was multiplied by 0.1, yielding a possible range of weights from 0.0 to 2.0. Resulting seriousness weights are presented in Table 1. Attesting to the validity of the weighting procedure, most of the 29 illegal items were rated as more serious than the norm violation items. Only four norm violation items' weights exceeded the mean seriousness weight (1.47) for the illegal items.

4.5. The 58-Item SRED

The 58-item "full scale" was calculated as the sum of seriousness weights for all of the scale items endorsed affirmatively by each subject. The means and standard deviations for the full 58-item scale were, for boys: $M = 6.93$ ($SD = 8.62$), and for girls; $M = 3.41$ ($SD = 5.52$). Figure 1 illustrates the distribution of male and female subject's SRED scores obtained by a simple sum of items endorsed. Extreme positive skew is the most notable characteristic of the distribution of scores. Skew is typical of self-reported delinquency instruments administered to unselected samples, and may be expected to be extreme in low-delinquency settings, although extremity of the skew may diminish with increasing age of the subjects.

4.5.1. Reliability. Test-retest reliability of the SRED was evaluated by correlation of the 58-item (unweighted) scale scores from two administrations separated by one month for 20 noncohort pilot subjects. The Pearson correlation obtained was .85, supporting the retest reliability of the scale for measuring total number of acts endorsed. Internal consistency reliability for the 58-item scale, as assessed by the Kuder-Richardson-20 coefficient, was .90. Both test-retest and internal reliabilities were well within the acceptable range for social science research instruments, and were comparable to reliability estimates

56

reported for previous measures (Elliott, Huizinga & Morse, 1986; Hindelang et al., 1981).

4.5.2. Content validity. Content validity requires that the universe of early delinquent behaviors be adequately represented by the items, and that the items reported by subjects be appropriate instances of the behavior the instrument is intended to measure (Elliott et al., 1983). The procedures for item selection described above (duplication of established instruments and consultation with local criminologists and constables) assured adequate sampling of the domain of illegal and norm violating delinquent acts.

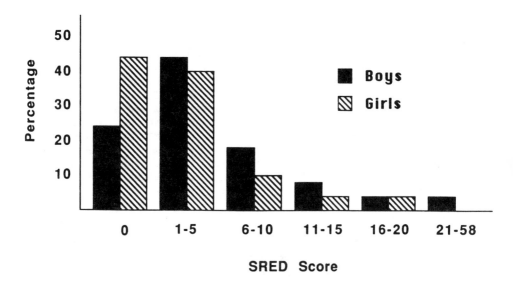

FIGURE 1. Percentages of girls and boys reporting self-report early delinquency at each item frequency level.

Validity check queries in the interview portion of the test protocol allowed subjects' card sort responses to be corrected if they were inappropriate to the objective of assessing delinquent behavior. Comparison of raw card-sort and post-interview scores revealed that as many as six item responses had been added and as many as 29 deleted from subjects' reports as a result of the interviewer's queries. Nevertheless, the interview had resulted in alteration of more than 2 items on only 38% of subjects' reports.

One exception to the confidence in item validity involves minor assault offenses (hit parents, hit peers, fighting). In fact, "hitting a parent" bore a zero item-total scale correlation. Other researchers have reported the problem of triviality of reported behavior for minor assault items. Elliott et al. (1983) estimated three quarters of minor assaults were of a trivial nature. Hardt & Peterson-Hardt (1977) found that 9 of 10 boys reported fist fighting. Pilot work with the SRED showed that many trivial hitting responses involved siblings, and most trivial fights occurred on school grounds. Therefore, these circumstances were excluded in the wording of SRED items. Nevertheless, the relatively large percentages of subjects reporting minor assault acts suggests that concerns about the validity of these items with early adolescents is warranted. Minor assaults accounted for 24.7% of the cohort's self-reported acts, whereas assaults made up only 5% of cohort arrests. A cross-cultural instrument should facilitate collection of information about the circumstances surrounding reported assaults.

4.5.3. External validity. External validity was examined by calculating the convergence of SRED scores with independent ratings of the subjects' antisocial behaviors obtained from parents and teachers, and by the "known groups" method of assessing concurrent criterion validity. The subjects' parents had completed the Revised Behavior Problem Checklist (RBPC, Quay and Peterson, 1983), a rating instrument for the major categories of child and adolescent psychopathology. The RBPC Socialized Aggression subscale provided a measure of parent report of antisocial problem behaviors. The subjects' teachers had completed the Rutter Child Scale B (RCSB, Rutter, Tizard & Whitmore, 1970), which is a 26-item questionnaire designed to be filled out by classroom teachers. The RCSB subscale of antisocial behavior was used as the teacher's report of subject's antisocial behaviors. Pearson product moment correlations calculated between the 58-item SRED scale and the parent RBPC and teacher RCSB antisocial subscales were .45 and .28, respectively (p <.001). These significant positive correlations suggested adequate convergent validity for the SRED.

A search for the 659 cohort subjects with local residence among district Youth Aid police files yielded 40 subjects, thus enabling application of the "known groups" method of assessing criterion validity (Hindelang et al., 1981; Hardt & Peterson-Hardt, 1977). Use of official data as validity criteria for self-report measures has been criticized on the grounds that evidence of the invalidity of police data was the original impetus for development of the self-report method. Although use of a police record criterion may appear paradoxical, Hindelang et al. (1981) have pointed out that such procedures are standard in validation of social science instruments that are hoped to be an improvement over existing measures. Also, despite the fact that the police certainly do not clear every delinquent act, there is evidence that police are likely to identify the most active offenders in a community (Chaiken, Lawless & Stevenson, 1974; Glaser, 1975). In addition to presence of a police file, two other measures of police contact were used to designate known criterion groups. Thirty-one parents had responded "yes" to the survey question, "Has your child ever been in trouble with the police?" During the interview, subjects were asked if any of their self-reported acts had resulted in contact with a police-

58

man, "so that the constable wrote down your name, took you to the
station, or contacted your parents." Forty-eight subjects reported
police contact of this nature. In cases where the subject's report of
police contact was not corroborated by police or parents, the precipi-
tating acts were trivial in nature, e.g., trespassing, swearing in
public, or throwing eggs at automobiles. (Although there was some
evidence of concealment or "deflation" of acts, in general the New
Zealand subjects demonstrated an overly compliant orientation to the
reporting task. Boys may have been inspired to exaggerate their aggressive prowess for the female interviewer, but girls also "tried to help
out." One girl proffered that, while she had done none of the acts on
the cards, she <u>had</u> once run in the school hallway, and could that
please count?) Comparison of the mean SRED scores of subjects with and
without police contact, as defined by the three sources of information,
is shown in Table 2. The mean scores of subjects in all three of the
police contact groups far exceeded the sample mean score.

TABLE 2. "Known groups" test of validity: Mean full and illegal SRED
Scale scores by police contact status.

	Full Cohort (N = 724)	Subject reports police contact (n = 48)	Parent reports S has had police contact (n = 31)	Police hold record (n = 40)
SRED scale		Group		
58-item Full Scale				
Mean	5.24	18.66	17.48	11.89
SD	7.50	13.14	16.10	13.93
29-item Illegal Scale				
Mean	1.75	7.30	7.47	4.66
SD	3.17	6.81	8.77	7.06

4.5.4. <u>Construct validity</u>. Evidence for the construct validity of a
new instrument is accumulated over time as studies are published that
have used the instrument to test theoretical predictions. One test of
the generaliza- bility of results from cross-cultural application of
the self-report method is cross-cultural replication of relations
between obtained delinquency scores and theoretical correlates. This
section presents results from preliminary investigations of theoretically predicted relationships between New Zealand early delinquency, as
measured by the SRED, and other variables. The variables, derived
primarily from the American and British literature, were social class,
intelligence quotient, history of reading disability, history of
conduct disorder, diagnosis of attention deficit disorder, family
constellation, and gender. Results for the full SRED scale are pre-

TABLE 3. Mean self-report early delinquency scores for differing subgroups of the sample[a]

Variable	Group		
Gender[*]	Boys(n = 376)	Girls(n = 348)	
Mean	6.93	3.41	
SD	8.62	5.52	
Family Constellation[b]	"Broken"(n = 177)	Stable(n = 547)	
Mean	7.21	4.60	
SD	9.22	6.74	
Reading Disability[c]	Disabled(n = 62)	Non-RD(n = 661)	
Mean	6.22	5.15	
SD	7.60	7.49	
Attention Deficit Disorder[d*]	ADD(n = 27)	Non-ADD(n = 697)	
Mean	14.63	4.87	
SD	14.07	6.89	
Early Conduct Disorder[e*]	CD(n = 13)	Non-CD(n = 711)	
Mean	18.43	5.00	
SD	13.78	7.13	
Socio-Economic Status[f**]	Low(n = 300)	Medium(n = 175)	High(n = 191)
Mean	5.96	4.88	4.18
SD	8.17	6.52	6.73
IQ[**]	Low(n = 224)	Medium(n = 253)	High(n = 245)
Mean	6.32	4.82	4.69
SD	8.74	6.14	7.50

[*] Student's t-test, separate variance estimate used where appropriate, $p < .01$.

[**] Analysis of variance, $p < .05$.

[a] Full 58-item SRED scale.

[b] "Broken" means single parent, step parent, or living with relatives for at least one full year of the subject's life. "Stable" means both biological parents had been present since the subject's birth.

[c] Assessed at age 11 by the Burt Word Reading Test (Scottish Council for Research in Education, 1976). Reading disabled was defined as more than two standard deviations below the sample mean reading score.

[d] Assessed at age 13 using agreement between subject report (Diagnostic Interview Schedule for Children, DISC; Costello, Edelbrock, Kalas, Kessler, & Klaric, 1982), parent report (Revised Behavior Problem Checklist; Quay & Peterson, 1983) and teacher report (Rutter Child Scale B; Rutter et al., 1970).

[e] Assessed at age 11 using the DISC (Costello et al., 1982).

[f] Father's social class, or if no father figure, mother's social class, as rated at age 13 by the Elley & Irving six-level scale for New Zealand (1976).

[g] Assessed at age 13 using the Wechsler Intelligence Scale for Children - Revised (Wechsler, 1974). Cutoffs were selected so as to divide the sample into thirds; Low = 100 or lower, Medium = 101 to 114, High = 115 or greater.

sented in Table 3. Group differences for all hypotheses tested were in the predicted directions, and differences were statistically signifi- cant for all variables except reading disability. These findings are consistent with those reported from research using previously developed self-report delinquency instruments (for review see Hindelang et al., 1981).

4.6. Subscales of the SRED

4.6.1. 29-item illegal and norm-violation scales. The expectation of low delinquency reporting rates had suggested that greater measurement variability might be obtained by inclusion of items representing "norm violation" as well as strictly legally defined offenses. However, self-report studies have frequently been criticized for overemphasis on relatively trivial items (Hindelang et al., 1979; 1981). Therefore, a subscale was formed that comprised the 29 items for which agreement was obtained between three Youth Aid constables on two criteria: the act is illegal for persons under age 17 in New Zealand, and the act is viewed by police as worthy of police intervention. (Truancy and expulsion from school, while not illegal, were included by the constables because they are the most frequently cited justifications for school referral of a youth to the Youth Aid Police Section.) These 29 items are list- ed first in Table 1. The remaining 29 nonserious items formed the "norm-violation" subscale (also listed in Table 1). For the cohort as a whole, an average of 1.13 illegal items and 2.60 norm-violation items were reported per child. Both the "norm-violation scale" and "illegal scale" were calculated as the sum of seriousness weights for all of the scale items endorsed affirmatively by each subject. The two scales were positively correlated, r = .79, p < .001. Their (unweighted) distributions are shown in Figure 2. The norm-violation items pro- duced less skew than the illegal items, as expected. If illegal acts alone had been assessed, over half (56%) of subjects would have report- ed no delinquent behavior. The inclusion of norm-violation acts re- duced to 35% the number of subjects with self-report scores of zero.

For the illegal scale (weighted for seriousness), the boys' mean score was 2.27 (SD = 3.81), and the girls' mean score was 1.20 (SD = 2.17). Internal consistency reliability for the illegal scale, as assessed by the Kuder-Richardson-20 coefficient, was .81. The illegal scale correlated at .46 with parent report and .27 with teacher report of antisocial behaviors. Correspondence of the illegal scale with "known groups" criteria is shown in Table 2.

The boys' mean weighted score for the norm-violation subscale was 4.66 (SD = 5.32). The girls' mean score was 2.20 (SD = 3.57). Inter- nal consistency was .84. The norm-violation scale correlated at .37 with parent report and .23 with teacher report of antisocial behaviors.

4.6.2. Categorical subscales. Many researchers have found it profit- able to develop homogeneous subscales representing categories of delinquent acts, and Hirschi et al. (1980) recommend analysis of homogeneous subscales prior to consideration of total item omnibus scales. Although exploratory factor analysis (Senna, Rathus & Seigal,

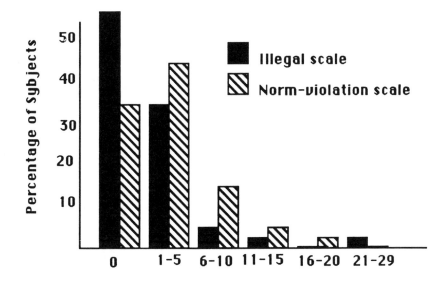

FIGURE 2. Percentages of subjects reporting illegal and norm-violation items at each item frequency level.

Sarbin, 1968) techniques have been used to develop subscales, results are often less than interpretable (see Hindelang et al., 1981, for review). Nevertheless, these studies commonly report item clusters approximating dimensions of aggression/ assaultiveness, property crime/-theft, and drug/alcohol offenses. For this study, items were grouped a priori according to face content as theft, interpersonal/aggressive, drug/alcohol, destruction/vandalism. (Subscales of school-related and home-related acts were also constructed, but reliability coefficients of less than .40 resulted in the omission of these scales.) The four item groupings were submitted to separate reliability analysis, and items demonstrating low item-total correlations were eliminated from each subscale. The resulting subscales are presented in Table 4. No subscale's reliability coefficient exceeded .80, suggesting caution in using the scales for research. Nonetheless, inspection of the correlation matrix of the four subscales revealed that inter-subscale correlations were not strong (range equaled .42 to .68). Some portion of this apparent "specialization" may be a spurious effect of gender differences in category frequencies. That is, while boys engaged in three times as much aggression and vandalism as girls, there was no significant sex difference for drug or alcohol related acts. The sex difference in onset of physical maturity yields 13-year-old girls who appear much older than boys of the same age, and who therefore may have more ready access to drugs and alcohol.

TABLE 4. Categorical subscales of SRED items:
Interpersonal/aggressive, theft, drug/alcohol,
destructive/vandalism

Subscale	Item numbers[a]	Reliability[b]	Boys Mean(SD)	Girls Mean(SD)
Interpersonal/ Aggressive	2,3,25 to 29, 57	.69	1.05(2.05)	0.31(0.94
Theft	9 to 16,47 to 52	.76	1.41(2.51)	0.80(1.65
Drug/Alcohol	17 to 21,53,55	.71	0.23(0.88)	0.16(0.69
Destructive/ Vandalism	3 to 7,37 to 41, 43 to 45	.79	1.68(2.84)	0.69(1.63

* Sex differences were significantly different, p < .01.
[a] Items are listed by number in Table 1.
[b] Assessed by the Kuder-Richardson-20 coefficient.

5. DISCUSSION

This paper described the Self-Report Early Delinquency scale
(SRED), as one example of a research instrument that was developed to
capture self-reports of illegal and norm violating behaviors from
adolescents in a low-delinquency setting. Test-retest reliability,
internal consistency, and criterion, convergent and construct validi-
ties were investigated using a sample of 724 New Zealand 13-year-olds.
All were found to be adequate for recommending the instrument for use
in further research. Relations between the SRED and selected theoretical correlates of delinquent behavior were in the predicted directions,
and were consistent with those obtained from self-report studies in
other countries. Data from the SRED, collected in 1985 and 1986, have
served as the dependent variable in seven studies to date. In 1987-
1988 the SRED is being administered in a second wave of delinquency
assessment at age 15, with results not yet available at this writing.
The exercise of designing a self-report instrument for use in a low-
delinquency setting seems to have been a success, but it very nearly
wasn't.

The SRED was developed through a series of successive accommodations to meet the demands of the research setting and the objectives of
the research. In the end, it bore almost no resemblance to its parent,
the structured interview from the United States National Youth Survey.
This chapter has described many of the conceptual issues considered and
practical steps taken in the development of the SRED. Certain of the
accommodations made were expedient for the New Zealand study's circumstances, and I would not recommend them for researchers undertaking
self-report research in a foreign setting. Nevertheless, we can learn

from those mishaps. What follows is a list of recommendations for
cross-cultural self-report researchers which has been gleaned from the
experience in New Zealand.
   (1) To insure generalizability and comparability, "key items"
generally viewed as illicit across cultures should be included.
   (2) Items unique in local opportunity may provide fascinating
information, and can be tagged for separate analysis.
   (3) Where circumstances predict low response rates to a sample of
illegal items, norm violation items may be included to tap a more
normal distribution of scores.
   (4) Locally derived seriousness weights can help to overcome the
problem of cultural discrepancies in the social meanings of items.
These weights can be obtained from respondent surveys or from
ratings of differential sanctions from the indigenous legal code.
   (5) Involvement of on-site consultants to the project is essential.
These individuals may be law enforcement personnel, high school
teachers, criminologists, or social welfare workers, anyone who
knows the wiles of native teenagers.
   (6) It is worthwhile to appraise ourselves of local sensibilities
regarding the appropriateness of inquiring about illicit behavior.
We should handle delicately concerns about why we would want to
document the extent of evil in their children. Many countries are
skeptical about social science research, and they often anticipate
exploitation from Americans (among others).
   (7) The interview format is recommended to overcome problems of
illiteracy and to ensure better control over the validity of
reports. Recruitment and training of suitable interviewers may be
more difficult away than at home, and will require more planning.
   (8) Although under-reporting is the norm in American and British
studies, we should anticipate culture-specific differences in
sources of invalidity. Collection of corollary data for validity
checks, such as police, parent or teacher reports is important for
cross-cultural research.
   The adjustments required for work in New Zealand were minor relative to those we should anticipate for most other countries. New Zealand is an industrialized, English-speaking, western culture, whose
legal code, like that of the United States, is based in English common
law. In a cross-national comparative study of delinquency where social
systems are unfamiliar, languages are alien, cultures are strange to
us, and local opportunities for crime are exotic, radical accommodations of our self-report measures may be imperative. Our task is to
sustain cross-cultural generalizability under those stringent conditions.

AUTHOR NOTES

   This work was supported by USPHS Grant 1 R23 MH-42723-01 from the
Antisocial and Violent Behavior Branch of the National Institute of
Mental Health. The Dunedin Multidisciplinary Health and Development
Research Unit is supported by the Medical Research Council of New Zea-

land. Appreciation is expressed for the methodological advice of Professor Sarnoff A. Mednick, and for the data collection efforts of Mrs. Pat Brasch.

REFERENCES

Chaiken, JM, Lawless, ME, & Stevenson, KA: The impact of police activities on crime: Robberies in the New York City subway system. Report No. R-1424-NYC, New York: The Rand Institute, 65, 1974.

Costello, A, Edelbrock, C, Kalas, R, Kessler, M, & Klaric, S: Diagnostic interview schedule for children - Child version, 1982.

Elley, WB, & Irving, JC: A socio-economic index for New Zealand based on levels of education and income from the 1966 census. New Zealand Journal of Educational Studies, 7:153-67, 1972.

-----: Revised socio-economic index for New Zealand. New Zealand Journal of Educational Studies, 11:25-36, 1976.

Elliott, DS, Ageton, SS, Huizinga, D, Knowles, BA, & Canter, RJ: The prevalence and incidence of delinquent behavior: 1976-1980. The National Youth Survey Report No. 26. Boulder, CO: Behavioral Research Institute, 1983.

Elliott, DS, Huizinga, D, & Morse, B: Self-reported violent offending. Journal of Interpersonal Violence, 1:472-514, 1986.

Erickson, ML, & Empey, LT: Court records, undetected delinquency, and decisionmaking. The Journal of Criminal Law, Criminology, and Police Science, 54:456-469, 1963.

Farrington, DP: Self-reports of deviant behavior: Predictive and stable? Journal of Criminal Law and Criminology, 64(1):99-110, 1973.

Glaser, D: Strategic criminal justice planning, Rockville, MD: National Institute for Mental Health Studies in Crime and Delinquency, 79-80, 1975.

Gottfredson, M, & Hirschi, T: The true value of Lambda would appear to be zero. Criminology, 24:213-234, 1986.

Hardt, RH, & Peterson-Hardt, S: On determining the quality of the delinquency self-report method. Journal of Research in Crime and Delinquency, 14:247-61, 1977.

Hindelang, MJ, Hirschi, T, & Weis, JG: Correlates of delinquency: The illusion of discrepancy between self-report and official measures. American Sociological Review, 44:995-1014, 1979.

Hindelang, MJ, Hirschi, T, & Weis, JG: Measuring delinquency. Beverly Hills, CA: Sage Publications, Inc., 1981.

Hindelang, MJ, & Weis, J: The bc-try cluster and factor analysis system: Personality and self-reported delinquency. Criminology, 10:268-294, 1972.

Hirschi, T: Causes of delinquency. Berkeley, CA: University of California Press, 1969.

Hirschi, T, Hindelang, MJ, & Weis, JG: The status of self-report measures. In Klein, MW, & Teilmann, KS (Eds.), Handbook of criminal justice evaluation. Beverly Hills, CA: Sage Publications, 1980, pp. 473-488.

Krohn, M, Waldo, G & Chiricos, T: Self-reported delinquency: A comparison of structured interviews and self-administered checklists. Journal of Criminal Law and Criminology, 65:545-555, 1975.

Kulik, JA, Stein, KB, & Sarbin, TR: Dimensions and patterns of adolescent antisocial behavior. Journal of Consulting and Clinical Psychology, 32:375-382, 1968.

Loeber, R: The stability of antisocial and delinquent child behavior: A review. Child Development, 53:1431-1446, 1982.

Magnusson, D, Anders, D, & Zetterblom, G: Adjustment, a longitudinal study. Stockholm, Sweden, 1975.

McGee, R: Response rates at phase XI of the Dunedin Multidisciplinary Health and Development Study. Unpublished report. Dunedin, NZ: Dunedin Multidisciplinary Health and Development Research Unit, Otago Medical School, 1985.

McGee, R, & Silva, PA: A thousand New Zealand children: Their health and development from birth to seven. Special report Series Number 8. Auckland, NZ: Medical Research Council of New Zealand, 1982.

Murray, CA: The link between learning disabilities and juvenile delinquency. Washington, DC: National Institute for Juvenile Justice and Delinquency Prevention, 1976.

Newman, G: Comparative deviance: Perceptions and law in six cultures. New York: Elsevier, 1976.

Olweus, D: Stability of aggressive reaction patterns in males: A review. Psychological Bulletin, 86:852-875, 1979.

Quay, HC, & Peterson, DR: Revised behavior problem checklist, interim manual. Coral Gables, FL: University of Miami, 1983.

Robins, L: Deviant children grown up. Baltimore: Williams & Wilkins, 1966.

Rossi, PH, Waite, E, Bose, CE, & Berk, RA: The seriousness of crime: Normative structure and individual differences. American Sociological Review, 39:224-237, 1974.

Rutter, M, Tizard, J, & Whitmore, K: Education, health and behaviour. London: Longman, 1974.

Scottish Council for Research in Education. The Burt word reading test, 1974 revision. London: Hodder & Staughton, 1976.

Sellin, T: Culture conflict and crime. A report of the subcommittee on personality and culture. New York: Social Science Research Council 1938.

Sellin, T, & Wolfgang, ME: The measurement of delinquency. New York: Wiley, 1964.

Senna, J, Rathus, S, & Seigal, L: Delinquent behavior and academic investment among suburban youth. Adolescence, 9:481-494, 1974.

Short, JF, & Nye, FI: Extent of unrecorded delinquency, tentative conclusions. Journal of Criminal Law, Criminology, and Police Science, 49:296-302, 1958.

Sturge, C: Reading retardation and antisocial behavior. Journal of Child Psychology and Psychiatry, 23:21-31, 1982.

Sudman, S, & Bradburn, NM: Response effects in surveys. Chicago: AVC, 1974.

Teilmann, K: Self-report criminality and interviewer effects. Unpublished Ph.D. dissertation, University of Southern California, Los Angeles, 1977.

Warner, C: A study of the self-reported crime of a group of male and female high school students. Australian and New Zealand Journal of Criminology, 15:255-272, 1982.

Wechsler, D: Manual of the Wechsler Intelligence Scale for Children - Revised. New York: Psychological Corporation, 1974.

West, DJ, & Farrington, DP: Who becomes delinquent? London: Heinemann Educational Books, 1974.

WORKING TOWARDS CLEARER DEFINITIONS: A NATIONAL SELF-REPORT STUDY OF
TEENAGE BOYS AND GIRLS IN ENGLAND AND WALES

Margaret Shaw and David Riley[1]
Formerly Home Office Research and Planning Unit
London, United Kingdom

1. INTRODUCTION

When in 1982 we began to think about the role of families in
adolescent delinquency, we were motivated by concern with what could be
done to reduce the chances of delinquency - by a concern with policy.
What, it was argued, could we say to parents to help them understand or
cope with the generation of adolescent delinquency? In a similar way,
situational crime prevention was at that stage concerned with providing
guidelines to various sectors of the community, on how to minimize
their chance of victimization (e.g., Clarke & Mayhew, 1980; Winchester
& Jackson, 1982). We were concerned with showing parents that many
children do things that could get them into trouble with the police.
We wished too to see whether there was still scope for parental action
by this stage, given the strength of evidence supporting the role of
parental supervision in prevention among younger children.[2]
     This indicated a need to know about the activities and inter-
relationships of a broad sample of girls and boys, their parents, their
friends and their daily lives, and suggested clearly a self-report
study. From the wealth of studies in Britain and America in particular
we knew about the peak ages of offending, about when young people are
most likely to offend, and that delinquent behavior is very widespread;
that much offending may be fairly trivial and goes undetected, and that

----

1. This study was conducted when both authors were members of the
Home Office Research and Planning Unit. Margaret Shaw now works as a
research consultant in Montreal, Canada, and David Riley is a member of
the Department of the Environment, London.

2. The decision to undertake a national cross-section study as a basis
for providing guidance to parents may shock those whose academic
sensibilities recoil at the notion of prescription based on cross-sectional
findings. We wish to make it clear that we regard cross-sectional studies
as having considerable policy relevance and to stress our firm belief in the
value of studies such as the current one for stimulating discussion and
providing information to policy makers, practitioners and the public.

M. W. Klein (ed.), Cross-National Research in Self-Reported Crime and Delinquency, 67–87.
© 1989 by Kluwer Academic Publishers.

most young people grow out of it. We knew that it was possible to identify at an early age the types of family circumstances associated with offending, and the children most likely to offend early, to continue, and to commit serious offenses. We knew a great deal about certain cohorts born in the 1940s and '50s in Britain (e.g., Wadsworth, 1979; May, 1975, West & Farrington, 1973; 1977), but much less abut those growing up in the 1970s and '80s. While one study related to a national birth cohort born in 1946 (Wadsworth), most others were based on specific areas or towns. For example, the rich data from the Cambridge study (West & Farrington) related to a single neighborhood with a limited range of backgrounds. In addition, that study, like most others, was concerned only with boys and the explanation of their delinquency.

Furthermore, we were interested in all delinquent behavior over a wide range of backgrounds, while official data only taps a very small proportion of such behavior. With the exception of West and Farrington, most existing studies used official measures of delinquency. The small number of self-report studies in Britain were all based on either restricted samples or small areas (Belson, 1975; West & Farrington, 1977; Shapland, 1978; Gladstone, 1978; Mawby, 1980; Campbell, 1981, 1986). And again, with the exception of those by Campbell and Mawby, these studies dealt only with boys. There was no national self-report delinquency data which covered both boys and girls, or even data on good unselected samples.

There had been a tendency too up to the 1970s for delinquency studies in Britain to concentrate on what West (1982) calls socio-psychological data, as well as, in the case of Wadsworth's National Survey, on biological, health and medical factors. Thus there had tended to be a strong focus on the developmental aspects of delinquency, but much less interest in the contemporaneous factors surrounding the period of greatest delinquent activity -- adolescence (with the exception, as usual, of West and Farrington).

On the whole, therefore, the kind of evidence available in Britain was concerned with the long-term generation of delinquency, and official delinquency. It did not provide much information about the patterns of the lives of most adolescents, their interactions with friends, school and family, their lifestyle. Nor could it take account of the social changes which had taken place in Britain through the 1960s and 1970s with the increased opportunities for offending (Felson, 1987), increased rates of divorce, and rising unemployment among young people, all of which might be expected to have an impact upon young peoples' lives.

Thus the factors which shaped the study reflected a number of different concerns. Foremost was the opportunity to examine self-reported delinquency in the medium and low risk populations likely to be found in a national sample, and to examine the potential for social crime prevention through the family. Along with schools, youth groups, and voluntary organizations, it had been suggested that both practical and theoretical problems, and lack of evidence of effectiveness, all militated against intervention in the family to prevent delinquency (Clarke, 1981). On the other hand, we were impressed with the strong evidence supporting the role of parental supervision in delinquency prevention among children (Wilson & Herbert, 1978; Wilson, 1980; West & Farrington, 1973), and among adolescents in the United States (Hirschi, 1969) and Canada (Biron & LeBlanc, 1977). The study presented, as well, an opportunity to test out social control and social learning approaches to delinquency in Britain, and using multivariate analysis to look at the interrelationships between the many factors associated with delinquency.

The resulting study, which forms the basis of this paper, took the form of a national household survey of adolescent girls and boys of 14 and 15 and their families in England and Wales in 1983. The project, which is reported more fully in Riley and Shaw (1985), comprised a sample of 751 families selected from a stratified random sample of households. Before turning to the details of the study, we take this opportunity to set out what in our view are the basic requirements of future surveys of this type.

2. CROSS-NATIONAL SELF-REPORT STUDIES

An obvious question is for what purpose do we want to develop cross-national self-report studies? We are clearly interested in rather more than providing differential counts of offense frequency, type or seriousness, from one country to another, or some brief plotting of cross-cultural differences which might provide clues to etiology. Theory-testing seems an essential component.

In our view, a worthwhile cross-national self-report study needs to fulfill a number of criteria. It should ideally be national, i.e., not limited to specific high-crime areas or targeted high-crime populations (although allowing for oversampling in some areas if desired). It is recognized that the ease with which national studies can be carried out -- and the cost -- is dependent upon a number of factors including the political system (federal, nonfederal), size of land mass, population density (compare Holland with Canada), and sampling frame used. Nevertheless, the point at issue is the desirability of national coverage, rather than the selection of one or two centers of population which may or may not be representative of that country, and where official delinquency rates may be subject to particular biases, or may not reflect changes in the overall amount of delinquent behavior.

Second, a cross-national self-report study should include both males and females. It is both unnecessarily restrictive and unacceptable to limit the development of self-report delinquency to boys as has frequently been the case in the recent past (see Loeber and Stouthamer-Loeber, 1986). To do so neglects the potential explanatory value of comparisons of gender differences and similarities in life-style, upbringing, attitudes, and behavior in relation to crime patterns. It is clear, too, that categorizations which are derived primarily from studies of males will fail to take sufficient account of factors which should be considered to assess fully the characteristics of both male and female lifestyles and delinquency (Smith & Paternoster, 1987). In addition, including both males and females provides an opportunity to map changes in such patterns with the apparent narrowing of gender differentials in offending (Rutter & Giller, 1982; Cernkovich & Giordano, 1979) and the by now well-documented finding that self-report rates for boys and girls show a far greater concordance than do official rates of offending (see e.g., Johnson, 1986; Riley, 1986).

Third, a cross-national self-report study should focus on crime-prone groups, particularly adolescents, but within narrow age ranges, or if a broad age range, sufficiently large and with clear age-specific definitions to enable differences and changes between age cohorts to be examined. An examination of the plethora of recent self-report delinquency studies indicates very wide divergence of opinion as to what constitutes adolescence. Some authors have defined adolescence as broadly as from 11 to 21 years, and samples of 11 to 19-year-olds are not uncommon (e.g., Morash, 1983, 1986; Cernkovich & Giordano, 1987). It has also been suggested (La Grange & White, 1985) that a static conception of adolescence dominates the literature, encouraging us to view it as a unitary period, and assuming findings "are applicable to adolescents of all ages," although "the processes related to delinquency change considerably as youths age through adolescence." From the point of view of child development, both prior and contemporaneous factors will have an influence on behavior, and since adolescence is a period of immense change both physiologically and culturally, it is important to map changes in and the development of such factors as family attachment and interaction, peer development, life styles, and exposure to opportunity by developing cross-national studies which are age-specific.

It is clear, nevertheless, that results from cross-national self-report studies set up on these criteria will provide different kinds of results from those using official data, or using different sampling techniques (snowballing interviews, police records, targeted high-crime areas). In some cases it may amount to polarized results; e.g., Johnson (1986) reports that family structural variables were related to delinquency when official records were used, but not when self-report data were applied. In other cases it may be a matter of the strength of effects. Thus Loeber and Stouthamer-Loeber (1986) note in their review of family factors in delinquency that comparison group studies contrasting, for example, samples of delinquents with nondelinquents, tend to produce larger effect sizes than do studies based on normal samples. If, as Hindelang and Hirschi (1979) argue, we are measuring different domains of behavior when we compare self-report findings with official delinquency, there still remains substantial evidence that they are related (West & Farrington, 1977). The purpose of this paper is to argue for the value of looking at self-report delinquency of the more common and less serious kind in our efforts to expand our understanding of delinquent behavior across cultures.

Having briefly considered what we take to be some of the main parameters for the development of cross-national self-report delinquency studies, what specific findings from our own study are of relevance to current discussions? Two issues in particular would seem, certainly in Britain, to need better definition: the relationship between self-report delinquency and routine activities, and measures of peer relations and their development. These are considered in the final section of the paper. The second part now considers the findings of the survey in relation to the overall criteria of national self-report studies discussed above.

3. THE STUDY

3.1. Sampling and Interviews

The primary focus of the national survey, which was carried out in the summer of 1982, was to examine the relationship between parental supervision and delinquency among a representative sample of boys and girls of 14 and 15 years. Two sets of structured questionnaires were developed following a developmental phase using group interview and focused interview techniques to isolate issues which seemed of particular concern to both parents and teenagers. All field work was conducted by a professional survey organization (SCPR). Final questionnaires covered a range of questions about family relationships, activities at home and outside, attitudes toward school, beliefs about offending, police contacts, as well as self-report delinquency.

A household-based survey was chosen as the most appropriate way of reaching a random sample of adolescents and their families. An approach through schools was rejected on a number of grounds, and not least because of the formidable difficulties in England and Wales of obtaining lists of addresses of pupils, and agreement to contact them which must be negotiated at the local level. The approach chosen, therefore, involved the screening of a stratified random sample of households on the electoral register. It was estimated on the basis of the 1981 population census that 8.3% of households in England and Wales would have a child of 14 or 15 (or one in 12 households). A target sample of 1000 double interviews with the child and a parent was set. This required 17,800 addresses to be screened, to take account of both the expected prevalence of eligible households and an expected response rate of 70% (see Riley and Shaw, 1985, Appendix I for fuller details).

Given the problems of screening for a minority population, a focused enumeration method was used, allowing interviewers to sample blocks of six households, and ask about the eligibility of adjoining households.[3] The total number of eligible households identified from 17,226 screened was 1,063. Among these, 751 double sets of interviews were finally achieved, 378 with boys and 373 with girls, and a respective parent.

For the purposes of the survey, families were defined as households where a target child was living with at least one natural or

---

3. This procedure, which had been successfuly developed by the survey company SCPR, considerably reduced interviewer contact time. Having established whether a 14- or 15-year-old lived in the initial household, they then asked whether children of between 12 and 16 lived in adjacent households. The wider age-range was used to eliminate mistakes over children's ages.

adoptive parent. Thus certain chldren, as well as those living away
from home, were excluded. The interviews were conducted at home, separately, and as far as possible, alone. In only 12% of the teenager
interviews was a third party present for some or all of the time -
usually this was another child or the mother. (The reported prevalence
of offending was not significantly different for these cases.) In 98%
of the cases the parent interviewed was the mother. Cost and considerations of intrusion weighed against interviews with both parents as well
as the teenager,[4] although it would have been useful to explore differences in fathers' and mothers' accounts of family intervention and
supervision (cf. Lewis, Newson & Newson, 1982). However, the parent
interviewed was asked specific questions about the partner's views.

3.1.1. Achieved sample. For any survey which claims to be national,
the representativeness of the final sample is of importance. Although
the proportion of households surveyed with a 14- or 15-year-old at 6.3%
never reached the estimated level of 8.3% in any region of the country,
and some concealed refusal may have been the explanation, there was no
evidence of serious imbalance in the composition of the sample.[5] There
is no published information which gives an accurate socio-demographic
profile of families with a 14- or 15-year-old in England and Wales.
The best estimate that could be made on the basis of the 1982 General
Household Survey (GHS) indicated little variation between socio-
economic groups in the GHS and the Survey: groups A and B, 34.4% and
31.4%; groups C1 and C2, 45.6% and 50,5%; D and E, 20.0% and 18.0% for
the GHS and the Survey, respectively.[6] This suggested that the lower
socio-economic groups where one "might expect" to find more serious
delinquency were not seriously under-represented. Nevertheless, as
Weis (1981) and others have pointed out, there is consistently a very
weak relationship, or none at all, between self-report delinquency and
socio-economic status. And indeed, in this study, none of the measures
of status were found to be related at the individual or aggregate level
with delinquency. It must also be noted that the economic profile of
families with children of 14 and 15 will be higher than that of

----

4. It was found during the developmental stage that interviews with
fathers as well as mothers took a very long time, but did not add
sufficient information to justify their inclusion. There was also a
tendency for fathers to refer questions about discipline and control to
mothers.

5. The original estimate may have been a "good" one, but still wide
of the mark.

6. The GHS is an annual sample survey of some 10,000 households in
England and Wales conducted by the Office of Population Censuses and
Surveys. The categories used here correspond to the following socio-
economic groups: A - professional; B - Employers/managers; C1 -
Intermediate/junior non-manual; C2 - Skilled manual/own account non-
professional; D - Semi-skilled manual and personal service; E - Unskilled
manual.

families at an earlier stage of their life cycle.

Nor did the study under-represent the unemployed; over 15% of the heads of households interviewed were unemployed. Given that double interviews had to be achieved for a family to be included in the study, the overall response rate was estimated as about 75%, which compares well with other household surveys.

In terms of family structure, 80% of the sample were living with both natural parents (a figure identical to that given by the Office of Population Census and Surveys for 10-15 year-olds in 1979), 8% were living with a natural parent and a step-parent, 10% with a lone mother, 2% with a lone father.[7]

3.1.2. The delinquency measure. The self-report measure used in the study was based on a set of 21 standard offenses, used in self-report studies in Britain and elsewhere, ranging from minor delinquency to more serious acts such as burglary and arson (see Appendix I). These were administered on cards, together with five more trivial forms of behavior (dropping litter, riding a bicycle without lights, etc.). The teenagers were asked to sort the cards into piles for acts ever commit-ted/never committed, and for each item committed, the number of times in the past twelve months. They were asked to tell the interviewer only the number of the card, not the offenses. Twelve of the items covered theft, six vandalism, and the remaining three were arson, carry-ing a weapon, and making hoax emergency calls.

Although a number of different definitions of delinquency were tested, the final analysis used a dichotomous delinquent-nondelinquent measure, delinquency being defined as one or more acts committed within the past twelve months. Reported drug use was also recorded at another stage of the interview, but not using the concealed-response card tech-nique, and drug use was not included in the delinquency measure.

3.1.3. Measures of parental supervision. The main explanatory vari-able, parental supervision, was defined by an age-specific measure. This was derived from Hirschi's (1969) concept of the psychological presence of parents, and recognized that supervision practices of parents of young adolescents will be different from those appropriate for 8-9 year-olds, for example. Adolescents, as part of their develop-ment away from the family, will often spend considerably more time out of the sight of parents and with their peers. Surveillance and chaper-onage techniques of parental supervision as described by e.g., Wilson (1980, 1987) are clearly no longer a major component, nor always appro-priate. And since teenage delinquency usually takes place away from home (although see Biron and LeBlanc, 1977) a measure of supervision based on parents' knowledge of their children's leisure time activities when away from home, who they are with, and what they are doing is more appropriate. For the purposes of analysis, those parents responding that they "almost always" knew where their children were, with whom, and what they were doing, were rated as exercising high supervision,

----

7. Interviewers were asked to record race by observation: 94% of the sample was classified as "white."

the remainder low supervision.

4. THE FINDINGS OVERALL

4.1. How Much Delinquency?

Given our initial decision to survey a normal population and to
look at the natural variation within that population to assess the
relative importance of factors associated with self-report delinquency,
what were the overall findings?

In the first place, the delinquency measure demonstrated a close
male-female ratio of offending, with 49% of the boys in the sample
admitting at least one offense in the past year, and 39% of the girls.
These rates of self-report delinquency are thus much higher than rates
of official delinquency based on police or court records for this age
group in England and Wales. Farrington (1981) for example, estimated
the prevalence rates for the more serious "Standard List Offenses" by
the age of 16 to be 12% for boys and 2% for girls. On the other hand,
the self-report admission rates are lower than those reported in less
respresentative samples. West and Farrington found generally higher
admission rates for their sample of inner-London boys at 14 years
(1973), as did Gladstone (1978) in his study of vandalism and delinquency among a sample of boys in Liverpool. Nevertheless, direct comparison
with other surveys is difficult, given the variety of samples, and
self-report instruments and methodology employed, as well as the possibility of real changes in the prevalence of delinquency over time.
Perhaps the most comparble data are those derived from the 1982 British
Crime Survey (Hough & Mayhew, 1983) for a small sample of 16-year-olds
(86 boys and 76 girls). Admission rates for that household-based national survey which used a similar technique of administration appeared to
be generally comparable with the present sample for similar offenses.[8]

To what extent were these admission rates a valid reflection of
the behavior of the sample? Certainly, there was a willingness to
admit items on the self-report measure. Thus, including the five very
minor items which were excluded from the delinquency measure, only 58
teenagers in the sample (8%) claimed they had <u>never</u> committed a single
item, and 88% admitted dropping litter at least once, 66% riding a
bicycle without lights (see also Appendix II). In terms of the relation between self-report admissions and official delinquency in the
sample, 16% of the boys' parents and 4% of the girls' reported that
their child had got into trouble with the police at some stage, and
this was significantly related to self-report delinquency. A search of
the Criminal Records Office (CRO) further revealed that 12 boys and 4
girls in the sample had a record. In only one such case did a parent
deny contact with the police. However, since most juveniles in England
and Wales are now cautioned rather than prosecuted initially, and

----

8. E.g., admission rates for graffitti were 6% and 8% for boys and
girls in the BCS, and 7% and 12% in the current study; 17% of boys in
each study admitted starting a fight.

cautioning data on juveniles are not centrally maintained or are slow
to be forwarded, it is difficult to obtain accurate information on
official delinquency for a sample of this age except perhaps retrospectively.

While the overall rates of admission for this sample suggest fairly minor delinquency involvement, around one-fifth of the sample admitted to offending five or more times over the past year (see Table 1
below). Given the reported association between official delinquency
and frequency of self-report admissions (e.g., West & Farrington,
1973), this group may be seen as the more serious offenders within the
sample.

TABLE 1. Number of delinquent acts admitted in past twelve months.

	0		1-4		5+		Total
Boys	194	51%	106	28%	78	21%	378
Girls	227	61%	82	22%	64	17%	373

It is of interest, too, that there was little to distinguish the
girls from the boys in terms of the types of offenses they admitted
(see Appendix I); roughly equal numbers of girls as boys admitted to
theft and/or vandalism during the past year, although the boys admitted
rather more aggressive behavior (carrying a weapon, breaking windows,
smashing bottles) than the girls. (It is, of course, the case that
differences in offense specialization may become more marked between
the sexes as they grow older. Junger-Tas and Junger, 1984, report that
girls in their broader age-range study were less likely to report
aggressive offenses than boys.) Nevertheless, among the girls who
admitted delinquency there was less contrast than might have been
expected, and indeed, the girls were proportionately just as likely to
have admitted five or more offenses as the boys (44% of all delinquent
girls as against 42% of the boys).

4.2. Explaining delinquency

Even with the comparatively low admission rates which are to be
expected in a national sample, and the low threshold measure of delinquency (one or more offenses in the past year) used in the study, a
wide range of factors concerning family, school, friendship and leisure
patterns, beliefs about offending and contact with the police was found
to be significantly related to delinquency. (A complete list will be
found in Riley and Shaw, 1985, Appendix 4.)

The measure of parental supervision used in the study proved both
to be related to self-report delinquency, and to show up some interesting differences between the girls and boys. Overall, those rated as

having high supervision were less likely to be delinquent (Table 2).
Girls, however, were much more likely to receive high supervision than
boys (60% compared with 47%).

TABLE 2. Percentage delinquent at two levels of parental supervision.

	High Supervision	Low Supervision	Total
Boys*	179 41%	199 56%	378
Girls**	224 29%	149 55%	373

* x^2 = 7.9, p < 0.005
** x^2 = 24.9, p < 0.001

Thus the effects of parental supervision on girls at this age
would appear to be much more powerful than for boys.

Since a major objective of the study was to attempt to take
account of competing correlates of delinquency, recognizing the complexity
of influences on adolescents in the generation of delinquent behavior, logistic regression analysis was used to allow the independent
effects of supervision on delinquency to be tested. Ten variables
which were strongly associated with delinquency at the 0.001 level, and
which had, in principle, some policy implications, were included along
with supervision in the analysis. For these teenage boys of 14 and 15,
four factors were found to explain a significant amount of the variation in delinquency:

* Those who reported that their friends were involved in delinquency were almost eight times as likely to be delinquent
  (7.7) as those reporting their friends not involved.

* Those who said they would not feel "very guilty" if they
  stole were about five times as likely to be delinquent (4.7)
  as those expressing guilt.

* Those who said they were closer to their mothers than their
  fathers or equally close to both were almost three times as
  likely to be delinquent (2.9) as those closer to their
  fathers.

* Those who usually went out three or more times a week to see
  their friends were about twice as likely to be delinquent
  (1.8) as those going out less often.

  (G square reduced from 450.3 + 324 df to 334.4 + 320 df).

Thus, our measure of parental supervision did not appear to have
an independent effect on delinquency among the boys once these four
factors had been taken into account.

The pattern for girls was somewhat similar but with the important exception that supervision did enter into the model. Six out of eighteen factors examined were found to explain a significant amount of the variance:

* Those who reported their friends were more involved in delinquency were about 15 times as likely to be delinquent (14.8) as those whose friends were less involved.

* Those with low parental supervision were about four times as likely to be delinquent (3.7) as those with high parental supervision.

* Those who felt their fathers did not understand their problems were about twice as likely to be delinquent (2.5) as those reporting understanding fathers.

* Those who felt stealing was not "very serious" were about twice as likely to be delinquent (2.3) as those who felt it was.

* Those who said their attitude toward school was not "very serious" were about twice as likely to be delinquent (2.2) as those who were serious.

* Those who thought it would make little difference to their friends if they stole were about twice as likely to be delinquent (1.8) as those reporting their friends would be concerned.

(G square reduced from 430.1 with 323 d. to 294.3 with 317 df.)

Thus, for the girls, parental supervision did appear to be an important factor in explaining delinquency.[9] However, the importance of the peer group among this age group was evident for both boys and girls, and appeared to be the strongest explanatory factor. Indeed, for boys it appeared to be an intervening variable in relation to supervision in that among those with delinquent friends, parental supervision did not seem to be related to delinquency.

It is to these aspects of the study that this paper now turns with a consideration of the role of the peer group and routine activity patterns in relation to self-report delinquency. These questions are put less to look backwards to past findings than to anticipate what

----

This is parental supervision as reported largely by the mother. There may be a cross-sex interaction, and fathers, had they been asked, might have reported more supervision over boys than girls. This seems unlikely, however, in the light of most studies which suggest -- as did this one -- that fathers have less contact with their children than mothers. It is also possible that fathers would be even stricter with daughters than with sons.

kinds of changes and improvements will need to be built into future
research on self-report delinquency.

4.3. Peers -- The Well-Known Secret

As Zimring puts it (1981) "adolescents commit crimes, as they live
their lives, in groups," although our treatment and punitive systems
and much research on delinquency continues to focus on individuals.
While he may be right that the role of peers has on the whole been
ignored of late, it has a "taken-for-granted" status which has a number
of implications for self-report delinquency. Thus it is a familiar
plaint that delinquency and delinquent friends are interchangeable
measures -- that the latter can be used as a surrogate measure of own
delinquency. Farrington and West (1973), for example, found a very
high correlation between self-report and friends' delinquency, and
Wilson (1987) argues that having delinquent friends is a concomitant,
not a facilitating factor. If this were the case, then it might be
simpler to develop friends' delinquency measures, rather than self-
report. Yet few would be prepared to go so far.
There is, after all, an equally respectable body of theory which
argues for the separate and contributory role of delinquent friends
(see Morash, 1986, for a discussion of the competing arguments). Nor
is all delinquent behavior at this age group behavior. Shapland (1978)
has demonstrated, as have others, variation in offending alone or with
friends according to type of offense with an overall rate of 70% group
offending, and Zimring only claimed 80% for the group. And what about
girls? Do we take it for granted that their peer relationships are the
same as boys and affect their delinquent behavior in the same way?
Also evident in the "taken-for-granted" status of peers is the too easy
assumption that having delinquent friends necessarily implies a delinquent peer group (or even the more emotive "gang"). It is much more
likely that the teenagers in the current study belonged to loosely
structured groups of peers, some of which were made up of friends or
acquaintances who were known to have committed offenses, others which
did not. There are certainly no grounds for assuming that those who
admitted delinquency in that study committed it in the company of the
friends they knew who had offended. (They were asked to sort the self-
report cards for friends' delinquency in terms of things "any of your
present friends have ever done," a much wider net.) And friendships,
after all, may be short or long-standing, casual, malleable, or intense
and close.
Part of the problem of dealing with peers of course relates to the
type of study used. As Farrington (1985) has argued, it is not possible to disentangle cause and effect relationships in cross-sectional,
as against longitudinal, research. Yet we would argue that there is
considerable scope for examining the role of peers in relation to self-
report delinquency with cross-sectional data. From the perspective of
the current study, it was important to allow for the influence of peers
as well as that of parents, school, beliefs, etc., an approach also
taken by Johnson (1979) and Elliott, Ageton and Canter (1979). The
concern was with the potential for increased parental supervision to

reduce the likelihood of delinquency among this age group, rather than with plotting the causal contribution of peers or supervision. Thus no assumptions were made about peers being part and parcel of their own delinquency (Riley, 1987). In addition, the fact that for girls, parental supervision was still an important factor in delinquency provided support for the importance of including peer delinquency in our model.

TABLE 3. Delinquency models for two groups of delinquents.

	1 or more offenses in past 12 months	5 or more offenses in past 12 months
Boys	N = 184	N = 78
Friends involved in delinquency	7.7	5.9
Would feel guilty if stole	4.7	2.7
Closer to mother than father or both parents	2.9	---
Went out three or more times a week	1.8	4.7
Girls	N = 146	N = 64
Friends involved in delinquency	14.8	7.8
Low parental supervision	3.7	---
Father didn't understand their problems	2.5	2.3
Stealing not very serious* would not feel very guilty**	2.3*	4.2**
Attitude toward school not very serious	2.2	---
Would make little difference if friends stole	1.8	2.3

What can be said about the contribution of peers to self-report delinquency in the current study? The table above compares the likelihood of delinquency among the more serious delinquents (five or more

offenses in the past year) with results for the whole group discussed
earlier, using logistic regression.

This suggests that for the more frequent offenders among both the
boys and the girls, having delinquent friends, while still the most
powerful factor, contributes rather less than for the whole delinquent
group, and that going out frequently for the boys, and attitudes to
offending among the girls assume greater importance than before.
And among these girls, parental supervision no longer enters the
model.

In Britain we know very little about the variety and development
of peer relationships through adolescence. Downes' study (1966) is one
of the few, but was based on a low income inner-London area. While
rather more work has been done on peer relationships of late in the
United States, this suggests that in the development of cross-national
self-report studies, it will be important to pay far more attention to
the context of offending -- and in relation to individual offenses --
who the respondent was with, how many others, what they did, who initiated the ideas (see Shapland 1978), how long they have known them, their
characeristic activity patterns, etc. But it also suggests that care
must be taken to build up measures which are both comparable and adapta-
ble to national characteristics.

Another way of looking at the development of adolescent relationships away from the family, however, is through the role of routine
activities. In the current study it would appear, for the boys at
least, that since by this age they spend so much of their leisure time
away from home, cutting down on time spent with their friends might
have little effect on delinquency. Perhaps more important is what they
do with their time, and the patterning of their activities. The following section considers how this might be done.

4.4. Routine Activities and Life-Style

There is quite a lot of evidence to suggest a systematic relationship between how, where and when individuals spend their time
away from home, and their likelihood of being victimized. It has been
shown that gender differences in teenage victimization, for example,
show little variation between males and females for types of victimization where both are equally at risk (Riley, 1986). This is consistent
with evidence from self-report delinquency studies which show that
male-female offending ratios vary according to specific types of
offending (e.g., Cernkovich & Giordano, 1979; Mawby, 1980; Canter,
1980). Thus the current study found the male-female offending ratio
was close to 1:1 for offenses such as stealing from relatives or family
and travelling without paying the correct fare, where opportunities for
both sexes are comparable. For other offenses likely to occur in public space away from supervision and surveillance, but where girls are
less likely to spend their time than boys, the ratio was around 3:1.

Exposure to risk forms one component of routine activities; the
second is how people normally spend their time. In the survey, two
different methods were used to assess lifestyle. Both parent and teenager were asked a series of structured questions about out-of-home

activities, including the number of times a week the teenagers went out to see friends, had friends in their home, the number of friends they usually met and where, when they were expected to be home at night, clubs and activities they took part in, and spending habits. In addition, a version of a time-budget diary was administered. This provided a detailed account of how they had spent their previous Saturday. This information was subsequently coded to provide data on (1) the duration and type of activity, (2) where it toook place (at home, at a friend's house or elsewhere), and (3) who else was present (no one, a parent, sibling, boy/girlfriend, one friend, two or more friends or others).

4.4.1. Teenage boys - lifestyle. For the boys in the study, significant differences between delinquents and non-delinquents on all but one of the indices examined were found: offenders were more often out with their friends, were expected home later in the evenings, more often met friends away from home, in larger groups, spent money on sport, in amusement arcades and on discos. In terms of the major predictors of delinquency derived from our model, peer group committment (defined as frequency of going out to see friends), peer delinquency (defined as having friends committing nine or more offenses), and parental supervision were all significantly associated with differences in how they spent their time (see Riley, 1988). By contrast, attitudes to crime and relationships with parents were not related to lifestyle differences.

The time-budget analysis provided an opportunity to corroborate responses to the structured questions, since it is more difficult for respondents to provide predictable responses. It also places fewer constraints on subsequent analysis. The Saturday analysis confirmed the differences between offenders and non-offenders in their use of time. Offenders spent significantly less time at their own homes than non-offenders (39% as against 49%) and more time elsewhere (54% as against 45%). They also spent less time with parents or on home activities and more with two or more friends. As with general lifestyle indicators, there was a similar relationship with the major predictors of delinquency in the model. The most marked differences were in relation to peer committment - those who went out a lot during the week spent more time away from home on the time-budget Saturday, on unstructured street activities (chatting, riding around on bicycles, walking), and with friends.

In order to assess whether a more specific measure of lifestyle would improve the fit of the model of delinquency for the boys, a specific measure of street time derived from the Saturday time-budget data was entered into the original logistic regession. While it did not improve the fit, it displaced the more general measure of peer committment, suggesting that the original model already took account of crime-relevant variations in lifestyle between delinquents and non-delinquents. On the whole, therefore, analysis of routine activities and lifestyle patterns among the boys contributed to our understanding of the implied relationship between peers and self-offending, in terms of increased opportunity for offending.

4.4.2. <u>Teenage girls - lifestyle</u>. How far does lifestyle analysis add to our understanding of gender differences in offending? One explana- tion for the higher offending rates found among teenage boys than girls, whether in official delinquency or self-report terms, may be differences in lifestyle patterns. Smith and Paternoster (1987) argue, for example, that gender differences in degree of deviance (in their study, marijuana use) reflect differential exposure to risk.

In the current study there were clearly differences between the genders in the role of parental supervision, and throughout the study evidence of differences in parental attitudes towards the behavior of girls and boys, and (consequent) lifestyles. Thus girls did not go out as much as boys, and parents were much stricter about asking where they were going and with whom; they were expected home earlier than the boys, and were more likely to have disagreements with parents about where they could go. They were also more likely to go out with parents more regularly, and to spend less time on out-of-door activities (33% compared with 55%). Thus whatever the prior socialization differences between the sexes, they clearly had less opportunity to offend.

Analysis of both general lifestyle measures and the time-budget data did confirm that delinquent girls, as with the boys, spent their time differently from non-offenders. They less often went straight home from school, were expected home later in the evenings, more often spent money on amusement arcades and discos, and were members of mixed- gender groups. The Saturday analysis confirmed that delinquent girls spent more time away from home, on unstructured street activity, and with their friends. However, the interpretation of these findings was more complex for girls (see Riley, 1988).

The link between leisure time and crime is less clear cut, and supervision seems to be more important in influencing what girls do, and particularly with whom they spent their time. Day-to-day leisure activity was more closely controlled by the parents, and time spent away from home was less often in crime-prone circumstances than for the boys. Only among the girls who were poorly supervised did their lei- sure activities resemble those of the boys.

In the present context, the purpose of this discussion has been to show that routine activity and lifestyle measures could significantly improve the interpretation of self-report delinquency data among this age group and that for cross-national comparisons it will be important to have sufficient detail in order to assess lifestyle differences across cultures. Few self-report studies have explored this area, and few have included measures which would allow us to locate time, place, activity, and companions in relation to delinquent behavior. A time budget approach such as that employed in the current study provides a useful, if more time-consuming, method for gathering such data. It proved of particular value for examining activity patterns among the girls and for comparisons between the sexes.

5. CONCLUSION

This paper relates to a specific application of self-report

methodology: a cross-sectional national study of teenagers and their families using structured household interviews. It reflects both our particular interests at the time of its initiation (in terms of parental supervision, and social control and social learning explanations of delinquency) and the policy-related context of the research. None of this is to deny the validity of other applications of self-report methodology, whether in terms of type of study (e.g., longitudinal rather than cross-sectional) or theoretical frameworks.

While the paper has stressed the need to explore contemporaneous factors in looking at self-report delinquency (e.g., in relation to peers and routine activities), we have done so in the knowledge that other issues -- family interaction, family structure, schools, early development factors and upbringing --are well represented in the existing literature and research. We have stressed too that it seems, in theory development terms, important to trace changes in family relationships, development of peer relations and changes in lifestyle through childhood and adolescence, and to undertake self-report studies which focus to different degrees on each of these areas at different ages, perhaps with in-depth studies on sub-samples of populations. This requires studies to be age-specific and to cover both males and females.

What the study demonstrated is that there are considerable benefits to be derived from using self-report methods on a broad-based household sample. While relatively low self-report rates and little serious delinquency compared with more focused populations are to be expected, there is considerable scope and explanatory power for exploring delinquency in such low and middle range populations. Clearly the kind of results derived in this study do not enable us to explore in detail some of the more familiar concerns of criminology -- offense specialization, relationships with serious offending or causal paths -- but there are gains to be made in looking at natural variations within a representative national sample. And for international comparisons, such an approach seems essential. For the future, it is hoped that data on self-report offending among a birth cohort of 15,000 16 year-olds in England and Wales, now being conducted by the International Centre for Child Studies, Bristol, will provide us with additional information on national report rates.

REFERENCES

Belsen, WA: _Juvenile theft: The causal factors_. London: Harper & Row, 1975.

Biron, L, & LeBlanc, M: Family components and homebased delinquency. _British Journal of Criminology_, 5:289-308, 1977.

Campbell, A: _Girl delinquents_. Oxford: Basil Blackwell, 1981.

Campbell, A: Self-report of fighting by females. _British Journal of Criminology_, 22:28-47, 1986.

Canter, R: Sex differences in self-report delinquency. _Criminology_, 2:373-393, 1980.

Cernkovich, SA, & Giordano, PC: A comparative analysis of male and
    female delinquency. The Sociological Quarterly, 20:131-145, 1979.
Cernkovich, SA, & Giordano, PC: Family relationships and delinquency.
    Criminology, 25:295-321, 1987.
Clarke, RVG, & Mayhew, P (Eds.): Designing out crime. London: HMSO,
    1980.
Clarke, RVG: The prospects of controlling crime. Research Bulletin
    No. 12. London: Home Office Research and Planning Unit, 1981.
Downes, D: The delinquent solution. London: Routledge & Kegan Paul,
    1966.
Elliott, DS, Ageton, SS, & Canter, RJ: An integrated theoretical per-
    spective on delinquent behavior. Journal of Research in Crime and
    Delinquency, 16:3-27, 1979.
Farrington, DP: The prevalence of convictions. British Journal of
    Criminology, 21:173-175, 1981.
Farrington, DP: Delinquency prevention in the 1980s. Journal of
    Adolescence, 8:3-16, 1985.
Felson, M: Routine activity and crime prevention in the developing
    metropolis. Criminology, 25:911-931, 1987.
Giordano, PC, Cernkovich, SA, & Pugh, M: Friendships and delinquency.
    American Journal of Sociology, 91:1170-1202, 1985.
Gladstone, FJ: Vandalism among adolescent schoolboys. In Clarke, RVG
    (Ed.), Tackling vandalism. Home Office Research Study, No. 47:
    London, HMSO.
Hindelang, MJ, & Hirschi, T: Correlates of delinquency: The illusion
    of discrepancy between self-report and official measures. American
    Sociological Review, 44:995-1014, 1979.
Hirschi, T: Causes of delinquency. Berkeley: University of
    California Press, 1969.
Hough, M, & Mayhew, P: The British Crime Survey first report. Home
    Office Research Study, No. 76. London: HMSO, 1983.
Johnson, RE: Family structure and delinquency: General patterns and
    gender differences. Criminology, 24:65-84, 1986.
Johnson, RE: Juvenile delinquency and its origins. Cambridge:
    Cambridge University Press, 1979.
Junger-Tas, J, & Junger, M: Juvenile delinquency: Backgrounds of
    delinquent behavior. The Hague: Ministry of Justice, 1984.
LaGrange, RL, & White HR: Age differences in delinquency: A test of
    theory. Criminology, 23:19-35, 1985.
Lewis, C, Newson, E, & Newson, J: Father participation through
    childhood and its relationship with career aspirations and
    delinquency. In Beail, N, & McGuire, J (Eds.), Fathers:
    Psychological perspectives. London: Junction Books, 1982.
Loeber, R, & Stouthamer-Loeber, M: Family factors as correlates and
    predictors of juvenile conduct problems and delinquency. In Tonry,
    M, & Morris, N (Eds.), Crime and justice, Vol. 7. Chicago:
    University of Chicago Press, 1986.
Mawby, R: Sex and crime: The results of a self-report study. British
    Journal of Sociology, 31:525-543, 1980.

May, D: Juvenile offenders and the organization of juvenile justice:
An examination of juvenile delinquency in Aberdeen, 1959-67.
Unpublished Ph.D. Thesis: University of Aberdeen.
Miller, WB: American youth gangs: Past and present. In Blumberg, AS
(Ed.), Current perspectives in criminal behavior. New York: Alfred
Knopf, 1974.
Morash, M: Gangs, groups and delinquency. British Journal of
Criminology, 23:309-335, 1983.
Morash, M: Gender, peer group experiences and seriousness of
delinquency. Journal of Research in Crime and Delinquency,
23:43-67, 1986.
Riley, D: Parental supervision re-examined. British Journal of
Criminology, 27:421-424, 1987.
Riley, D: Sex differences in teenage crime: The role of lifestyle.
In Research Bulletin No. 20. London: Home Office Research and
Planning Unit, 1986.
Riley D: Time and crime: The link between teenage lifestyle and delin-
quency. Journal of Quantitative Criminology, 3:339-354, 1987.
Riley, D, & Shaw, M: Parental supervision and juvenile delinquency.
Home Office Research Study, No. 83. London: HMSO, 1985.
Rutter, M, & Giller, H: Juvenile delinquency: Trends and
perspectives. Harmondsworth: Penguin, 1983.
Shapland, JM: Self-reported delinquency in boys aged 11 to 14.
British Journal of Criminology, 18: 255-266, 1978.
Smith, DA, & Paternoster, R: The gender gap in theories of deviance:
Issues and evidence. Journal of Research in Crime and Delinquency,
24:140-172, 1987.
Wadsworth, M: Roots of delinquency: Infancy, adolescence and crime.
Oxford: Martin Robertson, 1979.
Weis, JG: Delinquency from the self-report perspective. In Corrado,
RR, LeBlanc, M, & Trepanier, J (Eds.), Current issues in juvenile
justice. Toronto: Butterworth, 1983.
West, DJ, & Farrington, DP: Who becomes delinquent? London:
Heinemann Educational, 1973.
West, DJ, & Farrington, DP: The delinquent way of life. London:
Heinemann Educational, 1977.
West, DJ: Delinquency: Its roots, causes and prospects. London:
Heinemann, 1982.
Wilson, H: Parental supervision: A neglected aspect of delinquency.
British Journal of Criminology, 20:203-235, 1980.
Wilson, H: Parental supervision re-examined. British Journal of
Criminology, 27:275-301, 1987.
Wilson, H, & Herbert, GW: Parents and children in the inner city.
London: Routledge and Kegan Paul, 1978.
Winchester, S, & Jackson, H: Residential burglary: The limits of
prevention. Home Office Research Study, No. 74. London, HMSO,
1982.
Zimring, FE: Kids, groups and crime: Some implications of a
well-known secret. Journal of Criminal Law and Criminology,
72:867-885, 1981.

APPENDIX I. Self-report delinquency items showing numbers admitting each act in the past 12 months

		Boys (N=378)	Girls (N=373)
1.	Smashed bottles in the street	81	31
2.	Travelled on a bus or train without a ticket or deliberately paid the wrong fare	74	67
3.	Pinched something worth less than £1 from a shop	47	22
4.	Carried a weapon (e.g., a knife) intending to use it against someone if necessary	47	17
5.	Deliberately damaged school property	45	43
6.	Broke windows in an empty house	43	12
7.	Bought something you knew had been pinched	40	12
8.	Pinched something from family or relatives	30	33
9.	Written or sprayed paint on buildings	26	45
10.	Dialed 999 as a joke	19	19
11.	Damaged seats on buses and trains	10	23
12.	Pinched something worth between £1 and £5 from a shop	9	5
13.	Pinched something worth more than £5 from a shop	5	3
14.	Taken a bicycle with no intention of putting it back	8	3
15.	Got money from outside the family by threats	7	5
16.	Taken money from someone outside the family by force	4	5
17.	Pinched something from a parked car	4	3
18.	Deliberately damaged a parked car	3	3
19.	Tried to set fire to a building	1	1
20.	Snatched someone's wallet or handbag	1	1
21.	Got into someone's house while they were out and pinched something	0	1

For items excluded from the delinquency measure, overall admission rates for the past 12 months were: bought cigarettes, 172; kept something valuable they found, 133; dropped litter, 633; ridden a bicycle without lights, 359; started a fight, 109.

APPENDIX II.   Graph showing number of different acts ever committed by sample.

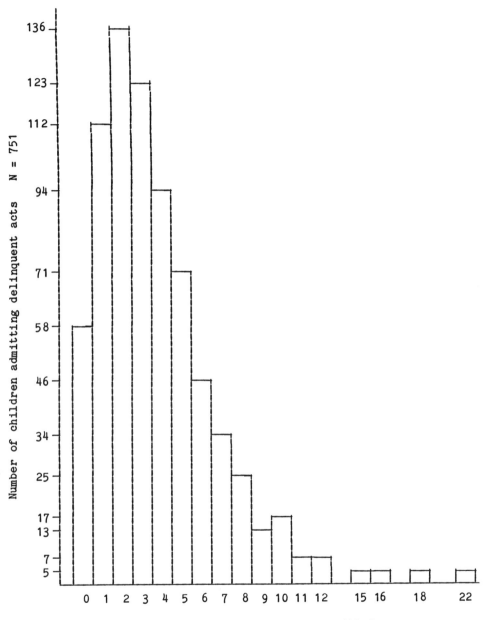

Number of different acts ever committed

ON THE USE OF SELF-REPORTS IN MEASURING CRIME AMONG ADULTS:
METHODOLOGICAL PROBLEMS AND PROSPECTS

Karl-Heinz Reuband
Zentralarchiv fur Empirische Socialforschung
University zu Koln
Cologne, Federal Republic of Germany

1. INTRODUCTION

The history of self-report research concerning the prevalence of
crime is a history of discontinuity. It is a history of changing foci
of interest and changing populations under investigation. At the beginning the focus was on the prevalence of crime. In later years it shift-
ed towards disentangling the causal patterns of delinquency; questions
of prevalence and epidemiology lost importance. At the beginning,
interest was in adults. The first self-report study actually centered
on adults, who were contacted more or less accidentally and handed a
questionnaire to return later to the researcher. Subsequent studies
relied on students, then finally almost all on school populations.
This partly intentional and partly accidental shift in the population
base had advantages: it made it possible to use more systematic frames
of sampling, assuring greater representativeness.[1] The shift, however,
also meant a loss in comparability and measuring social change via
trend studies. Due to the change in population, studies which allow a
comparison of the same population over time are scarce. Crime among
adults, although always a topic in criminological thinking, did not
gain any prominence in self-report research again. Apart from studies
on drug use there have been only a few surveys where an adult sample

----

1. The shift can be discerned for the USA as well as for Germany and
other countries. In Germany, the first self-report study was done by Magnus
Hirschfeld on homosexuality around the turn of the century. Students and
workers were used as the sample (Hirschfeld, 1914:480ff.). In the USA, the
first large study on crime of various natures was done among adults in the
1940s by Wallerstein and Wyle (1947); later studies in this realm referred
to students and then to the school population. The relatively high
prominence of student samples in all countries at the beginning might have
had something to do with the ease with which university researchers could
collect data from their daily clientele at low cost. Probably many of the
early studies, like the first one for Germany, done by Fritz Sack in Cologne
in 1964, were never published.

M. W. Klein (ed.), Cross-National Research in Self-Reported Crime and Delinquency, 89–106.
© 1989 by Kluwer Academic Publishers.

was used -- restricted, moreover, to a city or a region as the basis.[2] Nationwide studies are lacking.

In the following we shall report on two nationwide, representative studies we did of the adult population in West Germany. Along with questions on drug use, self-reports on selected types of crime were collected. We shall look at them mainly from a methodological point of view: How do the respondents react to such questions; to what extent do they perceive them as an invasion of their privacy; to what extent does the interview situation affect their willingness to admit deviance; and how do our prevalence data compare with anonymous data collected among young adults?

2. METHODOLOGY

The data were collected in face-to-face interviews as part of two omnibus surveys in April-June, 1982 and November-December, 1987. They were administered to representative samples of the West German population (including West Berlin) age 18 years onwards. The surveys were done by professional survey organizations, the first by Infratest and the second by GETAS. In both cases a random sample was used with a response rate of 68% and 70%, respectively. In 1982, 1993 people were interviewed and in 1987, 987. The questions on delinquent behavior ever committed were placed in the context of questions on attitudes towards illegal drug use and deviant behavior.[3] In the 1982 survey, respondents had to indicate the frequency of ever committing the offense, while in the 1987 survey only a simple "yes" or "no" response was required. In the 1982 survey, the self-report questions had to be answered by filling in a questionnaire handed to the respondent within the presence of the interviewer. After having done this task the sheet of paper had to be folded and handed back to the interviewer. In the 1987 survey, the response process was more public, requiring the interviewee to respond in the open and verbally.

In both studies the way in which the data were collected opened specific possibilities for methodological research. The procedure in 1982 made it possible to collect observational data. While the respondent was answering the questionnaire, the interviewer assessed the verbal and nonverbal reactions of the respondent to the questions on crime

---

2. For these studies of the adult population on a regional basis, see Vendrick's study in Groningen, quoted by Junger-Tas (1988) and, on a larger scale, the survey by Charles R. Tittle (1980).

3. The first survey in 1982 was part of a larger study on drugs and was financed by the National Institute on Drug Abuse (USA). The second in 1987, again with special emphasis on drug use, was financed by the Bundeszentrale für gesundheitliche Aufklärung (Federal Center for Health Education, Cologne). Both surveys were omnibus surveys with various topics apart from criminological ones. In the 1982 survey the self-report questions were asked in the first third, and in the 1987 survey at the end of the interview schedule.

according to a standardized coding scheme. In the 1987 survey, the
situation was different, since probing -- here on the experience of
illegal drug use -- was done in a standardized way and coded separately. Consequently, the interviewer had to know the answer explicitly
in order to know whether additional questions had to be posed or not.[4]
In both surveys a similar line of introduction was followed, calling
the subsequently mentioned behavior widely practiced behavior, thus
mitigating its appearance of deviance. In both cases the first behavior question referred to alcohol intoxication as some sort of mild and,
in some situations, even required deviation. In 1982 the following
questions pertained to hashish use, riding on public transport without
a ticket, and shoplifting. In 1987 the subsequent questions were on
attending cinema, concerts, sports or other meetings without paying,
riding on public transport without a ticket, and hashish use, in that
order.

3. REACTION TO QUESTIONS ON SELF-REPORT AND PREVALENCE RATES

Questions on self-reported delinquency do not seem to cause irrita-
tion on the part of the respondents to a noteworthy extent. Only 26%
conveyed the impression of being more nervous than before. Moreover,

TABLE 1. Reactions to self-report question according to age (multiple
responses in %).

Reaction	18-25	26-34	35-44	45-54	55-64	65+	Total
Nervous	22	22	24	36	23	30	26
Annoyed	3	1	3	7	6	7	4
Asks for anonymity	5	9	5	7	4	8	6
Other reactions	5	6	6	10	7	12	8
(N=)	294	352	362	308	304	358	1993

Source: 1982 survey. Here, and in the subsequent tables,
the unweighted sample is used.

----
4. For a more detailed discussion about the reactions to the
self-report questions and their effects on responses, see Reuband
(1988a). A report on the effect of probing is found in Reuband, 1988c.
In general, it shows that probing produces some more reported drug use,
although less than one might expect on the basis of "losses" in panel
interviews (for these losses in admission see also Reuband,
1986:94ff.).

the kind of nervousness it resembled was more often weak or moderate
than strong (3% strong, 11% medium, 13% weak). Only 4% seemed annoyed
and only 6% needed some kind of reassurance concerning the anonymity of
the data. When reactions are tabulated according to age of respondent
(Table 1) they tend to be remarkably similar across age, with the elder
respondents being affected only slightly more frequently by the special
type of questions than the younger ones.

As can be seen from Table 2, the use of public transport without a
ticket and the use of public facilities without paying is admitted by
roughly 30% of the respondents. Shoplifting has been practiced by 12%,
hashish use by 7-9%. When the 1982 and the 1987 figures are compared
for the sample as a total and within the respective age groups, no
clear cut trend can be discerned to show that the more public response
process produces lower figures than the more anonymous one. At least
for riding without a ticket, the data even go in the opposite direction, producing higher figures for the less anonymous (more recent)
study. It might well be that this difference, especially among the
young, reflects effects of interview administration less than real
change over time as more busses or trams had no entrance or exit
control (as might have happened in this period to some extent). Also,
increase of lifetime prevalence might somewhat reflect generational
change -- the younger respondents with their higher rates of delinquency grow older, causing a slight increase in lifetime prevalence among
the older respondents.

Lifetime prevalence in both surveys turns out to be the highest
among youth. Riding without a ticket is admitted by over 50% of the
18-25 year olds, but by slightly more than 10% of those 65 and older.
Shoplifting is admitted by 25% of the 18-25 year olds and by 4% of the
oldest group. The trends are similar for the other types of deviance.
Two reasons could account for this age relationship. First, it might
be that the older respondents are less willing to divulge their deviance in the interview than the younger groups. Second, the distribution might reflect real trends in generational experience. The opportunities to engage in these types of crime might have increased over the
years.

Both tendencies probably exist. On the one hand, older people are
more strongly tied to conventional routes of action and social roles
than younger ones. They are more committed to conformity, have more to
fear of public disapproval (see Becker, 1960). As a result they will
not only engage less in crime but might also be more selective in
giving details about their own past deviance in the interview.[5] The
way of answering might reflect the same kind of inclination which is

----

5. There are some indications concerning the direction of age effects:
In a British survey among adolescents, more respondents admitted ever hav
been before court than among an adult sample (see Blackmore, 1974 vs. May
& Hough, 1982). However, it is doubtful whether a strict comparability o
these studies exists. The adolescents were part of a longitudinal survey
which they had been asked about their own delinquency several times befor
They might have built up a stronger trust relationship than respondents i
the adult survey and therefore were more open.

TABLE 2. Self-reported delinquency according to age and year (multiple responses in %)

Age	18-25		26-34		35-44		45-54		55-64		65+		Total	
Year	82	87	82	87	82	87	82	87	82	87	82	87	82	87
Riding without a ticket	53	51	40	47	27	34	19	26	12	23	10	14	27	31
Shoplifting	25	-	22	-	10	-	8	-	4	-	4	-	12	-
Use public facilities without paying	-	50	-	37	-	35	-	32	-	19	-	19	-	30
Hashish use	16	21	18	16	5	14	1	5	*	3	*	1	7	9
(N=)	(294)	(95)	(352)	(173)	(362)	(176)	(308)	(167)	(304)	(159)	(358)	(217)	(1993)	(987)

Source: 1982 and 1987 surveys

* <0.5%

- Not ascertained.

reflected in deviance itself. On the other hand, generational opportunities to engage in the specified forms of deviance have increased as
well. In the 1960s, busses or trams had ticket collectors on board.
With the removal of the entrance or exit control during the 1970s, the
chance for free riding has improved. Similarly, with shoplifting, with
smaller shops being gradually replaced by large self-service stores,
opportunities for theft have become better than before. Drug use, in
forms of hashish use, finally, is a rather recent phenomenon which has
basically evolved in connection with the counterculture movements of
the 1960s (Reuband, 1988b). Given the fact that introduction into drug
use is concentrated in the youth period (BMJFG 1983:54), the earlier
generation will not catch up with the subsequent one, resulting in
lower prevalence rates.

4. EFFECTS OF THIRD PERSONS

     Face-to-face interviews take place in a non-anonymous setting.
The responses are made public to the interviewer and sometimes also to
other persons present. Although interview regulations advise keeping
others from the interview scene, this is not always done and not always
possible. Spouses might be present as well as children for whom the
respondent has to care and cannot leave alone. Third persons tend to
be present in about one quarter to one half of all face-to-face interviews (Reuband, 1984:120ff.).
     For the respondent, this might expose otherwise hidden and unknown
acts. Moreover, in the presence of children, admitting these acts
might mean negating the parents' role, denying for oneself what one
enforces in one's children. However, third persons may not always
represent a threat to validity of interview data. There might be
circumstances in which the respondent has told his spouse about his
behavior, but later forgotten about his own acts. The spouse present
during the interview might help in remembering the past.
     Bias due to third persons' being present might be reduced by
letting the respondent fill in a questionnaire handed to him in the
interview. In this case the other person will not hear the answer. He
could only become aware of it by standing directly behind the respondent, looking at the questionnaire. Using the questionnaire within the
context of the face-to-face interview was the strategy we employed in
the 1982 survey. In the 1987 survey no such device was employed, and
the response had to be given in public. Table 3 summarizes the figures
for the analyses. Even under the special situation of private questionnaire administration, there is a tendency among the 18-25 and the 26-34
year olds to admit deviance at a somewhat lower rate when third persons
are present. The effect, however, is not always strong and even coun-
terbalanced in one case by a reverse trend. Among the older respondents the effects are minimal, in one case again balanced in the other
direction. Whether this is a rather accidental finding, due to sample
size, or entails differential response tendencies in these categories

TABLE 3A. Self-reported delinquency according to third persons and age in 1982 (multiple responses in %)

Age Third person	18-25 Yes	No	26-34 Yes	No	35-44 Yes	No	45-54 Yes	No	55-64 Yes	No	65+ Yes	No	Total Yes	No
Riding without a ticket	44	58	37	41	31	24	19	20	13	12	9	11	26	27
Shoplifting	23	26	27	20	12	9	8	7	5	3	4	4	13	11
Hashish use	14	17	16	19	5	5	1	2	1	1	-	*	6	7
(N=)	93	201	118	234	118	244	106	202	91	213	95	263	625	1368

Source: 1982 survey

* <0.5%

TABLE 3B. Self-reported delinquency according to presence of third persons and age in 1987 (multiple responses in %)

Age Third person	18-25 Yes	No	26-34 Yes	No	35-44 Yes	No	45-54 Yes	No	55-64 Yes	No	65+ Yes	No	Total Yes	No
Riding without a ticket	64	46	31	56	35	33	21	27	17	25	14	15	29	31
Use public facilities without paying	55	48	31	40	32	36	40	29	17	19	18	19	31	30
Hashish use	23	21	12	18	7	18	6	4	3	2	-	1	8	9
(N=)	22	73	61	112	68	108	47	119	35	124	44	173	277	709

Source: 1987 survey

cannot be determined.[6]

In the 1987 survey, where no self-administered questionnaire was employed, the results tend to be similar although not identical; where third persons are on the scene respondents indicate less deviance than when nobody else listens to the interview. As expected, the less anonymous situation tends to produce somewhat stronger effects in the specified direction where identical offenses are compared. In case of riding without a ticket, third persons have a 25 percentage points effect among the 25- to 34-year-olds in the less anonymous situation, i.e., in the more anonymous situation the effects result in four percentage points only. There is an exception to this pattern however: among the 18- to 25-year-olds, more deviance is admitted whenever somebody is present. Given the relatively small number of respondents in the respective categories, this finding might be more accidental than substantive.

5. EFFECTS OF INTERVIEWER CHARACTERISTICS

Survey interviews are usually collected by professionally trained interviewers. They are trained not to indicate their attitudes and behavior and not to give any evaluations of the respondent's answers. But even if they keep to these rules, they cannot avoid conveying unwillingly an image of what they might think on various issues. Respondents tend to ascribe attitudes and beliefs to the interviewers on the basis of their visible social characteristics, such as age and sex. Given their basic interest in a smooth form of interaction, they give answers which minimize dissonance and potential conflict with the interviewer (c.f. Hyman et al., 1954; Steiner, 1984; Reuband, 1986b). They tend to reply similarly to people with the same characteristics as the interviewer.

In view of the fact that delinquency is widely practiced in youth, but is later reduced with increasing age (Kaiser, 1979:183ff.; Farrington, 1986), one should expect effects of interviewer age on self-reports on the basis of this reasoning: older interviewers should elicit less deviant behavior than younger ones in order to minimize conflict. In case of drug use, this has, in fact, already been shown for youth and young adult respondents (Reuband, 1985, 1986a). Whether it applies equally to other types of crime in the general population is not known. In Table 4 we have tabulated responses according to age of interviewer and respondent. The result replicates the findings for drug use mentioned above: in both the 1982 and 1987 surveys, a higher rate of Cannabis experience is obtained when interviewers are young. This applies above all to younger respondents, but can also be discerned among the older ones. What stands out further is that similar effects can be seen for riding on public transport without a

----

6. A general problem in assessing the effects of third persons is that presence and selection effects cannot be separated clearly. Possibly selection and presence effects together make up for the observed effects (see Reuband, 1987, on this problem).

TABLE 4A. Delinquency according to respondents' and interviewers' age - 1982 (in %)

Interviewers' Age	Respondent's Age						Total
	18 - 24	25 - 34	35 - 44	45 - 54	55 - 64	65+	
RIDING WITHOUT A TICKET							
18 - 34	64 (89)	42 (113)	25 (87)	18 (79)	11 (76)	9 (80)	30 (526)
35 - 49	45 (122)	36 (144)	28 (183)	20 (136)	12 (130)	10 (161)	25 (880)
50+	37 (78)	42 (88)	24 (87)	14 (89)	14 (97)	11 (114)	24 (557)
SHOPLIFTING							
18 - 34	25 (89)	22 (113)	10 (87)	4 (79)	5 (76)	4 (80)	13 (526)
35 - 49	28 (122)	20 (144)	12 (183)	8 (136)	3 (130)	4 (161)	11 (880)
50+	20 (78)	24 (88)	7 (87)	10 (89)	3 (97)	4 (114)	11 (557)
HASHISH USE							
18 - 34	20 (89)	23 (113)	6 (87)	3 (79)	3 (76)	- (80)	10 (526)
35 - 49	16 (122)	15 (144)	4 (183)	1 (136)	- (130)	- (161)	5 (880)
50+	13 (78)	15 (88)	7 (87)	1 (89)	1 (97)	1 (114)	6 (557)

Source: 1982 survey

TABLE 4B. Delinquency according to respondents' and interviewers' age - 1987 (in %)

Interviewers' Age	Respondents' Age						Total
	18 - 24	25 - 34	35 - 44	45 - 54	55 - 64	65+	
RIDING WITHOUT A TICKET							
18 - 34	62 (42)	56 (83)	38 (64)	15 (46)	16 (43)	18 (62)	34 (310)
35 - 49	43 (30)	39 (83)	31 (68)	33 (73)	33 (66)	16 (81)	31 (401)
50+	39 (23)	54 (37)	34 (44)	25 (48)	16 (50)	10 (74)	26 (76)
USE PUBLIC FACILITIES WITHOUT PAYING							
18 - 34	50 (42)	40 (53)	38 (64)	26 (46)	9 (43)	19 (62)	30 (310)
35 - 49	53 (30)	34 (83)	34 (68)	41 (73)	29 (66)	22 (81)	33 (401)
50+	44 (23)	41 (37)	32 (44)	25 (48)	14 (50)	15 (74)	25 (76)
HASHISH USE							
18 - 34	31 (42)	26 (53)	22 (64)	4 (46)	- (43)	- (62)	14 (310)
35 - 49	13 (30)	10 (83)	9 (68)	7 (73)	5 (66)	3 (81)	7 (401)
50+	13 (23)	14 (37)	9 (44)	2 (48)	2 (50)	- (74)	5 (76)

Source: 1987 survey

ticket. The effect is, however, restricted to the 18-25 year olds;
among the older respondents, the effect is less clear-cut.

Perhaps it matters that lifetime experience is asked for. Except
for hashish use (which is a rather recent and still youth-centered
phenomenon), the other types of delinquency have been practiced by the
members of the older generation as well. Under these circumstances the
middle-aged interviewer might be seen by the respondents as a person
with a somewhat similar biographical background. The less is his need
for adaptation -- except among the youngest who, still being treated as
youth by many adults, might see the older interviewer not only as a
representative of certain experiences but above all as authority.
Representatives of adult authority deal with youth educational aims in
mind; they preach conformity and enforce it. The young respondents
might take this into consideration when responding. If they do so they
do it regardless of the way the questions were administered - whether
given on a list for self-handling or by means of orally addressed
questions.[7]

6. COMPARISON WITH OTHER DATA

The validity of our data are difficult to assess. We do not have
other data on adults against which we can compare our results. What we
can do, however, is to take studies among young adults into consideration; these have been based mostly on anonymous questionnaires, administered in group settings. Such interviews are treated in the literature
as having the highest validity. They seem especially apt to elicit
information on deviant and nonconforming attitudes and behavior (Hyman
et al., 1954:182ff.; Sudman & Bradburn, 1974:40f.). The studies on
young adults available for Germany have been mainly restricted to
students and freshly recruited soldiers. Both samples have their
biases: whereas lower educated people are naturally excluded among
students, higher educated are somewhat under-represented among
soldiers. Still the studies on soldiers are probably the best approximation for generalization, the more so since they include the rural
areas and people with education like the average citizen. Two questions are of special importance in the following: Can we discern
trends over time in these data similar to those among the survey
respondents on a generational basis? And how similar are the prevalence figures to those reported earlier; how great is the bias of
using non-anonymous, face-to-face interviews?

We have drawn together the available evidence on self-report

----

7. Since we used a random sample, there is little likelihood that the
effect of interviewer characteristics are due to a selection process. Wh
cannot be ruled out altogether, however, is the possibility that third
factors, such as regional location, partially make up for the observed
effects. If in certain regions with certain traditions in behavior young
interviewers are more often used than in others, the effects would
theoretically take place. Only a strict random allocation of the
interviewer to the respondent can resolve this problem.

among young adults referring to lifetime crime and delinquency in Table 5.[8] The kind of region and the kind of population varies. Middle-sized and large cities and students in law school and sociology students are over-represented. No study is representative for a field of study, student body, or general population. Under these circumstances the only possibility of a comparison lies in looking at the range of variation and remembering the built-in biases when interpreting the data. According to the data, riding free by bus, tram, or subway is a rather widespread behavior in which a majority of men and women have engaged. Among students the rate for males is well above 80%, among females usually above 70%! In large cities (like Cologne and Hamburg) the rate is even higher, and in populations residing in more rural areas the rate is lower. The reason might lie in differential opportunities: in smaller regions where transport by bus rather than tram is common, entrance into the bus is often only possible by showing the ticket to the driver or buying it from him. In larger cities people have to obtain their ticket themselves in ticket machines. Given these differential opportunities, comparisons over time can only be made on the basis of the same locality and population.

Comparisons over a long time period can be done for a few types of offenses. The situation is best for shoplifting and drug use, less for riding without a ticket, or use of public facilities without paying. Shoplifting according to our overview has been committed by 42% to 45% of the men and by 29% to 35% of the women in surveys of the 1970s and 1980s. When compared with data from the sixties, the more recent data document an increase of prevalence (see no. 7 vs. 1, 5 vs. 2). In the mid-sixties the rate for theft was still about a quarter of the population. Data for the 1970s and 1980s turn out to be relatively stable.

Riding free without a ticket seems to have stayed equally stable during the 1970s with roughly 80% of the male students and more than 70% of the female students having engaged in it. The biggest increase might have taken place in the 1960s when in many cities the entrance and/or exit control in busses or subways was removed. Cannabis use has increased according to the overview since the sixties and has stabilized in the 20-30% range in the seventies and eighties (see also Reuband, 1988b). The above-mentioned generational data in our cross population surveys thus seem to reflect real changes to some extent.

Turning now to a comparison of these data with ours, there can be no doubt that non-anonymous interview situations lead to some underestimation of delinquency. Concerning riding without a ticket, the lowest rate for young adults in the 1970s is well above 50%; in the 1982 and 1987 surveys the rate in the respective age group is almost 50%, while in the subsequent age group (which should be the most similar to the ones covered in the 1970s surveys) it is even lower. It is only when

----

8. There are a few other studies which are not listed here because they ask for delinquency within the last year only. These kinds of studies probably provide better and more reliable results, but are beyond the scope to be discussed here. For one of the more recent notable studies on delinquency using a shorter time frame, see Villmow and Stephan (1985).

TABLE 5. Lifetime delinquency among young adults (in %).

	Study			N^1	Year of research	Riding without a ticket M	F	Shop-lifting M	F	Drug use M	F	Use of public facilities without paying M	F
Nr.	Population	Location	Author										

STUDENTS

Nr.	Population	Location	Author	N^1	Year	Ride M	Ride F	Shop M	Shop F	Drug M	Drug F	Pub M	Pub F
1	Sociology	Cologne	Sack	40/17	1964	-	-	20	24	3	6	-	-
2	Law	Giessen	Quensel/Quensel	-83-	1967	-	-	-24-		-4-		-61-	-
3	Law	Göttingen	Schwind/Eger	226/64	1971-73	85	72	-	-	-	-	-	-
4	Diverse*	Hamburg	Diekmann	114/68	1974	-93-		-	-	-	-	-	-
5	Law	Giessen	Kreuzer	296/132	1976-78	83	77	43	29	25	28	-	-
6	Law	Giessen	Kreuzer	191/159	1981-82	81	63	42	36	27	23	43	25
7	Sociology	Cologne	Reuband	68/64	1983	93	95	65	51	51	44	-	-
8	Law, Soc.,Econ.	Giessen	Kreuzer	755/595	1984-86	78	76	45	35	28	22	-	-

Table continued on next page.

TABLE 5. (continued)

	Study				Year of research	Riding without a ticket		Shop-lifting		Drug use		Use of public facilities without paying	
Nr.	Population	Location	Author	N[1]		M	F	M	F	M	F	M	F
OTHER POPULATIONS													
9	General population age 19-23 **	Hamburg	Gipser	-/125	1970-71	-	78	-	24	-	7	-	10[2]
10	School population age 19-22	Hamburg	Kreuzer	360/253	1973	84[3]	72[3]	48	21	45	22	-	-
11	General population age 20-30/34 **	Bad.-Württ.	Schöch	103/-	1971-73	54[3]	-	18	-	7	-	-	-
12	Soldiers	Bad.-Württ.	Schöch	256/-	1974	66[3]	-	42	-	10	-	-	-
13	Soldiers	Hessen	Kreuzer	727/-	1978	73	-	45	-	14	-	-	-

M = Male Respondents, F = Female Respondents, - = Not ascertained.
If not otherwise stated, anonymous self-administered questionnaires were used in a group setting:
* = self-administered questionnaire for individual response;
** = face-to-face interview;
*** = self-administered questionnaire in individual interview setting.
1 First number indicating number of male respondents, second number of female respondents.
2 Attending cinema without paying.
3 Riding without a ticket and use of public facilities without paying.

we take the social characteristics of the interviewer into consideration and refer to data where younger people did the interviewing that
the rate approximates the one in anonymous interviews. The situation
seems to be even worse for shoplifting, but not in the case of drug
use. The survey data in that case resemble closely the data from other
sources. Comparisons with other kinds of data on drug use among youth
confirm this impression (see Reuband, 1986a:92).

Perhaps it is the kind of delinquency which matters. Drug use is
a type of delinquency where nobody is harmed (except the deviant actor,
if so). Riding free on public transport entails an offense against
public amenities that cater to all and is also funded indirectly by all
(including the deviant actor himself). Shoplifting on the other hand,
though it might mean somewhat anonymous offending -- especially in
self-service stores -- still entails a victim. It could be that this
characteristic of the act makes for differential proneness to admit
deviance. The act itself can be constructed by the actor in a way that
allows for legitimacy. It entails differential possibilities of verbal
or nonverbal disapproval by the interviewer.

7. CONCLUSIONS

In our paper we have reported on one of the first nationwide
surveys on self-reported delinquency among adults. We have done so
from a methodological point of view and tried to assess its problems.
The analysis has shown that the general social desirability and the
situation of the interview both affect the results -- leading to some
underestimation of prevalence rates. Whether questions are handled in
a verbal way or by recourse to a questionnaire thus does not make any
difference. It could well be, however, that the use of other procedures improves the situation. One could, for instance, let the respondent seal the envelope and then hand it over to the interviewer. Or one
could hand him a questionnaire to be answered in private and then let
him send it to the institute. Only further methodological research can
find out.

At present, unfortunately, two positions prevail in the literature: on the one hand a rather uncritical attitude towards the validity of self-report, and on the other, an outspoken doubt about the use
of such data. However different they are, neither position implies an
interest in further, methodological research. But it is only by
finding out the limitations and sorts of biases which allow for improvement in design and interpretation. Self-report studies, regardless of
populations investigated, need more systematic research than has been
the practice in the past (especially so in Germany, but also in most of
the other European countries).

REFERENCES

Becker, H: Notes on the concept of commitment. American Journal of
Sociology, 66:32-40, 1960.

Blackmore, J: The relationship between self-reported delinquency and official conviction among adolescent boys. British Journal of Criminology, 19:172-175, 1974.

BMJFG (Bundesministerium fur Jugend, Familie und Gesundheit): Konsum und Missbrauch von Alkohol, illegalen Drogen, Medikamenten und Tabakwaren durch junge Menshen. Bonn-Bad Godesberg, 1983.

Diekmann, A: Die Befolgung von Gesetzen. Empirische Untersuchungen zu einer rechtssoziologischen Theorie. Berlin, 1980.

Farrington, DP: Age and crime. In Tonry, M, & Morris, N. (Eds.), Crime and justice. An annual review of research. Chicago/London, 189-250: 1986.

Gipser, D: Mädchenkriminalität. Soziale Bedingungen abweichenden Verhaltens. München, 1975.

Hirschfeld, M: Die Homsexualität des Mannes und des Weibes. Berlin, 1914.

Hyman, H, Cobb, W, Feldman, J, Hart, CW, & Stember, CH: Interviewing in social research. Chicago, 1954.

Junger-Tas, J: Self-report delinquency research in Holland with a perspective on international comparison. Paper prepared for the NATO advanced research workshop on "Self-report methodology in criminological research." The Hague, June 26-30, 1988.

Kaiser, G: Kriminologie. Eine Einführung in die Grundlagen. 4th edition, Heidelberg/Karlsruhe, 1979.

Kreuzer, A: Über Giessener Delinquenzbefragungen. In Triffterer, O, & Zezschwitz, Fv, (Eds.), Festschrift für Walter Mallmann. Baden-Baden, 129-150: 1978.

Kreuzer, A: Weitere Beiträge aus Giessener Delinquenzbefragungen. Monatsschrift für Kriminologie und Strafrechtsreform, 63:385-396, 1980.

Kreuzer, A: Kinderdelinquenz und Jugendkriminalitat. Umfang, Struktur und Entwicklung. Zeitschrift für Pädagogik, 29:49-70, 1983.

Kreuzer, A: Jugend, Drogen, Kriminalität. Third edition, Neuwied/ Darmstadt, 1987.

Landeskriminalamt Hamburg: Jugendkriminalität in Hamburg. Hamburg, 1975.

Mayhew, P, & Hough, M: The British Crime Survey. Home Office and Planning Unit Research Bulletin No. 14, 24-27: 1982.

Quensel, S, & Quensel, E: Delinquenzbelastungsskalen für männliche und weibliche Jugendliche. Kölner Zeitschrift für Soziolgie und Social-psychologie, 75-97: 1970.

Reuband, KH: Dritte Personen beim Interview - Zuhörer, Adressaten oder Katalysatoren der Kommunikation? In Meulemann, H, & Reuband, KH, (Eds.), Soziale Realität im Interview. Empirische Analysen methodischer Probleme. Frankfurt/New York, 117-156: 1984.

Reuband, KH: Methodische Probleme bei der Erfassung altersspezifischer Verhaltensweisen: Die Zusammensetzung von Interviewerstäben und ihr Einfluss auf das Antwortverhalten Jungendlicher. ZA Information, 17:34-50, 1985.

Reuband, KH: Zur Verbreitung illegaler Drogenerfahrung in der Bevölkerung der Bundesrepublik Deutschland - Versuche einer Messung im Rahmen der Umfrageforschung. Suchtgefahren, 32:87-102, 1986a.

106

Reuband, KH: Einflüsse der Interviewsituation auf den Inglehart'schen
Postmaterialismus-Index: die Bedeutung von Interviewermerkmalen
für das Antwortverhalten der Befragten. ZA Information, 18:35-55,
1986b.
Reuband, KH: Unerwünschte Dritte beim Interview. Erscheinungsformen
und Folgen. Zeitschrift für Soziologie, 16:303-308, 1987.
Reuband, KH: Reaktionen auf unangenehme Fragen - über den Einsatz
standardisierter Beobachtungsverfahren im mündlichen Interview. ZA
Information, 22:73-86, 1988a.
Reuband, KH: Drogenkonsum im Wandel. Eine retrospektive Prävalenz-
messung der Drogenerfahrung Jugendlicher in den Jahren 1967 bis
1987. Zeitschrift für Sozialisationsforschung und
Erziehungssoziologie, 8:54-68, 1988b.
Reuband, KH: Uber des "Vergessen" von Erfahrungen und Möglichkeiten
ihier Reaktivierung im Interview. ZA Information, 23:1988c.
Schöch, H: Ist Kriminalität normal? Probleme und Ergebnisse der
Dunkelfeldforschung. In Göppinger, H, & Kaiser, G (Eds.),
Kriminologische Gegenwartsfragen. Stuttgart, 426-443: 1976.
Schwind, HD, & Eger, H-J: Untersuchungen zur Dunkelziffer. Nichtent-
deckte Straftaten von Göttinger Jura-Studenten. Monatsschrift für
Kriminologie und Strafrechtsreform, 56:151-170, 1973.
Steinert, H: Das Interview als soziale Interaktion. In Meulemann, H,
& Reuband, KH (Eds.), Soziale Realität im Interview. Empirische
Analysen methodischer Probleme. Frankfurt/New York, 17-59: 1984.
Sudman, S, & Bradburn, NM: Response effects in surveys. A review of
studies. Chicago, 1974.
Tittle, CR: Sanctions and deviance. The question of deterrence. New
York, 1980.
Villmow, B, & Stephan, E (with collaboration of H. Arnold): Jugend-
kriminalität in einer Gemeinde. Eine Analyse erfragter Delinquenz
und Victimisierung sowie amtlicher Registrierung. Kriminologische
Forschungsberichte aus dem Max-Planck-Institut für ausländisches
und internationales Strafrecht. Freiburg, 1983.
Wallerstein, JS, & Wyle, CJ: Our law abiding law-breakers. Probation,
25:107-112, 1947.

SELF-REPORTED AND RECORDED DATA ON DRUG ABUSE AND DELINQUENCY ON 287
MEN IN STOCKHOLM

Jerzy Sarnecki
National Council for Crime Prevention
Stockholm, Sweden

1. INTRODUCTION

The 1956 clientele investigation is a longitudinal, projective
study of 287 men in Stockholm who are now about 40 years old. A large
number of different data collection methods have been used in the
study. For example, information has been obtained concerning the criminal behavior, drug abuse, and other anti-social behavior from police
records, other registers, and by interviewing the men themselves. This
was carried out on three occasions; when the subjects of the study were
11 to 15, about 18, and between 33 and 42 years old. This report compares information about anti-social behavior compiled by using these
methods.
The 1956 clientele study was inaugurated against the background of
a conspicuous increase in juvenile crime. The Crown authorized the
head of the Ministry of Justice to appoint experts to make "a study of
juvenile crime in order to discover its causes."
The expert group, some members of which changed in the course of
time, published altogether five reports from the project: "Methods of
the study. Debut of crime and recidivism" (SOU 1971:49), Gösta Carlsson: "Family, school and society in the light of official data" (SOU
1972:76), Birgitta Olofsson: "Home, upbringing, school and comrade
environment in the light of interviews and follow-up data" (SOU
1973:25), Sven Ahnsjö: "Physical-psychological development and status
in the light of parental interview and follow-up data" (SOU 1973:49)
and Kristina Humble and Gitte Settergren Carlsson: "Personality and
relations in the light of projective methods" (SOU 1974:31). These
five reports constitute one of the most extensive studies of juvenile
crime that has been made in Sweden.
In the report "Predicting Social Maladjustment" (Sarnecki, 1985)
some of the results from Stage One of the follow-up study, which was
started in 1983, are presented. This comprises a follow-up of records

107

M. W. Klein (ed.), Cross-National Research in Self-Reported Crime and Delinquency, 107–129.
© 1989 by Kluwer Academic Publishers.

about the individuals in the original study.[1] Work is at present in progress on <u>Stage Two</u> of the follow-up, which comprises interviews with individuals from the orignal study. This study is carried out together with Kristina Humble.

2. THE SUBJECT GROUP

The subject group for the clientele study consisted of the individuals included in a pilot study and in a main study. The pilot study comprised 42 boys with a criminal record and 42 controls matched to them. The main study comprised 150 boys with a criminal record and a control group of 53. The total number of subjects was thus 287, of whom roughly two-thirds have criminal records. When these boys were examined on the first occasion they were 11 - 15 years of age.

2.1. <u>The criminal group for the pilot study</u> was selected on the basis of reports from the Records Department of the Stockholm Criminal Investigation Department. The reports covered the period January 1959 - March 1960 and related to the first crimes against property committed by schoolboys aged 11 - 15 years. The group was selected randomly from boys whose crimes were not considered petty and who could definitely be considered guilty of them.

2.2. <u>The control group for the pilot study</u> was selected from the population records. For each boy in the criminal group, a boy was sought who resembled him with respect to age (11-13 and 14-15 years old), social group (group 3 corresponds to workers, manual laborers, etc., and groups 2 and 1 correspond to salaried employees, businessmen, etc.), type of urban area (areas with above or below average delinquency), and family type (broken and whole families, respectively). All of the matching variables were dichotomies. Among the boys complying with these requirements a random selection of 42 was included in the study.

2.3. <u>The criminal group for the main study</u> was selected on the same principles as for the pilot study from reports coming into the Stockholm Criminal Investigation Department in the period May 1960 - June 1963.

2.4. <u>The control group for the main study</u> was constructed on the same principles as for the pilot study, with the exception that one control was selected for every third criminal boy (SOU 1971:49, pp. 62-71). (The results of the matching for both the pilot study and the main study are presented in the appendix.)

----

1. A grant for Stage One of the follow-up study was made by the Sweden Tercentenary Fund. The follow-up work has been done by staff of the Research Division of the National Council for Crime Prevention.

3. THE DATA

3.1. Data on the Original Study

The data collected for the clientele study is very extensive. For every one of the subjects, about 2,000 variables have been measured. The data collection was done by different methods and at several different times by different research groups. On the occasion of the first data collection, when the boys were 11 - 15 years old, the following sources were used:

Data from <u>criminal records, social register</u>, etc., concerning the subject and his relatives;

Terman-Merrill <u>intelligence test</u>, supplemented by a non-verbal test method;

The projective tests, <u>Rorschach</u> and <u>AAT</u> (Adolescent Apperception Test): two psychologists independently evaluated all test responses;

<u>Sociological interview</u>: An interviewer and sociologist evaluated the results independently;

Revised edition of the "<u>criminality form</u>" that has been tried out on a large number of youths in Stockholm;

Simple <u>interests test</u> concerning leisure occupations and the like;

<u>Medico-psychiatric examination</u>;

Interview <u>with teacher</u>;

<u>Home visit</u> and interviews with parents;

<u>School grades</u> from the subjects' entire time at school (SOU 1971:49, pp. 23-24).

In the main study, some changes were made in comparison with the data collected in the pilot study. These consisted chiefly of shortening of the questionnaire and more precise wording of certain questions. The boys from the clientele study were followed up in conjunction with their enrollment for military service. The ordinary enrollment interview was extended by about 15 minutes per individual. They also received two questionnaires to fill in, one relating to their criminal behavior, the other to measure certain attitudes (SOU 1973;25, p. 57). All boys in the clientele study were also followed up in the Stockholm Child Care Committee's files, in the criminal records, in the records of the National Board of Excise, and in the Temperance Board.

3.1.1. <u>Registers and self-reported data at age 11 - 15</u>. The

self-report questionnaire was based on one which was implemented earlier with a representative range of school children of corresponding ages (Elmhorn, 1965). The form includes 24 questions about crime, from minor misdemeanors such as stealing in the home and stealing fruit, to thefts of mopeds, breaking into huts, the use of threats and force, and handbag snatching. The questionnaire also includes questions about the number of times each type crime was committed.

The answers were used to calculate the "criminal points" according to the system used in the school survey mentioned above. Each individual's points were then compared with the standard material provided by the school survey and awarded index points on a five-degree scale. Index point one means that the individual concerned had not committed more crimes than the 20% with the highest crime score in the school survey (SOU 1971:49). (There is a crime index only for the 203 individuals in the main study.)

TABLE 1. Sub-division of the boys according to criminal index points and crimes recorded by the police at age 15, in percentages.

Self-reported		Number recorded crimes			
Index	0	1	>2	Total	N
1	36	0	0	9	19
2	24	3	4	9	18
3	15	30	6	20	40
4	17	46	37	36	74
5	8	21	53	26	52
	100	100	100	100	203
Average index points	2.4	3.9	4.4	3.6	

The table indicates that there is a relatively strong relationship between the criminal index based on self-reported data and the information about the registered crime obtained from police records.

A multiple regression analysis compared crime at the age of 15 measured by police records with crime measured by the self-report method. The multiple regression variables included: psychiatric

prognosis (SOU 1971:49), psychological diagnosis from two projective
tests and IQ measurement (SOU 1974:31), adaptation to school according
to appraisal of teachers (SOU 1972;76), asocial environment of peers
according to an interview with the boy (SOU 1983:25), appraisal of the
home according to a parent interview (SOU 1973:25), and appraisal of
the overall social adjustment of the boy at an age of 11 -15 (Sarnecki,
1986). A total of 43% of the variation in self-reported crime and 50%
of the variation in police recorded crime was explained by these variables. The difference is not great, but does slightly favor the use of
official over self-report measures of youthful criminal behavior.

In connection with the construction of certain of the central
variables just listed, for example psychiatric prognosis, care had to
be taken to avoid confounding with information about criminal behavior.
The fact that the central study variables explain a greater proportion
of the variation in police-registered than self-reported crime could
result from awareness of police information. A model which consists of
the variables where the construction excluded consideration of the
criminal behavior of the young people explains 42% of the variation in
the registered crime and 40% of the variation in the self-reported
crime. The difference is insignificant. The model included: adjustment to school according to the teacher, appraisal of the home according to the parent-interview, the appraisal of delinquency of peers
according to the interview with the boy, psychological diagnosis from
two projective tests, and measurement of IQ.

As a result of matching, it should be noted, it is not possible to
study the classical questions in the dispute between the supporters of
the self-report and police register methods with respect to age, social
group, or family type, the three matching variables.

3.1.2. Self-report data when registering for military service. In a
survey carried out in connection with registration for compulsory military service, the boys were asked not only about crimes they had committed up to the age of 15, but also crimes up to the age of 18. The
relationship between self-reported crimes stated on the first survey
occasion and self-reported crimes up to age 15 stated when registering
for compulsory military service is positive but weak (R = 0.24, N =
203).

When processing the self-report questionnaire carried out during
military registration, it was found that the men in some cases stated
that they had committed certain crimes but not how often. Thus the
measure adopted was the number of types of crime committed, not the
number of crimes. It was felt that the number of types of crime would
be a good indicator of the crime levels of the study subjects (SOU
1973:25, p. 57). The correlation between this measure of crime up to
age 15 stated at the time of military registration, and the crime index
based on the self-reported survey actually obtained at age 15 was 0.33
(N = 203).

The relatively low relationship between self-reported crime stated
on two different occasions depends to a certain extent on the fact that
the time period covered by the questions is not exactly the same. On
the first occasion, the boys investigated were between 11 and 15, on

the average about 13 years old. Most of the boys were thus able to commit additional crimes during the period between the first survey occasion and age 15. Furthermore, the self-report forms used on the two different occasions were not completely identical. However, the complete difference in the answers in the two different surveys cannot be explained by "technical" factors. Thirty-three percent of the boys in the pilot criminal group neglected to report at the time of military registration one or more types of crime that they stated they had committed in the first survey. One quarter of the boys in the pilot control group also "forgot" what they earlier said they had committed. The crimes that the boys most frequently did not remember to report are offenses involving receiving stolen goods (purchased or used bicycles, mopeds, etc., which they believed or knew were stolen), bicycle theft, and housebreaking or burglary. The receiving offenses not reported make up almost half (43%) of those earlier reported by the boys. Unreported bicycle thefts, housebreaking, and burglary make up about one quarter of the crimes that should have been reported. "Forgetfulness" or negligence in connection with the reporting of crimes is just as common among the delinquent group as the control group (SOU 1973:25, p. 60).

TABLE 2. Report of comparison about crime obtained from police records and crime stated by the boys in the self-reported questionnaire on the occasion of registration for military service.

Number of crime questionnaires filled in by persons included in police records	213
Percent of persons stating wrong time for crime	9
Percent of persons who denied crimes registered by police	7
Percent of persons who did not report crimes registered by police because they were not covered by the questions or for other explicable reasons	21
Percent of registered crimes denied	5
Percent of registered crimes not covered by the questions or the denial of which can be explained	9
Percent registered crimes stated	85

Source: SOU 1973:75, p. 175

The three-grade scale of police-registered crimes up to age 15 correlates 0.44 (N = 281) with the crime index at age 15 based on

information from the self-report questionnaire at military registration
and 0.38 (N = 213) with the number of self-reported <u>types of crime</u> up
to 15 reported at the time of military registration. The correlations
are thus lower than those between registered crime and the crime index
based on information reported by the boys on the first survey occasion.

The report by Olofsson (SOU 1973:25) records the following comparison between information taken from police records when the boys were 18
years old and information from the self-report questionnaire in connection with registration for military service at the same age.

The relationship between the number of police-registered crimes
and the self-reported crime index at age 18 is 0.65 (N = 284). This is
a relatively strong relationship. The impression gained by Olofsson
concerning the answers given by the boys on the self-report questionnaires is that they really tried to answer these questions honestly.

3.2. Recorded Data in the Follow-Up Study

Data from the following registers was used in the follow-up in 1983
and 1984:

> The <u>SPAR Register</u> is a population register of all persons entered
> in parish registers having an income tax form or recorded in the
> Social Insurance Office in Sweden.
>
> The <u>Morbidity Register</u> is kept by the Central Bureau of
> Statistics.
>
> The <u>Social Insurance Register</u> is kept by the National Social
> Insurance Board.
>
> The <u>Police Register</u>, kept by the National Police Board.
>
> The <u>Judicial Statistics of the Control Bureau of Statistics</u>.
>
> The <u>Injection Mark Register</u> is a register of individuals who,
> after commitment to the Stockholm Remand Center, have shown
> injection marks from intravenous drug abuse (Bejerot, 1975).
>
> <u>Population and housing census</u> in 1965, 1970, 1975 and 1980.
>
> <u>National Board of Excise Register</u>, until 1977.
>
> <u>Register of Higher Education</u>.
>
> <u>National Labor Market Board Register of Persons Seeking Work</u>.
>
> The <u>Labor Market Training Register</u> of the National Labor Market
> Board.

3.2.1. <u>Interview data in the follow-up study</u>. Interviews were carried
out during the years 1984 - 1985 when the men were between 34 and 43

years old. The work was carried out by three experienced and middle-aged female interviewers. Most of each interview had a semi-structured character, with both psychological and sociological aspects covered. The conversation between the interviewer and the subject was tape recorded at the same time as the interviewer filled in the answers on the interview form. The survey also included a number of forms filled in by the men themselves under the supervision of the interviewer.

The semi-structured interview consisted of the following sections:
- Work
- Finances
- Family situation
    Present family
    Children
    Original family
    Foster families (if any)
- Schooling, education
- Views on society
- Alcohol habits
- Drugs
- Crimes
- Religious beliefs and moral matters.

Most of the sections were answered in chronological order so that the subject was able to state the various events in the order in which they occurred. For example, the interviewer could ask: When did you get your first job? What sort of a job was it? When did you finish working there? Where did you start working then? When did you finish working there? etc., all the way up to the current living situation of the subject. After this, the next section was taken up and answered in a similar way. The interview time varied to a marked extent but was never less than 1 1/2 hours. There were actually interviews lasting four hours and more.

The interviews were carried out at different places. Many took place in premises at the disposal of the project and which were located close to the Swedish National Council for Crime Prevention. Some interviews were carried out at another neutral place or at the home of the subject. Some were carried out at penal institutions to which the subjects were committed on the occasion of the interview.

The Swedish system using a social security number ("person number") provided the possibility, via the SPAR register mentioned earlier, of obtaining the current addresses of the men being investigated. The interview subjects were first contacted by letter which contained a reference to the study which had taken place about 25 years earlier. Some time after the letter had been received, the subject was contacted by telephone by the person who was to carry out the interview. During this conversation a time and place convenient to the subject was determined.

Of the original 287 boys, 199 were interviewed. The interview study thus suffered from a significant attrition of 31%.

The vast majority of the Swedish population has a telephone but it became obvious that a large number of the persons included in the

interview had unlisted telephone numbers. This created serious difficulties for the interviewers. However, most of those with unlisted
telephone numbers established contact with the interviewers themselves,
frequently after several letters. In certain cases the interviewers
made contact with subjects who had unlisted telephone numbers through
personal visits or by contacting relatives. But attempts to reach
certain of them failed in spite of repeated attempts. The non-response
also includes a small group of persons who did not live at the addresses shown in the registers and could not be traced.

A relatively small number of subjects, about 15 persons, refused
to let themselves be interviewed in spite of the fact that the interviewers were able to contact them by telephone. Some did not refuse
directly but failed to turn up at many meetings agreed upon.

On the follow-up occasion, 19 of the men in the survey were dead.
Mortality was considerably higher among those who, on the first study
occasion when the boys were 11 - 15 years old, were known to the police
for at least one significant property crime than in the case of the
boys without such a criminal record (Sarnecki, 1985). As a total,
however, the non-response was the same among sets of respondents.

On the other hand, the non-response does show a relationship with
registered crime in the follow-up:

TABLE 3. Missing individuals in the interview study by number of
recorded crimes, in percentages.

Number Recorded Crimes	Including dead	Excluding dead
No recorded crimes	28	22
1 or more recorded crimes	37	37
10 or more recorded crimes	36	36
20 or more recorded crimes	38	38
50 or more recorded crimes	32	32
Total	31	26

As the table shows, the non-response in the interview study is
greater among men whose names appear in police records. On the other
hand, the non-response does not increase with an increase in the number
of registered crimes. The table shows the non-response including and
excluding those dead. The deceased are automatically removed from
police records, which implies that the deceased are included in the
group without recorded crimes. Further analysis shows that individuals
with generally poorer social adjustment as adults had a higher

non-response rate than those with good social adjustment. The proportion of individuals who on the basis of register data were classified in the categories poor and very poor social adjustment was 21% of the entire study material, but only 16% of those interviewed (see the definitions on p. 21). The proportion of individuals in the good and very good social adjustment categories constituted 56% of all the men studied, but 67% of those interviewed. The proportion of individuals known for intravenous drug abuse, however, was almost as high among those interviewed (10%, 22 individuals) as among the entire group studied (11%, 32 individuals).

Even the individuals in the poorer social adjustment categories as 11-15-year-olds had a higher non-response rate in connection with the interviews as adults than those in the better social adjustment categories in the same age group. However, the connection between social adjustment in the 11-15 year old age group and the non-response rate is much weaker (barely significant). The reason seems to be that it is mainly an individual's adult social adjustment which affects the non-response rate. The correlation in the clientele material between adult social adjustment and adjustment in the 11-15 year old age group is .53. Apart from this, in regard to matching variables and other important variables of the study, the interview non-response rate does not differ from the material in general.

3.2.2. Drug abuse. The follow-up study includes three indicators concerning drug abuse among the subjects:
1. Information in police records of drug-related crime. (The records cover legal procedures for crimes committed by an individual after the age of 15.) Information about less serious crimes, not subject to prison sentences, is deleted after five years if no new crimes are committed. Information about more serious crimes, subject to prison sentences, is deleted after ten years if no new serious crimes are committed. (Yearbook of legal statistics, 1987, SCB.)
2. Register of injection needle puncture marks (Register of persons who, in 1965 or later, on admission into custody in Stockholm, were found to have marks resulting from intravenous drug abuse; Bejerot, 1975.)
3. Self-reported information from the interview study. According to the self-reports, 50% (100 individuals) of the men stated that they had used illegal narcotics on some occasion. The majority of them used hashish and only for a short period. It should be noted that the group studied is considerably more socially maladjusted than the normal population. Twenty individuals (10% of the men who replied to interview questions) were registered in police records for at least one drug-related crime and the same number were to be found in the register of injected drug abusers. None of the 48 men who stated that they only used hashish and no other drugs were registered for drug-related crimes in police records. Furthermore, none of these persons were noted in the Injection Mark Register.

Of the 23 men who stated that they used drugs other than hashish, not intravenously, however, four were registered in police records for drug-related crimes. One was noted in the Injection Mark Register.

Among the interviewed subjects who were registered by the police for drug-related crimes or who were noted in the Injection Mark Register, there were none who did not state in the interview that they had used drugs on some occasion in their lives.

Table 4 indicates that the probability of being registered for drug abuse increased among the injected drug abusers with the time stated for abuse. Among those with a drug abuse period of less than three years, only one was noted in police records. One explanation is that those who had a shorter drug abuse period stopped drug abuse a long time before the follow-up study. Some of these persons had probably stopped committing crimes at about the same time as they stopped drug abuse. This implies that even if they were registered for crimes during their drug abuse period, after a certain time without relapse into crime they had been deleted from the records. Of the 11 men who stated that they used drugs intravenously and who are not registered by the police for crimes, however, six were registered in police records for other offenses. The fact that these persons are not noted in records in connection with drug-related crimes cannot be explained by the deletion rules applying to police records.

TABLE 4. Self-reported intravenous drug addiction and arrests for offenses against the Narcotic Drugs Act.

Self-reported intravenous drug addictions Years of addiction	No arrests for offenses against the Narcotic Drugs Act	1 - 3 arrests	More than 4 arrests	N
None	165	4	0	169
Less than 1 year	1	0	0	1
1 - 3 years	4	1	0	5
More than 3 years	9	5	10	24
Missing excluding dead	62	5	2	69
Dead	19	0	0	19
N	260	15	12	287

Table 5 indicates that one of the men noted in the Injection Mark Register did not admit using drugs intravenously. However, he did admit extensive non-intravenous drug abuse. The other interviewed subjects registered for intravenous drug abuse admitted that they had used drugs in this way. On the other hand the questionnaire was not answered by 11 of the total 31 men who were registered for intravenous drug abuse.

Table 5 indicates that there were 11 (37%) of the men who,

according to their own information, used drugs intravenously but were
not registered for this in the Injection Mark Register. These men had
a shorter average drug abuse period than those who were noted in this
register. A closer examination also shows that the non-registered drug
addicts on the average used less drugs during their drug abuse period.
The primary explanation as to why their drug abuse was not registered
appears purely and simply to be that they were never taken to the
remand center where registration took place. Some of them also stated
in the interview that even during the drug abuse periods they worked
fairly regularly and led a comparatively normal life.

TABLE 5. Self-reported and recorded (injection marks) drug addiction.

Self-reported intrave- nous drug addiction	Recorded injection marks		
Years of addiction	No	Yes	Total
None	170	1	171
Less than 1 year	1	0	1
1 - 3 years	4	1	5
More than 3 years	6	18	24
Missing excluding dead	60	7	67
Dead	14	5	19
N	255	32	287

    Three of the non-registered drug addicts were registered in connec-
tion with extensive criminality. All three have also been taken into
the remand center in Stockholm; in our data there is no explanation as
to why they were not registered.

    The reader may recall that we collected self-report data about
drug abuse among the men studied both on the first survey occasion when
the boys were 11 - 15 years and on the occasion of military registration when they were 18. On the first occasion 12 of the boys stated
that they used drugs. These persons admitted drug abuse as adults. In
the interview at age 18, 53 stated that they used drugs. Among those
who were later interviewed, there were two who denied drug abuse.

3.2.3. Other forms of crime. In connection with planning of the interview in the follow-up study, it was not considered possible to ask
questions about actual crimes committed. For this reason we limited
ourselves to asking them if and when they were suspected of committing
crimes by the police and the types of crime covered by such suspicions.
Furthermore, they were asked if and during which periods they had
served prison sentences and been given other penalites for crimes. The
answers from the interviews can be compared with the information obtained from police records. (This is with the exception of the data deleted from the police records as well as suspicions which did not give

rise to legal actions.)

The correlation between the number of suspected crimes stated by the subjects and the number of crimes registered in police records was 0.50. The correlation between the number of months served in prison stated by the subjects and noted in police records was 0.87.

TABLE 6. Average number of crimes and months spent in prison as registered in police records and as stated in connection with interviews subdivided by appraisal of the social adjustment of the men as adults.

Total social adjustment		Very poor	Poor	Certain defects	Good	Very good	Total	R
Crime recorded by police	Mean	61.7	18.0	0.9	0.5	0.3	4.9	
Self-reported arrest	Mean	16.6	27.6	2.7	0.9	0.5	3.5	
	N	11	11	36	92	37	191	0.50
Recorded months of imprisonment	Mean	56.8	8.3	0.2	0.2	0.0	5.8	
Self-reported months of imprisonment	Mean	62.5	10.0	0.6	0.2	0.0	5.3	
	N	14	11	37	92	37	195	0.87

As Table 6 indicates agreement between the information provided by the men themselves and register data is considerably greater concerning the number of months spent in prison than concerning the number of suspicions of crime. This probably depends on the fact that the subjects interviewed simply remember better the penalties they received than the crimes of which they were suspected.

As far as the number of suspicions of crime is concerned, agreement between register information and interview answers increases as social maladjustment among the subjects decreases. This is also displayed in Table 6. Among those with heavy maladjustment, many could not on the whole answer questions about the crimes of which they were suspected and the times when these took place. These persons did not deny extensive crime during the interview but stated that they were absolutely in no condition to describe it. Those who tried to describe suspicions of crime reported considerably fewer crimes than those for which they were registered in police records. Those with fewer committed crimes, on the other hand, were able to describe most of the crimes for which they were registered. Furthermore, they often described crimes which had either been deleted from the records or which had never been registered, such as minor traffic offenses.

It is not possible to trace any clear pattern in the material for those of the registered crimes not described in the interview. On the contrary, the open attitude of the subjects was considerable, even including admission of serious crimes of violence. The exception consists of the few sexual crimes included in the register material; these were not described in any interviews.

The information provided by the subjects concerning the number of months in prison they were sentenced to agrees, as already mentioned, significantly better with register data. The relationship is very high, 0.87. The subjects tend throughout to state that they were sentenced to more months in prison than those appearing in the register. The difference cannot be fully explained by the deletion effect, since it also applies to the individuals with heavy criminal records, the register information for whom has not been subjected to any deletion.

3.2.4. Social adjustment at an age of 29 - 40. Social adjustment is defined in this paper as the individual's success in the adjustment to current societal norms. The term corresponds fairly closely to the "social adaptational status (SAS)", which Ensminger et al. (1983), define as the "...measure of the success or failure of the performance of an individual in a social field" (p. 74).

In evaluating the subjects' social adjustment, special emphasis was placed on the following criteria:
1. The individual's ability to provide for himself;
2. The law-abiding character of the individual;
3. Abuse, if any.

Apart from these three criteria, consideration was paid to such factors as self-inflicted death (by suicide or abuse), self-inflicted illness (by abuse), education, occupation, housing situation, and family situation. All of these criteria may be considered as describing the individual's success in adult life from the point of view of a traditional middle class ideal. They resemble those used in similar follow-up studies, e.g., Andersson's follow-up of Stockholm boys from the fifties (1976).

The evaluation of the subjects' social adjustment was made on a five-degree scale. Very poor social adjustment implies that the individual may be regarded as a complete reject or is dead owing to abuse or suicide. For an individual to be considered a complete reject he must fulfill several of the following criteria: wholly incapable of providing for himself by lawful means (has had no or practically no recorded income since the age of 25), has been sentenced to lengthy terms of imprisonment, internment or psychiatric care in detention, has no home of his own, lengthy and recurring admissions for rehabilitation of alcoholism, known for intravenous drug abuse.

For a rating as poor social adjustment, several of the following criteria had to be met: lengthy breaks in ability to provide for oneself, one or more sentences to imprisonment, alcoholic abuse, records of intravenous drug abuse, lengthy periods of illness owing to abuse, etc. The general picture of an individual classified in this category shows, despite manifest signs of maladjustment, that the individual makes efforts and periodically perhaps even succeeds in providing for himself in a lawful way and without intervention by the authorities.

For a rating as having <u>certain defects in social adjustment</u>, one or more of the following criteria had to be met: incomplete ability to provide for himself (low income or borderline to subsistence level, unstable maintenance conditions and the like), some criminal involvement (but of such character that only in exceptional cases did it lead to imprisonment and then of short duration), poor education, observation of alcoholic abuse (but not resulting in being taken into custody).

TABLE 7. Evaluation of subjects' social adjustment according to Recorded and Interview Data.

RECORDED DATA				INTERVIEW DATA				
	Very poor	Poor	Certain defects	Good	Very good	Missing data excl dead	Dead	N
Very poor	10	5	3	1	0	9	10	38
Poor	3	0	7	1	0	12	3	26
Certain defects	0	4	16	17	0	20	1	58
Good	3	1	8	63	15	26	1	117
Very good	0	0	3	16	23	1	0	43
Missing data	0	0	0	0	0	1	4	5
N	16	10	37	98	38	69	19	287

R = 0.72

For a rating of <u>good social adjustment</u>, the following criteria applied: full ability to provide for himself, no record of crime or abuse. In certain rare cases individuals with petty crime or an isolated case of drunkenness could be classifed in this category if they were otherwise well adjusted.

For a rating of <u>very good social adjustment</u>, the following criteria were met: high and stable income, no breach of the law or abuse, good education and good housing conditions (usually a houseowner) (Sarnecki, 1986).

Evaluations of social adjustment on this scale were made on the basis of register data collected in the follow-up study and independently on the basis of the data from the follow-up interview. The correlation between these two independent evaluations was 0.72.

The differences in classification of adult social adjustment on the basis of the two different data compilation methods were relatively small. Only in a total of 12 cases (6%), did appraisals based on the two different methods vary by more than one scale unit. It should be noted, however, that it was possible to make appraisals with the aid of register data for 83 more cases than with interview data.

4. DISCUSSION

The intention of the clientele study and its follow-up was not to determine the actual extent of crime. The intention was instead to find the causal relationship between crime together with other deviating behavior, and a number of other factors. This intention influenced the character of the measures of deviating behavior used. These yardsticks are intended primarily to rank the individuals studied with respect to the extent of crime and other types of anti-social behavior. The general conclusion of the comparison between such ranking with the use of self-report and register data shows that the results are fairly similar. The scales of anti-social behavior based on self-report data and register data respectively show a high relationship throughout.

In one case, namely that of drug abuse, a comparison can be made most directly between the self-report and the register methods. In this instance, the self-report interview proved itself to be superior to register data. This was particularly true of less serious drug abuse which is seldom discovered and registered by the authorities. Such minor abuse as the smoking of hashish and marijuana, as well as sporadic non-intravenous use of central nervous system stimulants, is not consistently found in the registers. It is unlikely that the result would be much better if other registers were used, such as those of the social services.

Even in the case of more serious intravenous drug abuse, the self-report method provided more information than the register method. The men who, according to register information, were heavy abusers, showed surprisingly great openness. The factors that probably made a strong contribution towards this openness were the construction of the interview study, in which the various "careers" in the life of the person concerned were followed in chronological order, and also the skill of the interviewers. Questions concerning abuse were put late in the interview. By this time the man concerned had revealed so much about his life, work, family conditions, and so on that it would be difficult for him to hide extensive drug abuse. As has been pointed out earlier, only one of the men registered for injected drug abuse did not admit intravenous abuse. However, he did admit extensive drug abuse of a non-intravenous type.

One serious problem in the interview study on the whole was the large non-response rate of 31%. In this sense, the register method with a small attrition (2%) was vastly superior. Not only was the non-response large but it was also larger among the most criminal individuals. This uneven allocation of the non-response was also due to the high level of mortality among those most criminal. The deceased persons were deleted from the police records so that we were not able to obtain data about their registered criminal record in the follow-up study. On the other hand, it was possible to find them in several other registers, particularly in the Injection Mark Register. All except four of the deceased who died at a very early stage were classified concerning adult social adjustment with the aid of register data.

The Injection Mark Register showed itself to be a considerably better source of information about serious drug abuse than notes in police records concerning contravention of the indictable drug offenses laws. Most of the men who stated in interviews that they used drugs intravenously could be found in the Injection Mark Register. Most of those who, in spite of reported intravenous abuse, could not be found in the Injection Mark Register, used drugs for a shorter period and not to any great extent. The good experience of the injection mark method has also been pointed out in other studies (Bejerot, 1975). Among the men who reported that they had committed fairly extensive drug abuse, there were, however, some who were not registered for any crime and had probably never been arrested. For this reason they had not been noted in the Injection Mark Register either. It would have been possible to include certain of these persons, if not all, if we had used information from the social services, national health services, etc. The self-report method appears to have been the most adequate in this respect.

Hindelang, Hirschi and Weis (1981) state that the self-report method functions to a different extent in different population groups. For example, it is less usable among individuals with extensive asociality. The conclusions drawn by Olofsson from the comparison between registered and self-reported crime in connection with military registration are the very opposite. According to Olofsson, it was primarily law-abiding boys on the whole who neglected to mention their offenses. The result from the follow-up of the adult men, on the other hand, agrees well with that of Hindelang et al., even though, in the follow-up of the clientele study, we never asked our subjects about their actual crime and limited ourselves to crime that was known to the authorities. The men in the follow-up study with the most marked criminal records proved to be completely incapable of describing all the crimes of which they had been suspected. However, this appears to be an actual lack of capacity and not a conscious attempt to conceal the truth. The lives of these men are so full of crime, abuse, and other anti-social behavior that it is unreasonable to expect that they can remember all their crimes. Furthermore, they do not know which of these crimes were included in their many sentences and other penalties. These men did not try to hide their anti-social behavior, were fairly well able to describe the number of months in prison, and they appeared to be truthful in their information about drug abuse. And finally, in spite of the particularly deficient reporting of their own crime, these men -- supported by interview answers -- in most cases were able to be appraised fairly correctly with respect to their overall social adjustment.

As was the case with the results of Hindelang et al., our study of adult men in Stockholm implies that the self-report method can be more useful for individuals with better social adjustment. Information

provided by them about their own crime agrees better with the information available in the register. Furthermore, they report in the interviews about crimes and penalties which cannot be found in the registers
because they were deleted or were never recorded. As already mentioned, the deletion rules are such that less serious misdemeanors are
deleted after five years if the individual concerned is not registered
for new misdemeanors. More serious crimes are deleted after ten years
if no recidivism has taken place. These rules mean that information
about individuals with lower crime levels generally disappears through
deletion while information about those with more crime remains. The
self-report method is therefore more useful for this group not merely
because it is this group that is best able to describe its crime but
also because register information about the criminal record of this
group has definite shortcomings through the deletion rules.

As indicated above, appraisal of the overall social adjustment of
the adult men based on registers and interview data gives a fairly
similar result. On average, social adjustment estimated on the basis
of interview data was considered to be somewhat better than social
adjustment based on register data. However, both sources do provide
good conditions to rank the individuals on the basis of their social
adjustment as adults.

Nye and Short (1957), followed by many others, demonstrated that
self-reported crime does not show any relationship with a number of
classical variables which are based on register data for criminological
research. This discovery resulted in a theoretical division of opinion
among supporters of the two methods. As Hindelang et al. point out,
differences in the research results obtained from studies of crime
using the self-report method and the register method respectively are
used as arguments to indicate that one or the other of the methods is
faulty. In spite of the differences, in the clientele material there
is obvious agreement between information obtained from the individuals
themselves and information about them obtained with the aid of register
data. We have thus been able to confirm that models for the prediction
of crime in the teenage period and social adjustment as an adult based
on variables noted when the boys were 11 - 15 years old are practically
identical, independent of whether the dependent variable is based on
register data or on self-report data. Models in which social adjustment is measured by means of register data, however, explain a somewhat
larger proportion of variance (35%) than models where social adjustment
is measured on the basis of interview data (30%).

It is always difficult to draw more general conclusions on the
basis of a limited investigation. This is also the case regarding the
results of the clientele study involving a small group of men in Stockholm. Furthermore, because of the matching procedure, the group has
been chosen in such a way that it includes significantly more individuals with serious social adjustment difficulties than the average for
men in Stockholm.

Carlsson (SOU 1972:76) has compared clientele boys with a normal
group of Stockholm boys (Jonsson, 1973). Based on this comparison, the
clientele material has been weighted in regard to the matching variables so that it corresponds to a normal population (Sarnecki, 1987).

Based on the weighted material it was possible to make certain general statements about Stockholm men born in the years 1943-51. However, the effects of the matching were so strong that certain individuals in the study's control group had to be weighted up to 82 times, which, along with the small size of the investigated group, substantially increased the risk of random error. The results of the analyses of the weighted material must therefore be interpreted with great care. A comparison between register data and interview data, of the same type which was carried out on the weighted clientele material above, provides results which on important points do not deviate from those presented in this paper. The non-response rate for the interview study regarding the weighted material is insignificantly lower than for the material presented here (27% compared to 31%). Thus if this study covered a normal population, the non-response problem would probably be about as large.

The question of whether today's young people would have answered the interview questions as truthfully as the boys interviewed 25 years ago remains. Another remaining question is if there are differences between the willingness to answer of people in Stockholm and people in other parts of the country. The answers to these questions must to a certain extent be speculative.

Within Swedish criminology the self-response method is used to only a relatively small extent. However, when it has been used, the experiences with the method have been consistently positive. In a recent study carried out in several schools in a Stockholm suburb, the non-response rate has been held to about 2%, and its validity and reliability are considered to be high. Even the experiences with the method in other parts of the country seem to be good (Olofsson, 1971; Henricsson, 1973).

The self-report method is used in Sweden to a relatively large extent in studies of alcohol, tobacco, and drug habits. The method has been used annually since 1971 in nationwide surveys of school pupils and with men who have been registered for compulsory military service. The method is also considered to function well here, even though it has been questioned. Kühlhorn and Aslund (1983) demonstrated in their study of the school surveys that there is a risk of significant underestimation of drug abuse among young people.

5. CONCLUSIONS

The conclusion that can be drawn on the basis of the result of the clientele study is that the register method appears to have certain advantages compared with the self-report method. Register data can be compiled in a considerably cheaper and faster way than interview data. Furthermore, the non-response rate in the interview study was large while it could be almost completely eliminated in the register study. Scrutiny of the crime of the most maladjusted men by using the self-report method was found to be least useful. The discussion going on in Sweden today about the use of the register method (Qwerin, 1987) includes the question of the ethics of using register data over which separate individuals have very little control. If this debate were to result in a deterioration of register data studies or even make them absolutely impossible, the self-report method can offer a largely acceptable alternative for longitudinal studies aimed at testing various models to explain shortcomings in social adjustment. In certain respects the self-report method is even superior to the register method. Furthermore, there are questions that can never be answered by using the register method, e.g., obtaining the viewpoint of the individual himself on his life situation and the reasons for it. This type of question is also relevant to criminological research.

Obviously, the most advantageous situation for research is when several different methods can be used to study the same question. Seen from this perspective, the self-report and register methods should not be considered as being opposed to each other but rather as a complement to each other.

REFERENCES

Andersson, M: Hur gar det för 50-talets Stockholmspojkar. Stockholms Kommunförvaltning, 1976.

Bejerot, N: Drug abuse and drug policy. Beta Psychatrica Scandinavica Supplement 256, 1975.

CAN 1986: Rapport 86, Alkohol- och narkotikautvecklingen i Sverige. Stockholm, 1986.

Elmhorn, K: Faktisk brottslighet bland skolbarn. En enkätundersökning, 1965.

Ensminger, M, Kellam, SG, & Rubin, BR: School and family origins of delinquency: Comparisons by sex. In Van Dusen, KT & Mednick, SA (eds), Prospective Studies of Crime and Delinquency, Kluwer-Nijhoff Publishing, 1983.

Farrington, DP: Self-reports of deviant behaviour. Predictive and stable? Journal of Criminal Law and Criminology, 64:99-110, 1973.

Henricsson, M: Tonaringar ich normer. (Teenagers and norms.) SO-rapport nr 4. Stockholm, 1973.

Hindelang, MS, Hirschi, T, & Weis, SG: Measuring Delinquency. Sage Library of Social Research 123, 1982.

Kühlhorn, E, & Aslund, P: The reliability of drug incidence studies. Commissioned by the Board of Education. Narcotic Drugs in Sweden. In Solarz, A (Ed.), BRA Rapport 1983:6, Stockholm.

Nye, FI, & Short, JF: Scaling delinquent behavior. American Sociological Review, 22:326-331, 1957.

Olofsson, B: Vad var det vi sa! Om kriminellt och konformt beteende bland skolpojkar. (What did we tell you! On criminal an conformist behavior among schoolboys.) Utbilidningsforlaget, Stockholm, 1971.

Qwerin, G: Metropolit i massmedia. En studie av hur Metropolitprojedtet bevadaes och besdrevs av TV och Stockholmstidningarna (Metropolit and the media). National Council for Crime Prevention. Sweden: BRA Frskning 1987:4.

Sarnecki, J: Predicting social maladjustment. The National Council for Crime Prevention, Sweden, 1985.

Sarnecki, J: Delinquent networks. The National Council for Crime
    Prevention, Sweden, 1986.
SOU: Unga lagövertrådare I. Undersökningsmetodik. Brottscdebut och
    aterfall (Methods of the study. Debut of crime and recidivism).
    Stockholm, 1971:49.
SOU: Carlsson, G. Unga lagövertrådare II. Familj, skola och samhälle i
    belysning av officiella data (Family, school and society in the
    light of official data). Stockholm, 1972:76.
SOU: Olofsson, B. Unga lagövertrådare III. Hem, uppfostran, skola och
    kamratmiljö i belysning av intervju och uppföljningsdata (Home,
    upbringing, school and comrade environment in the light of
    interviews and follow-up data). Stockholm, 1973:25.
SOU: Ahnsjö, S. Unga lagovertrådare IV> Kroppslig-psykisk utveckling
    och status i belysning föräldraintervju och uppföljningsdata
    (Physicalpsychological development and status in the light of
    parental interview and folow-up data). Sweden, 1973:49.
SOU: Humble, K & Settergren-Carlsson, G. Unga lagövertrådare V. Person-
    lighet och relationer i belysning av projektiva metoder
    (Personality and relations in the light of projective methods).
    Stockholm, Sweden: 1974:31.
Statistiska centralbyran: Rättsstatistisk Arsbok 1987 (Yearbook of
    Legal Statistics). Sweden, 1987.

128

APPENDIX 1.

Distribution of boys in the criminal and control groups, respectively,
in the main study.

Criminal boys					
Age	11-13		14-15		
Social group	Family type Whole	Broken	Whole	Broken	Total
1 and 2	15	9	23	14	61
3	30	15	28	16	89
Total	45	24	51	30	150

Control boys					
Age	11-13		14-15		
Social group	Family type Whole	Broken	Whole	Broken	Total
1 and 2	8	1	10	5	24
3	10	5	8	6	29
Total	18	6	18	11	53

Distribution of boys in the criminal and control groups, respectively, in the pilot study.

Criminal boys					
Age	11–13		14–15		
Social group	Family type Whole	Broken	Whole	Broken	Total
1 and 2	2	3	4	2	11
3	9	7	9	6	31
Total	11	10	13	8	42

Control boys					
Age	11–13		14–15		
Social group	Family type Whole	Broken	Whole	Broken	Total
1 and 2	3	3	4	2	11
3	7	8	9	6	31
Total	10	11	13	8	42

SCALING AND RELIABILITY PROBLEMS IN SELF-REPORTED PROPERTY CRIMES

Gerben J. N. Bruinsma
Faculty of Public Administration
University of Twente
Enschede, The Netherlands

1. INTRODUCTION

Since the early days of criminology as a scientific discipline, the way crime can and should be measured has been the subject of heated debates. Without a research method developed by themselves, criminologists in the early days used the official figures of registered convictions by the courts as a reliable and valid measurement instrument, later followed by the use of police crime figures. Since the rise of the labeling perspective and critical criminology, the value and usefulness of official figures have been questioned. After some preliminary efforts, the method of self-report was introduced by Nye and Short in 1957, and has since become commonplace, mostly in etiological research.

Nowadays the method of self-report is accepted among criminologists. This method is supposed to offer a solution for one major problem of their discipline: knowledge of the nature and the extent of (hidden) crime and its (unknown) offenders. During the last decade, some reflection has occurred about the method which could facilitate a deliberate evaluation of the advantages and shortcomings of the self-report method.

In this paper, some questions concerning the scalability and reliability of the self-report method will be posed. For this purpose an instrument will be presented that was constructed a few years ago to measure the frequency with which youngsters commit property crimes. This instrument was successfully employed in etiological research (Bruinsma & Zwanenburg, 1980; Bruinsma, 1981, 1983, 1985). It will be scrutinized here on survey data collected in two cities in the Netherlands in the years 1978 and 1980. In the first section, the instrument will be discussed and the research designs of the surveys will be outlined. In the second section, the univariate results of both measurements are presented and a comparison between the two surveys will be made. Next, the reliability and scalability of the self-report instrument will be subjected to close examination. By means of correlational, relability, and factor analyses, the 15 items of the questionnaire will be tested. Then the scalability and reliability of the instrument will be verified in several subgroups of the samples. Finally, the

M. W. Klein (ed.), Cross-National Research in Self-Reported Crime and Delinquency, 131–151.
© 1989 by Kluwer Academic Publishers.

results of the analyses will be discussed.

In this paper, the self-report method is considered as a measurement procedure like almost every other instrument in the social sciences constructed for the empirical assessment of abstract theoretical concepts. This means that the self-report instrument may be affected by systematic and random measurement errors. We will not accept the illusion of constructing a measurement instrument isomorphic with an ideal measure of crime.

2. THE INSTRUMENT AND RESEARCH DESIGN

The definition of deviant or criminal behavior has been the subject of discussion since the beginning of criminology as an academic discipline. For a long time criminologists relied heavily on official figures. But after the Second World War, a new strategy was developed: the method of self-report. With this method scholars in criminology were able to decide for themselves **how** and **what** kind of behavior was investigated and **by whom**. This kind of freedom has three advantages for criminology.

In the first place, researchers no longer run the risk that their own (etiological) theories are tested on the basis of data which are collected by others (officials), principally on the basis of common-sense theories. Instead, they can test their scientific theories with the help of data designed and collected especially for that purpose. Second, on the basis of this freedom, criminologists are able to set up their own domain of research, with all the succeeding opportunities for (unlimited) fundamental research. Last, the attention of criminologists can be directed to categories of people who never or hardly ever are registered in the official files, such as women or businessmen.

However, these opportunities do not imply any solution to problems, because there is a multitude of behaviors which fall under the common denominator of crime. Not all types of behavior can be observed or surveyed, so a selection must be made. This reduction problem implies the search for reliable and valid measurement instruments.

The method of self-report has been criticized heavily for its reliability and validity (for an overview, see Hindelang, Hirschi & Weis, 1981; Bruinsma, 1984). Some critics are very effective, while others are less so because of a lack of knowledge of social research methodology. Instead of rejecting the good together with the bad, however, criminologists must try to improve their measurement of crime.

This paper deals with an effort to measure the frequency of property crimes among youngsters aged 12 to 18. The scale, composed of 15 items, was originally developed for a test of differential association theory in the version of the German methodologist, K-D. Opp (Bruinsma & Zwanenburg, 1980; Bruinsma, 1985). The aim of this theory is to explain the frequency of deviant acts, not the seriousness of these crimes. A second consideration was that the measurement had to be attuned to the operationalization of the main independent concepts of the theory. In other words, on theoretical grounds it was decided to construct a scale with which the frequency of property crimes of youngsters could be measured. It was expected, because this kind of behavior constitutes about 70% of the officially registered crime, that this kind of behavior can be found more in a group of youngsters than other kinds of criminal behavior. At the time, there were no comparable Dutch self-report instruments available, so the construction of the measurement instrument was based more on face validity and on the theoretical grounds as mentioned before. But even the most informed and careful selection of indicators is marked by an unsuppressable element of arbitrariness.

The items consisted of concrete activities which are closely related to the everyday life of adolescents. Abstract or complex legal descriptions were avoided. The property crime items were selected in such a way that young people had the environmental opportunities to commit these acts. The items were strongly related to their own life domains, such as family, school, shopping, or leisure activities. More serious criminal acts like armed robbery or acts of tax evasion were not supposed to be of regular occurrence and were therefore excluded.

In both studies the data collection was organized as follows. The youngsters were anonymously asked whether they had committed any of the mentioned fifteen different concrete acts in the previous year. They could answer with never, once or twice, or more often. A more refined pattern of answers was not desired for it offers only pseudo-exactness, because for most youngsters crime is a low incidence phenomenon, not an everyday activity. And for those who commit many crimes it is assumed that they can not remember the **exact** number of acts in which they are involved.

The questions were put randomly in the form of: "Have you ever in the previous year ...?" The self-report questions were introduced by an announcement that anonymity and secrecy were guaranteed. Members of the schoolboard or teachers were not present during the surveys.

In this paper, data of two surveys are used to assess the scalability and reliability of this self-report instrument. The first data are derived from a sample of 244 youngsters aged 12 to 18 in a middle-sized city called Nijmegen (about 144,000 inhabitants) in the Netherlands. The sample can be described as a cluster sample.[1] Out of 12 randomly chosen secondary schools, four responded positively to the researcher's request for cooperation. These schools can be considered representative of all the secondary schools of Nijmegen. In every school, one class from the first three degrees was randomly selected by the researcher. A check on truancy found that one respondent was not present for that reason.

----

1. Both samples can be considered as cluster samples of which it is generally accepted that they are suitable for theory-testing. One disadvantage of this sampling procedure is that homogeneity may appear in the scores of the respondents in the several clusters. Clustering may reduce the number of independent observations, which may lead to an increase in the sampling error. As a consequence a bias in the test may occur. A check on homogeneity of the clusters by comparing the scores of several important variables between the respondents of the clusters and a random selection of the sample, however, yielded no homogeneity.

In the second survey, in 1980, the data were collected from a cluster sample of 1,196 youngsters aged 12 to 18 in the city of Arnhem (about 127,000 inhabitants). Out of 15 randomly chosen secondary schools, five responded positively to the researcher's request. In each school in all classes of the first three grades inquiries were made about their criminal behavior. Of the total population, seven pupils were ill at that time and only three were not present because of truancy.

Strictly speaking, the samples cannot be considered representative for Dutch youngsters, because the samples are not random. However, the youngsters in the samples are not atypical compared with other youngsters in the Netherlands.

3. SELF-REPORTED PROPERTY CRIMES

In Table 1, the responses to the property crime items by the youngsters of city A and of city B are presented. Because it is well known that girls and boys differ in their crime rates, the percentages by sex are presented in Table A and B of the appendix.

For both surveys the non-response rate is relatively very low. The non-response percentages of the city A sample vary from zero to 2.9% with a mean of 1.6% (for boys from zero to 4.2% with a mean of 2.2%, and for girls from zero to 2.6% with an average of .5%). In city B the non-response percentages are even lower and range from zero to .8% with an average of .3% (for boys from .2% to .8% with an average of .4%, and for girls there exists hardly any non-response, from zero to .8%, with a mean of .2%).

These figures suggest (but do not fully test) the tentative conclusions that (1) the questionnaire has been answered seriously by the respondents and, (2) they had no problem with the wording of the items.

It can be seen in the city A sample that, out of the fifteen offenses, shoplifting is reported most frequently, followed in decreasing order by free riding, changing price-tickets, taking money from parents, taking things from bicycle, and tilltap. In the category "more often" the percentages are highest for shoplifting, free riding, changing price-tickets, taking money from parents, and taking things from bicycles.

Offenses like taking things out of a dressing room, autobike theft, threatening to beat up unless given money, and taking things out of cars are reported the least.

Almost the same answers to the crime items can be observed for boys. For girls there exists a different response pattern. Girls report taking money from parents most frequently, followed by shoplifting, changing price-tickets, and free riding. Other felonies are seldom reported by them. If girls do report any involvement in property crimes, they confine themselves to these activities once or twice a year.

Comparing the self-reported frequencies of property crimes between boys and girls it can be observed that boys more often report involvement in property crimes and they report a greater variety of that kind of behavior than girls.

In the city B survey shoplifting is also reported most frequently by youngsters. Some 54.2% of them admit being involved in shoplifting in the previous year. Next to shoplifting, relatively most often reported are free riding, changing price-tickets, taking money from parents, taking things out of school, and tilltap. The least reported are breaking into a coin box of a public telephone, threatening to beat up unless given money, taking things out of cars, and autobike theft.

TABLE 1. Percentages, self-reported property crimes in city A (N=244) and city B (N=1196).

Type of crime	City A			City B		
	Never	Once or twice	More often	Never	Once or twice	More often
Taking things out of dressing room	97.1	2.0	.4	93.0	6.2	.8
Taking things from bicycle	77.9	15.6	4.5	80.9	15.1	3.8
Burglary	93.9	4.1	.8	94.1	4.3	1.3
Tilltap	82.0	12.7	2.5	73.9	19.8	5.5
Free riding	61.5	27.9	7.8	56.4	31.0	12.1
Breaking into a coin box of a machine	88.5	8.2	.8	93.1	5.1	1.6
Autobike theft	95.9	2.9	-	95.9	3.1	.9
Breaking into a coin box of a public telephone	94.3	2.5	1.2	97.5	1.3	.7
Shoplifting	54.5	34.4	10.2	45.8	39.0	14.7
Changing price-tickets	68.9	25.0	6.1	58.6	32.1	9.2
Taking things out of cars	93.4	3.3	.4	96.7	2.4	.5
Taking money from parents	68.9	24.2	5.7	67.6	26.3	5.9
Bicycle theft	90.6	7.0	1.2	89.0	7.3	3.4
Taking things from school	91.0	7.0	.8	71.7	22.6	5.4
Threatening to beat up unless given money	94.7	2.9	.4	97.2	1.5	.6

The highest percentages in the category "more often" can be found for shoplifting, free riding, and changing price-tickets. Boys again show a higher involvement and for girls a similar empirical conclusion as in the city A survey can be drawn, although they report for every crime item a lesser degree of involvement. Shoplifting, changing price-tickets, and free riding are reported most frequently. No or hardly any involvement is reported by girls in burglary, breaking into a coin box of a public telephone or of other machines, taking things out of cars, bicycle theft, or beating up unless given money.

Also in the second survey boys report relatively more involvement and a greater variety of property crimes than girls. Girls confine themselves more to a limited number of property crimes.

A comparison of the two surveys shows that in city B the youngsters report more involvement in property crimes than their peers in city A two years earlier, although the overall pattern is much the same. Exceptions are found for offenses like taking things from bicycle, burglary, breaking into a coin box of a machine or of a public telephone, and taking things out of cars. These kinds of crimes are reported slightly more frequently in the second survey. Remarkable is the increase in taking things from school. It can be observed that in city B about 20% more of the youngsters report having committed this property crime. For boys there is hardly any difference in the number of reported types of crime. However, in city B boys report relatively more frequently having committed the property crimes "more often."

The first global analysis of the response patterns of the two samples warrants the following conclusions:

1) the questionnaire has been answered seriously according to the overall low non-response rate;
2) there are no semantic problems with the wording of the property crime items;
3) youngsters do report their actual criminal behavior if they are asked about it. In general, boys report more involvement in property crimes than girls;
4) there are variations between the items as regards the response patterns. For some items the discriminative power can be questioned, especially when girls are involved;
5) the response patterns of nearly all items are negatively skewed. This implies that crime is still a low incidence phenomenon for youngsters, although, as we will see later, there exist great variations between them. Secondly, the skewed response scores may indicate some problems in respect to meeting the usual standards of scaling in the social sciences.

4. RELIABILITY AND SCALABILITY OF THE PROPERTY CRIME MEASUREMENT

The aim of social science is to explain and describe social reality, among other things, by means of relationships between concepts of a high level of abstraction. Criminologists have to bridge the gap between these abstract concepts and empirical indicators. And the more abstract and semantically rich a concept is -- and crime is such a concept -- the more numerous its indicators should be in a research design. The advantages of this procedure compared to one-item measurement are manifold: different indicators tap different facets of the same concept; idiosyncrasies and misunderstanding connected to a specific indicator are less damaging; and measurement errors tend to balance out. In other words, scaling is preferred over one-item measurement. Scaling models may be employed in criminology for three related but distinct purposes (McIver & Carmines, 1981):

1) scaling analysis may perform a hypothesis-testing purpose. In etiological research, for example, the scaling method can be used as a criterion to evaluate the relative fit of a given set of observed data to a specific theoretical or causal model;

2) scaling may be employed for the purpose of simply describing a data structure, that is, for discovering the latent dimensions underlying a set of obtained behavioral observations. In this case, the purpose of scaling analysis is mainly exploring to find the underlying dimensions of criminal behavior in order to describe and gain insight into the criminal behavior structure of people;

3) the purpose of scaling is to develop an unidimensional scale on which individuals can be given scores. Their scores on this particular crime scale can then be related to other measures of interest.

Until recently, criminologists just summed up all the answers of their self-report questionnaires in order to estimate the level of crime involvement of their respondents, assuming that their empirical indicators of crime represent one underlying theoretical dimension. Furthermore, these scholars ignored the fact that their instruments might be sensitive to serious random and/or systematic measurement error. Hindelang, Hirschi and Weis (1981) clearly show in their critical overview that such a practice may lead to biased estimates of crime involvement. They stated about the problem of homogeneity: "...from a statistical point of view, three polar arrangements of interrelationships in a collection of self-report "delinquency" items may obtain: (1) all items in the set may be uncorrelated, in which case a global scale consisting of these items is without empirical foundation; (2) all items in the set may be strongly intercorrelated, in which case a global scale composed of such items could be replaced by any item in the pool; (3) some items in the set may be strongly correlated with each other and uncorrelated with the remaining items" (Hindelang, Hirschi & Weis, 1981, 46-47). With other researchers they themselves locate in their self-report data five clusters (or subscales): a) an official contact index; b) a serious crime index; c) a delinquency index; d) a drug index, and e) a school and family offenses index. The lesson of their analyses can be stated as follows: employ correlational methods and reliability analyses before using the composite of your crime indicators. The results of self-reported research up to now indicates more or less that property crimes represent one underlying dimension. This hypothesis, however, will be tested now by way of the following procedure.

First, the intercorrelations of the property crime items for both surveys will be examined. Second, the relationships between the items and the composite scale will be studied and the reliability coefficient of the scale assessed. Next, principal component analyses will be carried out in order to locate possible clusters in the behavior of the youngsters. Last, the similarity of the component structure between both samples will be compared.

In Table 2, the bivariate relationships between the property crime

TABLE 2. Product-moment correlations between the self-report items in city A. Means (M), standard deviations (SD) and corrected item-to-scale correlations (I-T) (N = 208).

	1	2	3	4	5	6	7	8	9	10	11	12	13	14	15
1	-														
2	.24	-													
3	.07	.40	-												
4	.36	.45	.47	-											
5	-.05	.29	.20	.33	-										
6	-.19	.41	.49	.39	.28	-									
7	-.02	.35	.49	.31	.14	.36	-								
8	-.02	.28	.55	.28	.25	.40	.39	-							
9	.17	.39	.36	.32	.23	.40	.21	.25	-						
10	.18	.23	.19	.21	.10	.19	.23	.13	.01	-					
11	.20	.40	.64	.42	.20	.46	.45	.49	.29	.18	-				
12	-.03	.05	.05	.06	.19	.11	.09	.01	.21	.01	.09	-			
13	.05	.54	.55	.35	.17	.38	.40	.12	.33	.17	.39	.19	-		
14	-.04	-.04	-.06	-.05	.03	-.04	.04	-.05	.14	.05	.01	.09	.22	-	
15	-.02	.09	.21	.18	.01	.14	.24	.30	.06	.11	.25	-.03	.02	.10	-
M	1.01	1.13	1.06	1.09	1.45	1.10	1.03	1.05	1.55	1.37	1.04	1.36	1.10	1.09	1.04
SD	.19	.53	.27	.45	.64	.33	.17	.27	.68	.60	.22	.59	.33	.31	.21
I-T	.19	.57	.59	.55	.36	.57	.47	.42	.52	.29	.56	.18	.53	.11	.18

1 = Taking things out of dressing-room
2 = Taking things from bicycle
3 = Burglary
4 = Tilltap
5 = Free riding
6 = Breaking into a coin box of a machine
7 = Autobike theft
8 = Breaking into a coin box of a
    public telephone
9 = Shoplifting
10 = Changing price-tickets
11 = Taking things out of cars
12 = Taking money from parents
13 = Bicycle theft
14 = Taking things from school
15 = Threatening to beat up
     unless given money

items of the survey in city A are presented.[2] Row 16 contains the
means and row 17 the standard deviations of the items. Here again it
can be observed that the item scores are very skewed. Nevertheless the
correlations are moderately positive (ranging from zero to .64, with a
mean inter-item correlation of .22). Property crime involvement in any
of the life domains of youngsters has positive relationships with other
property crimes. Burglary, taking things out of cars, bicycle theft,
and autobike theft show the highest intercorrelations, although these
crime items have been reported the least. Taking things out of
dressing-room, taking money from parents, taking things from school,
and threatening to beat up unless given money constitute an exception
to this rule. These criminal behaviors show variable weak or no
relationships with the other property crime items. The weakness of
these four items is further highlighted by the corrected item-to-scale
correlations, which are presented in row 18.[3] All four items have a
correlation lower than .20, which means that there exists a weak fit
with the composite scale. The other items have moderately strong positive correlations with the composite scale, varying from .42 to .59.
The highest item-to-scale correlations can be observed for burglary,
taking things from bicycle, breaking into a coin box of a machine, and
bicycle theft.

Table 3 demonstrates that in the city B sample three items can be
considered as weak. The items breaking into a coin box of a public
telephone, taking money from parents, and threatening to beat up unless
given money, show weak or no relationships with the other items, and
their corresponding corrected item-to-scale correlations can be
observed for shoplifting, bicycle theft, and taking things from bicycle.

Both data sets point out that three items -- taking money from
parents, threatening to beat up unless given money and, taking things
from school -- contribute the least to the variance of the composite
scale.

In order to test the internal consistency of the property crime

----

2. The items are scored such that the response "never" is given the score
of 1, "once or twice" the score of 2, and the answer "more often" the score
of 3. All respondents missing any value on a single item are deleted from
all further analyses.

3. This correlation measures the relationship of an item and the
scale without that item.

140

TABLE 3. Product-moment correlations between the self-report items in city B. Means (M), Standard Deviations (SD) and corrected item-to-scale correlations (I-T) (N = 1157).

	1	2	3	4	5	6	7	8	9	10	11	12	13	14	15
1	-														
2	.20	-													
3	.22	.31	-												
4	.21	.33	.28	-											
5	.19	.28	.17	.26	-										
6	.12	.30	.36	.27	.17	-									
7	.13	.34	.40	.28	.19	.24	-								
8	.14	.20	.39	.16	.10	.26	.16	-							
9	.26	.40	.34	.39	.30	.26	.24	.20	-						
10	.17	.26	.21	.27	.30	.22	.19	.13	.43	-					
11	.09	.25	.38	.21	.12	.25	.34	.07	.24	.16	-				
12	.09	.08	.02	.06	.14	.08	.02	.03	.29	.10	.04	-			
13	.23	.47	.39	.40	.28	.38	.45	.24	.38	.25	.31	.06	-		
14	.19	.23	.12	.18	.16	.15	.02	.10	.35	.27	.09	.23	.15	-	
15	.10	.11	.10	.09	.18	.05	-.01	.15	.15	.08	.00	.11	.14	.08	-
M	1.08	1.23	1.07	1.32	1.56	1.09	1.05	1.04	1.70	1.51	1.04	1.38	1.15	1.33	1.02
SD	.30	.51	.31	.65	.75	.40	.27	.45	.79	.67	.32	.61	.49	.59	.21
I-T	.33	.52	.45	.48	.41	.41	.39	.29	.64	.45	.33	.21	.55	.36	.19

1 = Taking things out of dressing-room
2 = Taking things from bicycle
3 = Burglary
4 = Tilltap
5 = Free riding
6 = Breaking into a coin box of a machine
7 = Autobike theft
8 = Breaking into a coin box of a public telephone
9 = Shoplifting
10 = Changing price-tickets
11 = Taking things out of cars
12 = Taking money from parents
13 = Bicycle theft
14 = Taking things from school
15 = Threatening to beat up unless given money

scale, Cronbach's alpha is calculated.[4] For the 1978 sample, the unstandardized α is .76 and can be improved to .78 when the three mentioned items are deleted from the scale. For the second sample α is .77. After deletion of three weak items, α increases to .78. These alpha's can be considered as meeting the normal reliability standards of scaling in the social sciences. They are impressive when we keep in mind the fact that most of the items are very skewed.

Substantial corrected item-to-scale correlations like those found in the two data sets are often considered sufficient evidence that the items are measuring a single, common phenomenon. This evidence, however, is far from conclusive (McIver & Carmines, 1981). It is possible that two or more approximately equal and independent subsets of items are contained within the scale. Substantial correlations would be due to the fact that the items are only related to a subset of all the items in the scale. A more effective technique specifically designed to answer this question of dimensionality of multiple-item summative scales is factor analysis. It can be seen as a supplement to the other analysis techniques. In this study, principal component analysis is employed in order to test the unidimensionality of the property crime scale. According to Carmines and Zeller (1979, 60) one should expect, given the properties of principal components, if a set of items is measuring a single phenomenon:

1) the first extracted component explaining a large proportion of the variance in the items;
2) subsequent components explaining fairly equal proportions of the remaining variance except for gradual decrease;
3) all or most of the items having substantial loadings on the first component;
4) all or most of the items having higher loadings on the first component than on subsequent components.

With principal component analysis, the 15 items of the city A data set are reduced to four components, which explain 30.6%, 9.6%, 9.0%, and 7.3% of the variance. The majority of the items load positively on the first (unrotated) component. The exceptions are taking things out of dressing-room, changing price-tickets to buy things cheaper, taking things from school, and beating up unless given money. Close inspection of the factor loadings after varimax rotation, however, points out that the fourth component is dominated by the items taking things from school and taking money from parents, the third component by taking things out of dressing-room, and the second by threatening to beat up unless given money. The path of the eigenvalues shows a well-marked

----

. Cronbach's alpha is a maximum likelihood estimator of a parameter; the reliability of the composite scale cannot be less than the value of this parameter. From a practical estimation point of view, this means that alpha does not provide an optimal estimate of reliability when the items making up the composite are heterogeneous in their relationship to one another (and when N is small). In these conditions, Cronbach's alpha is smaller than the internal consistency of the composite. Thus the more the inter-item correlations diverge from one another, the more the value given by alpha understates the true reliability (see Zeller & Carmines, 1980, 56).

142

drop after the first component (4.58 versus 1.43, 1.34 and 1.09). The analysis warrants the conclusion that the last three components are formed by only one indicator and the error variance of the other items. As a consequence, the first component is judged to be the most theoretically and empirically meaningful.

TABLE 4. Principle component analyses after varimax rotation for property crimes in city A (N = 208) and city B (N = 1157).

Type of crime	City A				City B		
	Factor					Factor	
	I	II	III	IV	I	II	III
Taking things out of dressing-room	.14	-.16	.81	-.17	.17	.35	.28
Taking things from bicycle	.66	.13	.32	.02	.54	.36	.12
Burglary	.62	.55	.05	-.12	.67	.03	.36
Tilltap	.59	.19	.40	-.14	.49	.36	.07
Free riding	.60	-.03	-.22	.08	.21	.50	.15
Breaking into a coin box of a machine	.61	.31	.18	.02	.54	.12	.21
Autobike theft	.40	.59	.01	.08	.73	.01	-.05
Breaking into a coin box of a public telephone	.37	.67	-.11	-.15	.29	-.04	.72
Shoplifting	.53	.08	.30	.30	.37	.67	.12
Changing price-tickets	.11	.22	.56	.19	.28	.56	-.01
Taking things out of of cars	.52	.55	.17	-.08	.64	.06	-.18
Taking money from parents	.33	-.14	-.19	.61	-.13	.58	.02
Bicycle theft	.67	.12	.10	.20	.68	.23	.20
Taking things from school	-.08	.09	.10	.82	.03	.66	.02
Threatening to beat up unless given money	-.19	.76	.14	.13	-.12	.21	.69
% explained variance	30.6	9.6	9.0	7.3	27.6	9.9	7.3
Eigenvalue	4.58	1.43	1.34	1.09	4.14	1.49	1.10

From the self-reported data of city B, three components can be extracted, explaining 27.4%, 9.9%, and 7.3% of the variance. After varimax rotation it appears that the third factor is dominated by two items: breaking into a coin box of a public telephone and threatening to beat up unless given money. The second component is formed by taking things from school and taking money from parents. Here again we can observe a well-marked drop in the path of the eigenvalues after the first component (4.14 versus 1.49 and 1.10). These results indicate a confirmation of the analysis of the city A data.

Confronting these results of principal component analyses with the demands Carmines and Zeller put upon unidimensionality, the first three have been met. Their fourth demand is not met by the data of city B. Not all or most of the items load higher on the first component. In order to compare the two principal component analyses, Cattel's S was computed on the first components.[5] Between the two, S reaches .83, which means that there is a great similarity between the first components of the two samples and that the self-report instrument is relatively stable.

At first glance the results of the reliability and scalability analyses may not be very clear to the reader. However, the combination of the results of all the analyses together produces a structure in the self-reported property crimes. When analyzing this kind of data we have to keep in mind that we are dealing with behavior and not with attitudes or beliefs. The properties of the first differ from those of other measurements by their skewed scores. Most of the analysis techniques are more suitable for normal distributions of the scores. Thus, the "normal" criteria are more difficult to meet in self-report research. Second, crime is -- at least for most of us -- not an everyday activity, so it is remarkable to observe how relatively strongly the crime items correlate with each other.

The analyses of **both** surveys point out that, out of the 15 selected property crimes, three items have pronounced weak relationships with the other items; threatening to beat up unless given money, taking money from parents, and taking things from school. Two items, taking things out of a dressing-room and breaking into a coin box of a public telephone, can be considered ambiguous in the measurements. They do not fit in the scale constant, but they load positively on the first component in both surveys.

The other items are positively correlated with each other, and form one unidimensional component in both factor analyses. The item-to-scale correlations and the reliability correlations confirm these results. This can be regarded as evidence for the fact that involvement in any property crime activity tends to be at least slightly predictive of involvement in other property crime activities. Let's now look more closely at the three "deviant" crime items.

---

5. The question in factor comparison seems to be whether variables cluster together or are similarly interrelated in several groups of cases. The underlying factor variate, that construct the existence of which one is probing in different settings, might have more or less variance across groups. If it has less variance, then the variables sensitive to it would be expected to have less systematic variance, and thus would be expected to have low communalities. Levine (1977, 47) advises for factor comparison the use of Cattel's salient similarity index, S. The computation of this index is based on the classification of loadings into salient and hyper plane categories. The index may be

In Table 1 and in the Appendix it can be seen that youngsters report little or no involvement in threatening to beat up unless given money. Statistically speaking it is almost impossible to observe strong correlations with other property crime items. But that fact, of course, can not be the main reason for its weak fit. From a behavioral point of view this item **may** measure another aspect that has nothing to do with the commitment of property crimes: aggression.

It is obvious that the item taking money from parents does not fit into a property crime scale. Although 29.9% (in city A) and 32.2% (in city B) of the youngsters report stealing from their own parents, the item shows hardly any correlation with the other crime items (Tables 3 and 4). Consequently, this crime item has a low item-to-scale correlation and no loading on the first component. Tentatively it can be concluded that taking money from your parents is a more or less isolated activity which is not related to other criminal activities.

For the last item it is more difficult to find an explanation why it is not useful for the property crime scale. This activity is reported by 7.8% and 28% of the youngsters in both samples. Taking things from school, however, correlates positively only with shoplifting and bicycle theft in the city A sample, but it is related to more property crime items in the city B sample. Both principal component analyses point out that this item does not load on the first component. This isolated position may have something to do with the sampling procedure, in which pupils were selected through their schools and interviewed in their school setting. It remains unclear whether the weak fit of this crime item is due to sampling error or to other factors.

5. RELIABILITY OF THE PROPERTY CRIME SCALE IN SUB-SAMPLES

Our first examinations point out that the frequencies of property crimes can be measured relatively reliably. Besides that, the instrument proves its stability in the tests on data of two surveys.

It is common knowledge for criminologists that the statement, "We all do it once in a while" **may** be true; nevertheless, various population groups differ remarkably in their crime rate. All kinds of groups in society have their own criminal behavior structure, varying from hardly any involvement to forms of professional or organized crime. Hence, the demand must be made upon a self-report instrument that it be able to differentiate between crime rates of groups. For that reason it is supposed that groups of youngsters may differ in their criminal behavior structure and as a consequence differ in their average crime rate.

Footnote 5 (continued)
seen as a comparison of the difference between the number of hits and misses as a proportion of a weighted sum of the cell frequencies. S will reach a maximum value of unity when there is a perfect match, a minimum of minus one for a perfect match with one of the factors reflected, and zero when there is no congruence.

Up to now the reliability and the scalability were estimated for the total samples of youngsters. For several reasons three property crime indicators appeared not to be suitable for the composite scale (taking money from parents, taking things from school, and threatening to beat up unless given money) and were deleted from further analyses. In this section we will investigate to what extent the reliability changes when the instrument is used for different groups of youngsters. It may be, for example, that the reliability for very young persons (12 or 13 years old) drops to an unacceptable level according to normal evaluation standards. In addition, the property crime scale may vary systematically with the kind of sub-samples. In order to test this, the samples of both surveys are divided into several sub-groups based on such variables as sex, age, social class (measured by the occupation of the father; see Bruinsma, 1985), and type of education (LTS: junior technical education; MAVO, HAVO: general secondary education; VWO, Gymnasium, pre-university education). For each sub-group the reliability coefficient and the mean of the 12-item scale was computed.

In Table 5 it can be seen that in the city A sample the self-report shows some zero variance items in five groups. Girls, youngsters of 16 years and older, youth with an unemployed father, adolescents of the higher social class, and pupils with the highest level of education therefore cannot be compared with the other sub-samples. There is a combination of two reasons for this phenomenon: 1) the number of cases of these sub-groups is relatively small, and 2) the overall crime rate of the city A sample is lower than that of the city B sample. As a consequence, the reliability coefficients fluctuate. These variations are due to the property of α that is affected by the mean inter-item correlation and the number of items of the composite scale. Generally, the less the number of items, the lower α will be. Therefore, these sub-samples are excluded from further analyses.

For each of the remaining sub-samples, principal component analysis was carried out and the similarity between the results of these analyses were computed by means of Cattel's S. The similarity coefficients vary from .72 to .93 between the extracted components of the sub-samples and of the samples as a whole. These findings indicate a great similarity between the underlying behavior structure of the sub-groups of young people. The coefficients of the sub-samples range from .64 to .85. The lowest α's can be observed for girls (.64) and for youngsters in the age range 12 to 13 (.71). For girls, the relatively low reliability coefficient is due to the low inter-item correlations of property crime items. Girls, as stated in section 2, confine themselves to a limited number of property crimes, so the mean inter-item correlation is low. For very young adolescents the same conclusion can be drawn. With this subject we are faced with one of the problems of self-report: it is very difficult to judge whether the low reliability is the result of a bias in the instrument or whether it is due to the skewed scores of the respondents because of their low actual criminal behavior.

Comparing the mean scale scores of the sub-samples, it can be observed that the sub-samples do differ in their crime rate. Girls show the lowest involvement in property crimes and boys the highest.

146

Also in accordance with criminological research is that the older the age group, the higher the crime rate. No significant differences can be observed for social class in the city B sample. The results of this analysis warrant the conclusion that this property crime scale is able to differentiate between groups.

TABLE 5. Means and reliability coefficients of the property crime scale for sub-samples of city A and city B.

	City A			City B		
	Mean Score	Standard	N	Mean Score	Standard	N
Total	2.14	.83	224	2.72	.81	1166
SEX						
Boys	2.73	.84	150	3.61	.82	590
Girls	.93[a]	.30	73	1.82	.64	576
AGE						
12 and 13 years old	1.97	.81	102	2.34	.71	297
14 and 15 years old	2.01	.85	102	2.66	.80	646
16 years and older	3.89[b]	.88	18	3.28	.81	205
SOCIAL CLASS						
Unemployed	1.53[c]	.91	19	2.90	.75	116
Lower class	2.34	.80	75	2.64	.79	318
Middle class	1.72	.65	76	2.81	.82	383
Higher class	1.32[d]	.70	37	2.77	.84	239
EDUCATIONAL LEVEL						
L.T.S.	3.22	.84	92	2.87	.82	376
MAVO, HAVO	1.46	.82	86	2.96	.78	321
VWO, Gymnasium	1.24[e]	.40	46	2.09	.77	208

a. without bicycle theft, breaking into a coin box of a public telephone, burglary, and breaking into a coin box of a machine because of zero variances
b. without taking things out of dressing-room because of zero variance
c. without autobike theft because of zero variance
d. without autobike theft, breaking into a coin box of a public telephone, and taking things out of cars because of zero variance
e. without taking things out of a dressing-room, autobike theft, burglary, and taking things out of cars because of zero variance

6. DISCUSSION

Up to now the subject of validity of the self-report measurement has been neglected in this paper. The property crime scale has proven to be reliable and stable. This implies that the instrument is little affected by random error.

Reliability is basically an empirical issue, focusing on the performance of empirical measures. Validity, in contrast, concerns the problem of the extent to which the measurement is affected by nonrandom error, or in other words, does the instrument have systematic bias effects? Validity is usually a theoretical issue, because it inevitably raises the question: **"Valid for what purpose?"** As stated earlier, this self-report instrument was constructed for etiological research; the purpose was to build a scale to test differential association theory. The 15 empirical indicators were selected on face validity by the researcher in the conviction that the indicators cover most of the possible property crimes of youth. Each item is supposed to tap a part of the behavioral structure of youngsters in the age range from 12 to 18. Of course, more indicators may be added to this scale, but the surplus value of these additions can be questioned. Any addition may lead to disturbances which may affect the reliability of the scale.

In the literature, several strategies to evaluate the kinds of validity of the instrument are mentioned -- criterion validity, content validity, construct validity, and so on (Hirschi, Hindelang & Weis, 1981; Junger, 1987). In this paper, it is checked to see whether the instrument measurement errors vary systematically between groups. No such biases are observed. But how can a researcher judge whether systematic variations in the data are due to a bias in the instrument or to systematic variations in the actual criminal behavior? To answer this important question about criterion validity it is necessary to compare the self-report instrument with other instruments that are reliable and valid. But criminologists do not possess such an instrument. For most of the efforts to validate the self-report instruments, official figures have been used, for example police contacts, convictions, or observations by officials. It is a well known fact that these measures lack reliability and, as a consequence, validity. So the instruments constructed by criminologists are verified on unreliable and nonvalid standard measures.

Finally, some tentative remarks about the usefulness of the property crime scale can be made. In general it must be kept in mind that the self-report scale is a kind of questionnaire. Consequently, all known pros and cons of this methodology are appropriate to the use of self-report. Some purposes for which the property crime scale can be employed are:
1) etiological research with the aim "to assign some value of the property delinquency to each unit in the sample or population. The object is to explain variation in the values by reference to other variables whose values have also been assigned to the same units" (Hindelang, Hirschi & Weis, 1981, 19);
2) in situations where the aim of research is to study the criminal behavior structure of people;

3) as a sub-scale of a larger self-report research, when the aim is to gain an insight into the level of all kinds of crime involvement of certain well-defined groups;
4) in research projects aimed at studying young persons;
5) in international studies where the aim of research is to compare the crime figures of various groups of different nations. The main reason is that this property crime scale is made up of (non-serious) offenses punishable by law in all countries and is not composed of so-called "status offenses" like running away from home or defying your parents, which are more or less culturally and morally biased.

Like all other research instruments, this property crime scale has, of course, its limits.

1) It is not likely that this instrument can be employed with groups in society which are difficult to be contacted by researchers.
2) The instrument is less suitable as a (aggregated) social indicator in order to measure the actual crime levels of categories of people, cities, or countries.
3) It cannot be employed when the researcher's purpose is to measure the seriousness of self-reported criminal behavior.
4) Without adjustments of the scale it is not suitable for adults, because their everyday life differs in many ways from that of youth.

REFERENCES

Bridges, G: Errors in the measurement of crimes. In Wellford, C. (Ed.), Quantitative studies in criminology. Beverly Hills: Sage, 1978, 9-29.
Bruinsma, GJN: De controletheorie van Travis Hirschi: Toetsing van een causaal model. In Gunther Moor, LGH, e.a. (red), Grenzen Van de Jeugd. Utrecht: Ars Aequi Libri, 1981, 57-77.
Bruinsma, GJN: De controletheorie voor het grote en het kleine verschil, Tijdschrift voor Criminologie, 25e jrg., 1983a, 96-104.
Bruinsma, GJN: De methode van zelfrapportage van delicten, Tijdschrift voor Criminologie, 26e jrg., 1984, 295-308.
Bruinsma, GJN: Criminaliteit als sociaal leerproces. Een toetsing van de differentiële-associatietheorie in de versie van K-D. Opp. Arnhem: Gouda Quint, 1985.
Bruinsma, GJN, & Zwanenberg, MA: Deviante Socialisatie. Verslag van een pilotstudy. Nijmegen: Criminologisch Instituut, 1980.
Carmines, EG, & Zeller, RA: Reliability and validity assessment. Beverly Hills: Sage, 1979.
Elliott, DS: Review essays on measuring delinquency. Criminology, 20: 527-537, 1982.
Hindelang, MJ, Hirschi, T, & Weis, JF: Correlates of delinquency: The illusion of discrepancy between self-report and official measures. American Sociological Review, 44:995-1014, 1979.

Hindelang, MJ, Hirschi, T, & Weis, JF: _Measuring delinquency._ Beverly
    Hills: Sage, 1981.
Hirschi, T: _Causes of delinquency._ Berkeley: University of California
    Press, 1969.
Hirschi, T, & Gottfredson, M (Eds.). _Understanding crime. Current
    theory and research._ Beverly Hills: Sage, 1980.
Johnson, RE: _Juvenile delinquency and its origins: An integrated
    theoretical approach._ Cambridge: Cambridge University Press, 1979.
Junger, M: Validiteit van zelfrapportage van delinquentie bij jongeren
    uit ethnische minderheden. In De Jong-Gierveld & van den Zouwen, J
    (Eds.), _De vragenlijst in het sociaal onderzoek._ Deventer: Van
    Loghum Slaterus, 1987, 1953-174.
Levine, JP: The potential for crime overreporting in criminal victimi-
    zation surveys. _Criminology_, 14:307-330, 1979.
Levine, MS: _Canonical analysis and factor comparison._ Beverly Hills:
    Sage, 1977.
McIver, JP, & Carmines, EG: _Unidimensional scaling._ Beverly Hills:
    Sage, 1981.
Natalino, KW: Methodological problems in self-report studies. In
    Jensen, GF (Ed.), _Sociology of delinquency. Current issues._
    Beverly Hills: Sage, 1981, 63-77.
Opp, K-D: _Methodologie der Sozialwissenschaften._ Reinbek: Rowohlt,
    1976.
Opp, K-D, & Schmidt, P. _Einführung in die mehrvariabelenanalyse._
    Reinbek: Rowohlt, 1976.
Osterlind, SJ: _Test item bias._ Beverly Hills: Sage, 1983.
Petersilia, J: The validity of criminality data derived from personal
    interviews. In Wellford, C. (Ed.), _Quantitative studies in
    criminology._ Beverly Hills: Sage, 1978, 30-47.
Segers, JHG, & Hagenaars, JAP: _Sociologische onderzoekmethoden. Deel
    II: technieken van causale analyse._ Assen: Van Gorcum, 1980.
Swanborn, PG: _Methoden van sociaal onderzoek._ Meppel: Boom, 1987.
Thornberry, TP, & Farnworth, M: Social correlates of criminal involve-
    ment: Further evidence on the relationship between social status
    and criminal behavior. _American Sociological Review_, 47:505-518,
    1982.
Tittle, CR, Villemez, WJ, & Smith, DA: The myth of social class and
    criminality: An empirical assessment of empirical evidence. In
    American Sociological Review, 43:643-656, 1978.
Zeller, RA, & Carmines, EG: _Measurement in the social sciences. The
    link between theory and data._ Cambridge: Cambridge University
    Press, 1980.

APPENDIX

TABLE A. Percentages self-reported property crimes by sex in city A.

Type of crime	Boys (N = 165)			Girls (N = 78)		
	Never	Once or twice	More often	Never	Once or twice	More often
Taking things out of dressing room	97.0	1.8	.6	97.4	2.6	-
Taking things from bicycle	70.3	20.6	6.7	93.6	5.1	-
Burglary	90.9	6.1	1.2	100	-	-
Tilltap	74.5	17.6	3.6	97.4	2.6	-
Free riding	53.9	31.5	10.9	76.9	20.5	1.3
Breaking into a coin box of a machine	83.6	12.1	1.2	98.7	-	-
Autobike theft	94.5	3.6	-	98.7	1.3	-
Breaking into a coin box of a public telephone	91.5	3.6	1.8	100	-	-
Shoplifting	47.3	37.6	13.9	70.5	26.9	2.6
Changing price-tickets	66.7	25.5	7.9	74.4	24.4	1.3
Taking things out of cars	92.1	4.2	.6	96.2	1.3	-
Taking money from parents	70.9	23.0	4.8	64.1	26.9	7.7
Bicycle theft	86.1	10.3	1.8	100	-	-
Taking things from school	87.3	9.7	1.2	98.7	1.3	-
Threatening to beat up unless given money	93.9	2.4	.6	96.2	3.8	-

Source: Bruinsma and Zwanenburg, 1980, 124.

TABLE B: Percentages self-reported property crimes by sex in city B.

Type of crime	Boys (N = 607)			Girls (N = 589)		
	Never	Once or twice	More often	Never	Once or twice	More often
Taking things out of dressing room	89.6	9.1	1.2	96.4	3.2	.3
Taking things from bicycle	71.2	21.4	6.9	90.8	8.5	.7
Burglary	88.8	8.2	2.6	99.7	.3	-
Tilltap	69.2	21.1	8.9	78.8	18.5	2.0
Free riding	49.1	32.9	17.3	64.0	29.0	6.8
Breaking into a coin box of a machine	90.0	7.2	2.5	96.3	2.9	.7
Autobike theft	93.2	4.9	1.6	98.6	1.2	.2
Breaking into a coin box of a public telephone	95.7	2.3	1.3	99.3	.3	-
Shoplifting	33.9	43.5	21.7	58.1	34.5	7.5
Changing price-tickets	54.7	31.3	13.8	62.6	32.9	4.4
Taking things out of cars	94.6	4.3	1.0	99.0	.5	-
Taking money from parents	66.4	26.5	6.9	68.9	26.0	4.9
Bicycle theft	83.9	9.9	5.9	94.4	4.6	.8
Taking things from school	66.9	25.4	7.6	76.6	19.7	3.2
Threatening to beat up unless given money	95.7	2.5	1.2	98.6	.5	-

Source: Bruinsma, 1985, 114.

Part II. TECHNICAL ISSUES IN SELF-REPORT RESEARCH

In Part I, the rather comprehensive paper by Junger-Tas fore-
shadowed a number of the technical matters raised in Part II. Similarly, the Moffitt paper highlighted problems inherent in applying the
technology developed in a high-crime nation like the U.S. to a relatively low-crime nation such as New Zealand. In Part II, Elliott and
Huizinga give concrete shape to the struggles with self-report refine-
ments that have featured much recent work in the U.S.. Elliott and his
colleagues have been the leaders in this refinement process. The four
additional papers provide specific lessons in coming to grips with some
of the problems raised by Elliott and Huizinga, problems given much
attention in the workshop discussions as well.

Olweus clarifies in a non-pejorative fashion what he views as
major distortions among criminologists in the past in their use of
pivotal concepts such as prevalence and incidence. Loeber _et al_. illustrate the need and the procedures for dealing with a wider age range
of respondents than has been customary. Albrecht provides an unusual
discussion of the impact of penal codes on the considerations of cross-
national research. Dickes follows with a technically sophisticated
analysis of the structure of delinquent offense patterns; a resolution
of this issue has direct relevance for instrumentation with applications to international comparisons.

IMPROVING SELF-REPORTED MEASURES OF DELINQUENCY

Delbert S. Elliott
Institute of Behavioral Science and Department of Sociology
and
David Huizinga
Institute of Behavioral Science
University of Colorado, Boulder
USA

1. INTRODUCTION

Few issues are as critical to the study of crime and delinquency as the question of the reliability, validity and precision of our measures of this phenomenon. For many delinquency researchers employing self-report, offender-based measures, it would appear that these issues have been satisfactorily resolved. It is quite common for delinquency researchers today to reference the classic work of Hindelang, Hirschi and Weis (1981), cite their conclusion that the reliability and validity of self-reported measures of delinquency compare favorably to other standard measures employed routinely by social scientists, and proceed to report their findings without reference to the reliability or validity of their particular measure as employed in a particular sample or population.

There are some indications, however, that these issues are far from being resolved. Huizinga and Elliott (1986) note that while the levels of reliability reported for self-report delinquency measures (SRD) compare favorably with those of other social science measures, the reliability tests used may be inappropriate for this type of measure (see also Hardt & Bodine, 1965; Bachman et al., 1978), and while the standards cited for acceptable levels of reliability may be adequate for some research purposes, they are clearly problematic for others (e.g., individual differences or change scores).

The approach to validation has relied heavily upon official record measures of crime as the validation criterion. While correlation with alternative measures is a standard form of validation, the issues of the true validity of these separate measures is left unanswered by this procedure, since the validity of neither measure is beyond question, and not infrequently, the measures are conceptualized differently. There are also conceptual, methodological, or interpretation problems with much of the earlier validation work and a number of important validity issues have simply not been addressed. For example, there

155

M. W. Klein (ed.), Cross-National Research in Self-Reported Crime and Delinquency, 155–186.
© *1989 by Kluwer Academic Publishers.*

appear to be potentially serious effects of variation in item wording
(Schuman & Presser, 1981; Hindelang et al., 1981; Chaiken, Chaiken &
Rolph, 1983), inappropriate classification of behaviors or offenses by
respondents (Elliott & Huizinga, 1983), high levels of trivial events
being reported (Gold & Reimer, 1975; Huizinga & Elliott, 1986), and
double counting of single events (Elliott, 1982). In general, the
focus has been primarily upon problems of under-reporting with relatively little attention given to sources of error leading to over-reporting
(for example, see Weis, 1986). Further, there is some evidence for a
differential validity of SRD measures by race (Hindelang et al., 1981;
Weis, 1986; Huizinga & Elliott, 1986; Bachman et al., 1987; cf. Gold,
1970; Chaiken & Chaiken, 1982; Gottfredson & Gottfredson; 1984; English, 1988). There is also evidence of serious levels of under-
reporting for particular offenses, e.g., sexual offenses (Abel et al.,
1983) and tax evasion (Hessing et al., 1988). Finally, there is also
considerable confusion over types of measures employed in particular
studies (e.g., prevalence, incidence, general frequency rates and individual offending rates) and the adequacy of various approaches to scaling or scoring SRD measures (Elliott & Ageton, 1980; Elliott, 1982).

However one stands on the question of the adequacy of current
measures of self-reported delinquency, one thing is clear -- there is
room for improvement in these measures. Further, the increasingly
sophisticated theoretical propositions and methods for testing these
propositions frequently demand higher levels of reliability and validity. The primary focus of this paper is thus on practical ways of
improving our measures of self-reported delinquency.

In the following sections of this paper, we consider a number of
measure development, administration, scale construction and scoring
issues, each of which bears on the validity or precision of SRD measures. We will not consider those methodological issues surrounding
the measurement or assessment of reliability and validity, as these
issues have been addressed in a previous paper (Huizinga and Elliott,
1986). The primary focus will be upon task characteristics of self-
report measures rather than respondent or interviewer characteristics
as sources of response bias (Bradburn & Sudman, 1979). Bradburn (1985)
notes that task characteristics are a greater source of response
effects than either interviewer or respondent characteristics.

The data reported come primarily from a series of on-going analyses of self-report measures employed in the National Youth Survey, a
twelve year study of delinquency and drug use in a national panel of
American youth (Elliott & Ageton, 1980; Elliott & Huizinga, 1983; Huizinga & Elliott, 1986). Data from other studies are also discussed or
cited where appropriate.

2. CONSTRUCTION ISSUES

2.1. Reporting Inappropriate and Trivial Events

In the National Youth Survey, we conceptualized delinquency as
behavior in violation of legal statutes which involved some risk of

arrest if reported to or observed by the police. We were attempting to measure the offender behavior phenomena which put youth at significant risk for an arrest. Conceptually, this measure provides an upper limit to possible arrests, assuming that all "arrestable" behaviors specifically proscribed in criminal statutes (welfare statutes for status offense) constitute the behavioral domain for this SRD measure. The face validity and sampling validity (representativeness) of this measure are thus to be evaluated with reference to existing criminal statutes. Assuming that this conceptualization of delinquency is one frequently utilized in research, the reporting of trivial events, i.e., behaviors which logically fit the class of behaviors specified in the description, but are so minor that there is no significant risk of official response, presents a potentially serious problem for the face validity of this type of SRD measure.

Virtually all SRD measures continue to use the offense checklist format first used by Short and Nye (1957) in the mid-1950s. In this format, a series of short descriptions of a particular type of behavior are presented to the respondent who indicates whether he or she has engaged in that behavior (ever or during some specified time interval) and, in some cases, how frequently she or he have engaged in that behavior. Self-report delinquency scales reflect the sum of times checked, the variety of offenses acknowledged or the frequency of offenses reported across items. The check list format provides virtually no information about the details of the respondent's behavior.

In the 1967 and 1972 National Surveys of Youth (Gold & Reimer, 1975) details about the last three reported events of each offense type were obtained in personal interviews.[1] In an analysis of these follow-up questions, Gold and Reimer estimated that 22 percent of the responses were too trivial to be charged or considered delinquent acts.

During the 1979, 1980, and 1983 NYS surveys, a sequence of follow-up information was obtained for a subset of the self-reported delinquency items. When a respondent indicated that he or she had committed an offense described by one of the items included in this subset, information about the one most recent such event was obtained. In 1980 and 1983, information about the last three Index offenses (if reported) was obtained. This information included a behavioral description of that event. For example: What did you steal or try to steal? Where did you steal it from? About how much do you think was it worth? Were you alone or were others involved? or (for assaults) What kind of force did you use (punched, slapped, choked, beat, etc.)? Did you use a weapon? What were you trying to get (for robbery)? Was the person injured? How seriously? Based on this description, the degree of seriousness of the reported offense and whether the reported behavior was appropriate, in the sense that the behavior matched the offense described by the descriptive item, could be determined. Using this follow-up information, responses to self-reported delinquency items were classified into one of three categories -- inappropriate,

----

1. Gold used a card sort procedure rather than the Short-Nye checklist procedure, but the same type of short descriptive statements for each behavior/offense were used.

appropriate but trivial, or appropriate and non-trivial. Inappropriate responses included those for which the reported behavior did not logically fall into the class of behavior described by the self-reported delinquency item. For example, bicycle theft is not theft of a motor vehicle. If a response was judged appropriate, it was further classified as being either trivial or non-trivial. This latter classification was determined by judgments that a law enforcement officer upon observing or obtaining knowledge about the reported behavior would or would not have taken action against the offender. For example, slugging one's brother during an argument at home or stealing a friend's hair ribbon are unlikely to be officially treated as an assault or theft by the police; using the family car without permission in unlikely to be handled officially as a vehicle theft.

A summary of the information provided by this classification procedure for the total NYS sample, 1979-1983, is contained in Table 1. This table provides the percentage of responses to items judged to be inappropriate, trivial, or non-trivial.[2] For the totality of all item responses, approximately 5% were inappropriate, 30% were trivial, and 66% were non-trivial. The vast majority of responses to the minor assault items (i.e., hitting parents, teachers, other students, persons at work or others) were trivial (74.5%). Only 25% of the responses to these items involved behaviors considered to be appropriate and non-trivial. If these minor assault items were removed from the total set of items, only 13% of all remaining responses would be considered trivial and 81% would be considered appropriate and non-trivial.

Further examination of Table 1 indicates that 64% of the serious violent offenses (including robbery), are non-trivial, as are 71% of all reported Index offenses. For most theft items, 90% or more of reported events are non-trivial, the major exception being motor vehicle theft (60%). A relatively high proportion of reported fraud events were also considered trivial (37%) and a substantial proportion were classified as inappropriate (19%).

An analysis of differences in the reporting of non-trivial offenses revealed no evidence of a differential by sex, race, social class, or place of residence (urban, suburban, rural). Exactly why the interview situation, instruction sets, or wording of items causes some respondents to report trivial events to these rather typical SRD items is not clear, but some combination of those factors elicits reports of trivial events. This is problematic because, unless detailed information about each reported event is obtained, thereby greatly expanding the length of the SRD measure, knowledge about the triviality of reported offenses cannot be obtained and estimates cannot be adjusted for this over-reporting error. Perhaps investigative efforts directed at interview situations and item wordings that eliminate trivial

----

2. Since this classification was made only for the most recent reported event of each type, or the most recent three events in the case of Index offenses (1980 and 1983), the number of offenses by type reported here will not correspond with the totals reported in our general epidemiological reports (e.g., Elliott & Ageton, 1980 or Elliott & Huizinga, 1983).

TABLE 1. Percent of offenses classified as inappropriate, trivial and nontrivial, NYS 1979-1983.

Offense	Inappropriate N	Inappropriate %	Trivial %	Nontrivial %
1. Aggravated Assault	260	.01	33.8	65.4
2. Gang Fight	269	3.0	31.2	65.8
3. Sexual Assault	37	8.1	48.7	40.5
4. Robbery (Strongarming)	92	10.9	27.2	62.0
5. Motor Vehicle Theft	48	39.6	0.0	60.4
6. Theft Greater Than $50	141	5.7	0.0	94.3
7. Burglary	135	8.1	3.0	88.9
8. Stolen Goods	294	1.4	2.7	95.9
9. Theft $5-$50	190	7.9	0.0	92.1
10. Joyriding	211	8.1	.9	91.0
11. Hidden Weapon	130	3.1	.8	96.1
12. Bad Checks[a]	22	0.0	22.7	77.3
13. Theft Less Than $5	423	8.7	1.9	89.4
14. Fraud[b]	127	18.9	37.0	44.1
15. Credit Card Fraud[a]	20	0.0	0.0	100.0
16. Embezzlement[a]	11	8.3	16.7	75.1
17. Sold Hard Drugs[a]	31	0.0	0.0	100.0
18. Arson[a]	9	0.0	0.0	100.0
19. Vandalism (School)[b]	162	1.8	23.5	74.7
20. Hit Teacher[b]	89	0.0	92.1	7.9
21. Hit Parent[b]	98	0.0	83.7	16.3
22. Hit Student[b]	479	0.0	78.1	21.9
23. Hit Employee[a]	71	0.0	77.5	22.5
24. Hit Other[a]	214	1.9	53.7	44.4
Index Offenses(1-7)	982	6.2	22.4	71.4
Serious Violent Offenses(1-4)	658	3.5	32.8	63.7
Minor Assaults(20-24)	951	.4	74.5	25.1
All Offenses(1-24)	356	4.8	29.2	66.0

[a]Available only for 1983.
[b]Available only for 1980 and 1983.

responses without altering responses about non-trivial offenses would discover the factors underlying the trivial response problem and appropriate alterations to SRD instruments could be made. Since there are no sex, race, class or age differentials in the reporting of trivial events, this problem is not a serious one for estimating the social correlates of criminal behavior. But it poses a serious problem for accurate estimates of the volume of delinquent behavior and comparisons of self-reported offense rates with victim survey or officially recorded rates. It also poses potential problems for etiological studies since it may result in a misclassification of a significant proportion of respondents (i.e., an over-estimate of the prevalence rate) and their individual offending rates.

Our response to these data on the triviality of reported events has been to include follow-up questions about the most recent reported event for less serious offense items (misdemeanors) and for the last three reported events for more serious offenses (felonies) on subsequent NYS surveys. This procedure provides follow-up data on virtually all serious offenses reported and on a subset of less serious offenses. In those analyses where this source of overestimation can have some significant effect, we use adjusted SRD scores which take this follow-up information into account (e.g., Elliott & Huizinga, 1983). While this modification of the traditional checklist format for SRD measures does add significantly to the time required for administration, it does provide a means for correcting or adjusting individual SRD scores for this source of error. In addition, there are important other uses for the detailed follow-up data, e.g., establishing the proportion of offenses involving multiple offenders, the use of alcohol or drugs associated with each offense, levels of injury associated with particular offenses, and the average value of property stolen or destroyed.

It is also significant to note that this analysis revealed relatively low levels of inappropriate responses to these SRD items (5 percent overall). For the most part, respondents were correctly locating or assigning behaviors to the offense categories implied by the questions.

Another strategy for dealing with the triviality problem is to obtain wordings of items that describe offense behavior that carry a much higher probability of arrest. For example, rather than an item "hit other students," a more appropriate item might be (following Hindelang et al., 1981), "beat other students so badly they probably need a doctor." This latter item also illustrates a procedure suggested by Sudman and Bradburn (1982) for increasing the accuracy of responses to potentially threatening questions; longer and more specific questions are better than shorter general ones. Longer questions not only provide additional cues to help recall of past events, as these authors indicate, but also for delinquency questions they can provide cues as to the nature and seriousness of the question being asked. Thus, the addition of the phrase "so badly they probably needed a doctor" in the example above clearly adds a dimension of seriousness to the described behavior.

Even with longer items describing arrestable behavior, it is important to use follow-up items to obtain details of the reported offense

behavior. Both inappropriate and trivial responses are still likely to
occur and, without the more detailed descriptions of the behavior,
information about the scope and magnitude of this type of reporting
error would be unknown and any chance for correction would be lost.
Examples of the use of follow-up items can be found in the NYS (Elliott
& Huizinga, 1982; Gold & Reimer, 1975; and Hindelang et al., 1981),
although the latter do not discuss the follow-up data in any detail or
attempt to correct their estimates based upon these data. It should be
carefully observed, however, that the experience of the NYS and comments by Sudman and Bradburn (1982) clearly suggest that all follow-up
questions be delayed until the completion of the entire SRD checklist.
Otherwise some respondents quickly learn to avoid the follow-up questions by giving non-positive responses on the checklist items which
serve as a filter for the follow-up questions, as discussed by Thornberry elsewhere in this volume.

2.2. Item Specificity

In creating items for SRD scales, some concern for the level of
detail used in describing offense behaviors is needed. Clearly, asking
very many questions at a very fine level of detail is impossible within
the time limits of most interviews and the constraints of subject
cooperation and fatigue. However, the use of broad categories of
offenses, rather than more specific items subsumed in the broad categories, often results in lower scores and a presumed underreporting of
events (see, for example, Sudman & Bradburn, 1982; Hindelang et al.,
1981).

In the NYS, two examples of the effect of the specificity of items
can be illustrated. The first concerns alcohol use and the second
involves vandalism. For reasons described elsewhere (Brennan et al.,
1981), two roughly equivalent halves of the national sample were
created for the 1978 survey. One half of the sample received the
single item, "How often in the last year have you used alcoholic
beverages (beer, wine and hard liquor)?" The other half were asked
three separate two part items, "Have you ever used beer?" (If yes)
"During the last year how often did you drink beer?" A similar set of
questions was asked for wine and for hard liquor. The average rate of
alcohol use under the one-item condition was "once every 2-3 months"
while under the three-item condition it was "once a week." Similarly,
the proportion of individuals using alcohol under the one-item condition was 58% and under the three-item condition it was 72%. Although
part of the difference could be attributed to the additional lead-in
filter in the three-item condition (as suggested by Sudman and Bradburn, 1982) it is likely that much of the difference was due to the
increased frequency obtained by summing across the three items. Similar results for alcohol use when single and multiple items are employed
is reported by Sudman and Bradburn (1982).

In the vandalism example, one half of the sample received the one
item, "How many times in the previous year have you purposely damaged
or destroyed property that did not belong to you?" The other half
received one similar item for each of three contexts: belonging to your

parents or other family members, belonging to a school, and any other property not belonging to you. The average number of vandalism events reported under the one-item condition was .62 while under the three-item condition the average was 2.29. Similarly, the proportion of individuals reporting one or more property offenses under the one-item condition was 16% compared to 30% under the three-item condition. Based upon the regression of 1978 scores on 1977 scores in the half-sample receiving three items each year, the expected mean vandalism score for the 1978 half-sample receiving the single item in 1978 was 1.62. The actual mean was .62, 38% of the expected value. The level of underestimation thus appears to be substantial. Similar findings involving vandalism items are reported in Hindelang et al. (1981).

As these examples illustrate, the level of item specificity can have sizeable effects on the reporting rates of delinquent behavior. Separate items about similar offenses occurring in different contexts and items that involve different substances (and presumably different objects) increase the rate of reporting. Conceivably, longer questions providing more cues in a single question may reduce the difference between single and multiple items. However, the longer questions cannot simply be a listing of contexts or specific offenses, but require a more detailed description of a single offense in a particular context.

While the level of specificity is an issue of importance, it appears that it is one for which fixed guidelines cannot be given. Where to draw the line in obtaining a balance between item specificity (with its potential effect on levels of reporting), subject fatigue and cooperation, and the needs of the research project is a difficult question but one that should not be ignored.

2.3. Item Overlap -- The Double Counting of Specific Events

An issue affecting the accuracy of summative scales or indices is the inclusion of items for which a single behavioral event leads to a positive response on two or more of the SRD items. For example, an item about theft under five dollars and theft in a public place could both be answered positively even though a respondent has engaged in only one theft behavior. In a summative theft scale that included these items, the one theft event is quite likely to be double counted.

While there is little empirical evidence on this issue of logically overlapping items, it is a potential problem that can be seen in many SRD measures and may result in serious overcounts of delinquent behaviors. For example, this appears to be a potentially serious source of error in the Hindlang et al. (1981) SRD scales (see Elliott, 1982). In some instances, overlapping items have been deliberately included as a means of examining the reliability (internal consistency) of the SRD measure. Hardt and Petersen-Hardt (1977) included two items concerning police contact. The first concerned being warned or questioned and the second being ticketed or arrested. While these two items are not synonymous nor necessarily refer to the same event, 98 percent of those ticketed also reported being warned or questioned, and if both items were included in a count of police contacts, the potential for overcounting is clear.

During the fifth and sixth waves (1980 and 1983) of the National
Youth Survey, the SRD follow-up questions for certain SRD items
included a question about whether the reported behavior had also been
reported on any other item in the checklist. The items with this
follow-up question are not a representative sample of the full set of
SRD items but were limited to items in which double counting was
thought to be more likely. In the construction of the NYS measure, a
deliberate attempt was made to eliminate overlapping items. Yet 11% of
the events reported in response to this select set of items were double
counted, based upon responses to the follow-up questions for these
items. These data are presented in Table 2. Double counting was most
pronounced for motor vehicle theft (56%), with 40% of the events also
being reported as joyriding and 23% as theft over fifty dollars. A
high rate of double counting also occurred with responses to burglary,
with 15% of these reported events also being reported as thefts over
fifty dollars.[3]
Although the use of similar or even essentially identical items to
examine the internal consistency of SRD measures and the inclusion of
items that have some degree of logical overlap may have profitable use
in particular research designs, it is important that such overlapping
items not be included in the same summative index or scale. To include
them in the same scale may result in significant overcounts of the
delinquent behavior of individuals or groups.

2.4. Reference Periods

The primary validity issue in establishing the length of the reference period concerns several forms of memory bias or distortion (e.g.,
forgetting events, forgetting the details of events, or recalling these
events inaccurately) which are associated with the length of the recall
(reference) period (Garofalo, 1977). In general, the research findings
suggest that the longer the reference period, the greater the omission
of relevant events; the shorter the period, the greater the telescoping
bias (i.e., inaccurate location of events in or out of the reference
period). There is also evidence that these memory failures are not
random, but are related to the type of crime, the offender-victim relationship, and the salience of the event for the person reporting (LEAA,
1972; National Research Council, 1976; Sparks et al., 1977; Sudman &
Bradburn, 1974, 1982; Garofalo & Hindelang, 1977; Schneider, 1978;

----

3. Again, because these item frequencies were obtained from
follow-up questions for the most recent or three most recent events
reported, they cannot be compared to frequencies reported in other
epidemiological reports for the NYS. The estimates of double counting
are based upon items contained in our General Delinquency B scale, with
vandalism considered a single offense, i.e., combining vandalism items.

TABLE 2. Multiple reporting of specific offenses: 1980 and 1983.

Offenses	Unduplicated Number of Events Reported	Double Counted Offenses																										Inflation Over-report[b]	
		1	2	3	4	5	6	7	8	9	10	11	12	13	14	15	16	17	18	19	20	21	22	23	24	25	26	N	%
1. Motor Vehicle Theft	25	3				1			10																			14	56.0
2. Theft Greater Than $50	96	5		10			1		1		3	2																21	21.9
3. Stolen Goods	187		16			2														1			1					21	11.2
4. Arson[a]	14																				1							1	7.1
5. Theft Less Than $5	267			4				1			9							4	2	15							2	13	4.9
6. Aggravated Assault	175																			3							2	25	14.3
7. Gang Fight	147																	1	1									8	5.4
8. Joyriding	128	13										1	1					1		1								15	11.7
9. Robbery	36																											2	5.6
10. Theft $5-$50	111	5	4			9					4	2														1		23	20.7
11. Burglary	86	1	13	2																						3		25	29.1
12. Illegal Checks[a]	22													1														1	4.5
13. Sold Marijuana[a]	113																1											1	0.9
14. Sexual Assault[a]	17																											0	0.0
15. Hit Teacher[a]	6																											1	16.7
16. Hit Parent[a]	32			2																								0	0.0
17. Hit Student[a]	86															1	1	1								2	2	7	8.1
18. Hit Employee[a]	70						3									1	1	1	2	2						1	1	7	10.0
19. Hit Other[a]	212						16	5											2	1	1						6	31	14.6
20. Sold Hard Drugs[a]	29																											0	0.0
21. Fraud	54																											4	7.4
22. Credit Card Fraud[a]	11																											0	0.0
23. Pickpocket[a]	6																											0	0.0
24. Embezzlement[a]	12													1														1	8.3
25. Vandalism	142							1											1									4	2.8
Total N/%	2084	19	38	22	0	12	23	7	14	3	17	5	1	2	0	2	0	6	6	22	2	0	2	0	1	9	12	225	10.8

a = For 1983 data only

b = Offense for which no follow-up questions were asked. These offenses could be reported as a double count for some other offense, but other offenses cannot be double counted in direct response to these offenses. Included are

Weis, 1986).[4] Several additional issues are involved in the selection
of the reference period: 1) the longer the reference period the larger
the number of reported offenses; 2) for relatively rare events, the
length of the reference period will affect the number of reported
events and thus the sample size necessary for analyses (e.g., when
asking about index crimes, a three month reference period requires
approximately four times the sample size to achieve the same number of
reported offenses as a survey that uses a twelve month reference
period); 3) if comparison with national estimates is desired, most of
these measures are aggregated on an annual basis; and 4) as a result of
seasonal variations and recall errors, there may be difficulties associated with adjusting fractions of years to whole year estimates (Bachman
& O'Malley, 1980). Sudman and Bradford summarize the dilemma:

> If the behavior is highly salient, so that the percentage of
> omissions is small, substantial overstatements will occur if
> the time period is too short. In this case, the researcher's
> desire for a longer time period to obtain more data coincides
> with the selection of a time period to get the most accurate
> recall. Since both telescoping and omissions are occurring
> simultaneously, and since the effects of time work in the
> opposite directions for these two forms of forgetting, there
> is some time period at which the opposite biases cancel and
> the overall levels of reported behavior are about right
> (1982:45).

After an extensive investigation of this issue, the National Crime
Surveys adopted a six month reference period. However, this decision
was influenced by the design of the National Crime Surveys (which
involved a rolling reference period and the need to locate reported
victimizations by month within the reference period) and by the a
priori decision to publish reports on a quarterly basis (National
Research Council, 1976). In fact, the available research indicated
that for determining whether a victimization occurred or not (memory
omissions), a six month reference period was not demonstrably better
than a twelve month reference period (National Research Council, 1976;
Garofalo & Hindelang, 1977). Sparks et al. (1977) in a separate study
also found no difference in overall reporting accuracy for a twelve as
compared to a six month reference period.

All things considered, a twelve month reference period seems
preferable for self-report epidemiological studies if there is no need
for establishing a more precise location of events within the reference
period. Recall errors are not substantially greater than for a six
month period and the advantages are substantial with respect to smaller
sample sizes and direct comparisons with existing crime measures

---

4. Sparks et al., report that in the London Survey, memory error
(both the failure to recall an event and inaccuracy with respect to
when the event occurred) was a "...more or less random phenomenon which
is unlikely by itself to introduce any serious biases into estimates
from victim survey data" (1977:61).

166

aggregated on an annual basis.

With respect to using reference periods longer than twelve months, analyses of NYS data provide evidence of serious levels of under-reporting for two and three year reference periods as compared to a one year period (Menard & Elliott, 1988). The first five NYS surveys were conducted annually and each involved a twelve month reporting period. The sixth NYS survey was conducted three years after the fifth survey. The primary reference period was again twelve months (the twelve months immediately preceding the interview), but SRD data were also obtained retrospectively for the intervening years involving a two- and three-year recall.[5] Annual prevalence rates for 1976 through 1983 are presented in Figure 1 for measures of general delinquency, Index offenses, marijuana use and polydrug use. The solid trend lines in Figure 1 are based on the annual one-year recall data for 1976-80 and 1983. The dashed lines and the points they encompass (1981 and 1982) are based upon two- and three-year extended recall data. For all four offenses, the two- and three-year recall data form a "dipper" below the trend line established with the one-year recall data. Assuming a linear relationship over the entire 1976-1983 period, the estimates for 1981 and 1982 are significantly lower than expected (p = .001) for all four offenses (for a more detailed analysis see Menard and Elliott, 1988). The magnitude of the underestimation in this comparison also appears to be related to the length of recall required for the esti-mate. A similar analysis involving age-specific estimates for each year, essentially controlling for maturation effects over this period, reveals the same consistent underestimates for 1981 and 1982 for each birth cohort.

These findings have obvious relevance for the current controversy over the need for longitudinal data collection (Gottfredson & Hirschi, 1987, 1988; Greenberg, 1985; Blumstein et al., 1988a, 1988b). If we consider only the retrospective cross-sectional data collection at wave six for the years 1981-1983 to estimate the over-time trend in preva-lence, these data suggest an upward or increasing trend for all four offenses which is spurious or exaggerated, at least in comparison to the prospectively collected annual data which reveal an increasing rate of prevalence only for polydrug use.

The length of recall issue is more problematic for etiological stud-ies, particularly longitudinal studies where there is an interest in measuring change. The advantages of a longer reference period with respect to sample size and comparability to existing national crime measures are less important. The more critical issue concerns the appropriate lag for measuring change on the independent and dependent variables under consideration. Our own experience in theory testing with NYS data indicates that a twelve month reference period is

----
5. To protect the consistency of the one-year recall period across all waves of the NYS, the SRD measure involving the one-year recall (1983) wa administered first. The format for this measure was identical to that utilized in the first five surveys. Later in the interview, respondents were asked to respond to another set of SRD items for the years 1981 and 1982.

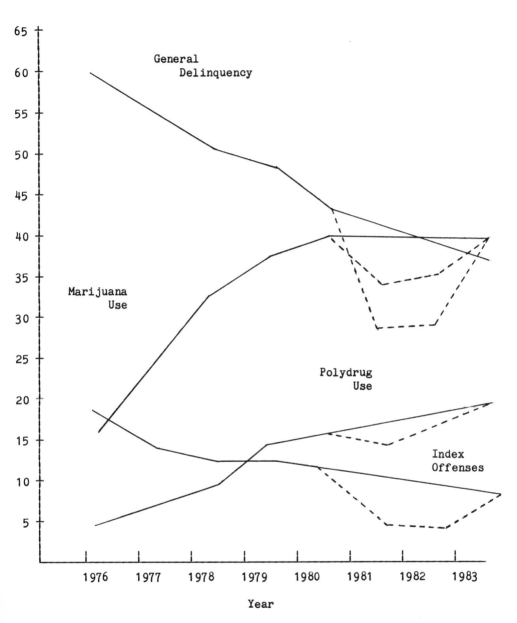

FIGURE 1.   Prevalence of selected offenses, 1976-1983.

probably too long, and that a shorter reference period would facilitate
theory testing.[6] However, the use of multiple data collection waves
with shorter reference periods increases telescoping error and greatly
escalates the cost. A more cost-efficient strategy might be to use a
data collection design similar to that used in NCS victimization
surveys, employing a twelve month (or six month) data collection
cycle, but locating reported offenses in six or three month reference
periods with follow-up questions after a general twelve month filter.
This is the procedure we are currently using in the Denver Youth Study,
a longitudinal study of self-report delinquency and drug use among
youth aged 7 to 15 in 1987 (Huizinga, 1986).

The use of bounding techniques helps to minimize the inaccurate
location of events in time. Two types of bounding techniques have been
used. In the first, a panel study is normally required, and data from
the preceding interview is used to remind respondents of behaviors
previously reported. Additionally, interviewers check currently
reported behaviors to see if they are similar to behaviors reported on
the earlier data collection wave, and if a similar offense is found,
probe to insure that the same event is not being reported. A similar
procedure has been suggested for cross-sectional studies (Sudman &
Bradburn, 1982), by first asking respondents about offenses in a time
period prior to the period of interest. This same procedure could be
used for the first wave of panel studies so as not to lose first wave
estimates.

This type of bounding procedure is somewhat difficult to implement
since it requires that all questionnaires or interview schedules be
"tailor-made" for each respondent with data from his or her prior data
collection wave. It also adds significantly to the administration time
required for the SRD measure. On the other hand, it is probably the
most effective approach to minimizing recall errors.

The second bounding technique involves the use of anchor points
that clearly delineate the time period of interest. In most instances,
events that are particularly salient for the population under study
provide good choices for the anchor points. Thus New Year's Day,
Christmas, July 4 in the U.S., and other dates of particular historical
interest to the respondent appear to be good choices. In addition to
asking questions about the interval between two anchor points, before
beginning the actual behavioral questions it may be helpful for interviewers to spend a brief period discussing with a respondent personal

----

6. In a series of 16 fold table analyses examining the relationship
between change in peer associations and delinquent behavior, a substantia
number of subjects changed on both measures during a given year, renderin
the causal order ambiguous for these subjects. We suspect this problem m
be fairly widespread. Further, relatively little is known about appropri
lag periods for change analyses involving delinquent or criminal behavior
There is evidence that if the lag period is too long, incorrect conclusio
concerning causal order are possible (Pelz & Lew, 1970). In the absence
knowledge about appropriate lag periods, Pelz and Lew recommend using
shorter lag periods (which can be collapsed, if necessary) rather than
longer ones.

events that occurred within the bounded time interval. This may not only bring the time frame into clearer focus but also may provide a memory aid to specific behaviors.

The use of anchor points under a number of conditions has been examined by Loftus and Marburger (1983). They consistently found evidence of reduced telescoping errors with the use of anchor points. The NYS self-reported offender measure has made use of both yearly anchor points (Christmas) and discussion with respondents of personal events occurring in the time frame for the 1980 and 1983 surveys. While there is no firm evidence, the subjective impressions of interviewers suggest that both procedures have worked reasonably well. Thus, the use of some type of bounding technique in self-report offender surveys is strongly recommended as a procedure to minimize recall errors.

3. METHODS OF ADMINISTRATION

It has often been assumed that a less personal interview would result in more accurate and valid information about sensitive subjects such as criminal behavior, and that anonymous, self-admininstered questionnaires would be more appropriate than non-anonymous, face-to-face interviews. In general, however, the research evidence does not support this assumption. In a thorough examination of this issue, Hindelang et al., (1981) compared results from anonymous and non-anonymous interviews and questionnaires. They found that the test-retest reliability (and internal consistency) was essentially the same under all four conditions for both variety scores and last year frequency scores. Using ever variety scores, the correlation with measures of official data was similar in all four forms of administration. Official record checks also showed little difference between forms of administration for either males or females, but there were some small differences by race. These authors conclude that overall the results of self-report offender research are not dependent on administration method and that no one method is consistently better than another. It was noted, however, that self-administered questionnaires resulted in higher levels of missing data, especially for items that requested information following a filter question (i.e., Have you ever ...? If so, how many times?).

Similar conclusions about methods of administration are reached by Sudman and Bradburn (1982), who point out that there is evidence of only small differences by form of administration and that for potentially threatening questions, it is the threat that is the dominant factor resulting in underreporting and not the type of administration. Krohn et al. (1975), using a sample of college students, also found that there was no statistical difference between interview and questionnaire methods in the percentage of students giving positive responses to delinquency items. Bale (1979) reports a similar finding in an analysis of questionnaire and interview data from a sample of heroin addicts. On the other hand, Bayless et al. (1978) and Gold (1966) present some evidence that interviews generate more valid self-report data than questionnaires.

Thus, it appears that major differences by type of administration (anonymous vs. non-anonymous and face-to-face interview vs. self-administered questionnaire) are not to be anticipated, and that the choice of administration method depends on other factors. There is, however, a need for further investigation of this issue. Administration of anonymous questionnaires to groups of respondents may increase the feeling of anonymity and thus affect responses. (The questionnaire condition used by Hindelang et al., involved questionnaire administration to single subjects.) The need for such information about group administration is also noted by Sudman and Bradburn (1982). In addition, the emphasis of research on types of administration has centered on underreporting and on the percentage of individuals who under-report. Because self-reported offender data are also affected by over-reporting, it would be helpful to know if the level of over-reporting is affected by method of administration and to determine whether the actual level of frequency responses is dependent on the method of administration. For example, Erickson and Empey (1963) noted that habitual offenders had difficulty estimating the number of times they had committed offenses and that some probing was required to reach reasonable estimates. Thus, at least among this group, face-to-face interviews might be required to obtain accurate estimates of the number of offense behaviors.

Although face-to-face interviews and self-administered questionnaires have been almost exclusively the only methods of administration for self-reported offender surveys, other methods have been considered. Among these are randomized response (randomized questions), telephone surveys, and automated individualized interviewing. The randomized response method is a technique that could be used with any form of interviewing and is designed to increase the anonymity of respondents and reduce the threat of sensitive questions. Essentially each item consists of two questions, one the question of interest, which is potentially threatening, and the second, some question of neutral content. By flip of a coin or some other random device, one of the questions is selected and a response obtained for the question. However, by using identical response sets and allowing the respondent to "flip the coin," the interviewer or researcher never knows which question was in fact answered. Knowing the probability of selecting questions, statistical procedures are employed to estimate total scores within the sample of respondents. The randomized response method has been shown to produce estimates similar to those of other interviewing methods. However, from our perspective the loss of individual information, the administration complexity, and the need for large sample sizes to achieve the same level of statistical accuracy as other procedures, suggest that it is not a very useful procedure (cf. Sudman & Bradburn, 1982; Hindelang et al., 1981).

Telephone interviews provide a different method of interview administration that is reported to have a great potential for cost savings. While noting that little is known about the effect of telephone surveys in collecting self-reported offender data, Bradburn and Sudman (1982) report that for a question about arrests for drunk driving, there were no substantial differences between telephone interviews, face-to-face interviews, and self-administered interviews. Telephone interviews have also been used in relatively long victimization surveys with results similar to those obtained in face-to-face interviews (Ruchfarber & Klecka, 1976).

In 1986, we conducted a study comparing telephone and face-to-face interview data obtained from two random samples of NYS panel members (N=188 each) stratified by race and prior reported delinquency levels. Our objective was to establish the feasibility of using telephone interviews in subsequent waves of the NYS as a cost reduction technique and to examine the comparability of SRD estimates and reliabilities derived from these two types of interviews.

The analysis of the differences in 1985 annual prevalence rates for SRD scales by interview method revealed only one statistically significant difference (for minor theft; face-to-face = .12; telephone = .26). There were no statistically significant differences in mean frequency scores on SRD scales by type of data. There was a general tendency in these estimates for those based upon telephone interview data to be higher than those based upon face-to-face interview data, but the differences were not statistically significant (except as indicated above). Because the NYS is a longitudinal study attempting to measure change over time, we also compared the mean change in annual rates from 1983 to 1985 for the two samples. For changes in annual prevalence, there were no statistically significant differences for either type of interview, although for the face-to-face interview sample, differences on felony theft and General Delinquency (B) approached statistical significance (p $\leq$ .06). There was general consistency between types of interviews with respect to the direction of changes in annual prevalence rates. For SRD frequency measures, there were no statistically significant changes from 1983 to 1985 on any scale for either type of interview. However, there was less consistency in the direction of change by type of interview. In general, however, there was no evidence for any systematic differences in annual prevalence or frequency estimates associated with type of interview; nor did there appear to be significant differences in the magnitude of sample changes in prevalence or mean frequency from 1983 to 1985.

In this study, then, there did not appear to be any systematic difference in SRD estimates derived from telephone or face-to-face interviews. However, one word of caution is in order. These were not initial interviews with these respondents. Those who were interviewed by phone had nearly all been interviewed six times previously with face-to-face interviews. Rapport with these respondents had been established much earlier and they were quite familiar with the general structure and content of the interview. Thus, the results of this comparison should not be generalized to initial interviews.

It should also be noted that approximately 20% of youth in the telephone sample had no phones at their residence and although we sent them letters requesting that they call us collect, left messages for them with parents and friends, and indicated that we would pay them $20 for the interview, relatively few of these youth actually completed interviews. Those without phones were disproportionately black and the overall completion rate among blacks in the telephone sample was 40%

compared to 66% in the face-to-face sample. This suggests a potentially serious differential loss rate associated with telephone interviews.
The loss rates were not associated with delinquency level (strata)
within either the white or black subsamples; the loss was associated
with race within the telephone sample only.

While telehone surveys may thus have potential, we would recommend
caution when using this method for cross-sectional surveys or first
waves of panel surveys. The potential for selective loss rates, potential difficulties in convincing respondents of the validity of confidentiality guarantees without showing them written consents, difficulties
in implementing human subject informed consent procedures and establishing the legitimacy of the survey and sponsoring organization, all
suggest that additional research is needed on this question. Our
analysis also suggests that the cost savings associated with telephone
interviews is not as great as originally anticipated.

Another form of interview administration is computer-assisted
interviewing. Two types of this kind of interviewing have been used.
In the first, an interviewer sits at a CRT-keyboard and reads items
displayed on the CRT-screen and types in the respondents' answers. In
the second, the computer acts as an interviewer and records typed-in or
touch-screen responses. A major advantage of either of these procedures is the ease with which complex skip patterns and tailored testing
techniques can be employed. A discussion of the advantages and disadvantages of computer assisted interviewing is beyond the scope of this
paper. However, with the coming of portable terminals and portable
computers, such procedures may prove beneficial. Since little is known
about computer assisted interviewing in collecting self-report offender
data, it currently is an administration procedure that cannot be recommended. However, it should be noted that this procedure has been
successfully used in other behavioral areas and may, in fact, hold
promise in collecting offender data as well.

Given the above considerations and particularly the observation
that face-to-face interviews may reduce the black-white underreporting
differential (Weis, 1986), it would seem that face-to-face interviews
would currently provide the safest method of administration to obtain
accurate and valid self-reported offender information. Provided confidentiality is guaranteed, complete anonymity is not required. Although
self-administered questionnaires are a viable option, the potential
problems of increased amounts of missing data, difficulties in using
bounding procedures, and the demonstrated value of interviewer probes
and assistance to respondents on particular items, suggest this method
would be less profitable. Other procedures, such as telephone interviews and computer assisted interviews have promise and may prove to be
beneficial both in having at least equal accuracy and in reducing overall cost. However, the successful use of these latter two procedures
for obtaining accurate self-reported offender information remains to be
demonstrated.

4. SCORING, SCALE CONSTRUCTION AND TYPES OF MEASURES

4.1. Response Sets and Scoring Procedures

The type of response sets used with self-report offender measures of crime may clearly have an effect on the accuracy and validity of these measures. A major concern has been the use of normative response categories such as "never," "sometimes," and "often," since this kind of response set is open to interpretation by respondents and provides no meaningful count of behaviors. The use of categorical response sets involving frequency ranges is also of concern. Many of these response sets have used only low frequency categories such as "none," "once or twice," and "three or more times." These response sets not only prevent accurate numerical estimation but, perhaps more importantly, they seriously truncate the upper end of the numerical distribution. As a result, an individual with a high involvement in a particular behavior is given the same score as an individual involved in relatively few such behaviors. For items that often have some high frequency scores among respondents (e.g., shoplifting, minor assault, drug use) this response set is particularly problematic. For frequency categories that provide a more encompassing frequency range and for response sets that categorize frequency by using time periods, e.g., "never," "once a month," "once a week," "once a day," a response bias of never picking the most extreme category may result in inaccurate responses. Bachman and O'Malley (1984) report such a tendency for blacks as compared to whites. In addition, it may be very difficult for a respondent to select the appropriate category, since none may reflect the actual frequency of offending. This is especially true if a respondent engages in the behavior only episodically. In the NYS we have discovered a significant occurrence of episodic events, e.g., ten shoplifting offenses, all occurring within a two-month period during the summer. This pattern of offending is difficult to report on a categorical frequency continuum which assumes an even distribution of offending over the reference period. Further, Hughes and Dodder (1988) report that even minor changes in a categorical response continuum (e.g., from "never," "1-2 times/month," "1-2 times/week," "1-2 times/day") are accompanied with significant differences in mean score values. Patterns of correlations between these scores and measures of theoretical variables were very similar however, suggesting that this difference in response continuum was more important for epidemiological than etiological studies. It is, however, critical to comparisons across surveys. These types of problems led to the use of open-end questions in the NYS SRD measure. Sudman and Bradburn (1981) also recommend the use of this type of response format.

The use of open-end frequency responses avoids many of the above problems, but the accuracy or reliability of this response mode is also troublesome. While an individual infrequently engaged in a particular behavior may not have difficulty recalling each occasion of that behavior, an individual frequently involved in the behavior may have great difficulty remembering each such incident and can only give an approximate response. The error committed, however, is probably no

174

larger than that occurring when frequency categories are used.

The open-end response format also tends to generate some extremely high scores. This is a source of some concern, since these scores, if exaggerations or falsifications, should be "corrected" or modified so as not to effect unfairly the estimates of mean frequencies. In a special review of NYS respondents with extreme scores, all subjects reporting frequencies of 24 or greater to any SRD item for 1976-80 were identified. Several checks were made on these respondents and their responses. First, all high frequency reports were examined individually to determine if the response seemed reasonable, unlikely or impossible. For example, reporting drunkenness 100 times a year, while not impossible, does appear unlikely. Second, these respondents' entire interviews were examined to determine if there was any evidence of a consistent pattern of unlikely responses, or high levels of inconsistency in responses (like reporting being drunk 100 times in the SRD section, but drinking beer, wine or liquor only once a week in the drug use section of the interview). Third, interviewer comments relative to specific items written in the margins or in the written observations at the end of the interview were examined for impressions about the validity of these responses.[7] This review led to several conclusions. First, the vast majority of interviewer comments relative to extreme scores provided positive justification for these scores, rather than suggestions or impressions about deliberate exaggeration or falsification. Second, virtually none of the responses was logically impossible. Third, many of the highest frequency responses were reasonably justified by interviewer notes of verbatim respondent comments. For example, a report of 400 thefts under $5 was accompanied by a note in the margin in which the respondent said "I work at a grocery store every day after school and steal oranges to eat every day." Fourth, those reporting high frequency responses were rarely identified as unreliable on the basis of the pattern of their responses or inconsistencies in their responses. Obviously, these observations do not verify the accuracy of these extreme scores, but there is no compelling evidence from any of these checks that extreme scores were reported as "jokes," obvious exaggeration, or deliberate falsification. The fact that many were accompanied by some comment explaining the response is one indication that respondents' were attending to the questions and providing meaningful answers. Finally, there is no general rule for altering or "correcting" extreme scores that is not arbitrary and likely to produce errors of underestimation.

As a result of this analysis, we have not attempted to correct any individual SRD frequency estimates for extreme scores. We have eliminated complete interviews or sections of interviews when the internal

---

7. All interviewers were trained to write down unsolicited comments made by the respondent, in the adjacent margins or on a special page in the ba of the interview schedule. For every interview there was also a special page where interviewers were to write down immediately after leaving the respondent's home or place of the interview, their impressions of the interview and any unusual circumstances that would help us understand the responses.

response patterns indicated a respondent was essentially unresponsive, but we have not eliminated or corrected specific frequency estimates. Rather, we have attempted to alert readers to the presence of extreme scores by indicating the maximum score and standard deviation for each item or scale, as well as mean frequencies (Elliott et al., 1983).

However, even with these problems, the use of an open response set that obtains actual frequency counts of behaviors and avoids the difficulties of categorical response sets would seem more appropriate and affords a simpler, more direct interpretation, particularly for epidemiological studies estimating rates of delinquency in the population.

Because there is almost no empirical information about the relative adequacy of open-end frequency responses in comparison with a response set of multiple frequency categories that cover the full range of possible behavioral frequencies in the literature, we have conducted a number of analyses comparing these two response formats. The SRD measure in the NYS has employed both an open-end and a multiple categorical response set. The initial response solicited is the open-end frequency response. If this response is 10 or more, the interviewer then asks the respondent to select one of the following categorical responses: 1) once a month, 2) once every 2-3 weeks, 3) once a week, 4) 2-3 times a week, 5) once a day, or 6) 2-3 times a day. A comparison of individual frequency scores based upon these two response formats, using the midpoint of the category selected for the categorical score, is moderately high (r = .65, 1976). Comparing the two frequency distributions, the major difference involves the last two (high frequency) categories. At this end of the continuum, estimates based upon the midpoint of the category are substantially higher than the direct open-end frequency response. Surprisingly, the open-end response format provides a more conservative estimate of the number of delinquent offenses reported.

A comparison of the test-retest reliabilities of the open-end and categorical scales is presented in Table 3. While there are substantial differences in reliability estimates for open-end as compared to categorical forms of a given scale, there is no consistent pattern favoring either form. For males, a slightly larger proportion of category scales have higher reliabilities, but for females the opposite is true. There were no consistent patterns when considering black-white differences. In sum, neither form is clearly superior to the other with respect to reliability estimates. For a more complete discussion of the reliability issue, see Huizinga and Elliott (1986).

A major difference between open-end and categorical forms of scales is that the open-end forms are very skewed. This characteristic may have important consequences for analyses involving relationships between measures, for example, regression analysis. Multiple R and zero-order correlations for the two types of SRD scales (for 1977 and 1980) are shown in Table 4 with a selected set of predictor variables. The differences in the zero-order correlations are consistent and substantial. Categorical scores produce higher correlations for both the general measure and the Index measure of delinquency and for both 1977 and 1980. For the Index offense scale in 1977, all but one of the correlations is non-significant when using the open-end measure,

176

whereas they are all significant when using the categorical measure. Levels of explained variance associated with these two types of SRD measures in multiple-regression analyses reveal the same consistent pattern. For General Delinquency in 1977, the explained variance is three times as great with the categorical measure as compared to the open-end measure; for 1980, it is five times as great. These are not trivial differences. The skewness in the open-end SRD scales is extreme, and although regression analyses are assumed to be quite robust in the face of skewness, there are serious problems with these measures when used in regression analyses and one is well advised to use some transformation of raw frequency scores; one can always rescore raw frequencies into a categorical score; the reverse transformation, however, is problematic.

TABLE 3. Test-Retest Reliability Coefficients: 1980 NYS SRD Scales – Males and Females.

	MALES (N = 102)		FEMALES (N = 75)	
	Frequency Scores	Category Scores	Frequency Scores	Category Scores
General Delinquency	.625	.903	.909	.827
Index Offenses	.644	.872	.835	.709
Felony Assault	.660	.797	.825	.642
Robbery	.853	.771	*	*
Felony Theft	.578	.759	.970	.942
Minor Theft	.878	.854	.718	.692
Property Damage	.886	.704	.649	.717
Illegal Services	.929	.837	.707	.743
Public Disorder	.601	.810	.974	.861
Status	.479	.864	.541	.758

*The number of robberies reported by females was insufficient for obtaining a reliable estimate.

In the light of the above findings, we have opted to use open-end frequency based measures in NYS epidemiological analyses and categorical based measures in all etiological analyses. However, the same effect could be realized with only an open-end response set, using raw scores for estimates of the frequency of offending in epidemiological analyses and logit transformations of raw frequency data in etiological analyses. The open-end measures are most easily interpreted when presenting estimates of population rates as they involve simple counts of offenses. They also may provide slightly more accurate estimates at the high end of the frequency range. If only one type of response set is possible, the open-end response set seems clearly preferable to the

TABLE 4. Zero Order and Multiple Correlations: Open-End and Categorical SRD Frequency Measures with Selected Predictor Variables.

Predictor Variables[a]	Wave[b] '76-77	Wave[b] '79-80	1977 General Delinquency 2 Open-End r	Open-End Beta	Categorical r	Categorical Beta	1977 Index Offenses 2 Open-End r	Open-End Beta	Categorical r	Categorical Beta	1980 General Delinquency 5 Open-End r	Open-End Beta	Categorical r	Categorical Beta	1980 Index Offenses 5 Open-End r	Open-End Beta	Categorical r	Categorical Beta
Family Normlessness	1	4	.11	.03*	.22	.04*	.03*	-.01*	.15	.03*	.16	.05*	.22	.01*	.14	.04*	.17	.04*
School Normlessness	1	4	.11	-.03*	.24	.00*	.04*	.01*	.17	.01*	.13	.02*	.29	.07*	.17	.01*	.20	-.00*
Family Involvement	2	5	-.07	-.03*	-.19	-.02*	-.02*	.02*	-.12	-.01*	-.06	-.02*	-.14	-.02*	-.02*	.03*	-.05	.03*
School Involvement	2	5	-.09	-.02*	-.19	-.03*	-.00*	.03	.11	.01*	-.10	-.05*	-.14	-.04*	-.09	-.02*	-.12	-.02*
Conventional Beliefs	1	4	-.15	-.03*	-.30	-.05*	-.03*	.04*	.17	.04*	-.17	.00*	-.32	-.03*	-.17	.02*	-.22	-.01*
School Strain	1	4	-.12	-.04*	-.22	-.07	-.03*	-.00*	.16	-.06	-.05	.03*	-.20	-.05*	-.12	-.03*	-.18	-.08
Involvement with Delinquent Peers	2	5	.35	.29	.59	.50	.19	.17	.46	.42	.26	.17	.54	.46	.35	.27	.42	.34
R			.31		.57		.14		.43		.21		.54		.29		.39	
R²			.10		.33		.02		.19		.05		.29		.09		.15	

* = Nonsignificant. All other correlations are statistically significant, p = .01.

a = For a description of these measures and their psychometric properties, see Elliott et al. 1985.

b = These numbers designate the data collection wave the measure was obtained. For example, correlations in the first two columns (1976) involve Family Normlessness wave 1 with General Delinquency wave 2, i.e., a lagged correlation; or for Family Involvement wave 2 with General Delinquency wave 2, a contemporaneous correlation. The time location of each measure is indicated by the wave designation on each predictor measure.

use of a categorical response set.

One type of response set commonly utilized in self-reported delinquency studies has not been included in the above discussion. This
format asks if a respondent has ever engaged in a particular behavior
during some reference period such as the last six months, the last
year, or an entire lifetime. A simple yes or no response is obtained.
"Variety" scale scores are then obtained by counting the number of
behaviors that received a positive response. While Hindelang et al.,
(1981) recommend an ever-variety prevalence measure as the basic measure for etiological research, we see little to recommend it. First,
no evidence is presented by Hindelang et al. (1981) in support of the
claim that ever-variety prevalence measures have better validity than
last year (annual) prevalence or frequency measures. We have re-scored
NYS scales using this procedure and the reported differences in test-
retest reliability for annual prevalence, ever-variety prevalence and
general offending measures are small and of questionable significance
(Huizinga & Elliott, 1986). But the major problem of ever-prevalence
measures for etiological research concerns the temporal ordering of
independent and dependent variables: with this measure there is simply
no way to establish the time location of reported delinquent offenses
relative to the measures of relevant independent variables; there is no
way to rule out the rival hypothesis that delinquency is the independent variable in each of the observed relationships. Further, these
measures have limited utility for any longitudinal study or program
evaluation in which there is an interest in changing involvement in
crime or delinquency over time (as acknowledged by Hindelang et al.,
1981) and they have no direct comparability to other routinely collected national crime rates (e.g., UCR or NCS in the United States). Finally, the use of a simple yes-no categorization can readily be obtained
from actual frequency counts or a categorical response set. Thus, the
loss of information with a simple yes-no response coupled with other
analysis problems suggests that this type of response set has very
limited utility.

The use of the yes-no set as a filter question is recommmended.
Sudman and Bradburn (1982) note that events occurring sometime in the
past may be less salient and thus questions covering a longer period
may be less threatening than questions about the recent past. They
thus suggest asking items of the form "Have you ever..." as a precursor
to obtaining actual frequency information of a more recent time period,
such as the past year. It is assumed that the lead-in question will
reduce the sensitivity of the later question and thus reduce under-
reporting. Again there is little empirical information about this
issue, so whether the time taken in asking double questions about each
behavior is worth the possible gain in reporting accuracy must currently be left to individual judgment.

4.2. Combining items into scales

Within the field of crime and delinquency, the creation of summative
scales or indices most often depends on the assumption that a heterogeneous phenomenon is being observed and the summative scale is being

used to obtain a more complete picture of the extent of criminal or delinquent behavior. In this case, several potentially diverse items are combined into a scale. Within this framework, whenever items are combined into scales or indices some information is lost and the scale distribution may not reflect the distribution of particular items. Scales may obscure or even reverse the distribution of scores occurring at the item level. As a result, there is a danger of misleading or incorrect interpretation of findings, especially if differences at the item level are ignored.

Of particular importance is the inclusion of both low and high frequency items in the same scale, since the high frequency items tend to dominate the scale totals. In this situation, it would be incorrect to assume that the distributional characteristics of the scale adequately reflect the distributions of separate items included in the scale. Commonly, seriousness of offense and frequency of offense go hand in hand, and the combination of serious and non-serious items in the same scale results in a scale that is dominated by and characteristic of the non-serious offenses and uncharacteristic of the serious offenses. Such scales are often entitled with names reflecting the more serious offenses, and findings based on these scales and titles are often misleading.

Illustration of some of these problems using NYS data can be found in Elliott and Ageton (1980) and Elliott et al. (1983). For example, substantial racial differences are reported for the prevalence of sexual assault, aggravated assault, and minor assault. However, because the differences in aggravated and minor assault are in opposite directions, when these measures are combined into a general assault scale, no racial differences are found. Thus, the unqualified conclusion that there are no racial differences in assault would be very misleading.

A second example involves the finding reported in Elliott and Huizinga's (1985:160) analysis of differentials in social class that middle-class females report significantly higher levels of public disorder offenses than lower-class females. An examination of the individual items in this scale reveals that this difference can be attributed to a single offense item -- disorderly conduct. This class differential was not observed for the other offenses in the scale (hitchhiked, drunkenness, panhandled, and obscene phone calls).

In view of the above, care should be taken in the construction of summative scales from individual SRD items. The simple combining of items into general or specific offense subscales should be approached with caution. Attention should be given to the levels of frequency and seriousness of the items and the nature and distributional properties of the items. Without careful consideration of the composition of scales, misleading or erroneous conclusions are likely to be made. We have recommended elsewhere that individual items be examined carefully before drawing conclusions from summary scales so as to be aware of the exceptions to generalizations based upon scales (Elliott et al., 1983).

4.3. The Basic Parameters of Delinquency -- Types of Measures

Prior self-report delinquency studies have often confused offender-based and offending-based measures and at least some of the inconsistency in findings relative to the social correlates of delinquency can be attributed to inappropriate comparisons of different measures. In this regard, it is useful to distinguish between three general types of delinquency rates: prevalence rates, general offending rates, and individual offending rates. Prevalence is an offender-based measure, i.e., it is a count of the persons who have committed one or more offenses of a given type or class within a designated period of time. The prevalence rate is typically expressed as the proportion of persons in the population who have reported some involvement in a particular offense or set of offenses. The time interval is usually designated, as in an annual prevalence, a three year prevalence, or a lifetime (ever) prevalence rate.

The general offending rate refers to the relative number of offenses or behaviors which occur in a given population during a specified time period. It is offenses which are being counted, not persons. General offending rates may be expressed as an average number of offenses per person, or as the number of offenses to some other population base (e.g., per 100, 1000 or 100,000 persons). For example, the Uniform Crime Report of annual arrest rates is a general offending rate per 100,000.

The individual offending rate refers to the offending rate in the active offender population as opposed to a general population. The base again may involve a mean number of offenses per offender active during the reference period, or a rate per 100, 1000, or any other designated base number of offenders active during the reference period. The individual offending rate is thus a function of the combined prevalence and general offending rates, i.e., it is the general offending rate divided by the prevalence rate.

If the general offending rate remains constant in a population while the prevalence rate declines, the individual offending rate will have increased, i.e., while there are fewer active offenders, each one is committing more offenses. While seldom reported in epidemiological studies employing self-report surveys, the general offending rate is very useful in describing the dynamics of delinquent involvement in a general population (see Elliott et al., 1985). The individual offending rate is also an important rate for the study of criminal careers and the potential effects of selective incapacitation and other crime control policies (Blumstein & Moitra, 1980; Wolfgang et al., 1972; Blumstein & Cohen, 1979; Shinnar & Shinnar, 1975; cf. Gottfredson & Hirschi, 1987, 1988).

Several comments about these proposed standard measures are in order. First, the offending measures obtained in self-report surveys involve counts of person-offenses, not crime events. To our knowledge, self-report offender surveys have not attempted to provide any direct estimate of crime event rates. Further, the UCR arrest rates (as opposed to crimes known to the police) are person-offense frequency rates, not crime event rates.

Second, neither the UCR nor the NCS provide any direct estimates of offender prevalence rates. While there are some estimates of annual prevalence and lifetime prevalence based upon official record data (Wolfgang et al., 1972; Blumstein et al., 1986), the primary source of national annual prevalence rates are self-report offender surveys.

Third, we have deliberately not used the term "incidence" in the discussion of proposed standard measures. This term has been used in our own prior work (Elliott & Ageton, 1980; Elliott & Huizinga, 1983) and that of others (e.g., Tracy, 1978; Reiss, 1975; Biderman, 1972) with the same definition as that given above for the general offending rate. However, the term incidence has a long history with medical researchers studying the epidemiology of infectious disease (Hunt, 1979) and refers to a distinctly different kind of rate (i.e., the proportion of the uninfected population at risk at the beginning of the year that becomes infected during the year). In the interest of avoiding confusion, we propose to use the term general offending rate as the measure of the frequency of offending in a population rather than the term incidence.

Finally, we recommend that both prevalence and offending (general and individual) measures be obtained in self-report offender studies. To facilitate an assessment of onset, it is generally advisable to obtain an ever-prevalence measure in cross-sectional studies and for the first wave of longitudinal studies. But the basic measure of self-reported offending should afford estimates of annual prevalence, general offending, and individual offending. Ever-prevalence variety measures have a limited utility for all types of criminological research, whether it be etiological, epidimiological or program evaluation research. If we could achieve a general consensus on the definition and use of these measures, it would greatly facilitate the comparisons of findings across studies and the accumulation of knowledge over time.

5. SUMMARY

It has been over 30 years since the pioneering work of Porterfield (1946), Murphy et al. (1946), Wallerstein and Wyle (1947), and Short and Nye (1957) introduced self-report measures of delinquent behavior. Surprisingly, there has been little modification of the basic checklist format for SRD measures. We have suggested that some major modifications in this basic format are needed if we are to improve the validity of SRD measures. Specifically, two major format changes have been recommended: 1) the use of detailed follow-up questions to probe specific details of events reported in response to checklist items so as to eliminate inappropriate and trivial responses and correct for the double (and sometimes triple) reporting of single events, and 2) the use of open-end frequency response sets rather than categorical or normative response sets. It is acknowledged that the concern over trivial events is based upon a particular conceptualization of delinquency or crime as illegal behaviors which carry some significant risk for official action if observed or reported. If one is defining delinquency more broadly as antisocial behavior, the issue of trivial events is less problematic.

The reporting of trivial events and logical overlap in SRD items both contribute to inflated estimates of prevalence, general offending, and individual offending rates. Given the NYS data presented earlier, these two sources of error may account for as much as 40% over-reporting of offenses on global SRD scales. Estimates of underreporting derived from official records comparisons suggest a 20 to 32% under-reporting (Hindelang et al., 1981; Huizinga & Elliott, 1986). Over-reporting thus appears to be as serious a source of error as is under-reporting. It is possible that these errors offset one another and that general population estimates and estimates for particular demographic subgroups are relatively accurate, but there is some reason to believe that they may not offset one another. There did not appear to be demographic differentials in the reporting of trivial events, but there is some evidence for these differentials in under-reporting. Further, for individual levels of analysis, these sources of error present a much more serious problem, as they directly influence who is and is not classified as delinquent and the levels of individual offending for any given reporting period.

The problems associated with item specificity, reference periods, scoring, scale construction, and type of SRD measures all lead to a recommendation for some standardization of at least a core set of SRD items, scales and types of measures. The recent longitudinal studies funded in the U.S. by the Office of Juvenile Justice and Delinquency Prevention have made a significant start in this direction, with all three projects agreeing to a standardized set of core SRD items and scales (along with standardized measures of a number of other key variables).

In addition to standardization, we have suggested a number of practical procedures which can be utilized to minimize response bias and enhance the validity of our SRD measures. These include increased question length and specificity, the use of multiple items, aided recall, bounded recall, shorter reference periods, open-end response sets, detailed follow-up questions, and careful attention to the content and construction of SRD scales. A greater commitment to the use of these procedures should result in a substantial improvement in the validity and accuracy of our self-reported measures of delinquency and crime.

AUTHOR NOTES

This research was supported by grants from the Antisocial and Violent Behavior Branch, National Institute of Mental Health (MH 27552 and MH 41761); and the National Institute for Juvenile Justice and Delinquency Prevention (78-JN-AX-003) and the National Institute of Justice (83-IJ-CX-0063) and 82-IJ-CX-0011) both of the U.S. Department of Justice.

REFERENCES

Abel, GC, Gunningham-Rathner, J, Becker, JV, & McHugh, J: Motivating
    sex offenders for treatment with feedback of their psychophysiologic
    assessment. Paper presented at the World Congress of Behavior
    Therapy, Washington, DC., 1983.
Bale, RN: The validity and reliability of self-reported data from
    heroin addicts: mailed questionnaires compared with face-to-face
    interviews. The International Journal of the Addictions,
    14:993-1000, 1979.
Bachman, JG, & O'Malley, PM: When four months equals a year: Inconsis-
    tencies in students' reports of drug use. Ann Arbor: Survey
    Research Center, University of Michigan, 1980.
-----: Yea-saying, nay-saying and going to extremes: Black-white dif-
    ferences in response styles. Public Opinion Quarterly, 48:491-509,
    1984.
Bachman, JF, O'Malley, PM, & Johnston, J: Adolescence to adulthood:
    Change and stability in the lives of young men. Youth in
    Transition, Vol. VI. Ann Arbor: Institute of Social Research, 1978.
Bachman, JG, Johnston, LD, & O'Malley, PM: Questionnaire responses
    from the nation's high school seniors, 1982. Ann Arbor: Institute
    of Social Research, University of Michigan, 1984.
-----: Monitoring the future: Questionnaire responses from the
    nation's high school seniors, 1986. Ann Arbor: Institute for
    Social Research, University of Michigan, 1987.
Bayless, D, Boesel, D, & Piper, L: Effects of survey conditions on
    victimization response and response quality in surveying school
    crime. Paper presented at the American Statistical Association
    meetings, San Diego, California, 1978.
Biderman, AD: Notes on prevalence and incidence. Unpublished manu-
    script. Washington, DC: Bureau of Social Science Research, 1972.
Blumstein, A, Cohen, J, & Farrington, D: Criminal career research: Its
    value for criminology. Criminology, 26:1-35, 1988a.
-----: Longitudinal and criminal career research: Further clarifica-
    tions. Criminology, 26:57-74, 1988b.
Blumstein, A, & Cohen, J: Estimation of individual crime rates from
    arrest records. The Journal of Criminal Law and Criminology,
    70:561-585, 1979.
Blumstein, A, & Moitra, S: The identification of 'career criminals'
    from 'chronic offenders' in a cohort. Law and Policy Quarterly,
    2:321-334, 1980.
Bradburn, NM: Response effects. In Rossi, PH, & Wright, JD (Eds.),
    Handbook of survey research. New York: Academy Press, 289-328,
    1985.
Bradburn, NM, & Sudman, S (Eds.): Improving interviewing method and
    questionnaire design. San Francisco: Jossey Bass, 1979.
Brennan, T, Elliott, DS, & Huizinga, D: Patterns of multiple drug use.
    Unpublished paper. Boulder, Colorado: Behavioral Research
    Institute, 1981.
Chaiken, JM, & Chaiken, MR: Varieties of criminal behavior. Santa
    Monica: The Rand Corporation, 1982.

184

Chaiken, JM, Chaiken, MR, & Rolph, JE: Self-reported commissions of crime: Comparisons of two questionnaire formats. Santa Monica: The Rand Corporation, 1983.

Elliott, DS: A review essay on 'Measuring delinquency' by Hindelang, MJ, Hirschi, T, & Weis, JG. Criminology, 20:527-537, 1982.

Elliott, DS, & Ageton, SS: Reconciling race and class differences in self-reported and official estimates of delinquency. American Sociological Review, 45(1):95-110, 1980.

Elliott, DS, & Huizinga, D: Social class and delinquent behavior in a national youth panel: 1976-1980. Criminology. 21:149-177, 1983.

Elliott, DS, Ageton, SS, Huizinga, D, Knowles, BA, & Canter RJ: The prevalence and incidence of delinquent behavior: 1976-1980. National Youth Survey Project Report 26. Boulder, Colorado: Behavioral Research Institute, 1985.

Elliott, DS, Huizinga, D, & Ageton, SS: Explaining delinquency and drug use. Beverly Hills: Sage Publications (in press).

English, K: Assessing the quality of self-reported crime rate data. MA thesis. Boulder: University of Colorado, 1988.

Erickson, M, & Empey, LT: Court records, undetected delinquency and decision-making. Journal of Criminal Law, Criminology, and Police Science, 54:456-469, 1963.

Garofalo, J: Time: A neglected dimension in tests of criminological theories. In Meier, RF (Ed.), Theory in criminology. Beverly Hills: Sage Publications, pp. 93-116, 1977.

Garofalo, J, & Hindelang, J: An introduction to the National Crime Survey. Washington, DC: U.S. Government Printing Office, 1977.

Gold, M: Undetected delinquent behavior. Journal of Research in Crime and Delinquency, 3:27-46, 1966.

Gold, M: Delinquent behavior in an American city. Belmont, CA: Wadsworth, 1970.

Gold, M, & Reimer, DJ: Changing patterns of delinquent behavior among Americans 13 through 16 years old: 1967-1972. Crime and Delinquency Literature, 7:483-517, 1975.

Gottfredson, DC, & Gottfredson, GD: The validity of self-reports. Paper presented at the annual meeting of the American Society of Criminology, Cincinnati, Ohio, 1984.

Gottfredson, M, & Hirschi, T: The methodological adequacy of longitudinal research on crime and delinquency. Criminology, 25:581-614, 1987.

-----: Science, public policy and the career paradigm. Criminology, 26:37-55, 1988.

Greenburg, D: Age, crime and social explanation. American Journal of Sociology, 91:1-21, 1985.

Hardt, RH, & Bodine, GF: Development of self-report instruments in delinquency research. Syracuse, NY: Youth Development Center, Syracuse University, 1965.

Hardt, RH, & Peterson-Hardt, S: On determining the quality of the delinquency self-report method. Journal of Research in Crime and Delinquency, 14:247-261, 1977.

Hessing, DJ, Elffers, H, & Weigel, RH: Exploring the limits of self-reports and reasoned action: An investigation of the psychology of tax evasion behavior. Journal of Personality and Social Psychology, 54:405-413, 1988.

Hindelang, MJ, Hirschi, T, & Weis, JG: Measuring delinquency. Beverly Hills: Sage Publications, 1981.

Hughes, SP, & Dodder, RA: Alcohol consumption indices: Format comparisons. Journal of Studies on Alcohol, 49:100-103, 1988.

Huizinga, D, & Elliott, DS: Reassuring the reliability and validity of self-report delinquency measures. Journal of Quantitative Criminology, 2:293-327, 1986.

Hunt, LG: Incidence and prevalence of drug use and abuse. In DuPont, RI, Goldstein, A, & O'Donnell, JO (Eds.), Handbook on drug abuse. Washington, DC: U.S. Government Printing Office, 1979.

Law Enforcement Assistance Administration: San Jose methods test of known crime victims. Washington, DC: U.S. Government Printing Office, 1972.

Loftus, EF, & Marburger, W: Since the eruption of Mt. St. Helens, has anybody beaten you up? Improving the accuracy of retrospective reports with landmark events. Memory and Cognition, 11:114-120, 1983.

Menard, S, & Elliott, DS: Longitudinal and cross-sectional data collection and analysis in the sociological study of crime and delinquency. Unpublished paper. Boulder, Colorado: Institute of Behavioral Science, 1988.

Murphy, FJ, Shirley, MM, & Witmer, HL: The incidence of hidden delinquency. American Journal of Orthopsychiatry, 16:686-696, 1946.

National Research Council: Surveying crime. Panel for the evaluation of crime surveys. Washington, DC: National Academy of Sciences, 1976.

Pelz, DC, & Lew, RA: Heise's causal model applied. In Borgatta, EF, & Bohrnstedt, GW (Eds.), Sociological Methodology. San Francisco: JosseyBass, pp. 28-37, 1970.

Porterfield, A: Youth in trouble. Fort Worth, TX: Leo Potisham Foundation, 1946.

Reiss, AJ, Jr: Inappropriate theories and inadequate methods as policy plaques: Self-reported delinquency and the law. In Demerath, NJ, III et al. (Eds.), Social policy and sociology. New York: Academic Press, 1975.

Schneider, AL: Portland forward records check of crime victims. U.S. Department of Justice, Washington, DC: U.S. Government Printing Office, 1978.

Schuman, H, & Presser, S: Questions and answers in attitude surveys. New York: Academic Press, 1981.

Shinnar, R, & Shinnar, S: The effects of the criminal justice system on the control of crime: A quantitative approach. Law and Society Review, 9:581-611.

Short, JF, Jr., & Nye, FI: Reported behavior as a criterion of deviant behavior. Social Problems, 5:207-213, 1957.

Sparks, RF, Glenn, HG, & Dodd, DJ: Surveying victims. New York: John Wiley and Sons, 1977.

186

Sudman, S, & Bradburn, NM: Asking questions: A practical guide to questionnaire design. San Francisco: Jossey-Bass, 1982.

Sudman, S, & Bradburn, NM: Response effects in surveys: A review and synthesis. Chicago: Aldine Press, 1974.

Tracy, PE: An analysis of the incidence and seriousness of self-reported delinquency and crime. Unpublished Ph.D. dissertation. University of Pennsylvania. Ann Arbor: University Microfilms International, 1978.

Wallerstein, JS, & Wyle, CJ: Our law abiding law-breakers. Probation, 25:107-112, 1947.

Weis, JG: Issues in the measurement of criminal careers. In Blumstein, A, & Cohen, J (Eds.), Criminal careers and career criminals, Vol. II. Washington, DC: National Academy Press, pp. 1-51, 1986.

Wolfgang, ME, Figlio, RM, & Sellin, T: Delinquency in a birth cohort. Chicago: University of Chicago Press, 1972.

PREVALENCE AND INCIDENCE IN THE STUDY OF ANTISOCIAL BEHAVIOR:
DEFINITIONS AND MEASUREMENTS

Dan Olweus
Department of Personality Psychology
University of Bergen, Bergen, Norway

1. CURRENT DEFINITIONS IN EPIDEMIOLOGY

In epidemiology, the concepts of prevalence and incidence are
central (Bradford Hill, 1977; Last, 1983; Morris, 1975). Basically,
prevalence (or prevalence rate) refers to the number of diseases or
spells of disease existing at a particular point in time or within a
specified time period related to the total number of persons exposed to
risk (a population or a defined group of people). Incidence (or incidence rate) on the other hand measures the rate of appearance of new
cases in the group or population, i.e., the number of diseases/spells
of disease beginning within a specified period of time related to the
total number of persons exposed to risk during that period.[1]
In definitions of prevalence and incidence the basic units of
observation are usually persons, but they can also consist of events/
diseases/spells of disease (Cooper & Shepherd, 1972; Morris, 1975). As
an example of the latter usage, health service statistics typically
deal not in persons but in events, i.e., in spells of episodes of diseases. This practice is convenient and useful for providing estimates
of the demands made on the health services or of services delivered
(Morris, 1975). At the same time, there are certain disadvantages
associated with this usage which make it less desirable for many other
purposes.[2]
The basic characteristics of the concepts of prevalence and

----

1. The terms prevalence and incidence are often used as synonymous
with prevalence rate and incidence rate, a practice that is followed in
this chapter. It should be noted, however, that prevalence and
incidence sometimes refer to the absolute number of diseases (persons
having the disease) existing, or absolute number of new cases
beginning, within a specified time period etc., in a defined population
(see Last, 1983).

2. These problems are basically the same as those discussed in connection
with the measure "average frequency of antisocial acts per group member;"
see section entitled "Comments and recommendations."

M. W. Klein (ed.), Cross-National Research in Self-Reported Crime and Delinquency, 187–201.
© 1989 by Kluwer Academic Publishers.

incidence as commonly used in epidemiology are evident from the definitions given in Table 1.

TABLE 1. Current definitions of prevalence and incidence in epidemiology

Cumulative prevalence rate	=	Number of diseases (persons having the disease) existing at any time within period from birth up to specified age/time point x 100
		Number of persons exposed to risk (a group or population) during that period
Period prevalence rate	=	Number of diseases (persons having the disease) existing at any time within specified time period x 100
		Number of persons exposed to risk during that period
Incidence rate	=	Number of diseases beginning (persons contracting the disease) within specified time period x 100
		Number of persons exposed to risk during that period

As mentioned above, incidence is based on the rate with which a disease or disorder arises during a defined period of time. The incidence rate is considered to be of particular value in discovering risk factors -- causes and precursors -- "which lead up to the onset of disease, and in judging the outcome of attempts at primary prevention" (Morris, 1975, p. 266). Factors existing at the time of onset or preceding onset of the disorder can be related, possibly in a causal way, to the disorder. The incidence rate is also essential for describing age-related development and historical trends.

Since prevalence is an expression of the amount or "volume" of disease existing in a population at a specified point in time (point prevalence), during a particular period (period prevalence), or up to a certain time point or age (cumulative prevalence), independent of time of onset, this rate is considered less useful than the incidence rate in searching for causes of a disease. The prevalence rate depends both on incidence and the duration of a disorder, and a change in prevalence rate may reflect a change in incidence, in duration of the disorder (outcome), or both. The causal factors as well as the disease have often come into existence at some period before the time of observation. (However, the prevalence rate also includes all cases of the disease beginning within the specified time period.) It is obvious that the factors affecting the incidence or onset of a disorder may be partly different from those influencing its prevalence. For example, the "causes" leading to onset of smoking behavior (incidence) which are mainly social-psychological in nature (peer pressure, modeling), are at least partly different from the factors contributing to its maintenance or continuation (reflected in the prevalence rate), e.g., physiological dependence (in this example we regard smoking behavior as a "disorder").

2. "TRANSLATIONS" OF THE CONCEPTS. SOME PRELIMINARY CAUTIONS

When we want to apply the concepts of incidence and prevalence to the field of criminology or antisocial behavior, we face certain problems. One problem relates to the specification of a counterpart of a "disease" or "spell of disease." The most natural counterpart seems to be <u>an antisocial or criminal act (a crime)</u> defined, for example, as an act or a behavior that can be viewed as a <u>violation of a legal/formal or informal social rule</u> (Olweus & Endresen, in preparation). However, in using this "translation" of the disease concept, we must note certain features that distinguish an antisocial act from a disease. Most diseases can be described as having an onset, a course of development, and an outcome, but this is not the case with an antisocial act, or only in a very superficial way. The completion of a particular antisocial act cannot readily be interpreted as signifying the end of "an antisocial process" in the way a spell or process of influenza can be considered finished when the infected person has recovered.

A second and related problem is associated with the fact that a criminal act such as breaking into the coin box of a pay phone, committed by a teenager for the first time in his or her life, in many cases can be viewed as an expression or reflection of a more or less stable tendency or predisposition to antisocial behavior that has been in evidence a long time before this particular criminal act was carried out. It is often possible to identify early forms of antisocial behavior of a similar nature in the life of the offender. Accordingly, one may ask in what sense the breaking into the coin box represents a completely new behavior (cf. discussion of predisposing factors in the section entitled "Some conceptual distinctions").

The preceding considerations certainly do not preclude a meaningful use of the concepts of incidence and prevalence in the field of antisocial or criminal behavior, but they should caution us against employing them in an uncritical and indiscriminate way without due consideration of the nature of the phenomena under study. In addition, to get a fuller understanding of the acts and processes involved, I believe it is necessary to specify a kind of broad conceptual model which can serve as a framework for our thinking about these issues and for guiding our research efforts. Some suggestions about the specification of such a model will be briefly presented in a later section.

3. CURRENT USES IN CRIMINOLOGY

In criminology, the concept of prevalence has usually been defined in a way that corresponds naturally to the usage found in epidemiology (e.g., Ball, Ross, & Simpson, 1964; Gordon & Gleser, 1974; Farrington, 1986). Thus, there has been little ambiguity or controversy about the definition of prevalence. As in epidemiology, it has been common practice to make a distinction between cumulative, period, and point prevalence rates. Generally, we can state that the <u>cumulative prevalence rate</u> measures the proportion or <u>percentage of individuals</u> in a specified group or population <u>who have ever committed a certain antisocial act</u> or offense (defined by some explicit criterion, usually on the basis of self-reports or official records) up to a certain time point or age. This measure is thus obtained by dividing the number of persons (usually multiplied by 100) in the group/population who have <u>committed the act a least once</u> up to the specified time point or age by the (average) total number of persons in the group/population ("exposed to risk"). The <u>period prevalence rate</u> measures the proportion of individuals in the group or population who have committed the antisocial act at least once within certain age or time limits, for example, between the thirteenth and fourteenth birthday or during the past year. The concept of <u>point prevalence,</u> defined as the proportion of individuals in a group or population who have committed an antisocial act at a specified point in time, e.g., on a particular day of the month, does not seem to have been much used in criminology.

Although there has been considerable consensus in the criminological literature on the definition of prevalence measures, this is not the case with <u>incidence.</u> At least three different definitions (or derivatives of them) have been employed.

1) Incidence has been used to refer to the <u>average frequency</u> with which a certain antisocial act or offense has been committed in the whole group/population of interest within certain age or time limits. This measure is obtained by dividing the number or frequency of acts by the total number of individuals in the group (offenders as well as nonoffenders) which thus gives the <u>average offense rate per group member</u> (possibly multiplied by 100 to give average frequency for the act per 100 persons; e.g., Elliott & Huizinga, 1983; Empey, 1982). Official statistics on (age-specific) aggregate arrest or crime rates are typically of this kind (though usually expressed as number of crimes or arrests per 100,000 population).

2) The <u>individual crime rate or lambda</u> (Blumstein & Cohen, 1979) has also been used as a measure of incidence (e.g., Farrington, Ohlin, & Wilson, 1986; Wilson & Herrnstein, 1985). In this case the number of antisocial acts is divided by the number of persons who have committed at least one antisocial act within the specified time or age limits. This measure thus reports the <u>average offense rate of the active offenders</u> in the group within the defined period.

3) Finally, incidence has been defined as the <u>proportion of new cases, new offenders or "newcomers"</u> in the group during the specified time span (e.g., Ball, Ross, & Simpson, 1964; Nettler, 1984). As will be elaborated in a later section, newcomer status can be specified in

two different ways. It is obvious that this definition of the incidence concept is basically the same as the one typically used in epidemiology.

4. COMMENTS AND RECOMMENDATIONS

I will briefly comment on the three definitions of incidence presented above and conclude by recommending a version of the last one for use in criminology.

The first usage of the term incidence as the average frequency (or total number) of antisocial acts (crimes/arrests, etc.) per group member (or per standard unit) may be of some utility for certain purposes such as giving information on the level of criminality or average (or total) number of crimes within a particular time period or geographical area (as compared with corresponding measures for other time periods or other geographical units, etc.). There is, however, a basic limitation to this measure in that it does not permit separation of the two distinct components making up this measure: the number of individuals having committed at least one antisocial act in the specified time period (prevalence) and the average number of acts committed by those involved in the antisocial activity in the period. Accordingly, a difference on this measure between two geographical units or time periods may be a reflection of different numbers (proportions) of offenders, different levels of antisocial activity by those involved, or both. The inherent ambiguity of this measure has contributed, for instance, to a lack of knowledge of, and controversy about, the form of the age-crime curve, for representative populations as well as for particular groups of active offenders (Blumstein, Cohen, & Farrington, 1988; Gottfredson & Hirschi, 1986; Hirschi & Gottfredson, 1983).

In addition, this "incidence" measure does not focus on the frequency of new cases arising during the defined period of time, which is a key element in the traditional epidemiological definition of incidence. In the study of epidemiological issues, such a focus is essential for several reasons, some of which were indicated in the introduction. It can thus be concluded that the "average frequency per group member" definition of incidence has very little in common with the incidence concept as used in epidemiology. I suggest that this definition of incidence be abandoned in criminology (although the measure as such may be retained and used for particular purposes but preferably with a designation such as "average frequency of antisocial acts per group member" rather than incidence).

The second measure of "incidence" defined as the individual crime rate or the average offense rate of the offenders does not suffer from the inherent ambiguity of interpretation characterizing the first measure of "incidence" (above). This measure is useful for describing the level or "degree of individual criminal activity by those who are active offenders" (Blumstein et al., 1988, p. 4). However, as was the case with the first definition of "incidence," this measure has very little to do with the incidence concept as defined in epidemiology. Accordingly, I suggest that this way of specifying incidence also be avoided in criminology.

As indicated, the third definition of incidence as the proportion of new cases (i.e., new offenders or newcomers) in the group/population during the specified time span is very similar to the one typically found in epidemiology. And as in epidemiology, status as a new case can be specified in two different ways. One is to define a new case as a person who commits the antisocial act (or any antisocial act) in the period of concern but who has never before committed the act (or any antisocial act). Such a measure thus gives the proportion of first-time offenders in the group (with regard to a specific antisocial act or to any antisocial act). This way of defining status as a new case is clearly the most common in connection with incidence estimates in epidemiology (although, generally, the concept of incidence defined along these lines has not been much used in criminology).

A second way of deciding upon status as a possibly new case is to relate the current behavior not to the individual's whole foregoing life as in the first definition, but to a specified previous period in which the individual has or has not committed the antisocial act (see, e.g., Eaton, 1986). If such a usage is adopted, committing the antisocial act after a period of a certain length during which the individual did not commit the act (a period of desistance) would be counted as a new case, even if the person had committed the act in a still earlier period. Specifying a new case in this way would be similar to what is done in epidemiology in connection with certain diseases: A person who falls ill with influenza in a certain period would be classified as a new case even if s/he had had the same illness some time ago (and recovered).

In conclusion, incidence (rate) has a well-established definition in epidemiology and when applying the term to the field of criminology, it would seem useful to retain its basic meaning as the proportion of new cases in the population or group of interest within a specified time period. As explained above, status as a new case can be defined in two different ways and, consequently, it is important to be quite specific about which procedure was followed in the particular research.

The definitions of prevalence and incidence that I would like to recommend (or some variation of them) for use in criminology are presented in Table 2.

In calculating prevalence or incidence rates in a particular research project, one may focus attention on a specified antisocial act/offense or on groups of acts or any antisocial act (such as convictions, independent of the kind of antisocial act committed). Official records, self-reports and other methods involving information from teachers, peers, or parents and the like can all be used to measure the acts concerned. It should be noted, however, that use of prevalence/incidence rates in connection with composites or scales (commonly employed in self-report methods), which generally comprise a number of different antisocial acts, poses special problems which must be handled by somewhat arbitrary decision rules (see e.g., Elliott & Huizinga, 1983).

TABLE 2. Prevalence and incidence: Definitions recommended for use in criminology.

Cumulative prevalence rate	=	Number of persons having committed antisocial/criminal act at least once (offenders) up to specified age/time point x 100 ÷ Number of persons exposed to risk (a group or population) during that period
Period prevalence rate	=	Number of persons having committed antisocial/criminal act at least once (offenders) within specified time period x 100 ÷ Number of persons exposed to risk during that period
Incidence rate	=	Number of new offenders/new cases within specified time period x 100 ÷ Number of persons exposed to risk during that period
New offender/ new case defined as:	a)	Person committing antisocial/criminal act for the first time in his/her life
	b)	Person committing antisocial/criminal act for the first time after specified period of desistance

5. SOME CONCEPTUAL DISTINCTIONS

Incidence and prevalence are concepts characterizing a population or special group of interest and are not used to describe the behavior, conditions or characteristics (such as a disease or a disorder) of a single individual. In order to obtain an estimate of the incidence rate for a specified antisocial behavior or act, it is necessary to collect information at the individual level about the onset of the behavior or characteristic of concern. Such information will also be useful in describing the first phase, the stage of onset, of the "natural history" (developmental course) of the behavior/characteristic at issue. Furthermore, by systematically relating data about onset to immediately preceding or approximately concurrent changes in the individual's external or internal (such as biological) environment, it is possible to develop an understanding of factors that initiate, elicit, or precipitate the behavior/characteristic under study.

However, it is important to study not only the onset of a characteristic, but also its duration/continuation and possible termination or discontinuation (offset). Such information is valuable in describing other aspects of the "natural history" of a behavior/characteristic and will be relevant to estimates of e.g., period prevalence rates. Also, data about termination can be systematically related to approximately concurrent factors in the individual's external or internal environment (<u>terminating factors</u>) and give important clues about how to change the behavior/characteristic or its degree of changeability. Conversely, information about the continuation of a behavior/characteristic is of value in identifying factors that tend to maintain or reinforce the behavior in question (<u>maintaining factors</u>).

In certain kinds of epidemiologic studies, e.g., of simple infectious diseases, it may often be sufficient to restrict attention to initiating/precipitating factors on one hand and maintaining versus terminating factors on the other. In the field of criminology, however, it is often necessary, in particular in explanatory contexts, to take another class of variables into account.

It is well known that an individual's level of antisocial or criminal behavior in adolescence or young adulthood can be predicted more or less successfully from relatively early child rearing patterns (e.g., Loeber & Stouthamer-Loeber, 1986) or from the individual's own behavior (such as aggression) several years before the onset of criminal behavior proper (e.g., Olweus, 1979). There is also a good deal of evidence to suggest that the individual's genetic endowment is likely to affect his or her propensity to engage in antisocial behavior. As a group, this set of variables can be designated <u>predisposing factors</u>. Such factors can be regarded as precursors (e.g., aggressive behavior) of the later antisocial behavior or as factors that have an effect on the precursors (e.g., the effects of certain child rearing patterns on aggressive behavior; see Olweus, 1980). They can also have a direct (causal) effect on the later antisocial behavior itself. What the <u>predisposing factors have in common</u> is the fact that they are associated with an individual's probability of engaging in antisocial behavior (i.e., an increased probability) and that they have been in operation or can be identified, at least in principle (such as genetic endowment), considerably before initiation of the antisocial/criminal behavior proper.

For an adequate understanding of the determinants and development of antisocial behavior, in particular in a causal-analytic framework, it is important to take into account not only <u>initiating, maintaining, and terminating but also predisposing factors</u>. If such variables are not included in our conceptual models, there is considerable risk that our estimates of the causal determinants of antisocial behavior will be partly in error. In particular, we are likely to overestimate the importance of concurrent factors (such as peer pressure, school failure; see Olweus, 1983) at the expense of biological factors or environmental conditions that operated at an earlier age. Stated in more technical language, our causal model may be mis-specified and lead to biased estimates.

In sum, the preceding considerations underscore the importance of a comprehensive and differentiated conceptualization along the lines suggested for an adequate understanding of the determinants and development of antisocial behavior.

6. A NEW SELF-REPORT INSTRUMENT OF ANTISOCIAL BEHAVIOR

In the concluding sections I will give a brief description of a
new self-report instrument designed to measure different aspects of
antisocial behavior in relatively young people, primarily preadoles-
cents and adolescents. The empirical analyses to be reported were
based on data collected on four largely representative samples, each
consisting of 600-700 boys and girls in grades four through seven with
modal ages of 11-14 years. The subjects belonged to 112 classes drawn
from 42 primary schools (comprising grades one to six) and junior high
schools (comprising grades seven through nine) in Bergen, Norway. The
self-report instrument was administered, together with several other
questionnaires, at three time points separated by a one-year interval.
In this chapter, only data from the first administration, in May 1983,
will be used. For more detailed information about the project and the
self-report instrument, see Olweus, 1978, 1984, 1987a, 1987b, in press,
and Olweus and Endresen, in preparation.

In constructing the self-report instrument, we examined a number
of existing instruments, including the recent developments of Elliott
and Ageton (1980) and Hindelang, Hirschi, and Weis (1981). Although it
is clear that the latter instruments were very carefully constructed
and are quite valuable in the contexts they were designed for, we felt
that they could not be used without considerable modification in our
developmental project. In particular, they were too heavily loaded
with items concerning relatively serious offenses/crimes which would
not be very useful with our samples because of very low or zero response frequencies at all age levels. In addition, it is likely that
at least some teachers and parents would have strongly objected to the
inclusion of such items, in particular for the youngest children.[3]
Conversely, these instruments contained relatively few items on disciplinary problems and other rule-breaking behavior in school, and we
were particularly interested in including a fair amount of items of
this kind. Finally, the Elliott and Ageton and Hindelang et al. instruments were somewhat too long. Accordingly, we chose to construct our
own items, although we drew on previous instruments in selecting and
formulating several of the items.

The 23 core items of our inventory were selected from two broad

---

3. Because of resistance from some teachers and parents, approximately 20
additional items on antisocial behavior, mostly of a relatively serious
kind, including the use of narcotics, were given only to the two highest
grades, six and seven, in the first wave of measurement. These items were
placed after the items discussed in this chapter. The psychometric
characteristics of these additional items and their relationships with the
scales used here (above) will be reported in a later publication. A
complete set of items including the twenty additional items can be obtained
by writing to the author.

conceptual domains.[4]   One concerned disciplinary problems and other
rule-breaking behavior in school, while the second covered more general
and non-school related antisocial acts such as vandalism, theft, burglary, and fraud (two items could belong to either domain). The division of the items into these two broad areas, General Antisocial Behavior and School-Related Antisocial Behavior (see Table 3), was based on
both conceptual and psychometric considerations (see Olweus & Endresen,
in preparation).

A comparison of these sets of items with the contents of the instruments of Elliott and Ageton and Hindelang et al., show the expected similarities and differences. Briefly, there are items concerning
theft, burglary, vandalism, and fraud in all of these instruments, but
items on more serious crimes such as rape, robbery, assault, and prosti-
tution are missing in our inventory. On the other hand, we have included more items related to school problems.

6.1. Format

To permit estimates of cumulative and period prevalence, incidence
(when measurements at two or more time points are available), average
frequency of antisocial acts per group member, and average frequency of
antisocial acts per offender, we used a two-stage questioning technique
in the first version of the inventory. First, the subjects had to
respond YES or NO to the question whether they had ever committed the
antisocial act concerned. If they answered in the affirmative, they
were asked to estimate about how many times they had committed the act
"this spring (from Christmas until now)." The reference period thus
comprised the past five months which constituted a natural time unit
for the subjects.

The format of the inventory looked like this:

	a) Have you ever done (taken part in) this?	b) If YES, about how many times this spring (from Christmas until now?
1) Stolen money or other things from members of your family?	YES	..... times this spring
	NO	no time this spring

----

4. Since one of the overriding goals of this project was to study
bullying and other forms of aggressive behavior (e.g., Olweus, 1978,
1984, 1987a, 1987b, in press), a number of items dealing specifically
with these aspects were included in the project (in separate
inventories). Several of these items could be easily adapted to the
format of the present instrument and included in the assessment of
antisocial behavior.

Detailed instructions about how to respond were written on the
front page of the inventory. These instructions were read aloud in the
class by the research assistants administering the questionnaire.
There was also a test example on the front page, which the research
assistants went through with the subjects, allowing ample time for
questions and clarification.

Although this question-and-response format seemed to function
quite well, we decided after some experimentation to make a slight
modification in order to simplify responding further. This change was
introduced in the third wave of measurement, two years after the first
phase of data collection. The questions in that version of the inventory had the following appearance:

Have you done (taken part in) this?

1) Stolen money or other things from members of your family?	NO, never YES, in the past, but not this spring Yes, about ...... times this spring

We have not made a detailed comparison of the data obtained with
the two different designs of the inventory, but it was the research
assistants' impression, based on their contact with the students, that
the latter format made responding slightly simpler and quicker. We
recommend that this format be used in future studies with the present
instrument.

6.2. Cumulative Prevalence Values

Though it is possible to derive several different measures from
the instrument, as previously indicated, only cumulative prevalence
values (rates) for each item are reported in Table 3 (i.e., the percentage of individuals of the relevant group who had committed the act at
least once in the past five months or previously). The values for the
different items are grouped according to domain, grade/age, and sex.
Items within each domain are listed in descending order of mean cumulative prevalence rate (averaged across grade or sex without weighting in
the column farthest to the right). The number preceding the items
refers to the order in which they were presented in the inventory.

The mean cumulative prevalence rates for all of the items within a
domain are shown at the bottom of each domain table, separately for
each combination of grade and sex (again without weighting).

As evident from Table 3, there was considerable variation in the
seriousness of the antisocial acts included, as reflected in the mean
cumulative prevalence rates for the individual items. In the
domain of General Antisocial Behavior, the range was from 25.7% to
0.6%; corresponding figures for the domain of School-Related Antisocial
Behavior were 64.8% and 8.0%

198

TABLE 3. Cumulative prevalence values for the different subsamples

A Items belonging to General Antisocial Behavior Scale (GAS)	Boys Grade 4 5 6 7	Mean value for boys[a]	Girls Grade 4 5 6 7	Mean value for girls[a]	Mean for boys & girls[a]
12. Scribbled on the school building, outside or inside, or on things belonging to your school?	16 20 28 39	25.8	6 20 28 48	25.5	25.7
1. Stolen money or other things from members of your family?	22 22 29 45	29.5	14 18 16 38	21.5	25.5
22. Avoided paying for such things as movies, bus or train rides, or food?	10 11 26 47	23.5	1 3 9 34	11.8	17.6
7. Taken things worth less than 200 N.Cr. from a shop or a kiosk without paying?	10 15 22 39	21.5	2 7 9 19	9.3	15.4
19. Taken part in a "gang fight"?	22 31 21 23	24.3	3 7 6 5	5.3	14.8
11. Without permission, taking a bicycle or moped not belonging to you ("borrowed" it?)	13 14 19 22	17.0	4 6 7 11	7.0	12.0
20. Purposely destroyed or broken such things as windows, benches, telephone boothes, or mailboxes?	9 11 14 29	15.8	4 2 2 7	3.8	9.8
23. Drunk so much beer, wine, or liquor that you clearly felt drunk?	4 3 4 25	9.0	0 2 2 16	5.0	7.0
5. Falsified someone's signature to get money or other advantages?	4 1 2 12	4.8	0 0 3 4	1.8	3.3
17. Purposely destroyed seats in a bus, a movie, or other places?	2 4 3 10	4.8	0 0 1 3	1.0	2.9
10. Purposely destroyed chairs, tables, desks, or other things in your school?	1 2 4 11	4.5	0 0 0 3	0.7	2.6
15. Taken things worth more than 200 N.Cr. from a shop or kiosk without paying?	1 1 4 10	4.0	0 1 2 1	1.0	2.5
16. Broken into a shop, house, or apartment and taken something?	2 2 2 8	3.5	0 0 0 1	0.3	1.9
3. Stolen a wallet or purse while owner wasn't around?	0 0 2 3	1.3	0 0 0 1	0.3	0.8
9. Broken into a parking meter or the coin box of a pay phone?	1 1 1 2	1.3	0 0 0 0	0	0.6
Mean value	7.8 12.1 12.7 (9.2 21.7)	12.7	4.4 12.7 (2.3 5.7)	12.7 (6.3)	9.5

TABLE 3. (continued)

B Items belonging to School-Related Antisocial Behavior Scale (SAS)	Boys Grade 4	5	6	7	Mean value for boys[a]	Girls Grade 4	5	6	7	Mean value for girls[a]	Mean for boys & girls[a]
8. Come late for school in the morning?	60	66	67	75	67.0	49	69	63	69	62.5	64.8
4. Been sent out of the classroom?	49	51	47	50	49.3	9	16	18	21	16.0	32.6
13. Been detained in school after ordinary lessons were finished?	37	28	30	37	33.0	14	15	11	19	14.8	23.9
18. Sworn at a teacher?	17	20	22	38	24.3	2	4	15	25	11.5	17.9
21. Been called up to the headmaster for something wrong you had done?	22	31	20	38	27.8	2	5	3	10	5.0	16.4
14. Skipped one or two classes?	9	9	13	31	15.5	2	4	6	21	8.3	11.9
6. Had a violent quarrel with a teacher?	7	10	11	18	11.5	1	7	8	16	8.0	9.8
2. Skipped school a whole day?	5	9	5	21	10.0	3	3	4	14	6.0	8.0
Mean value	25.8	26.9	29.8		15.4 24.4						23.2
	28.0 38.5					10.3 16.0 16.5					

Note: The cumulative prevalence values were calculated as the proportion of subjects in the group who received a score of 2 (committed the act this spring) or 1 (committed the act previously but not this spring). The four male subsamples consisted of 297-368 boys each, and the four female subsamples of 264-311 girls each.
[a] Mean values were calculated without weighting according to number of subjects in the respective groups.

For all of the items, the mean cumulative percentage values were higher for boys than for girls, although the difference was small for one of them (number 12). Many of the remaining items showed fairly substantial sex differences. As regards grade/age trends, the percentages at the bottom of each domain table revealed increasing average levels from lower to higher grades for both boys and girls and for both domains.

Summarizing the results in Table 3, we can conclude that the theoretically expected sex and age/grade differences were obtained by and large, attesting to the validity of the instrument.

In addition, a number of analyses of the psychometric properties of the inventory were carried out, including internal-consistency and test-retest analyses of the three basic scales of the instrument (derived from grouping and adding the individual items): The scale of General Antisocial Behavior (GAS, fifteen items), the scale of School-Related Antisocial Behavior (SAS, eight items), and the scale of Total Antisocial Behavior (TAS, 23 items) which comprised all of the items in GAS and SAS. In addition, these scales were related to other dimensions of theoretical relevance such as scales of bullying behavior and opposition to parents, respectively, and school grades. Overall the results from these analyses were quite encouraging, indicating that the scales had satisfatory or good reliability, stability, and validity as well as theoretical relevance.

As a preliminary conclusion, it can be stated that the self-report instrument described is likely to be useful in the study of the developmental course, correlates, and antecedents of antisocial behavior.

AUTHOR NOTES

The research reported was supported by grants from the William T. Grant Foundation, the Norwegian Ministry of Education, and the Swedish Delegation for Social Research (DSF). Several of the ideas presented were developed while the author was a Fellow at the Center for Advanced Study in the Behavioral Sciences, Stanford, California, USA. He is indebted to the University of Bergen, the Spencer Foundation, the Norwegian Research Council for the Humanities and the Social Sciences, and the Center for Advanced Study in the Behavioral Sciences for financial support during his year at the Center in 1986-87.

REFERENCES

Ball, JC, Ross, A, & Simpson, A: Incidence and estimated prevalence of recorded delinquency in a metropolitan area. American Sociological Review 29:90-93, 1984.

Bradford Hill, A: A short texbook of medical statistics. London: Hodder & Stoughton, 1977.

Blumstein, A, & Cohen, J: Estimation of individual crime rates from arrest records. Journal of Criminal Law and Criminology, 70:561-585, 1979.

Blumstein, A, Cohen, J, & Farrington, DP: Criminal career research: Its value for criminology. Criminology 26:1-35, 1988.

Cooper, B, & Shepherd, M: Epidemiology and abnormal psychology. In Eysenck, HJ (Ed.), Handbook of abnormal psychology (2nd ed.). London: Pitman, 1972.

Eaton, WW: The sociology of mental disorders (2nd ed.). New York: Prager, 1986.

Elliott, DS, & Ageton, SS: Reconciling race and class differences in self-reported and official estimates of delinquency. American Sociological Review, 45:95-110, 1980.

Elliott, DS, & Huizinga, D: Social class and delinquent behavior in a national youth panel. Criminology, 21:149-177, 1983.

Empey, LT: American delinquency (rev. ed.). Homewood, Ill.: Dorsey, 1982.

Farrington, DP: Age and crime. In Tonry, M, & Morris, N (Eds.), Crime and justice, Vol. 7. Chicago: University of Chicago Press, 1986.

Farrington, DP, Ohlin, LE, & Wilson, JQ: Understanding and controlling crime. New York: Springer, 1986.

Gordon, RA, & Gleser, LJ: The estimation of prevalence of delinquency: Two approaches and a correction of the literature. Journal of Mathematical Sociology, 3:275-291, 1974.

Gottfredson, MR, & Hirschi, T: The true value of lambda would appear to be zero: An essay on career criminals, criminal careers, selective incapacitation, cohort studies, and related topics. Criminology, 24:213-233, 1986.

Hindelang, MJ, Hirschi, T, & Weis, JG: Measuring delinquency. Beverly Hills, CA: Sage Publications, 1981.

Hirschi, T, & Gottfredson, MR: Age and the explanation of crime. American Journal of Sociology, 89:552-584, 1983.

Last, JM (Ed.): A dictionary of epidemiology. New York: Oxford University Press, 1983.

Loeber, R, & Stouthamer-Loeber, M: Family factors as correlates and predictors of juvenile conduct problems and delinquency. In Tonry, M, & Morris, N (Eds.), Crime and justice, Vol. 7. Chicago: University of Chicago Press, 1986.

Morris, JN: Uses of epidemiology (3rd ed.). New York: McGraw-Hill, 1984.

Nettler, G: Explaining crime (3rd ed.). New York: McGraw-Hill, 1984.

Olweus, D: Aggression in the schools: Bullies and whipping boys. Washington, DC: Hemisphere, 1978.

Olweus, D: Stability of aggressive reaction patterns in males: A review. Psychological Bulletin, 86:852-875, 1979.

Olweus, D: Familial and temperamental determinants of aggressive behavior in adolescent boys: A causal analysis. Developmental Psychology, 16:644-660, 1980.

Olweus, D: Low school achievement and aggressive behavior in adolescent boys. In Magnusson, D, & Allen, VE (Eds.), Human development: An interactional perspective. New York: Academic Press, 1983.

Olweus, D: Aggressors and their victims: Bullying at school. In Frude, N, & Gault, H (Eds.), Disruptive behavior in schools. New York: Wiley, 1984.

Olweus, D: Bullying and harassment among school children in Scandinavia: Research and a nationwide campaign in Norway. Mimeo, 1987a.

Olweus, D: Bully/victim problems among school children in Scandinavia. In Myklebust, JP, & Ommundsen (Eds.), Psykologprofesjonen mot ar 2000: Arbeidsliv, internasjonalisering og utdannelse. Oslo: Universitetsforlaget, 1987b.

Olweus, D: Bully victim problems in school: Basic knowledge and effects of an intervention program. In Rubin, K, & Pepler, D (Eds.), The development and treatment of childhood aggression. Hillsdale, NJ: Erlbaum, in press.

Olweus, D, & Endresen, J: Assessment of antisocial behavior in preadolescence and adolescence. Manuscript, in preparation.

Wilson, JQ, & Herrnstein, RJ: Crime and human nature. New York: Simon and Schuster, 1985.

DEVELOPMENT OF A NEW MEASURE OF SELF-REPORTED ANTISOCIAL
BEHAVIOR FOR YOUNG CHILDREN: PREVALENCE AND RELIABILITY

Rolf Loeber, Magda Stouthamer-Loeber, Welmoet B. Van Kammen
Western Psychiatric Institute and Clinic, School of Medicine,
University of Pittsburgh, Pittsburgh, Pennsylvania, USA
and
David P. Farrington
Institute of Criminology, University of Cambridge
Cambridge, United Kingdom

1. INTRODUCTION

Delinquent careers, typically, have been thought to begin in adolescence (ages 12 to 16) rather than during late childhood (7 to 11).
The commission of offenses by elementary school aged youngsters, however, has attracted more attention from criminologists in recent years,
which has resulted in some new insights. First, offenders now are said
to engage in delinquent acts at an earlier age than was previously
thought. Second, an early onset of offending, according to some
studies, is predictive not only of longer offending careers but also of
higher rates of offending during the career. Third, surveys show that
a surprising proportion of elementary school age children commit offenses that do not lead to criminal prosecution, and thus do not show up in
crime statistics (Loeber, 1987).
      Self-reported offending questionnaires have rarely been given to
pre-teenage children. Richards, Berk, and Forster (1979), however,
reported results obtained from a questionnaire completed by 748 5th and
6th grade children (aged 11-12 mainly) living in a middle class Chicago
suburb. Nearly three quarters (74%) reported ever having had beer or
wine, 23% had had hard liquor, 26% had committed minor shoplifting, 45%
had fought with another student, 22% had defaced property, 21% had
cheated on a test, 9% had damaged property, 5% had been truant, 3.9%
had used marijuana, 2.7% had run away from home, and 1.5% had stolen a
bicycle. These results are reinforced by findings from other studies.
Klemke (1978) found that by age 10, 50% of a sample of boys and girls
had reported shoplifting. Likewise, Elliott, Knowles, and Canter
(1981), reporting on the findings from the National Youth Survey, found
that 8% of a sample of 11-year-old boys and girls had stolen something
of less than $5 value in the past year, and 14% had stolen from their
family. Remarkably, none of the studies surveyed reported on sex specific prevalence rates.
      Prevalence rates of antisocial behaviors based on children's self-
report can be compared with that based on parent or teacher report.
Typically, prevalence rates of theft based on information from parents
or teachers were lower than the rates based on the child's self-report

M. W. Klein (ed.), Cross-National Research in Self-Reported Crime and Delinquency, 203–225.
© *1989 by Kluwer Academic Publishers.*

in late childhood (Achenbach & Edelbrock, 1981; Glidewell, 1968; Loeber, 1987; Rutter, Tizard, and Whitmore, 1970). Whether this is also the case for very young children, however, is not yet known.

The study of offending in late childhood is severely hampered by the lack of self-report instruments designed for use with young populations. Not uncommonly, instruments designed for older age groups have been used for 10 to 12 year-olds, sometimes with only minor modifications (Richards, Berk, & Forster, 1979; Loeber & Dishion, 1984). As far as we are aware, no studies have examined the reliability of self-report antisocial measures for children of that age, much less younger children.

Prior efforts to measure self-report delinquency in elementary school age youngsters were inhibited by concerns that the children (a) might not understand the language of existing survey instruments, (b) might have limited knowledge of the types of offenses to be measured, and (c) might have difficulties in accurately estimating the frequency of their delinquent acts. The crucial question of how to establish the reliability of children's responses to delinquency surveys has not been fully addressed. For young children, under the age of criminal responsibility, reliability cannot be established by comparing the youngsters' self-reports to official records of arrests as has been done for adolescents (Hindelang, Hirschi, & Weis, 1981). Since such an external criterion cannot be used, we must assess the reliability of a self-reported measure for children's antisocial behavior by various, less direct ways. One of these is to measure the concordance between the youngster's self-report and reports by parents and teachers on the child's antisocial behaviors noted within the same time frame.

There has been a great deal of prior research on the agreement between self-reports, teacher ratings and parent ratings of child problems. Achenbach, McConaughy, and Howell (1987) carried out a meta-analysis of 119 studies. The average (weighted) correlation between self-reports and teacher ratings was .20, and between self-reports and parent ratings was .25. The correlations were higher for undercontrolled problems (such as aggression, delinquency, and hyperactivity) than for overcontrolled ones (such as anxiety and withdrawal); the correlations were also higher at age 6-11 than at age 12-19. Along that same line, it is not uncommon for parents of older children to be less aware of the mischief their children get into than it is for parents of younger children (Loeber & Schmaling, 1985). On the basis of these studies, we do not expect very high concordance of parent-child and teacher-child reports. However, whether or not a child reported a behavior, given that the parent reported the same behavior, may be a more important criterion of agreement than a correlation.

This chapter addresses the following questions:
1) How well do 1st and 4th grade boys understand questions in a survey of self-reported antisocial behavior?
2) What is the "ever" and "six-month" prevalence of antisocial behaviors reported by these boys?
3) To what extent is the child report reliable or concordant when compared with the parent or teacher report?

These questions are addressed in a longitudinal study entitled

"Progressions in Antisocial and Delinquent Child Behavior," currently underway at the University of Pittsburgh School of Medicine. The present paper is a preliminary step toward the development and evaluation of a new self-report delinquency measure for elementary school aged boys. The measure estimates the boys' understanding of selected items, uses simple language, and has categorical rather than frequency answers.

2. METHODS

2.1. Subjects

The subjects were 2573 first, fourth, and seventh grade boys enrolled in public schools in Pittsburgh, PA., who were included in the initial assessment of a prospective longitudinal survey in the Spring of 1987 (n=743) and 1988 (n=1830), when their average ages were 6.9, 10.2, and 13.2 years. In the first year of subject acquisition, eighteen elementary and six middle schools were selected, leaving the remaining 29 elementary and eight middle schools to be covered in the second subject acquisition wave. Four out of the 47 elementary schools declined to participate; in order to have a sufficient number of subjects, one randomly selected middle school participated in both subject acquisition waves. The effect on the representativeness of the available pool of subjects in participating schools, averaged over the two years of subject acquisition, compared with all subjects in the Pittsburgh Public Schools was minimal with regard to racial distribution (a difference of 1.7 percentage points for grades 1 and 4, and .6 for 7th grade), and achievement scores (no difference for grades 1 and 4; a difference of 1 percentage point for grade 7).

The procedures in both subject acquisition waves were similar; therefore, the figures given below are those of the two waves combined. Names and addresses of all 1st, 4th, and 7th grade boys in participating schools were provided to us by staff of the Board of Public Education. Parents were sent a letter briefly explaining the study and announcing that an interviewer would contact them. Families were paid $12.50 per interview, while seventh grade boys received an additional $5. Of the 4482 names and addresses, a random selection of 3452 names was gradually released to the interviewers. At the end of the interview period, 2584 boys had been interviewed, of whom 11 proved to be ineligible, resulting in a sample of 849 first graders, 868 fourth graders, and 856 seventh graders. A total of 465 families refused to participate. The remaining 403 names, released to interviewers, included a number of ineligible children (N = 82) such as girls, children in wrong grades, those not in participating schools, and more than one qualifying child per family. Another 82 names were ineligible because the children moved to an address outside the city. In addition, 62 children could not be located, even with the help of the schools, most likely because their parents had deliberately provided false addresses in order to enroll children in particular schools (in which case these children would be ineligible, if found). At the close of the interview phase, 177 families remained uninterviewed, of whom 50 (28%) had already agreed to participate; however, these could not be interviewed within the time frame and were not required to reach the target sample size of 750 in the first wave and 1800 in the second wave. Contact had been made with the remaining 127 families, those contacts ranging from the leaving of a letter, to actually talking with them.

However, the contact had not progressed to the point of either a commitment to participate or a refusal before the closing date of the subject acquisition wave. It is reasonable to assume that these 177 families did not constitute a group which is different from the remainder of the sample in regard to their refusal rate. The overall cooperation rate has been calculated as the number of completed eligible interviews divided by the number of completed eligible interviews plus the number of refusals, yielding a rate of 84.7%.

The cooperation rate was not uniform across grades; it was 84.6% for first grade, 86.0% for fourth grade, and 83.5% for seventh grade. The slightly higher refusal rate for seventh graders reflects the fact that, although at all ages the boy as well as the parent were required to give consent to participate, the seventh graders exercised their right to refuse (and disagreed with the parent) more often than the younger boys, who generally went along with the parent's decision.

The cooperation rate in the current study compares favorably with that of other longitudinal studies on antisocial child behavior. A review of such studies by Capaldi and Patterson (1987) showed a participation range from 52% to 100%, with a median of 75%. In most of the reviewed studies, however, the parental involvement was limited to giving permission. In their own study, Capaldi and Patterson (1987) achieved a 74.4% participation rate by utilizing a more lavish financial incentive system for both interviewers and families than is generally feasible in research studies.

Table 1 shows some characteristics of the sample of the current study. First and fourth grade boys came from classrooms in the same elementary schools, while 7th grade boys came from middle schools. The percentages of Black boys in the final sample were 54.3, 51.8, and 53.5 for first, fourth and seventh graders, respectively. This compares to 56.4%, 54.0% and 54.2% for the first, fourth, and seventh grade Black enrollment district wide, averaged over the two years of subject acquisition (Pittsburgh Public Schools, 1986, 1987).

A little over half of the boys (56.2%) lived in households where the main caretaker (in 92.3% of the cases the natural mother) was separated, divorced, widowed, or never married. In 42.3% of the households there was no father or acting father. About one fifth (21.2%) of the mothers or acting mothers living with the child had not completed high school, while at the other extreme 17.3% had a college degree; for fathers or acting fathers living with the child, these figures were 30.6% and 20.9%, respectively.

2.2. Procedure

Boys were interviewed in their homes while, simultaneously, the caretaker completed several questionnaires. The person designated as the main caretaker was, in 91.1% of the cases, the natural, step, or adoptive mother. In 3% and 5.6% of the cases, the main caretaker was the grandmother or the father, respectively. The remainder of the children lived with various other relatives or foster parents. For ease of exposition, the main caretaker will be called the parent. The interview with the boy lasted approximately an hour, and care was taken to conduct it in private. All interviews were conducted within three month periods in the Spring of 1987 and 1988. Soon after all the families had been interviewed, the teachers completed questionnaires for each of the boys participating in the study. Cooperation by the teachers was on a voluntary basis, and the school district did not allow us to remunerate teachers for their time. Nevertheless, complete questionnaires were obtained for 95.4%, 94.6%, and 97.5% of the 1st, 4th, and 7th graders, respectively.

TABLE 1. Characteristics of the sample.

	Grade 1	Grade 4	Grade 7
Number of subjects	849	868	856
Average age	6.9	10.2	13.2
% Black	54.3	51.8	53.5
% Living with natural mother	94.2	91.7	90.9
% Living with natural father	45.0	45.6	40.8
% Not living with (acting) father	43.9	39.5	43.5
% (acting) mother not completed high school	20.5	20.6	22.5
% (acting) mother with college degree	16.0	16.4	19.5
% (acting) father not completed high school	29.0	29.1	33.9
% (acting) father with college degree	20.6	20.0	22.3

2.3. Measures

2.3.1. Seventh grade boys. Seventh graders were administered a 40-item self-report delinquency questionnaire (SRD) and a 16-item drug questionnaire, based on the National Youth Survey, developed by Elliott and his colleagues, which has been evaluated extensively (Elliott, Huizinga, & Ageton, 1985). For each delinquency or drug item, the boys were asked whether they had ever done it, and how often they had done it in the past six months. The "ever" questions had a yes-no format, whereas for the questions pertaining to the past six months the actual frequencies were recorded.

2.3.2. First and fourth grade boys. The self-report delinquency questionnaire (SRD) used with the seventh grade boys was judged to be too difficult for first and fourth graders to understand, and not all items applied to this younger age group. Therefore, a new 33-item Self-Report Antisocial Behavior Scale (SRA) was developed. Another rationale for developing the SRA was that a number of the behaviors in the SRD were age-inappropriate, or would have an exceedingly low base rate for early elementary school-age boys. Examples of the former in the SRD were: being drunk in a public place, lying about one's age to get into a movie or to buy alcohol, using checks illegally, and committing rape. One example of the latter in the SRD was: theft (categorized according to value), which in the SRA was split into theft in different locations without specifying the value; another example in the SRD was hitting to hurt without specifying the victim, which was changed in the SRA to hitting specific victims such as teachers, parents, students, or siblings. Thus, the SRA was shorter and at times used wording slightly different from the SRD (e.g., taking something that does not belong to you vs. stealing). In addition, certain items were repeated, specifying different situations or persons in order to make the content less abstract (this was done for damage, stealing, and hitting). An abbreviated listing of the SRA items can be found in Appendix 1.

When there was doubt about whether young children would understand what was meant, a series of questions preceded the item to ascertain whether the boy knew its meaning. First, the interviewer would read a sentence containing the behavior and ask the child whether he knew what that meant. If the child said yes, he was asked to give an example. If the child did not understand the behavior or had difficulty giving an example, the interviewer gave an example and then asked the child again to give an example. If the child still did not understand the behavior, the question was skipped. Exceptions to this procedure were the items for smoking marijuana and sniffing glue, for which no explanation was provided by the interviewer to the child. The reason for this was that, whereas items such as damage, hitting someone, or taking something, fall within the child's experience, either as part of his own repertoire or by observation; this may not be the case for smoking marijuana and sniffing glue. The explanation of these two behaviors was withheld for ethical reasons in order to avoid any possibility of raising the child's curiosity about those acts. As with the scale for the older children, "ever" and "past six months" information was collected. For the "ever" questions the answer format was "yes-no;" for the "past six months" questions the answer format was "never," "once or twice," and "more often."

For all children, the time frame of the past six months was discussed before the questions were asked, and personal events, as well as dates such as Christmas or the beginning of school, were used to delineate the time period.

2.3.3. Parent. The parent completed an extensive demographic questionnaire on the entire family. In addition, a revision of the Child Behavior Checklist (CBCL) was administered (Achenbach, 1978; Achenbach & Edelbrock, 1979, 1983). The CBCL is a 112-item questionnaire about a wide range of child behavior problems, such as anxiety, depression, compulsions, oppositional behaviors, hyperactivity, and delinquency. The instrument has been widely used and has adequate test-retest reliability (Achenbach & Edelbrock, 1983). However, specific delinquent behaviors and concealing rather than aggressive antisocial behaviors, such as various forms of dishonesty and minor forms of property infraction, were under-represented. Therefore, 88 items were added in this study to cover concealing antisocial behaviors and most of the behaviors from the self-report delinquency scale. The time frame for the CBCL was the past six months. The answer format is "not true," "somewhat or sometimes true," and "very true or often true." In addition, an "ever" scale was created for 21 antisocial items with a "yes-no" answer format.

2.3.4. Teacher. Teachers completed a revised version of the Teacher Report Form of the Child Behavior Checklist (TRF) (Edelbrock & Achenbach, 1984). Twenty-three delinquent and concealing antisocial behavior items were added to this scale in order to increase its comparability with the child and parent reports. The answer format for the TRF was the same as for the parent CBCL. It was, of course, not possible to ask teachers the "ever" questions.

2.4. Variables

The various instruments did not all have the same items, and the items in common were not always phrased in exactly the same way. We will compare only those items which were phrased the same way or in which the meaning had not been materially altered. The wordings of the majority of the items in the CBCL and the TRF were identical, and the wordings of the items added to the original CBCL and TRF were the same as in the SRA. Original items on the CBCL and the TRF, however, vary sometimes from the SRA and the SRD items, e.g., shoplifting in the CBCL vs. taking something from a store without paying for it in the SRA and SRD.

2.5. Analyses

The primary aim of the analyses is to examine the reliability of the child report on the SRA. First, findings on the children's understanding the questions are presented. Second, the prevalence patterns found for first and fourth graders will be compared, with the expectation that prevalence is higher for fourth than for first graders. Comparisons will refer to the prevalence of specific behaviors and total prevalence rates summed across different antisocial acts. Third, we will compute the association between parent and child reports of selected antisocial behavior observable by parents. A fourth form of reliability consists of the percent of children who report a particular antisocial behavior, given that the parent reported that behavior within the same time frame. This is based on the assumption that parents are usually more reliable informants, and that, at a minimum, the child would be expected to report those acts of which the parent has knowledge. (The reverse probability that the adult reports the child's antisocial behavior, given that the child reports the same behavior, appears less useful as an indicator of reliability, because many anti-social child behaviors occur outside the purview of adults.)

Finally, the degree of concordance between the child and parent reports can be expressed by means of Relative Improvement Over Chance (Loeber & Dishion, 1983). This is an index of association which, compared to other indexes, such as phi, has the advantage of correcting for chance and for differences in the marginal totals of 2 by 2 tables. Specifically, Relative Improvement Over Chance (RIOC) is related to phi in that RIOC = phi/maximum phi, and is related to Kappa in that RIOC = Kappa/maximum Kappa (Farrington & Loeber, 1988). RIOC is more interpretable than either phi or Kappa because it ranges from 0 to 1 for associations stronger than chance.

3. RESULTS

3.1. Understanding

The first issue addressed was the degree to which 1st and 4th grade boys understood eight questions concerning antisocial behavior. The results are presented in Table 2. With only two exceptions, the great majority of boys appear to have understood each item. For example, 91.3% of the 1st grade boys and 98.5% of the 4th grade boys understood the question about stealing a bicycle. The least understood questions were those pertaining to smoking marijuana (24.5% and 81.4% for grades 1 and 4, respectively), and sniffing glue (18.3% and 35.7%, respectively). Table 2 shows that children's understanding of the questions increased with grade, as would be expected.

TABLE 2. Percent of 1st and 4th grade boys who understood certain questions.

	% Boys who understood question	
	1st Grade	4th Grade
damage on purpose	85.1	97.9
steal bicycle	91.3	98.5
cheat on school tests	92.0	99.7
hit someone	98.8	99.6
skip school	75.0	99.6
smoke marijuana	24.5	81.1
sniff glue	18.3	35.7
avoid paying	81.0	95.5

3.2. Reliability of "Ever" Prevalence

Table 3 shows the "ever" prevalence for particular antisocial behaviors, based on youngster's self-report and, wherever possible, the report by the parent on the same behavior. For example, 7.9% of the 1st graders and 19.5% of the 4th graders reported having stolen from

TABLE 3. Ever prevalence rates (%) based on boys' self-reports and parents' reports of child antisocial behavior.

	Grade 1 (N = 849)		Grade 4 (N = 868)	
	B	P	B	P
damage at home	14.5	---	26.7	---
damage at school	3.7	---	10.3	---
damage at other places	9.9	---	26.7	---
street vandalism	5.3	4.8	13.3	4.5
fire setting	3.5	10.0	6.0	13.2
Total damage	26.0		51.2	
steal bike	2.6	.6	2.8	2.5
shoplift	7.9	7.7	19.5	11.2
steal money at home	8.7	---	22.6	---
steal other at home	7.2	---	20.5	---
(steal at home)	---	13.5	----	19.7
steal at school	4.6	5.1	11.8	7.2
steal elsewhere	4.9	12.4	8.9	17.1
steal from car	1.8	---	3.1	---
steal from building	.8	1.2	2.9	2.8
avoid paying	6.2	---	9.7	---
robbery	.8	---	2.2	---
Total theft	26.0	21.6	53.1	29.8

B = Boy as informant; P = Parent as informant.

(Table 3 continued)

	Grade 1 (N = 849)		Grade 4 (N = 868)	
	B	P	B	P
hit teacher	5.1	1.4	6.9	2.5
hit parent	8.5	12.5	8.5	7.6
hit student	38.3	34.4	72.2	55.5
hit sibling	48.9	54.2	64.3	61.9
hidden weapon	2.9	1.6	7.3	2.1
rowdy in public	10.0	---	19.4	---
thrown rocks	11.0	---	23.5	---
Total violence	66.3	66.7	91.2	77.3
drink beer	7.8	---	11.9	---
drink wine	3.1	---	4.5	---
drink liquor	1.1	---	1.8	---
smoke	3.4	---	9.3	---
use marijuana	.4	---	.5	---
sniff glue	1.2	---	1.8	---
Total substance use	12.7		21.0	
school suspension	9.0	7.5	26.3	30.4
cheat test	7.5	3.3	14.1	4.4
skip school	5.2	1.5	7.8	5.9
run away	3.8	1.9	6.6	5.2
trespass	12.0	---	21.0	---
Total status offenses	28.5	13.2	47.0	36.5

B = Boy as informant; P = Parent as informant.

shops. The respective figures for parent report were 7.7% and
11.2%. The most prevalent antisocial behavior was hitting siblings,
admitted by 48.9% of the first and 64.3% of the fourth graders, fairly
close to parents' estimates. In fourth grade, hitting other students
was about as prevalent as hitting siblings (72.2%).

It should be noted that prevalence estimates presented in Table 3
are based on the assumption that boys who did not understand the question had not engaged in the behavior. We cannot entirely exclude,
however, the possibility that some of those who did not understand the
question had engaged in the behavior. If we assume that the maximum
prevalence of the behavior among those who did not understand the question would be the same as the prevalence for those who understood it,
then we can establish an upper limit for the prevalence of the entire
sample. In most cases the range thus established was quite narrow
(i.e., within one percentage point). The range was larger, however,
for those questions which a sizeable number of children did not understand. For first graders the following behaviors fell into this category: smoking marijuana (prevalence range from .4% to 1.4%), sniffing
glue (1.2% to 6.5%), and skipping school (5.2% to 6.9%). For fourth
graders only sniffing glue had a relatively wide range (1.8% to 5.2%).

Table 3 shows that, as expected, the prevalence of most antisocial
behaviors in 4th grade was higher than the prevalence in 1st grade.
The prevalence doubled or almost doubled from grade 1 to grade 4 for
all damage items, all theft items except bike theft and avoid paying,
and all status offenses, except skipping school. There was also an
increase in the prevalence for the violence items. The prevalence for
hitting teachers was slightly higher in grade 4 compared with grade 1.
Hitting a sibling, the item with the highest prevalence in grade 1, was
only one third higher in grade 4. The least increase in prevalence was
found for the substance use items, with the exception of smoking, which
is substantially higher in grade 4 than in grade 1. The summary
scores, shown in Table 3, reflect these increases, with the total prevalence of damaging or stealing property being about twice as high for
4th graders compared to 1st graders (51.2% vs 26.0%, and 53.1% vs.
26.0%, respectively). The total admitted violence was 66.3% for 1st
graders, and 91.2% for 4th graders, compared to 12.7% and 21.0% for the
total prevalence of substance use. The total prevalence of status
offenses was 28.5% for the 1st graders and 47.0% for 4th graders. In
summary, the ever prevalence showed that a large proportion of boys,
especially those in the fourth grade, had engaged in some types of
antisocial behaviors. Presumably, many of these behaviors were of
minor seriousness, but this was not clear from the data.

One method for establishing the reliability of the youngsters'
self-report is to compare the child's ever prevalence with that of the
parent report. This is possible for those items in the questionnaires
where it can be assumed that parents would probably be aware of the
child's behaviors. Examples are the child's suspension from school and
overt antisocial acts. Table 3 shows that the ever prevalence of
school suspension based on 1st graders' report (9.0%) compares reasonably well with that based on parent report (7.5%). The figures for the
4th grade were 26.3% and 30.4%, respectively, again fairly comparable.

TABLE 4. Percent child report given the parent report of the same antisocial behavior.

	Grade 1 (N = 849)	Grade 4 (N = 868)	Grade 7 (N = 856)
street vandalism	9.8 (41)*	10.3 (39)	
fire setting	12.9 (85)	18.3 (115)	15.9 (88)
steal bike	60.0 (5)	45.0 (20)	
shoplift	26.2 (65)	45.4 (97)	58.7 (121)
steal at school	18.6 (43)	30.4 (69)	
steal elsewhere	7.6 (105)	20.3 (148)	
steal from building	.0 (10)	25.0 (24)	29.6 (27)
hit teacher	33.3 (12)	38.1 (21)	
hit parent	19.2 (104)	30.1 (66)	
hit student	53.8 (292)	85.4 (481)	
hit sibling	63.3 (452)	78.5 (530)	
hidden weapon	14.3 (14)	22.2 (18)	50.0 (40)
school suspension	39.1 (64)	64.4 (264)	83.8 (444)
cheat test	18.5 (27)	36.8 (38)	44.2 (52)
skip school	22.2 (9)	57.1 (49)	68.2 (170)
run away	56.3 (16)	51.1 (45)	60.2 (83)

* The numbers in parentheses show the number of parents admitting the particular child behavior

The correspondence between parent and child estimates of the prevalence of total violence was similarly high, although better for 1st graders than for 4th graders (66.3% and 66.7% for 1st graders, and 91.2% and 77.3% for 4th graders). It should be noted in all of these examples, however, that the child's and parent's total scores did not always reflect the same, specific questions.

Whereas the prevalence estimate for theft as reported by parents of the 1st graders was generally similar to that of the boys themselves, the gap had increased by 4th grade, with boys reporting a higher prevalence than their parents. For example, theft at school was reported by 4.6% of 1st graders, which was very similar to the 5.1% reported by their parents. In contrast, 11.8% of the 4th graders reported having stolen at school, compared to only 7.2% reported by their parents. The agreement between child and parent ever prevalence of total theft was reasonably high for 1st graders (26.0% vs 21.6%), but lower for 4th graders (53.1% vs 29.8%). Only for two behaviors - fire setting and stealing elsewhere other than home or school - did the prevalence reported by parents exceed that of the child in both the first and the fourth grade.

Another way to examine the reliability of the child report is to calculate the percent of children admitting a particular behavior, given that the parent reported that behavior. In order to make comparisons possible with grade 7 parent-child dyads, Table 4 shows the results for that grade and grades 1 and 4 only for items which were comparable across the SRD and the SRA. Of particular interest were those behaviors that the parents were in a position to observe or see the results of. For example, 64.4% of the 4th grade boys reported ever having been suspended from school, given that their mother reported that behavior; the comparable figure was 39.1% for 1st graders. Also, 63.3% of the 1st graders reported ever hitting siblings, given the parent report of the child hitting siblings, compared to 78.5% for the 4th graders. Overall, the average conditional prevalence was higher for aggression than for theft in either grade (the means for all theft items were 22.5% and 33.2% for 1st and 4th graders, respectively, compared to a mean of 36.8% and 50.9% for all aggression items).

Table 4 includes the figures for grade 7 as well for comparable items. These reinforce the notion that the ever prevalence reported by the child, given the parent report, increased with age, with the largest increase taking place from grade 1 to grade 4. This increase with age is to be expected since older children will have a higher life-time frequency, and, therefore, a higher chance of concordance with parents. The trend of a higher conditional prevalence in the older grades was not evident in all behaviors. For example, the conditional percentages for firesetting were 12.9%, 18.3%, and 15.9% for grades 1, 4, and 7, respectively, and for run away 56.3%, 51.1%, and 60.2%.

A final method for investigating the reliability of youngsters' ever report on the SRA was the calculation of RIOC to show parent-child agreement on specific behaviors. The results of these analyses are shown in Table 5; stars indicate that the N reported by either the parent or the child was smaller than ten and that RIOC in these instances was not calculated due to increased variance of this measure with small N's. Therefore, comparison of average levels of RIOC were possible only for some but not for other behaviors. The average RIOC for 1st graders (24.5%), based on 15 antisocial behaviors, was somewhat lower than that of 4th graders (33.3%); for the eight antisocial behaviors that were in common between the SRA and the SRD, the average RIOC for 4th and 7th graders were similar (37.2%, and 39.2, respectively),

with the average RIOC for 7 out of the 8 behaviors at 22.3% for the
first graders. The relatively low RIOCs may partially reflect the fact
that parents often do not know about children's antisocial behaviors.

TABLE 5. Concordance between child and parent report of ever
occurrence of antisocial child behavior, expressed in RIOC.

	Grade 1 (N = 849)	Grade 4 (N = 868)	Grade 7 (N = 856)
street vandalism	4.6	.2	
fire setting	29.6	36.2	17.4
steal bike	58.8	43.4	
shoplift	19.8	32.1	40.5
steal at school	16.2	21.1	
steal elsewhere	7.6	26.4	
steal from building	*	22.7	21.8
hit teacher	29.7	33.4	
hit parent	17.6	23.8	
hit student	24.8	47.4	
hit sibling	24.0	28.9	
hidden weapon	11.6	16.1	39.7
school suspension	33.0	63.4	63.9
cheat test	11.2	26.4	20.1
skip school	16.4	53.4	55.3
run away	56.3	47.6	55.5

Note: Open space indicates that a comparable item was not
available in the SRD; * indicates that RIOC was not computed
when N < 10 in either the row or the column of the table.

3.2.1. Summary of reliability of the ever prevalence data. First and
fourth graders' responses to the ever questions of the SRA appear to be
largely reliable in that: (1) the prevalence rates reported by children

tend to be lower for 1st than for 4th graders; (2) for antisocial
child behaviors for which parents have direct knowledge, such as aggression and school suspension, prevalence figures based on child report
were very similar to those based on parent report, but the discrepancy
between parent and child report was larger for 4th than for 1st
graders, reflecting the fact that, as children grow older, parents may
be less aware of their activities; (3) prevalence based on the child
report given that the parent reported the same behavior was high in a
number of instances, and was larger in the higher grades, as expected,
given the larger number of occurrences on which the congruence for
life-time prevalence may be based; when the figure was low for the 1st
and 4th graders, this was true for the 7th graders as well; (4) when
parent-child agreement was measured by means of RIOC, the average RIOC
was very similar for fourth and seventh graders for those behaviors
which could be compared. The average RIOC was lower for the first
grade.

3.3. Reliability of the Six-Month Prevalence

Table 6 shows the prevalence of self-reported antisocial behavior
over the past six months, and compares these figures with the prevalence reported by the parents and teachers. Dashes denote that a behavior was not included in an instrument for a particular informant. For
example, the teacher would rarely know if the child had damaged
property at home, and so the teacher was not asked this. The prevalence of some behaviors reported by youngsters was very low, presumably
reflecting their low occurrence in the rather narrow time window of six
months.
As with the findings on ever prevalence, the six-month prevalence
for 4th graders was consistently higher than that for 1st graders. For
example, the prevalence of total damage was 15.5% for 1st graders
and 32.4% for 4th graders, and 15.4% and 31.9% for total theft, respectively.
Prevalences based on parent's or child's reports were more similar
for those antisocial behaviors which are observable by parents than
for less observable behaviors; however, this applied more to 1st
graders than to 4th graders. Thus, the six-month prevalence of school
suspension for 1st graders was 6.2% when based on the child report
and 5.4% when based on the
parent report, while the comparable figures for 4th graders were 17.5%
and 23.5%. Similarly, the six-month prevalence of total violence was
53.8% and 63.7% for 1st graders and their parents, respectively, compared to 80.6% and 70.4% for 4th graders and their parents. In general, for a number of antisocial behaviors prevalence figures were more
similar between parents and their 1st grade sons than for parents and
their 4th grade sons. For example, the prevalence of street vandalism
by 1st graders was 3.8% and 3.1%, when based on either child or parent
report, compared to 6.3% and 2.9% in the case of 4th graders. The prevalence of total theft was 15.4% and 14.1% as reported by first grade
children and their parents, respectively, compared to 31.9% and 18.9%
for fourth graders.

TABLE 6. Six-month prevalence rates (%) based on boys' self-reports and reports from parents and teachers.

	Grade 1			Grade 4		
	B	P	T	B	P	T
damage at home	7.5	---	---	15.0	---	---
damage at school	2.6	---	---	6.8	---	---
damage at other places	5.3	---	---	15.2	---	---
street vandalism	3.8	3.1	---	6.3	2.9	---
fire setting	1.6	4.8	.9	1.5	6.0	1.5
Total damage	15.5			32.4		
steal bike	1.3	.6	---	.6	---	---
shoplift	3.7	3.1	---	6.7	5.6	---
steal money at home	5.1	---	---	11.5	---	---
steal other at home	3.9	---	---	10.7	---	---
(steal at home)	---	9.3	---	---	12.3	---
steal at school	3.1	2.9	9.4	7.8	5.3	11.7
steal elsewhere	2.7	7.8	---	4.3	9.2	---
steal from car	1.2	---	---	1.2	---	---
steal from build.	.7	.4	---	1.7	1.5	---
avoid paying	3.9	---	---	6.0	---	---
robbery	.7	---	---	1.7	---	---
Total theft	15.4	14.1		31.9	18.9	

B = Boy as informant; P = Parent as informant; T = Teachers informant.

(Table 6 continued)

	Grade 1			Grade 4		
	B	P	T	B	P	T
hit teacher	3.9	.8	2.0	5.2	1.0	2.4
hit parent	4.9	6.1	---	5.2	3.9	---
hit student	29.1	23.2	25.2	55.1	39.7	31.3
hit sibling	37.2	48.4	---	56.0	52.2	---
hidden weapon	2.1	.6	---	4.5	.5	---
rowdy in public	6.6	29.0	---	12.7	23.8	---
thrown rocks	6.1	---	---	14.7	---	---
Total violence	53.8	63.7		80.6	70.4	
drank beer	3.7	---	---	6.7	---	---
drank wine	1.6	---	---	1.8	---	---
drink liquor	.7	---	---	1.0	---	---
smoke	2.1	---	---	4.0	---	---
marijuana	.1	---	---	.2	---	---
sniff glue	.7	---	---	.9	---	---
Total substance abuse	6.8			10.7		
school suspension	6.2	5.4	---	17.5	23.5	---
cheat test	5.7	1.9	---	8.1	2.3	---
skip school	4.0	1.1	12.5	3.9	3.1	11.7
run away	2.4	.9	---	2.3	2.4	---
trespass	6.9	21.8	15.2	14.2	18.9	24.6
Total status offenses	19.1	26.6		32.6	37.3	

B = Boy as informant; P = Parent as informant; T = Teacher as informant.

Table 6 also allows for comparison between child and teacher reports for a number of school-related behaviors. The six-month prevalence of stealing at school, as reported by teachers was 9.4% for 1st graders and 11.7% for 4th graders, much higher than the child's self-report (3.1% and 7.8%), suggesting a possible under-reporting by children. A similar trend was found for truancy and trespassing. There was a consistent discrepancy between the teacher and child report of the prevalence of the child's hitting of teachers, with the former being lower than the latter. It is possible that teachers other than the one who filled in the questionnaire were victimized, but this possibility is less likely for 1st grade boys, who interacted mainly with their homeroom teacher. The prevalence of hitting students by 1st graders was similar when based either on the teacher or the child report (29.1% vs. 25.5%), but diverged for 4th graders (55.1% vs. 31.3%).

We did not attempt to calculate other forms of reliability for the child report of six-month prevalence. The generally low frequencies made it less useful to calculate the percent of boys displaying a particular behavior given that the mother or teacher reported the same behavior. Likewise, the calculation of RIOC was less feasible for the six-month estimates.

3.3.1. Summary of the reliability of the child's six-month prevalence.
Only limited checks could be made on the reliability of the youngsters' self-reported antisocial behavior over the past six months. These checks, however, indicated that: 1) the prevalence for 4th graders was higher than for 1st graders, as expected; and 2) that the prevalence of selected child behaviors was similar whether based on parent, teacher or the child's self-report, but the similarity was higher for 1st than for 4th grade boys.

3.4. Discussion

We will return now to the questions raised in the introduction concerning the use of a measure of self-reported antisocial behavior for 1st and 4th grade boys. We have demonstrated that the majority of youngsters appear to have understood the questions they were asked. The 1st graders' understanding was poorest for illicit substance use; overall, 4th graders' understanding of antisocial behaviors was higher than that of 1st graders.

The prevalence of antisocial behaviors also was higher for 4th than for 1st graders, for answers to both the "ever" and the "six-month" questions. It is evident from the data that a significant proportion of elementary school aged children engage in antisocial acts. Self-report survey instruments often have revealed that delinquent-type activities frequently occur prior to the first arrest which, in Pennsylvania at least, rarely takes place prior to the age of 12.

We are aware of only one data set with which to compare the current findings on 4th graders, the one collected by Richards et al. (1979) which focused on 5th and 6th grade (11-12 year old) children from an upper class Chicago suburb. Because the authors did not break down the ever and 6-month prevalence rates by sex, it is unclear whether any different prevalence rates in that and the current study can be attributed to sex, social status, or other factors. The findings for 4th graders in Pittsburgh, with the exception of substance use, were not dramatically different from the findings on slightly older children in the Chicago study. For example, 45.4% of the Chicago children reported ever having fought with students, compared with 62.7% of the Pittsburgh boys who had hit students. Substance use was much higher in the Chicago than in the Pittsburgh sample; for instance, 23.3% of the Chicago children ever had used liquor, while this was reported by 1.6% of the Pittsburgh boys. The prevalence of cheating on tests was more comparable (20.7% in Chicago vs. 17.7% in Pittsburgh), but the prevalence of skipping school was somewhat less (5.2% vs. 8.4%). Similarly, six-month prevalence rates for each sample provide broad agreement for some but not for other antisocial behaviors. For example, 9.7% of the Chicago youngsters engaged in minor shoplifting, and 2.1% in major shoplifting, compared with 8.9% of the Pittsburgh boys, irrespective of whether the theft was minor or major. Unfortunately, findings on the 1st grade boys in the Pittsburgh study could not be compared with other studies due to the absence of other studies on 1st graders.

In the present study, for many specific behaviors based on either the child's or the parent's report, comparisons between the ever prevalence rates showed a surprising level of agreement. This agreement was slightly higher for 1st graders than for 4th graders, probably reflecting parents' decreasing level of awareness of their child's activities. We also calculated the conditional probability that a child would report on a specific behavior given that the parent had ever noted the behavior. This analysis was restricted necessarily to those behaviors that were readily observable to adults. It showed relatively high values for behaviors such as 4th graders' suspension from school and hitting siblings but lower values for a number of other, less visible behaviors. Overall, conditional agreements were higher for aggression than for theft, and higher for 4th as compared with 1st graders. Thus, a tendency for children to underreport was noted; this was not restricted to the young children, but was also evident from analyses done on the 7th grade boy-parent dyads. The average RIOC between child and parent report of the same behavior was very similar for 4th and 7th graders, but lower for the 1st graders.

Further analyses on the six-month estimates confirmed that for many behaviors the prevalence rates, based either on child's vs. parent's or child's vs. teacher's report, were very similar. As could be expected, the prevalence rates were higher for 4th than for 1st grade boys. Other reliability comparisons for the six-month data, however, were less feasible due to low N's.

The current study indicates that information from adults is essential in order to piece together a more comprehensive picture of a child's antisocial acts, especially as a retrospective indicator of the occurrence of the acts over the life of the child. The study did not address the possible reasons for discrepancies between the parent's and the son's reports. Low concordance could be attributed to children's failure to remember past events, different interpretations of the questions by the youngsters and their parent, or a genuine unwillingness on the part of the child to reveal misbehavior to the interviewer. The concordance was higher for 4th than for 1st graders. The tendency to under-report, however, was not unique to the SRA instrument, but was also found for the 7th grade boys' responses to the self-report delinquency questionnaire.

The results demonstrate that substantial numbers of the 7- and 10-year-old boys in the study had engaged in delinquent types of acts. The finding underscores that criminal careers are likely to start prior to the first arrest. In Pennsylvania, first arrests prior to age 12 are rare, since this is the age at which youngsters become criminally responsible for their behavior. We can draw several conclusions from the results. First, the data reinforce the need to seek information from other informants, such as a parent or a teacher, to complement the child's self-report of his antisocial or delinquent behavior. The question, therefore, is not whether young children's self-reports are one hundred percent reliable, but whether their information complements that provided by adults. Second, even when parent-child agreement is incomplete, a finding shared with many other studies in the realm of child psychopathology (Achenbach et al., 1987), it remains to be seen to what extent the report of young children has predictive utility in forecasting later delinquent involvement, over and above the predictive utility that is generally known from parent and teacher ratings (Loeber & Dishion, 1983). This most important test of the usefulness of both the ever and the six-month versions of the SRA for young children is yet to come. Five hundred boys in each of the three grade cohorts of the Pittsburgh Youth Study are now being followed up at half-yearly intervals over a period of three years, which will provide the necessary predictive validity missing in the current analyses. Eventually, the current data will be linked to various longitudinal outcomes, such as official records of law-breaking.

AUTHOR NOTES

The authors are grateful to Celia Nourse Eatman for her comments on an earlier draft. Particular thanks are due the staff of the Life History Studies section (Western Psychiatric Institute and Clinic, School of Medicine, University of Pittsburgh, Pittsburgh, PA.) for their valiant efforts and enthusiasm that made the data collection possible. The paper was written with financial support of Grant No. 86-JN-CX-0009 of the Office of Juvenile Justice and Delinquency Prevention, Office of Justice Programs, U. S. Department of Justice. Points of view or opinions in this document are those of the authors and do not necessarily represent the official position or policies of the U.S. Department of Justice.

REFERENCES

Achenbach, TM: The child behavior profile: I. Boys aged 6-11. Journal of Consulting and Clinical Psychology, 46, 478-488.

Achenbach, T. M., & Edelbrock, C. S. (1979). The child behavior profile. II. Boys aged 12-16 and girls aged 6-11 and 12-16. Journal of Consulting and Clinical Psychology, 47, 223-233, 1978.

Achenbach, TM, & Edelbrock, CS: Behavioral problems and competencies reported by parents of normal and disturbed children aged four through sixteen. Monographs of the Society for Research in Child Development, 46:1-82, 1981.

Achenbach, TM, & Edelbrock, CS: Manual for the Child Behavior Checklist and Revised Child Behavior Profile. Burlington, Vt., 1983.

Achenbach, TM, McConaughy, SH, & Howell, CT: Child/adolescent behavioral and emotional problems: Implications of cross-informant correlations for situational specificity. Psychological Bulletin, 101(2):213- 232, 1987.

Capaldi, D, & Patterson, GR: An approach to the problem of recruitment and retention rates for longitudinal research. Behavioral Assessment, 9:169-178, 1987.

Edelbrock, C, & Achenbach, T: The teacher version of the Child Behavior Profile: I. Boys aged six through eleven. Journal of Consulting and Clinical Psychology, 52:207-217, 1984.

Elliott, DS, Huizinga, D, & Ageton, SS: Explaining delinquency and drug use. Beverly Hills: Sage Publications, 1985.

Farrington, DP, & Loeber, R: RIOC and Phi as measures of predictive efficiency and strength of association in 2 x 2 tables. Unpublished manuscript, 1988.

Elliott, DS, Knowles, BA, & Canter, RJ: The epidemiology of delinquent behavior and drug use among American adolescents, 1976-1978. Progress report to the National Institute of Mental Health, Behavior Research Institute, Boulder, Colorado, 1981.

Glidewell, JC: Studies of mothers' reports of behavior symptoms in their children. In Sells, SB (Ed.), The definition and measurement of mental health. U. S. Public Health Service, National Center for Health Statistics. Washington, D. C.: Government Printing Office, 1968.

Hindelang, MJ., Hirschi, T, & Weis, JG: Correlates of delinquency: The illusion of discrepancy between self-report and official measures. American Sociological Review, 44:995-1014, 1979.

Klemke, LW: Does apprehension for shoplifting amplify or terminate shoplifting activity? Law and Society Review, 12:391-403, 1978.

Loeber, R: The prevalence, correlates, and continuity of serious conduct problems in elementary school children. Criminology, 25:615-642, 1987.

Loeber, R, & Dishion, TJ: Early predictors of male delinquency: A review. Psychological Bulletin, 94:68-99, 1983.

Loeber, R, & Dishion, TJ: Boys who fight at home and school: Family conditions influencing cross-setting fighting. Journal of Consulting and Clinical Psychology, 52:759-768, 1984.

Loeber, R, & Schmaling, KB: The utility of differentiating between mixed and pure forms of antisocial child behavior. _Journal of Abnormal Child Psychology_, 13:315-336, 1985.

Pittsburgh Public Schools Membership report as of September 22, 1986. Pittsburgh, PA: [Board of Education], 1986.

Richards, P, Berk, RA, & Forster, B: _Crime as play - delinquency in a middle class suburb_. Cambridge, MA: Ballinger, 1979.

Rutter, M, Tizard, J, & Whitmore, K: _Education, health and behavior_. New York: Wiley, 1970.

APPENDIX: Self-reported antisocial behavior items used for 1st and 4th grade boys.

1) Broken or damaged or destroyed something belonging to your parents or other people in your family on purpose?
2) Broken or damaged or destroyed something belonging to a school on purpose?
3) Broken or damaged or destroyed other things that did not belong to you, not counting things that belong to your family or school?
4) Stolen or tried to steal a bicycle or skateboard?
5) Taken something from a store without paying for it?
6) Taken some money at home that did not belong to you, like from your mother's purse or from your parents' dresser?
7) Taken anything else at home that did not belong to you?
8) Taken anything at school from the teacher or other kids that did not belong to you?
9) Taken something out of somebody's house or yard or garage that did not belong to you?
10) Taken something that does not belong to you from a car?
11) Cheated on school tests?
12) Hit a teacher or other grown-up at school?
13) Hit one of your parents?
14) Hit other students or got into a physical fight with them?
15) Hit your brother or sister or got into a physical fight with him or her?
16) Gone into somebody's garden, backyard, house or garage when you were not supposed to be there?
17) Run away from home?
18) Skipped school without an excuse?
19) Secretly taken a sip from a glass or bottle of beer?
20) Secretly taken a sip from a glass or bottle of wine?
21) Secretly taken a sip from a glass or bottle of liquor?
22) Secretly smoked a cigarette, smoked a pipe or chewed tobacco?
23) Smoked marijuana?
24) Sniffed glue?
25) Been sent home from school for bad behavior?
26) Written things or sprayed paint on walls or sidewalks or cars, where you were not supposed to do that?
27) Been loud, rowdy, or unruly in a public place so that people complained about it or you got into trouble?
28) Purposely set fire to a building, a car or other property or tried to do so?
29) Carried a hidden weapon other than a plain pocket knife?
30) Gone into or tried to go into a building to steal something?
31) Avoided paying for things such as movies, bus or subway rides, or food?
32) Snatched someone's purse or wallet or picked someone's pocket?
33) Thrown rocks or bottles at people?

COMPARATIVE RESEARCH ON CRIME AND DELINQUENCY - THE ROLE AND RELEVANCE
OF NATIONAL PENAL CODES AND CRIMINAL JUSTICE SYSTEMS

Hans-Jorg Albrecht
Max Planck Institute, Freiburg im Breisgau
Federal Republic of Germany

1. INTRODUCTION

In the fields of criminology and criminal law probably everybody
can agree with two propositions. First, throughout the world, criminal
and delinquent acts are observed, recorded and counted. Rates of crime
are interpreted as rather important indicators of a paramount social
problem. Second, we can agree that throughout the world -- and independent from cultural and political systems -- criminal laws as well as
criminal justice systems exist, displaying (to varying degrees) successful attempts to define and classify behavior or events as requiring
punishment or some other societal reactions, be it treatment or education. Offenders or delinquents are processed through various stages of
criminal justice. On the other hand, it is equally easy to conclude
that despite rather uniform roles and functions law has been assigned
in industrialized countries (Luhmann, 1972), there do not exist universal definitions of crime and delinquency. Agreement has not been
reached on what is or what should be considered to be a criminal act or
delinquent behavior (neglecting here rather meaningless abstract definitions such as: a crime is an act violating criminal law without justification or excuse). The answer to the question of whether there are
universal crimes thus points to the rather trivial idea that law and
norms, crime and deviance, represent relative concepts which vary along
the dimensions of culture and nations as well as over time (Chang &
Blazichek, 1986).
Although we might agree with the argument that everybody knows
what murder, rape, robbery, or theft is and that "no one must consult
the law to know that murder, rape and theft are criminal acts" (Gross,
1979); and although every language provides morally-based terms to
denote certain behavior as unacceptable, there remains the question,
nonetheless, of what kinds of behavior or what range of behavior should
fall under concepts such as murder, rape, robbery, and theft. Even
crimes considered almost everywhere as "crimes mala per se" -- the most
serious crimes or traditional crimes -- will probably invoke different
legal labels and definitions (Junger-Tas, 1978, p. 10). Obviously,
these crimes usually referred to as being "mala per se" are rather

M. W. Klein (ed.), Cross-National Research in Self-Reported Crime and Delinquency, 227–248.
© *1989 by Kluwer Academic Publishers.*

"crime antiqua," old crimes, which no longer attract much attention or interest as far as their definition and the range of behavior covered by these definitions are concerned (Wilkins, 1980). If we had a broader or even universal legal understanding of various crimes, there would be fewer problems in framing conventions and treaties on mutual assistance in criminal law matters, on extradition, and similar issues, and there would be more success in developing an international penal code.

There have, in fact, been a number of efforts to harmonize national criminal and procedural laws as well as efforts defining common areas of concern or problems within the field of crime and criminal justice. But the work done so far by international organizations such as the United Nations and regional UN institutes or the Council of Europe has not led to much reduction in the differences in the legal construction of crime and delinquency, processing offenders through the justice system, or in the response to crime and delinquency. Obviously, it is much easier to harmonize civil or trade law than criminal laws. Efforts to harmonize criminal statistics have also revealed major problems in standarizing crime definitions, classification procedures, etc. (Junger-Tas, 1978, p. 24; Vetere & Newman, 1977).

On the other hand, rapidly growing mobility, the decreasing meaning of distance, and internationalization of commerce bring about considerable convergence of opportunity structures and behavior patterns (Luhmann, 1972, p. 333). The spread of new drugs or leisure time activities is rather rapid, indicating that behavior and problems associated with certain types of behavior cannot be confined to those areas where they originally took root. Thus, common and similar concerns in controlling behavior by means of criminal law can now be observed on an international level.

2. HOW MUCH DIFFERENCE CAN BE FOUND BETWEEN DIFFERENT NATIONAL CRIMINAL LAWS?

Although the international comparative approach to the study of criminal law and criminal justice has a long tradition, systematic comparisons do not exist between various criminal codes covering the whole range of crime definitions which would allow an assessment of similarities and differences in legal definitions of crime and delinquent behavior. There exist partial comparisons covering single offenses or offense groups in limited numbers of countries, e.g. abortion (Eser & Koch, 1987), drug offenses (Albrecht, 1986; Meyer, 1987), violent crimes (McClintock, 1973), serious property crimes (Waller & Okihiro, 1978), petty fraud and property crimes (Council of Europe, 1980), environmental crimes (Heine, 1986), or main features of juvenile justice systems (see le Poole, 1977; Klein, 1985, or Dünkel & Meyer, 1985, 1986) or criminal justice systems (see HEUNI, 1985). But even within the rather narrow concept of comparative legal research on single offenses, rather serious problems are obvious; they raise the question of whether in-depth legal comparative work on definitions alone actually can help to improve comparative criminological research on crime and delinquency. It is argued that comparative research on single issues in criminal laws must inevitably lead to a comparison of systems at large in order to understand the meaning and the relevance of differences or similarities found (Kaiser, 1978; Anttila, 1978). Certainly there exist deficits in information on the legal systems of various nations; there is limited access to legal materials such as statutes and court decisions, creating further problems with respect to the analysis of criminal law in a comparative perspective. It is evident that many countries do not provide systematic information on basic criminal law and procedural law for comparative purposes. Whether the global crime and criminal justice information network planned by the United Nations Committee will lead to improvements is still an open question (see Joutsen, 1987).

Before assessing differences and similarities between countries, one must consider whether there exist differences in crime definitions within a country. Although we are used to talking about legal crime definitions or legal norms as providing uniform concepts, legal structures in terms of substantive and procedural law are far from being self-evident. Obviously, the first problem is a problem of choice as to who should define the reach of criminal or delinquency laws and the range of behavior fallng under these definitions within one jurisdiction. Should it be a legal scholar commenting on criminal laws, judges, public prosecutors, defense councils, police or civil servants within a Ministry of Justice? There are, in addition, the victims of crime or bystanders reporting incidents of crime who influence the input which may be subjected to definitional procedures at the police level. It goes without saying that crime definitions will depend on the position held by those defining and interpreting crime and criminal law.

However, we could agree also with the proposition that problems of definition in terms of dissensus and conflict usually occur only in marginal areas of criminal law, with most cases probably being classified according to criminal statutes in a routinized and non-conflicting way. This corresponds to the observation that a great deal of operations, interactions and decision-making within the criminal justice system is not characterized by conflict and dispute between different justice agencies (Albrecht, 1987, p. 51). But there also exist certain areas in criminal law where conflict and dissensus with respect to crime definitions do emerge because of the sensitivity of certain types of behavior or as a consequence of umbrella-type laws serving as elastic frameworks for the implementation of various and varying policies. Public order offenses and -- most important -- statutes or laws referring to children or juveniles in need of care and supervision or neglected children belong to this category of law.

It has been argued that application of criminal law in a substantial proportion of criminal cases does not lead to any conflicts or dissensus on the question "has a crime actually occurred?" and "what kind or type of crime did occur?" and we are therefore likely to conclude that national criminal laws serve as a uniform point of reference within a given territory or jurisdiction for the various criminal justice agencies and courts. But the fact is that criminal law and its application by the justice agencies are always embedded in a local

political and social culture and community which might be quite
powerful in producing different meanings and conceptions of criminal
behavior.   Thus criminal law and appropriate reactions (Swanson, 1979;
Duffee, 1980) should receive more attention than they have attracted up
to now.

This is especially true with respect to those umbrella-type crime
definitions which seem to become more prevalent in modern criminal
legislation, at least in industrialized countries.   This type of law
may on the one hand display the inability of legislative bodies to
achieve a final consensus about the types of behavior which fall under
criminal statutes, leaving considerable discretionary power to local
administrative bodies and agencies implementing the law.   On the other
hand this kind of law is more flexible and therefore better adapted to
rapid changes within modern societies.   Therefore, it seems plausible
to conclude that within-country variation with respect to crime definition or operationalization of criminal law is more likely to be prevalent when the type of law concerned is rather open or incomplete.

With respect to differences between national penal codes and juvenile delinquency laws, we may consider the following types of differences:

1. Behavior may be regarded as a criminal offense everywhere,
    although the legal label is different.   As an example, we can
    take property crimes.   An offense such as "burglary" according
    to U.S. statutes may be defined as "break and enter" in Canada
    or as "attempted theft under aggravating circumstances" in
    West Germany or in Austria.   Destroying something by means of
    fire may be a crime of arson in one country and mere destruc-
    tion of property in another.   Differences between legal labels
    can also be observed with respect to aggravating and mitigat-
    ing circumstances.

2. Behavior may be criminalized in one country but not in an-
    other.   Drug laws can be cited as an example, with some states
    not defining the possession or purchase of small amounts of
    drugs, with the intent to consume, a crime at all (for an
    overview see Albrecht, 1986; Meyer, 1987).   Sexual or moral
    offenses represent other important areas for such differences
    in the extent of criminalization (see Junger-Tas, 1978).

3. Behavior may be punishable in theory according to criminal law
    in various countries but may be de facto decriminalized in
    some countries.   For example, possession of small amounts of
    soft drugs or using public buses without paying the fare in
    many countries is regulated by civil means although according
    to penal codes it is technically a criminal offense.

4. Behavior may be defined as a criminal offense with the conse-
    quence of criminal penalties in one country, but as misdemean-
    or, contravention, or administrative offense with the conse-
    quence of administrative or civil penalties in other coun-
    tries.   Various traffic offenses, petty property crimes, or
    petty fraud represent some categories which are assigned dif-
    ferentially to these legal categories of delinquent behavior.

5. Criminal laws may potentially cover a wide range of behavior,

thus opening fields of control rather than defining precisely which behavior should be controlled. This type of law may be differentially operationalized in various countries and/or enforced to varying degrees. Public order offenses, victimless crimes (e.g. pollution crimes, drug crimes), and some traffic laws are likely to lead to such differences.

6. A great potential difference is embedded in laws specifically referring to the behavior of children or juveniles. While there exist countries providing a special body of juvenile "offenses" (status offenses) allowing intervention in the lives of children or juveniles, other countries do not allow intervention on the basis of behavior alone which would not constitute a crime if committed by an adult. Juveniles are subjected to the same criminal law in these latter countries as are adults, with the age of criminal responsibility varying, but normally by way of special juvenile criminal laws or procedural laws requiring different court proceedings and, most important, sanctions different from those for adults. Special juvenile criminal laws may not exist in some countries, as is the case of Switzerland or the German Democratic Republic, but the regular criminal law provides for other kinds of penalties in the case of juveniles and adolescents (see Dünkel & Meyer, 1985, 1986; le Poole, 1977).

Nevertheless, in those countries which do not have status offenses or corresponding definitions of delinquent behavior, interventions may be justified when a child or a juvenile is judged to be neglected or in danger of neglect, and parents fail to fulfill their duties towards their child's education. Indicators of neglect or the danger of neglect partially coincide with behavior defined as status offenses in other jurisdictions. Truancy, going to places forbidden for children or juveniles, alcohol or other drug problems, or criminal acts committed by children under the age of criminal responsibility may serve as indicators for the need of intervention on the part of administrative agencies responsible for the implementation of juvenile protection laws. The basic difference with respect to definitions and conceptions between these systems of juvenile law and juvenile control probably concerns the degree to which children or juveniles must show up with problem behavior mentioned above in order to justify the definition of a state of neglect on the one hand and a status offense on the other. While normally one act of truancy, drunkenness in public, etc., will not justify intervention into the life of the juvenile or into parental authority on the basis of juvenile protection laws, this may well suffice for a status offense.

On the basis of these considerations we may conclude that:
1. differences between national criminal laws and criminal justice systems are but one source of variation in crime definitions and conceptions of crime and delinquency;
2. the differences between criminal statutes and delinquency

or juvenile laws may have a different impact on the design of
comparative studies on crime and deviance depending on the
type of crime definitions used in criminal legislation as well
as the type of differences in various crime or delinquency
definitions. Furthermore, we may differentiate between crimes
where criminal law is involved almost exclusively by the public and victims on the one hand, and, on the other, those
criminal statutes or (partially) juvenile laws where, due to
the lack of victims or other reasons, reactions are almost
exclusively dependent on operational concepts and activities
of criminal justice or other agencies.

The relevance of differences and/or similarities between national
criminal laws and criminal justice systems therefore cannot be restricted to methodological problems but should also be located in the theoretical field as well as around the questions which should be answered by
comparative studies on crime and deviance.

This creates a somewhat ambivalent situation with respect to variation introduced by the international and national dimensions of criminal and delinquency laws, processing of offenders, and the response to
delinquency and crime. While on the one hand similarity and functional
equivalence are needed with respect to crime and delinquency definitions in order to identify culturally independent correlates of deviance and crime, on the other hand, variation in crime and delinquency
definitions may be useful when attempting to assess the impact of different methods of control on the magnitude of crime, justice, or other
social problems. Within the first approach, criminal law serves as an
important point of reference in constructing a dependent variable which
is equivalent in terms of conception and definition across nations and
cultures, thus separating crime and deviance definitions from the overall cultural or social system on various levels, including national
levels. Within the second approach, these crime and delinquency definitions are regarded either as parts of a set of independent variables or
as dependent variables requiring variation with respect to definitional
or conceptual aspects.

Problems associated with differences between criminal law and
delinquency laws in various countries with respect to comparative studies of crime and deviance therefore should be located along a range of
methodological and theoretical questions which take as a point of departure existing variation in criminal law, processing offenders, and
information on offenses and offenders. The problem is not to accommodate penal codes or legal offense categories, but rather how to cope
with those differences in terms of methodology and theory.

When discussing variations in crime definitions and their relevance for comparative research, one important similarity between most
countries should not be forgotten. This similarity concerns the phenomenon of not knowing the law. Not knowing the law is rather widespread
with most people in any society; they are unable to assign behavior
correctly to the abstract offense categories in criminal statues. The
ultimate power and the knowledge required to be capable of assigning
certain events or behavior to a rather broad set of specific criminal
statutes are embodied in a small group of experts and specialists. So,

the different levels of information-gathering about crime and delinquency imply not only different views on what should be a crime or what might be defined a crime, but also different levels of capability in evaluating events and behavior in the light of penal statutes.

Taking into account this kind of distribution of knowledge we might expect that problems of comparability of crime and delinquency definitions increase with increases in the amount of expertise and professionalism vested in definitions preceding the event of counting crime and delinquency. As police and court information on criminal acts cannot be separated from expertise once the event has gone through the process of definition and has been assigned to a specific category of crime, the most promising means of gathering comparative data on crime and delinquency is the use of self-reports or victimization surveys.

3. INTERNATIONAL COMPARATIVE RESEARCH ON CRIME AND DELINQUENCY

When reviewing international research on crime and delinquency, we find that there are very few predesigned comparative studies. Although the approach of the United States-based national victim surveys has been widely adopted (see Arnold, 1987 for a review of victimization studies), questions and items normally have been adapted to the respective national laws, statutes, etc., as well as to national research interests. But there is some hope, in that these surveys are based on crime definitions presented to respondents in everyday language which might be easier to equate across various nations and make the data more appropriate for the purpose of international comparisons [van Dijk & Steinmetz, 1980; Block & Block, 1984; Kerner, 1978; see also Clinard, 1978; Stephan, 1976, pp. 317, 327 with comparisons between Zürich, Switzerland and Stuttgart, FRG as well as Stuttgart and North American cities, on the basis of victimization survey data. Comparisons of crime definitions and questions referring to single crimes show that, although the focus is in general on the same types of offense, there are differences which cannot be controlled (p. 471)].

Basically, we may consider four types of international comparative research on crime and delinquency:
1. Comparative research with official crime and delinquency data;
2. Comparative self-report surveys;
3. Comparative victimization studies;
4. Comparative research on perceptions of crime and delinquency, including ratings of seriousness of crime.

The bulk of comparative research centers around analysis of official crime and justice data. This type of research has addressed questions about correlates of crime rates such as the degree of urbanization, social and economic development, or has used variations in punishment between countries as quasi-experimental designs for examining the impact of certain penalties on trends in crime (Landau, 1984; Archer & Gartner, 1984; Wolf, 1971; Wellford, 1974; Gurr, 1977). Another type of research based on official crime data addresses the decision of the justice system, e.g., examinations of the stability of punishment rates

234

or the effect of crime rates on imprisonment rates (Moitra, 1987; Bennett, 1982). Since all of them have to be based on police-recorded crime, suspects or arrested offenders, convicted and sentenced offenders, etc., a common problem is whether the crime categories and offense types used in the analysis are equivalent between the different units. Besides the well-known problems of differences in the organization of information sampling and counting procedures between national criminal justice systems, the use of legal labels has created serious problems as well. These problems stem partially from differences in the general conception of penal code offenses. Some countries make distinctions between crimes or criminal offenses on the one hand and administrative offenses or misdemeanors and contraventions on the other hand. Some have statutes which partial out from the range of punishable offenses those acts which yield only minor damage or injuries (e.g., Austria and some socialist countries).

Most of this type of research is based either on Interpol statistics or on data from the two world crime surveys carried out by the United Nations (Redo, 1986). But with respect to Interpol statistics which are compiled on the basis of standardized questionnaires, we must acknowledge that the problems associated with different legal definitions, etc., could not be overcome. This is officially acknowledged in the introductory remarks in publications of Interpol statistics, pointing out that "because of the variations in the definitions of crime in different countries the forms only referred to several wide categories of crime more or less universally recognized and indictable in ordinary law," and furthermore, "the definitions of these categories are very wide in order to allow the use of national crime statistics without too many modifications." Thus, we do not know much about the equivalence of the data about the cateories of crime: the same is true of the world crime surveys. But this is not only a consequence of differences in the crime categories or crime definitions; major problems concerning the equivalence question also result, e.g., from differential definitions regarding attempts to commit a crime or out of the definition of intentional acts versus mere negligence and the separation of those acts. Problems also arise with respect to how different kinds of participation in crime are labelled, and how different acts committed during a single crime event are counted (e.g., the most serious only or all offenses; see Reiss, 1983; Collmann, 1973). Even comparisons based on official crime data between countries with rather uniform and common criminal law and criminal similarities seem to involve considerable difficulties when trying to interpret differences or similarities in official accounts of crime (see Smith, 1983 for England, Wales, and Scotland; Hauge, 1983 for the Scandinavian countries).

The consequences of this dilemma and the suggestions made to overcome at least some of the problems of non-equivalence consist mainly in pointing out that crime data stemming from different countries should not be compared in the strict sense of the term, but that only national trends in crime rates should be compared (see e.g., Martin & Conger, 1980). But this seems to be a feasible approach only when assuming that within each country crime definitions and counting procedures remain stable over time. We also encounter other warnings such as that only "cautious" comparisons should be made or that data are "more or less" comparable, warnings which really indicate that comparisons should not be made at all.

Another type of comparative research based on official crime and delinquency data concerns studies using individual though official crime data derived from national court information systems. Such comparative work has been done in the area of youth crime and juvenile delinquency including several European countries (France, Hungary, Poland, Yugoslavia; Malewska & Peyre, 1973; Chirol et al., 1975). The questions put forward in this piece of research focussed on the relationship between various indicators of socio-economic development and delinquent and criminal behavior of juveniles and young adults, 14 to 24 years old, using several wide categories of crime (crimes against persons, crimes against property, crimes against public morals). Although a special working group had been set up to study the legal definitions of the various countries included (Henry, 1977), the final conclusion was that "it's hardly needed to be said, that given the differences of definition, apprehension and measurement of delinquency in the various countries, the data were not directly comparable" (Malewska & Peyre, 1973, p. 16). An interview administered to two samples of French and Polish delinquents who had appeared before a juvenile court provided further data on delinquent behavior such as alcoholism, running away, and truancy. The problems associated with this type of research are obvious, too. Although better approximations can be reached in using individual data derived from files than is possible with aggregate official data that can seldom be regrouped or disaggregated, preselection by the police or public prosecutor cannot be taken into account.

Comparative surveys on the basis of self-reported behavior are also rare. Besides self-reported delinquency studies carried out consecutively in several Scandinavian countries in the sixties and seventies, there was a comparative, predesigned study on self-reported delinquency involving Canada and Switzerland (Vaz & Casparis, 1981). The results of the self-reported delinquency studies in Scandinavian countries have been described as rather depressing (Hauge, 1983, p. 32), when addressing the question of comparability of the data on crime and delinquency. This is mainly due to differences between the questionnaires used to adapt to the different research interests, etc. (Christie, Andenaes, & Skirbekk, 1965).

In the Canadian-Swiss study of delinquency (13-19 year old students), 14 items were introduced in the questionnaire to give a measure of delinquency/crime, items which were said to "commonly be considered in law as delinquent or criminal conduct" (Vaz et al., 1981, p. 72). But out of these 14 items at least four are neither delinquent nor criminal according at least to Swiss juvenile or criminal law (e.g., trying to get intimate with a girl, taking a drink, feeling high from liquor, gambling) or could be said to be delinquent or criminal only under very specific circumstances (e.g., gambling or drinking). Furthermore, the Swiss-Canadian study, together with other comparative crime studies also involving Switzerland, can be taken as an example of how big the difference in outcomes of assessing crime problems of a country can be when using different measures of crime or delinquency or different types of crime or delinquency. While on the basis of the self-report data it has been concluded that more masculine, aggressive acts, destroying property, and serious theft are much more common among Swiss boys than among Canadian boys, on the basis of data gathered in the world crime survey, Switzerland was chosen as a low-crime country (Adler, 1983), as one of the ten countries with the lowest crime rates throughout the world. In contrast, no differences in the rates of victimized people are found between large regions in the Federal Republic of Germany and Switzerland (Stadler, 1987) when using the same set of questions concerning serious crime [general property crimes (theft), burglary, auto theft, rape, robbery, serious and minor assault, and destruction of property].

The third type of comparative research on crime concerns predesigned victimization studies which are also quite rare but have made some progress toward a common and comparable set of victimizing events. Two predesigned comparative victimization studies using different operationalizations of victimizing events have been carried out up to now (but see also the Scandinavian survey on violence based on a questionnaire first used in Finland and then consecutively in other Scandinavian countries, Hauge & Wolf, 1974). One of these studies focused on "sexual victimization" in student populations of two university cities in the FRG and in the U.S. (Kirchhoff & Kirchhoff, 1979). The items introduced to measure sexual victimization were derived from the specific statutes criminalizing sexual behavior, thus employing quite different conceptions of sexual victimization. While American criminal law covers a wide range of sexual behavior, the German criminal sexual law is restricted to more or less serious sexual offenses. In Germany, moral crimes or offenses concerning consenting deviant sexual behavior are eliminated from the penal code.

As can be expected from these differences in the questionnaires, a 95% victimization rate was obtained in the American sample while the corresponding rate in the FRG was approximately 50%. It goes without saying that the use of different measures of sexual victimization does not allow valid comparisons between the two countries involved.

The questions which can be answered are properly restricted to the problem of how sexual victimization, as measured by operationalizing strictly legal categories of sexual offenses, is coped with in each jurisdiction. Thus, comparisons are not even possible on the question of whether differences in criminal law lead to differences in the distribution of events or the magnitude of certain problems, because events measured and counted are not the same.

While it has been argued that stressing differences in criminal law could be fruitful too (Croft, 1979), the general impression is that the strict reference to national penal codes in delineating items representing crime or deviance (with the consequence that these items do not overlap) leads instead to carrying out two different studies simultaneously.

The second predesigned comparative victimization study was carried out in three countries using the same standardized questionnaire, a mail survey, in Texas, U.S., Baden-Württemberg, FRG, and Baranya,

Hungary (Arnold, 1986; Arnold & Korinek, 1985). The German questionnaire was used again later in a German speaking Swiss canton (Stadler, 1987). The aims of this study concerned (1) measuring criminal victimization in different countries with differing legal and criminal justice systems, (2) identifying correlates of fear of crime and criminal victimization, and (3) assessing official aggregate crime data through examining reporting behavior and its correlates. The research group suggested a set of standardized definitions of crime categories which should be used as guidelines in the systematic comparison of two or three penal codes (Arnold & Teske, 1982). The study then concentrated on serious crime, on the one hand taking as its point of departure the Uniform Crime Report definitions (burglary, auto theft, larceny, assault with and without a weapon, robbery, rape, arson) while including on the other hand less serious crimes such as destroying property, and a general category of "other crimes" as well as victimizing events which are non-events vis-à-vis the criminal code (e.g., accidents) but nonetheless might have influence on "fear" and other variables.

In order to avoid "shopping basket" problems as much as possible (wide definitions of crime which may cover a wide range of behavior differing in seriousness) and to ensure comparability (within and across nations), additional questions related to each victimizing event asked for information on the type of property stolen or vandalized, the value of items lost through criminal events, the place where the crime occurred, injuries suffered, and victim relationship to the offender. With respect to the comparative approach related to police-recorded crime, two aspects had to be differentiated: the first aspect concerns comparability of survey data with police-recorded crime data within one country, while the second concerns comparability of police-recorded crime data between the countries. In-depth analysis of recording and counting procedures within police information systems as well as in-depth analysis of the content of the national penal codes allowed esti- mates about the degree to which police crime categories may in fact overlap or cover differing ranges of criminal behavior when focusing on police recorded crime. But the comparability of police-recorded crime data between countries as well as the comparability of survey data with police data are dependent on the degree to which police data can be disaggregated and broken down by characeristics of crimes introduced in questionnaires and seen as relevant within the theoretical framework of research. Thus, approximations are possible but strict comparability cannot be achieved. Nevertheless, survey data on victimizing events and reporting behavior actually could be compared and used in assessing differences in police-recorded crime rates between countries. Obvious- ly lower official crime rates in Hungary, as compared with the FRG, do not coincide with a similar relationship on the basis of victimization data (with a fairly higher rate of victimization in Hungary). This can be explained by differences in the reporting behavior which in turn might be related to different attitudinal patterns vis-à-vis the po- lice. What seems to be important for international comparisons of survey-based crime data is that comparability of crime events is depen- dent on two factors. The first is the amount of additional information which can be gathered about the event; the second is information on the meaning and relevance this event had for the respondent in terms of attitudes, perceptions, and behavior (e.g., reporting to the police, protective measures, fear, etc.).

It has been argued that the dimension of national penal codes and justice systems introduces a conceptual bias which should be avoided by making studies independent from the legal structures of the countries concerned (Wilkins, 1980, p. 39). Most important in this respect are attempts to get measures of severity of crime focussing on the harm caused via damage or injuries (Sellin & Wolfgang, 1964; Wolfgang et al., 1985; OECD-indicators of crime: van Dijk & Steinmetz, 1980; OECD, 1974). This kind of study has been carried out in various countries and has been interpreted as producing quite similar rank ordering of seriousness of different criminal events (Villmow, 1977). However, the results of these studies have been challenged by suggesting that it is not even possible to find a nationwide uniform measure of seriousness of crime, but that there are instead different groups within a country adopting quite differing views of crimes and deviance as defined in the penal code (Winberger, Jacubowics, & Robert, 1977; Christianson, 1970; see also Rose, 1970, stressing the relativity of measures of seriousness because of the lack of a clear-cut absolute base, p. 51). As measuring seriousness of crime requires assumptions about a basic consensus on what should be punished and on the seriousness of various acts, these findings suggest that measurement of crime seriousness should be multi-dimensional. Furthermore, replication of the first study on the severity of crime (Sellin et al., 1964) has been proven to be difficult without adapting the items to the legal structure of another country because harms described in the original questionnaire were not at all meaningful in another country. Thus in Denmark, from the original 141-item list, 20 items had to be eliminated (Christianson, 1970, p. 108).

A more radical solution of the problem of differing crime and delinquency definitions has been suggested by radical criminologists, arguing that it would be better to adopt a conflict view of juvenile behavior and to avoid the terms deviance and crime totally (European Group for the Study of Deviance and Social Control, 1983, p. 5).

Still other suggestions stress the differences in defining youth crime and juvenile delinquency, stating that no single unique definition of youth crime and juvenile delinquency can be adopted for purposes of comparative research, but that comparative research should attempt to understand how juvenile delinquency or juvenile crime are defined and experienced in everyday life (UNSDRI, 1984; UNSDRI, 1986), or should cover aspects of delinquency as an operational concept with different meanings in the community, in the police, and the court system (Peters, 1968). A rather similar proposal concerns the definition of delinquency as behavior which is dealt with through non-primary socializing agencies while behavior which is coped with by the family, etc., should be regarded to be non-delinquent, be it technically a crime or a delinquent act (Lejins, 1984, p. 3). Consequently, we may note the advice to refrain from the "crime in different countries syndrome" (Robertson & Taylor, 1973) and to focus on the relationship between controlled and controllers, to adopt a "wait and see approach" rather than relying on methods of agreement on the one hand or methods of difference on the other hand (Robertson et al., p. 28).

International comparative research on perceptions of crime and deviance has been carried out on the question of transcultural and transnational elements of crime and deviance norms (Newman, 1976; Scott & Al-Thakeb, 1980). While with these latter approaches, interests switch from measurement or explanation of criminal or deviant behavior to definitional problems, the other approaches to crime and delinquency uphold the question of crime and delinquency measurment or explanatory interests while trying to avoid legal definitions of crime and delin- quency. As Wilkins (1980) argued: "We should not assume that the con- cept of mala per se is valid but it is just possible that we might empirically find something like it as a basis for international data on the phenomena we now call crime." But it is rather difficult to ima- gine a phenomenological or empirical approach to the study of crime and deviance without reference to norms. To substitute the norm concept through terms such as "harm" is not avoiding definitional problems but is rather substituting one problem of definition for another. It is really hard to believe that it would be possible to get meaningful information through means like questionnaires and interviews by avoid- ing evaluative words which have some relation to the (deviant) behavior which is to be studied. This represents a kind of a scientific double bind: trying to get information, for example, about how often an indi- vidual has committed theft without using the term theft.

So, the problem is not to make data independent of the legal struc- ture but rather to organize data-gathering independently from assign- ment procedures normally embedded in processing an offender through the system.

4. WHICH OFFENSES OR DELINQUENT ACTS SHOULD BE COVERED BY AN INTERNATIONAL COMPARATIVE SELF-REPORT SURVEY?

Summarizing the above and attempting to arrive at conclusions about the type of offenses which should be included as well as the way they should be included in an international comparative study based on self-reports, we may consider the following aspects:

a) Reference has to be made to criminal law in deriving items which are used in questionnaires or interviews, with the intent of touching on criminal or delinquent behavior. There does not exist an empirical way to study crime and deviance which is independent from the legal norms, providing consequences in terms of punishment or reactions labelled otherwise (Gibbs, 1981).

b) For the purpose of international comparative studies on crime and delinquency, a standardized set of items referring to crimi- nal and delinquent statutes is needed (Clinard & Junger-Tas, 1979, p. 168) so that theoretical questions may be asked con- cerning the correlates of crime and delinquency, and the assess- ment of the impact of differences in the use of criminal law in

        controlling behavior.
- c) Standardization of items as a prerequisite for equivalent measures of crime and delinquency within or across nations requires:
1) appropriate choice between the different types of criminal or delinquent behavior as defined in criminal codes or delinquency laws,
2) appropriate operationalization of offenses or delinquent acts satisfying the need for equivalence across cultures or nations with respect to the meaning attached to specific behavior, the need for appropriate representation of legal crime definitions, and the need for comparability with other information systems concerning crime and delinquency (on police and/or court level).
- d) Standardization of items requires an appropriate translation (back and forth method), a more or less technical problem which, judging from experiences so far, can be solved adequately (Scott et al., 1980; Peyre, 1983).

As far as the appropriate choice of offenses or delinquent behavior is concerned, we have first to consider that the question of which crimes and delinquent acts should be covered must reflect the boundary of criminal law and delinquency laws as set up by all national codes. As any questionnaire or interview can only contain a sample from the population of criminal or delinquent acts, the question arises how this sample should be drawn from the general population of acts. Since it is not possible to draw a representative sample from all acts covered by legal crime definitions -- something which is not possible even if research is restricted to one jurisdiction -- the problem of choice of criminal delinquent acts has to be based on other procedures. In deciding upon this question we may resort to the research already done on the basis of self-report surveys. The first aspect we may consider concerns the advice to include serious crimes in order to avoid the problem of gathering too much data on trivial acts (Burcart, 1977; Huizinga & Elliott, 1986). But there are further aspects which have to be considered when the focus is on the appropriate choice among crimes. First of all, obviously the most serious crimes (murder, homicide, manslaughter) can seldom be included in questionnaire research because reliable data cannot be expected. Second, while there exist offense types (e.g., theft, assault) which can be translated into everyday language and can be circumscribed in a way guaranteeing that the range of behavior falling under the legal crime descriptions is adequately covered, there exist other serious offenses which cannot easily be translated into every language. Those have to be transformed into descriptions covering but a small part of the range of behavior potentially falling under the legal definitions (e.g., fraud, forgery, sexual offenses other than rape). Research which focussed on this problem has demonstrated that there are serious problems with respect to the understanding of certain types of offenses (Villmow, 1977; Villmow & Stephan, 1983; Elmhorn, 1965). To assure adequate understanding of these types of crime, rather lengthy explanations would be required, some kind of legal training during an interview or the administration of a questionnaire, which clearly is not a practical solution.

4.1. Specific categories

We can identify five areas of criminal or deviant behavior which should be included in international comparative research on crime and delinquency, because they display common main concerns about crime patterns and common interests in controlling behavior, at least among nations with comparable general opportunity structures:

4.1.1. Traditional, serious offenses. In the case of so-called traditional crime, a great deal of overlapping of legal definitions across countries can be expected, though legal terminology may vary.

4.1.2. New crime/modern crimes. In this area of criminal offenses, differences between penal codes can be expected on the question of how far criminal law actually goes in criminalizing or penalizing certain behavior. The most important type of crime which should be considered here is drug crime.

4.1.3. Petty offenses. With respect to petty offenses such as small theft, using public transportation systems without paying the fare, etc., differences between penal codes can be expected in terms of the degree of de facto decriminalization or the use of civil or administrative law.

4.1.4. Public order offenses. While most nations provide penal provisions at the community or state level which justify interventions in situations where public peace or public order are endangered, the focus in this area should be on the question of how these provisions are operationalized by police, courts, or other authorities.

4.1.5. Delinquency statutes, youth laws. The differences which exist with respect to the handling of youth problem behavior in legal definitions and delinquency or youth laws have been described earlier. Coping with these differences should mean the identification of problem behavior which might be relevant as a basis for official intervention, be it technically a delinquent act or serving as an indicator of neglect.

4.2. Specific Dimensions

Before going into some details with respect to the areas of offenses and crime types described above, we should acknowledge that there are several dimensions of equivalence which should be considered in international comparative research on crime and delinquency. The following figure displays the various dimensions.

242

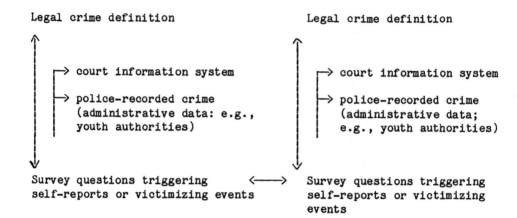

Nation A   Nation B

Legal crime definition   Legal crime definition

→ court information system   → court information system

→ police-recorded crime   → police-recorded crime
  (administrative data: e.g.,   (administrative data;
  youth authorities)   e.g., youth authorities)

Survey questions triggering   ⟷   Survey questions triggering
self-reports or victimizing events   self-reports or victimizing
                                            events

There are both vertical and horizontal dimensions of comparability and equivalence which should be considered. The vertical dimensions of comparability are essential for assessing the representativeness of survey questions with respect to legal crime definitions, for record checks as a measure of reliability, for the inclusion of complementary data on crime and delinquency (gathered from police and court information systems), and for assessing the involvement in crime on the part of non-respondents. The horizontal dimension focusses on the equivalence of survey questions across nations.

The need to ensure comparability within nations on the one hand and across nations on the other hand can be satisfied only when additional information on the offenses considered is collected. This allows accommodation to the varying crime definitions and estimates on equivalence between countries. Additional information should cover the following dimensions:

1. Characteristics of the criminal act;
2. Characteristics of the victim (if any);
3. Characteristics of crime objects;
4. Value of objects; intensity of injuries caused;
5. Perceived consequences of the act;
6. Experienced consequences of the act;
7. Participation in crime via groups, gangs, etc.

While some of these issues are general in nature, being relevant to each act, considered other categories apply only to certain types of crimes.

4.3. Specific Acts

Among the five areas of offenses or offense types enumerated earlier, for the traditional, serious crimes the following should be addressed in comparative surveys:

a)   Property crimes (theft, larceny, burglary, breaking and en-
     try): With respect to the general category of theft compara-
     bility of responses to questions addressing acts such as
     "taking away property without the intent to give it back"
     should require information on the value of items taken away,
     the place where a theft has been committed (school, at home,
     on the street, in another apartment, etc.), the kind of items
     taken (motor vehicle, bicycle, money, parts of bicycle,
     etc.), and the degree of force used. Information about these
     characteristics should allow assignment to the varying legal
     definitions of property crimes as well as accommodation to
     other data sources on crime.

b)   Robbery: Offense characteristics with respect to robbery
     which should be covered include the degree of violence or the
     degree of threat of violence, whether a weapon was used in
     exerting threat or violence, the type of object which the
     offender sought (money, other items) as well as its value,
     the place where the offense occurred (street, indoors, etc.),
     and finally, information concerning injuries suffered by the
     victim.

c)   Assault: With respect to assault, basically the same infor-
     mation as in the case of robbery should be sought.

d)   Rape: As in the case of assault, the degree of violence or
     threat of violence should be considered. Other questions
     should cover the place where the offense was committed, whe-
     ther a weapon was used, and whether there were injuries to
     the victim.

e)   Destruction of property: While basic information required to
     ensure comparability concerns the type of items destroyed,
     acts should be described as well; some acts may be labelled
     destruction of property in some countries that are not in
     others, e.g., graffiti.

f)   Arson: Additional information on arson should include the
     type of object burnt as well as the way the offense was com-
     mitted.

g)   Traffic offenses or traffic-related offenses: Some of these
     offenses, too, could be included in survey research, namely
     using a car without a license and using a motor vehicle with-
     out sufficient insurance.

h)   Receiving stolen property: Additional information should be
     related to the value of items received.

The second area of offenses which should be covered include so-
called new or modern crimes. Although there exist considerable differences in the specification of controlled drugs and the extent of criminalizing certain drug-related behavior, the following standard questions should be included in a survey: Type of behavior vis-à-vis
drugs: use/possession, purchase, selling drugs; the type of drug
(soft, hard), the amount of drugs involved and the intensity of use.

Another type of new crime which could be included in comparative
survey research concerns computer or information-related crime (e.g.,
copying, purchase of or selling computer programs, etc.).

With respect to petty crimes and behavior, the most commonly used in self-report research on crime and delinquency, most should be covered by questions addressing traditional (property) crimes. But there exist several other types of petty offenses which should be included in comparative research, as well.

   a) Using motor vehicles without the consent of the owner (joyriding).
   b) Using public transportation systems without paying the fare.
   c) Fraudulent behavior such as slipping into concerts, movies, etc., without a ticket.

Within the fourth area of offenses, public order offenses, questions should touch on those situtions and events which include the risk of being defined as disturbing public order and peace. These situations concern participation in riots or demonstrations, squatter movements, and certain types of youth movements or membership in soccer clubs. The emphasis should be on whether conflicts (and what kind of conflicts) with police or other authorities were involved while engaging in these types of activities.

With respect to the fifth area of concern, delinquency or juvenile laws, we may differentiate between several types of relationships between juveniles or adolescents and the institutions which may respond to their behavior. As has been mentioned earlier, the questions should not only address the mere occurrence of such behavior, but should touch also on the dimension of intensity and frequency.

At least three types of behavior should be included in comparative surveys aiming at delinquent behavior:

   a) Running away from home or staying away from home;
   b) Truancy or playing hooky from school;
   c) Under-age activities: use of alcohol, going to places such as discos, bars, etc., getting access to x-rated movies or videos, etc.

5. CONCLUSIONS

The problem of accommodation of penal code categories and juvenile delinquency definitions across countries may be resolved in comparative self-report research, whereas on the basis of official accounts of crime and delinquency, only rough approximations can be reached. The degree to which accommodation can be carried out depends on the amount of additional information which can be gathered in self-report surveys, which in turn is dependent on the method used. While accommodation of penal codes at large between various nations surely is not feasible, main areas of concern (as far as crime and delinquency are concerned) can be identified whereby behavioral and controlling dimensions should be included.

REFERENCES

Adler, F: <u>Nations Not Obsessed with Crime</u>. Littleton, 1983.

245

Albrecht, H-J: Criminal law and drug control: A look at Western Europe. *International Journal of Comparative and Applied Criminal Justice*, 10:17-40, 1986.

Albrecht, H-J: Particular difficulties in enforcing the law arising out of basic conflicts between the different agencies with regard to the best suited reaction upon highly sensitive kinds of crime. In European Committee on Crime Problems (Ed.), *Interactions Within the Criminal Justice System*,. Strasbourg, 1987, p. 13-20.

Anttila, I: Problems of comparative research on the use of discretion in criminal justice. *Annales Internationales de Criminologie*, 17:43-81, 1987.

Archer, D, & Gartner, R: *Violence and Crime in Cross-national Perspective*. New Haven, London, 1984.

Arnold, H: Kriminelle Viktimisierung und ihre Korrelate. *Zeitschrift für die Gesamte Strafrechtswissenschaft*, 98:1014-1058, 1986.

Arnold, H, & Korinek, L: Kriminalitätsbelastung in der Bundesrepublik Duetschland und Ungarn: Ergebnisse einer international vergleichenden Opferbefragung. In Böhm, H et al., (Eds.), *Kriminologie in Sozialistischen Ländern*. Bochum, 1985, p. 65-136.

Bennett, RR: The effect of police personnel levels on crime clearance rates: A cross national analysis. *International Journal of Comparative and Applied Criminal Justice*, 6:177-193, 1982.

Block, CR, & Block, RL: Crime definition, crime measurement, and victim surveys. *Journal of Social Issues*, 40:137-160, 1984.

Burcart, JM: Measuring delinquency through self-report instruments: A bibliographic essay. Institute of Policy Analysis, 1977.

Chang, DH, & Blazicek, DL: *An introduction to comparative and international criminology*. Durham, 1986.

Chirol, Y et al.: *Delinquance juvenile et developpement socio--economique*. Paris: La Haye, 1975.

Christiansen, KO: Method of using an index of crime of the kind devised by Sellin and Wolfgang. In Council of Europe (Ed.), *The Index of Crime. Some Further Studies*. Strasbourg, 1970, p. 7-30.

Christie, N, Andenaes, J., & Skirbekk, S: A study of self-reported crime. *Scandinavian Studies in Criminology*, 1:86-116, 1965.

Clinard, MB: *Cities with little crime*. Cambridge, 1978.

Clinard, MB, & Junger-Tas, J: Probleme und Resultate beim Vergleich ubernationaler Victim Surveys. In Kirchhoff, GF & Sessar, K (Eds.), *Das Verbrechensopfer*. Bocum, 1979, p. 159-176.

Collmann, H-J: *Internationale Kriminalstatistik. Geschichtliche Entwicklung unde gegenwärtiger Stand*. Stuttgart, 1973.

Council of Europe (Eds.): *Report on decriminalization*. Strasbourg, 1980.

Croft, J: *Crime and comparative research*. HORS 57. London, 1979.

van Dijk, JJM, & Steinmetz, CHD: *The RDC victim surveys 1974-79*. The Hague, 1980.

Dünkel, F & Meyer, K (eds.): *Jugendstrafe und Jugendstrafvollzug. Stationäre Massnahmen der Jugendkriminalrechtspflege im internationalen Vergleich*. Vol. 1, Freiburg, 1985. Vol 2, Frieburg, 1986.

246

Duffee, DE: Explaining Criminal Justice. Community, Theory and Criminal Justice Reform. Cambridge 1980.

Elmhorn, K: Study in self-reported delinquency among school children in Stockholm. Scandinavian Studies in Criminology, 1:117-146, 1965.

Eser, A & Koch, H-G (Eds.): Schwangerschaftsabbruch im Internationalen Vergleich. Baden-Baden, 1988.

European Group for the Study of Deviance and Social Control: Disputing deviance: Experience of youth in the eighties. Working papers in European Criminology No. 4.

Gibbs, JP: Norm, deviance, and social control. Conceptual matters. New York: Oxford, 1981.

Gross, H: A theory of criminal justice. Oxford, 1979.

Gurr, TR: Crime trends in modern democracies since 1945. Annales Internationales de Criminologie, 16:41-85, 1977.

Hauge, R: Definition and scope of comparative studies in crime trends, including a review of work carried out since about 1945. In Council of Europe (Ed.), Trends in crime: Comparative studies and technical problems. Strasbourg, 1983, p. 25-49.

Hauge, R, & Wolf, P: Criminal violence in three Scandinavian countries. Scandinavian Studies in Criminology, 5:25-33, 1974.

Heine, G: Erkennung und Verfolgung von Umweltstraftaten im Europäischen Rechtsraum. Umwelt & Planaungsrecht, 1987, p. 281-291.

Henry, M: Etude de la comparabilite des criteres juridiques. Annales de Vaucresson, 1977, p. 61-97.

Huizinga, D, & Elliott, DS: Reassessing the reliability and validity of self-report measures. Journal of Quantitative Criminology, 2:293-327, 1986.

Joutsen, M: Computerization and the international exchange of information on crime and criminal justice. In HEUNI (Ed.), Computerization of criminal justice information systems: Realities, prospects, methods and effects. Helsinki, 1987, p. 253-266.

Junger-Tas, J: Some issues and problems in cross-cultural research in criminology. The Hague, 1978.

Kaiser, G: The comparative method in criminology. NCJRS, 1978.

Kerner, H-J: Fear of crime and attitudes towards crime. Comparative criminological reflections. Annales Internationales de Criminologie, 17:83-99, 1978.

Kirchhoff, C, & Kirchhoff, GF: Untersuchungen im Dunkelfeld sexueller Viktimisation mit Hilfe von Fragebögen. In Kerchhoff, GG, & Sessar, K. (Eds.), Das Verbrechensopfer. Bochum, 1979, p. 275-299.

Klein, MW (Ed.): Western systems of juvenile justice. Beverly Hills, Sage Publications: 1984

Landau, SF: Trends in violence and aggression: A cross-cultural analysis. Annales Internationales de Criminologie, 22:119-150, 1984.

Lejins, PP: A speculative note on the meaning of juvenile delinquency.
    In Brusten, M et al., (Eds.):   Youth crime, social control and
    prevention: Theoretical perspectives and policy implications.
    Studies from nine different countries.   Pfaffenweiler, 1984, p.
    3-8.
Luhmann, N: Rechtssoziologie.   Reinbek, 1972.
Malewska, H, & Peyre, V: Delinquance juvenile, famille, ecole et soci-
    ete.   Vaucresson, 1973.
Martin, RG, & Conger, RD: A comparison of delinquency trends: Japan
    and the United States.   Criminology, 18:53-61, 1980.
McClintock, FH: The phenomenological and contextual analysis of crimi-
    nal violence.   In Council of Europe (Ed.), Violence in society.
    Strasbourg, 1973, p. 115-162.
Meyer, J. (Ed.):   Betäubungsmittelstrafrecht in Westeuropa.   Freiburg,
    1987.
Moitra, S: Crimes and punishments.   Freiburg, 1987.
Newman, G: Comparative deviance.   Perception and law in six cultures.
    New York, Oxford, Amsterdam, 1976.
OECD: Social indicators: Recommended list of social concerns.   In
    Zapf, W (Ed.):   Soziale Indikatoren.   Knozepte und Forschung-
    sansätze.   Frankfurt, New York, 1974, p. 229-230.
Peters, AAG: Comparative survey of juvenile delinquency in Asia and
    the Far East.   UNAFEI, Tokyo, 1968.
Peyre, V: Technical problems in the design and execution of compara-
    tive studies.   In Council of Europe (Ed.):   Trends in crime:
    Comparative studies and technical problems.   Strasbourg, 1983, p.
    53-69.
le Poole, F: Law and practice concerning the counterparts of "persons
    in need of supervision" in some European countries, with a partic-
    ular emphasis on the Netherlands.   In Teitelbaum, LE, & Gough, HR
    (Eds.):   Beyond Control.   Status Offenders in the Juvenile Court.
    Cambridge, 1977, p. 115-160.
Redo, SM: The United Nations Crime Trends Surveys: Comparative crimi-
    nology in the global context.   Annales Internationales de
    Criminologie, 24:163-179, 1986.
Reiss, AJ: Problems in developing statistical indicators of crime.   In
    Connaitre la criminalité: Le dernier etat de la question.   Aix,
    Marseille, 1983, p. 25-61.
Robertson, R, & Taylor, L: Deviance, Crime and Socio-Legal Control.
    Bristol, 1973.
Rose, GNG: The merits of an index of crime of the kind devised by
    Wolfgang and Sellin.   In Council of Europe (Ed.):   The index of
    crime.   Some further studies.   Strasbourg, 1970, p. 33-52.
Scott, JE, & Al-Thakeb, F: Perceptions of deviance cross-culturally.
    In Newman, G. (Ed.), Crime and deviance. A comparative perspec-
    tive.   Beverly Hills, London: Sage Publication, 1980, p. 42-67.
Sellin, T, & Wolfgang, ME: The measurement of delinquency.   London,
    1964.
Smith, LJF: Criminal justice comparisons.   London: Home Office, 1983.

248

Stadler, H: Kirminalitat im Kanton Uri. Eine Opferbefragung. Jur.
    Diss, Entlebuch, 1987.
Stephan, E: Die Stuttgarter Opferbefragung. Wiesbaden, 1976.
Swanson, C: A comparison of organizational and environmental influ-
    ences on arrest policies. In Meyer, FA, & Baker, R (Eds.),
    Determinants of law-enforcement policies. Lexington, Toronto,
    1979, p. 15-33.
Teske, RHC, & Arnold, H: Comparison of the criminal statistics of the
    United States and the Federal Republic of Germany. Journal of
    Criminal Justice, 10:359-374, 1982.
UNSDRI: Juvenile social maladjustment. Rome, 1984.
UNSDRI: Action oriented research on youth crime. An international
    perspective. Rome, 1986.
Vaz, EW, & Casparis, J: A comparative study of youth culture and delin-
    quency: Upper middle-class Canadian and Swiss boys. In Shelley,
    LI (Ed.), Readings in comparative criminology. Cabandale,
    Edwardsville, 1981, p. 56-77.
Vetere, E., & Newman, G: International crime statistics: An overview
    from a comparative perspective. Abstracts on Criminology and
    Penology, 17:251-267, 1977.
Villmow, B: Schwereeinschätzung von Delikten. Berlin, 1977.
Villmow, B, & Stephan, E: Jugendkriminalität in einer Gemeinde. Frei-
    burg, 1983.
Waller, I: La criminalité au Canada et aux Etats Unis: Tendences et
    explications comparatives. Annales Internationales de Crimino-
    logie, 14:51-84, 1981.
Waller, I, & Okihiro, N: Burglary: The victim and the public. Toron-
    to, 1978.
Weinberger, J-C, Jakubowicz, P. & Robert, P: Sociète et perceptions
    des comportements déviants incriminiès. Paris, 1977.
Wellford, LF: Crime and the dimension of nation. International Jour-
    nal of Criminology and Penology, 2:1-10, 1974.
Wilkins, LT: World crime. To measure or not to measure? In Newman,
    GR (Ed.): Crime and deviance. A comparative perspective. Bever-
    ly Hills, London: Sage Publications, 1980, p. 17-41.
Wolf, P: Crime and development. An international comparison of crime
    rates. Scandinavian Criminology, 3:107-120, 1971.
Wolfgang, ME, et al.: The national survey of crime severity. Washing-
    ton, D.C.: Department of Justice, 1985.

WHAT KIND OF HOMOGENEITY FOR SELF-REPORT DELINQUENCY ITEMS?

Paul Dickes
Centre d'Etudes de Populations de Pauvrete et de
    Politiques Sociales
Walferdange, Luxembourg

1. INTRODUCTION

Since the seminal work of Nye and Short (1957), delinquency has commonly been defined operationally by the responses subjects give on self-report delinquency items. This methodology was the origin of a productive research trend. In 1965, different reports on self-report delinquency questionnaires were presented at a conference at Syracuse University (Hardt & Bodine, 1965). Reviews were published by Nettler (1974) and particularly by Hindelang, Hirschi and Weis (1981). The book Measuring Delinquency by Hindelang, Hirschi and Weis (1981) is a very comprehensive contribution to the measurement of delinquency with self-report material. It included a review of the main issues in the English-speaking literature and results of a vast quasi-experimental study on conditions affecting reliability and validity of self-report procedures.

The purpose of this paper is to go back to structural aspects of measurement of delinquent behavior through self-report items. Traditionally, scales or indicators are constituted by adding the subject's responses to the self-report items. Can this procedure be justified from a psychometric point of view? In other terms, is it possible to presume that the items of the scale belong to a single dimension, or the same latent trait? The answer to this question, according to Hindelang et al. (1982) is based on the structure of the correlation matrix between the items: they propose three competing models which may occur theoretically (Hindelang et al., 1981, 46-47):

1. all items in the set may be uncorrelated, in which case a global scale consisting of these items is without empirical foundation;

2. all items in the set may be strongly intercorrelated, in which case a global scale composed of such items could be replaced by any item in the pool;

3. some items in the set may be strongly correlated with each other and uncorrelated with the remaining items.

The main issues of the review of Hindelang, et al. (1981), as far

M. W. Klein (ed.), Cross-National Research in Self-Reported Crime and Delinquency, 249–267.
© 1989 by Kluwer Academic Publishers.

250

as the measurement problem is concerned, can be summarized as follows:

1. Most authors don't justify methodologically the operation of adding the responses of subjects for a composite score. They either create a global score or several subscores without any empirical basis.

2. If reliability coefficients are estimated, they agree with the best psychometric standards (test-retest reliabilities vary between 0.80 and 0.95; internal consistency coefficients and split-half reliabilities vary between 0.85 and 0.95).

3. The correlations between the items are positive and greater than zero.

4. Some authors (Nye & Short, 1957; Slocum & Stone, 1963; Dentler & Monroe, 1961; Arnold, 1965; Liska, 1973) apply the hierarchical deterministic model of Guttman to the data. The fit is generally bad, unless the numbers of items are less than 10.

5. Factor analysis gives divergent results. Some are unidimensional (Gold, 1970), others are bi- or multidimensional (2, 3 or even 10 factors). If multidimensional solutions are found (Quay & Blumen, 1963; Short & Strodtbeck, 1965; Winslow, 1967; Heise, 1968; Ferdinand & Luchterhand, 1970; Senna et al., 1974; Walberg et al., 1974), they often cover the traditional categories of delinquent behavior like thefts, assaults, withdrawal.[1]

6. Cluster-analysis of the items leads to different clusters. In general, cluster interpretation corresponds to the traditional domains of self-report items. The sub-scores computed with the items of same clusters are positively intercorrelated.

Considering these results, Hindelang et al. (1981) reject the first theoretical possibility (independence between items) and the second one (global solution). They adopt a "moderate" version of the third possibility (positively intercorrelated subscores).

We consider that this position may not be the definite answer to the general problem of homogeneity of self-report items.

Responses are usually dichotomized and the probability of occurrence of many severe delinquency behaviors is generally low. Or, the size of the correlation coefficient between binary items is sensitive to the probability of occurrence of the responses. The smaller the probability, the smaller the correlation. So the correlation between infrequent items and frequent items cannot be high, even if a strong relation exists. The particular structure of the correlation matrix of the authors' third possibility can thus be explained by the marginal probability of the items. This can influence all analyses performed from a correlation matrix (like internal consistency, factor analysis, and cluster analysis of items).

The negative results of the application of the hierarchical model is not surprising. The conditions for the deterministic Guttman-model are severe; no error components are allowed. So the application of

----

1. Fréchette and LeBlanc (1979) obtain a two factorial solution: delinquency and misconduct.

other hierarchical models with less severe conditions is tempting.

If one can observe correlations between sub-scores (stemming from factor analysis or cluster analysis) the problem of the structure of this correlation matrix is still not solved. We will apply structural and measurement models -- which can handle responses with low marginal probability -- to our own data, in order to test the homogeneity of self-report items. Several years ago we studied[2] self-report delinquency in Belgium (Universite de Liege) and France (Universite de Nancy II). We used self-report instruments in the theoretical context of Hirschi's control theory (Hirschi, 1969). Although our main concern is theoretical aspects, this paper is specifically focused on measurement problems. Several publications and communications set the context: Dickes and Hausman (1983), Hausman (1984), Dickes and Hausman (1984), Dickes (1985a, 1985b), Dickes and Hausman (1986). Our theoretical position concerning measurement of delinquency through self-report items can briefly be recalled (Dickes, 1985a):

1. The measurement of delinquency is a **behavioral** one. It doesn't matter much whether the measurement of delinquency is unidimensional or multidimensional, but the index or score constituted with self-report items has to be considered as a behavioral one.

    Of course, the meaning of "behavior" differs from the meaning given by experimental psychologists and ethnologists. We measure behavior indirectly through verbal responses. We ask subjects about their own behavior retrospectively, so typical distortions and errors may occur. But Hindelang et al. (1981) show that these errors are known and could reasonably be controlled.

2. Self-report items belong to the behavioral class of **involvement**.

    In the context of "facet theory" (Canter, 1985) one can basically distinguish several behavioral variables by the meaning assigned in principle by the researcher to the response category.

    Levy (1985) makes the distinction between three varieties of behavioral variables: intelligence, attitude, and involvement. The formal definition of involvement is given by the following mapping sentence (Levy, 1985, p. 61):

    > An item belongs to the universe of involvement
    > items if and only if its domain asks about the
    > amount of contacts in a (cognitive/affective/in-
    > strumental) modality with an object, and its
    > range is ordered from (very high to very low)
    > amount of contact with that object.

----
2. Together with Pierre Hausman.

Self report items belong to the instrumental (or behavioral) modality of the definition. Involvement is defined with respect to some object. This object refers precisely to the content of self-report items.

3. Self-report items belong to the class of **derogatory conducts**.

In the literature of self-reported studies, one can find two kinds of practices in defining the content of the items. The first practice is the inclusion in the questionnaire of only those items which are offenses against the law (see Hirschi, 1969). The second practice stretches the definition and also includes misconducts and misdemeanors. Debuyst (1975) sees offenses and misconducts as "problematic behavior."

The empirical results of Hindelang et al., (1981) support the second practice. Many researchers regard misconducts as belonging to the same dimension(s) as offenses. For theoretical and practical purposes, it is important that the definition of the content is independent of local official norms. This is extremely important, if comparative research is to be done.

That is the reason we opt for the second practice. But we prefer the term "derogatory conduct" to "problematic behavior."[3] The meaning of "derogatory conduct" is closer to the definition of the object we want to measure than the meaning of "problematic behavior." It includes the ideas of "nonconformity" and "affect someone or make prejudice."

We shall now present basic material, models, and results of our own investigation. The same self-report questionnaire is administered under standardized conditions to five different samples. We use material collected by students for their dissertations and make secondary analyses on the merged file of self-report items.

2. RESEARCH DESIGN

The questionnaire contains 30 items. The items cover all those aspects which are traditionally included in self-report instruments: vandalism, drug and alcohol abuse, assaults, thefts, and misconducts at home and school. Only 27 items are retained for treatment. The official contacts with police and the reactions of teachers serve as control variables.

The response categories for each item are ordinal, as follows: never, once, sometimes, often, and no answer.

----

3. The term was suggested by our colleague Jacques Selosse.

The questionnaire is anonymous and applied collectively in class-rooms.

The reference population is young people (boys and girls) of secondary schools (first level). Three independent samples are drawn at random from the list of student's classes in two French towns in 1983 and 1984. The sample size is respectively of 363, 380 and 149. Data are merged into a unique file and contain 892 observations. Of the sample, 50.6% are boys and 8% of the students are not of French nationality. All school-types and socioeconomic levels of families are represented. Age ranges between 14 and 16 years.

3. MODELS AND METHODS

Data analysis concerns mainly the items. We test hypotheses concerning the relations between items and/or structure of response vectors of the subjects. Four competing models can be defined.

1. Model of maximum heterogeneity: Self-report items are independent.

2. Model of differential homogeneity: Delinquency is multidimensional. It is possible to derive several distinct dimensions from self-report items. Dimensions may be independent or correlated.

3. Model of maximum global homogeneity: Self-report delinquency is global or unidimensional.

4. Model of maximum hierarchical homogeneity: Self-report delinquency is unidimensional, and between the items one can observe a hierarchical structure.

There exists a network of logical relationships between the four models. If model number one is true, the other three are false. If model number two is true, the third and fourth are false. If model number four is true, model number three is true also. If model number three is true, model number four may be true or false.

We adopt the principle of triangulation (Denzin, 1970) for testing the models. Different methods are applied to the same data. Each method has specific limitations or constraints. The convergence of results leads to a final interpretation. We particularly use the following exploratory and confirmatory techniques.

Item analysis, internal consistency, and principal component analysis are well known and need no special developments. The methods are used by Hindelang et al., (1982). The two other methods are confirmatory measurement models. They may directly test hypotheses about homogeneity. Our demonstration is principally based on the results obtained with these two methods.

254

TABLE 1. Methods used for testing the models.

Method	Type of technique	Type of data	Type of association
Internal consistency	exploratory	relation between items	Bravais-Pearson correlation
Principal component analysis	exploratory	relation between items	Bravais-Pearson correlation
The measurement component of LISREL	confirmatory	relation between items	polychoric correlation
Rasch model	confirmatory	structure of the response vector	-----------

LISREL (Analysis of Linear Structural Relationships) is a general model, developed by Jöreskog (1969, 1970) for analyzing covariance matrices. It consists of two parts: a measurement model and a structural equation model. We are only interested in the measurement model which specifies how the latent variables (or factors) are measured in terms of the observed variables. The confirmatory approach proceeds as follows:
- Computation of a correlation matrix from empirical material (observed correlation matrix).
- Formulation of hypotheses concerning the factorial structure.
- Translation of the hypotheses into parameters (fixed, free, and constrained parameters are allowed).
- Estimation of free parameters with least squares or maximum likelihood methods.
- Computation of a theoretical correlation matrix.
- Testing the fit between observed and theoretical correlation matrix.

We adopted the suggestions of Jöreskog and Sörbom (1981), concerning the handling of discrete variables and we calculated the polychoric correlation coefficient between the items.

The Rasch model, a Guttman-like procedure for dichotomous items, belongs to the class of latent-trait models. It was developed in the sixties by the Danish psychologist Rasch (1960, 1966). Computational problems in relation to the model are mastered (Fischer & Allerup, 1968; Wright and Panchapakesan, 1969; Gustafsson, 1977). All latent-trait models have in common that a set of parameters is used for the description of the items and that a single parameter represents the latent trait. The function relating the latent trait and the probability of response to the item is explicitly stated: a logistic function is used. The Rasch model is the simplest of all latent-trait models. Only one parameter is used for each item: its difficulty. Thus the Rasch model is labelled as a <u>one-parameter model</u>. The Rasch model asserts that the probability of a correct answer by person v to item i is:

$$P\left(A_{vi} = 1 \mid \xi_v, \sigma_i\right) = \frac{\exp\left(\xi_v - \sigma_i\right)}{1 + \exp\left(\xi_v - \sigma_i\right)} \qquad \text{(Eq. 1)}$$

σ_i = The difficulty parameter of item i.

ξ_v = The ability parameter of person v.

A_{vi} = A binary response variable with the value 1 if answer of person v to item i is correct and the value 0 if incorrect or omitted. A particular realization of this stochastic variable is given the algebraic notation of a_{vi}.

k = The number of items in the test.

Here are some important properties of the model:
1. If items are model-conform, they measure all the same latent-trait: involvement in derogatory behavior. Items are unidimensional and homogeneous.
2. Items and persons are measured on the <u>same</u> latent-traits: involvement in derogatory behavior.
3. The relation between probability of occurrence of a derogatory behavior and latent-trait is a <u>logistic function</u>. The slope of the <u>item-characteristic curve</u> is the same for each item. So there exists a hierarchical probabilistic relation between the items. If a person is intensely involved in derogatory behavior, it is highly probable that items with lesser intensity, like minor delicts or misconducts, are also performed by this person. The lower the intensity of the items on the latent-trait is, the higher is the probability of occurrence of the behavior by that person.
4. Stochastic independence between items is assumed. The response to an item i is independent of the response to an item j. Correlation between two items depends only on the correlation the items have with the latent trait.
5. The raw score (number of derogatory behaviors) is a sufficient statistic for estimating the position of the person on the latent-trait.

This model imposes rather demanding conditions for a unidimensional measure. But if the application leads to positive results, an <u>objective</u> measure of delinquency is realized. We speak of objectivity if

the person-specific parameter (on the latent trait) is constant for a
given person regardless of the items that person attempts, and if the
item-specific parameter (on the same latent trait) is taken constant
for a given item regardless of the person's attempting that item.

4. TESTING MODELS

Which of the four hypothetical models is now consistent with the
data? Our answer stems from the confrontation of the results obtained
by different methods. We can easily discard the model of maximum heterogeneity with the results from the confirmatory techniques. The choice
beween the model of differential homogeneity and the model of maximum
global homogeneity is done by LISREL. The results confirm the maximum
global homogeneity hypothesis. The main features of this test have
been published (Dickes, 1985b), so here we will only summarize our
results. The test of maximum hierarchical homogeneity is done by means
of the Rasch model. We present these results with more details, because they have not been published elsewhere. We will see that the
structure of our data is consistent with the hierarchical hypothesis of
the Rasch model.

4.1. Model of Maximum Heterogeneity

There is enough experimental evidence for discarding the model of
maximum heterogeneity. The review of Hindelang et al. (1982) shows
that the correlation coefficients between the items are positive and
that the internal consistency is greater than 0.80. Our results are
consistent with those of Hindelang et al. (1982).
- The mean correlation between the items is 0.30 with a standard
  deviation of 0.09. All the correlations are located between
  0.11 and 0.63.
- Internal consistency (measured with the alpha coefficient of
  Cronbach) equals 0.92.
- Principal component analysis shows that the first factor,
  before rotation, explains 33% of the total variance. Satura-
  tions of the items on the first component are greater than
  0.40.

4.2. Models of Differential and Global Homogeneity

Different factor-analytic structural hypotheses are analyzed with
LISREL. The results are summarized in Table 2.
Several global indicators evaluate the fit between the observed
and the theoretical correlation matrix. It is sufficient here to exam-
ine the goodness-of-fit index adjusted for degrees of freedom (AGFI).[4]
The nearer the index is to the value 1, the better is the adjustment.
The inspection of Table 2 shows that solutions B2 and C2 are

----

4. Use of Chi square makes no sense because the estimation of the
parameters was done with an unweighted least square technique.

TABLE 2. Confirmatory factor analysis of different theoretical representations with LISREL. (NF = number of factors: AFGI = adjusted goodness of fit index; RMS = root mean square residual; Item numbers refer to the list - Table A - in appendix).

Factorial representation	NF	NP	AGFI	RMS
A. One general factor (27 items)	1	54	0.974	0.081
B. Two factors (number of items) factor 1: 2,4,5,6,7,8,10,12,13,14, 15,16,17,18,19,20,24,25, 26,28,29; factor 2: 1,9,11,22,27,30				
- B1: oblique solution: correlation between factors is estimated	2	55	0.977	0.076
- B2: orthogonal solution: correlation between factors is fixed = 0.	2	54	0.717	0.266
C. Three factors (number of items) factor 1: 2,5,6,8,12,14,18,19,24, 25,26; factor 2: 1,9,11,15,17,22,27,30; factor 3: 4,7,10,13,16,20,28,29.				
- C1: oblique solution: correlations between factors are estimated	3	57	0.983	0.065
- C2: orthogonal solution: correlations between factors are fixed = 0.	3	54	0.376	0.395

- A: one general factor: test of the model of maximum global homogeneity.
- B: two-factorial representation: delinquency and retreatism.
- B1: correlation between factors is allowed (oblique solution).
- B2: correlation between factors is fixed to be equal to 1 (orthogonal solution).
- C: three-factorial representation: thefts, retreatism-vandalism, assaults.
- C1: correlations between factors are allowed (oblique solution).
- C2: correlations between factors are fixed to equal 1 (orthogonal solution).

258

unsatisfactory and can be rejected. Solution A is equivalent to solution B1 or C1, and solution B1 is equivalent to solution C1. The correlations between oblique factors are substantive (greater than 0.80). Thus, we cannot reject the model of maximal global homogeneity. Between the three well-adjusted models we choose the global factorial representation. In doing so we adopt the principle of economy of science: If three competing models fit the data as well, the simplest solution is the best.

4.3. Model of Maximum Hierarchical Homogeneity

The test of this theoretical representation is performed with the Rasch model. The responses of the subjects are dichotomized. If the answer of the subject is "never" he obtains the score 0. All other response categories are coded 1. After eliminating the subjects whose raw score equals 0 (no derogatory behavior) or 27 (the subject is involved in all the derogatory behaviors),[5] estimation of the parameters is performed with a maximum likelihood function (Fischer, 1974).

Different tests are applied for evaluating the qualities of the solutions. Some procedures are concerned with the analysis of the items; others are global.

The item-specific tests allow discarding those items which are not model-conform. The following procedure is adopted here:

Different sub-samples are created. If the Rasch model holds for these items, estimation of item-parameters must remain stable between the different samples. We have tested the stability of item-parameters on five different samples:

ECH1: total sample (N=892 subjects);
ECH2: study number 1 (N=363);
ECH3: study number 2 (N=380);[6]
ECH4: subjects without official self-report delinquency (N=718);
ECH5: subjects with official self-report delinquency (N=174).

The overall quality of the solutions is evaluated with global tests. We use here the tests of Andersen and Martin-Löf (Gustaffson, 1977). The fit is evaluated through a chi-square function.

The global test of the 27 derogatory items are presented in the following table.

The fit between the observed and the expected theoretical structure is far from being satisfactory. The discrepancies evaluated with Chi square tests are important.

The application of the item-oriented tests reveals that instability of estimation of item parameters results mainly from inadequacies in the formulation of the items. Stochastic independence is offended with items number 5, 6, 22, and 25, while formulation with double meaning occurred in items number 12, 13, and 15. These seven items are thus

----

5. It is impossible to estimate the parameters for these subjects.

6. We reject the application of the study number 3, because the number of subjects (N=149) is too low.

TABLE 3. Global tests of adequacy of the Rasch model with the 27 items (df = degrees of freedom: p = probability).

Analysis	N	Nr	Martin-Löf Chi^2	df	p	Andersen Chi^2	df	p
ECH1 total sample	892	824	890.5	650	0.000	125.6	78	0.011
ECH2 study no. 1	363	330	848.6	598	0.000	40.5	26	0.037
ECH3 study no. 2	380	361	934.6	624	0.000	61.1	26	0.000
ECH4 no official contacts	718	654	580.6	416	0.000	75.8	52	0.020
ECH5 official contacts	174	170	702.1	650	0.138	42.0	26	0.012

discarded. The remaining item-pool of 20 items is then tested again.
    The results of the overall tests with the set of the 20 remaining items is presented in the following table.

TABLE 4. Global tests of adequacy of the Rasch model with the 20 items (df = degrees of freedom: p = probability).

Analysis	N	Nr	Martin-Löf Chi^2	df	p	Andersen Chi^2	df	p
ECH1 total sample	892	793	469.6	342	0.000	82.3	76	0.299
ECH2 study no. 1	363	315	442.2	323	0.000	22.4	17	0.269
ECH3 study no. 2	380	354	381.5	323	0.029	65.0	38	0.005
ECH4 no official contacts	718	624	321.9	228	0.000	46.5	38	0.167
ECH5 official contacts	174	169	402.8	342	0.030	22.1	19	0.279

The improvement of the adjustment is impressive. Chi square tests show that the discrepancies between observed and theoretical structure are reduced and become insignificant. The estimation of item parameters, performed on each sub-sample, is also stable. All the correlations between the estimations of item-parameters performed on each sub-sample are greater than 0.99.

Thus, the model of maximum hierarchical homogeneity of these 20 items cannot be rejected. The hierarchical ordering of the items and the corresponding magnitude of the items on the latent trait are presented in Table 5. The values are expressed in a metric, called the WITS scale (Wright, 1968), and presented and discussed as the W scale (Woodcock & Dahl, 1971). The norming is performed from a single reference item, with a theoretical WITS value of 50.

5. DISCUSSION

The results from the analysis are in favor of maximal global homogeneity. If self-report items are constructed with contents covering that which we call derogatory behavior -- delinquency and misconducts -- the prevalence of one latent variable can empirically be sustained.

TABLE 5. Ordered list of the 20 items which conform to the Rasch model (* = norming item).

Item	WITS
30. Retort to teacher	32.17
11. Get drunk seriously	42.15
18. Enter into a cinema without paying a ticket	42.28
1. Stay away from school without excuse	42.87
24. Take things worth less than 100 frs.	44.67
10. Quarrel and hurt someone	45.36
7. Destroy candy, coin ... machine	46.35
9. Run away from home and stay overnight	49.49
20. Slashing the seats in a bus ...	49.64
28. Purposely destroy tires, aerial ...	50.76
2. Take things worth less than 1000 frs.	51.27*
27. Use hashish, downers, marijuana ...	52.41
17. Use speed, heroin, LSD ...	54.11
19. Take a car for a ride ...	55.07
8. Take a wallet, handbag ...	55.65
14. Take a bicycle ... (no returning)	56.17
4. Purposely destroy the windows of a car	56.28
26. Take hubcaps, wheels, the battery ...	57.22
29. To fire at persons, cars, ...	57.47
16. Intentionally started a building on fire	58.60

This factor reproduces the original correlation matrix as well as

several multidimensional oblique factor-analytic solutions. The
substantial correlation between oblique factors supports the general
factor interpretation.

These results don't agree with the position of Hindelang et al.
(1981). They adopted a "moderate" version of the differential homogeneity model. Although they observe high intercorrelations between
different delinquency scores, they prefer the differential hypothesis.
In view of our results, this interpretation is not false. One can also
reproduce the correlation matrix if the emergence of oblique factors is
allowed. But the same fit is performed with the one-factor solution,
so we prefer the simpler maximum global homogeneity model to the differential homogeneity model.

We can thus accept the usual practice in criminological research
consisting of summing up the responses to self-report items in order to
construct global indicators. This is a legitimate measure of the latent trait. Results from different questionnaires, items and settings
can thus legitimately be compared. This appears to be an important
point for the generalizations of the results performed with self-report
material.

The generalizations hold also if one considers specific domains of
the items. If different authors study some preferential subsets of
behavior (like thefts, drug abuse, or school misbehaviors), they measure with self-report items the same global hypothetical construct:
involvement in derogatory behavior. Local theories on these domains
are thus preferably reformulated in general terms.

Age-specific limits have to be underlined. Our samples are 14-16
year-old children. From longitudinal research (West & Farrington,
1977; LeBlanc & Biron, 1980) we know that delinquent involvement is
maximal at that age. Application of the maximum global homogeneity
hypothesis to the self-report behaviors of younger or older subjects
has to be demonstrated.

As far as the maximum hierarchical homogeneity model is concerned,
the findings are provocative for further research. Within the limits
of our research and if given conditions are fulfilled, the maximum
hierarchical homogeneity model, measured with the Rasch measurement
procedure, cannot be discarded. This is an encouraging issue, because
the theoretical properties of the Rasch model throw new perspectives on
theoretical and practical features of self-report measures. Our results suggest that the Rasch model holds for different sub-sets of
items if one is careful about the formulation of the items.

Can these conclusions be generalized? The answer is, of course,
no. Replications and further testing are needed. The assumptions
about three main features of the Rasch model merit further consideration.

(1) The first one is concerned with the hierarchical property of
the items. Our results are in contradiction to the results of the
application of the Guttman scaling method (especially if the number of
items is greater than 10). The explanation lies in the deterministic
version of the Guttman scale used in the previously cited research.
The deterministic conditions, with the assumptions of error-free
measurement, are too restricting and not very realistic for social

research.

If the Rasch model holds, the hierarchical properties are given. In fact, the one-parameter model supposes that the item-characteristic curve has the same slope. This leads to a hierarchy between the items on the latent continuum. The more delinquent a subject is, the higher is the probability of occurrence of minor delinquencies. A person who will usually commit serious delicts will, with a high probability, also commit minor delicts or misconducts. The smaller (expressed in WITS) the delicts are, the greater the probability of occurrence. If these conditions are fulfilled -- as the findings from our research do suggest -- we need further research in order to explain this regularity.

Even the probabilistic hierarchical assumptions of the Rasch model impose heavy constraints on the data. Need for replications is crucial for the generalizations of the results. Rasch analysis must be applied to other data. In the case of negative results, other homogeneity models (like two- or three-parameter models) -- where hierarchical conditions are relaxed -- have to be applied.

(2) The second point concerns the items. Results are very sensitive to the formulation of the items. Care has to be taken against propositions offending stochastic independence. Double meaning in the wording of the items has to be avoided. If, in an empirical sense, the application of the Rasch model on a subset of items was quite possible, we need further theoretical refinement to define more exactly the concepts (involvement in derogatory behavior) and the transformation rules for translating concepts into items. Explicit rules seem necessary for generating an item-universe. Relevance of the rules has to be tested in order to know the circumstances under which latent-trait models hold.

As soon as this research is realized successfully, tailored testing is possible. Each subset of the item-pool will measure the latent continuum equally well. If estimations of item parameters are known, the sensitivity of tailored scales is known. Measures of change and intergenerational and intercultural comparisons are possible.

(3) The most obvious developments in self-report research are based on the sample-free property of the latent-trait model. Theoretically, estimations of item-parameters are independent of subsamples of persons. In our research, stability of estimations was performed through five different subsamples. We don't know if this is true in other settings.

The challenge of international comparative research is thus provocative. A coordinated international research program -- even a modest one -- on measurement of self-report questionnaires with latent-trait models should be promising. One can hope to achieve internationally valid standards, whose utility, from a fundamental point of view, can then be demonstrated.

Our main conclusion about the structure of self-report items is the support of a maximum homogeneity model. We have enough experimental evidence for considering seriously the hierarchical nature of the hypothetical relationships between self-report items, revealed by the one-parameter latent-trait model. Further research is needed for assessing the generalizations of the findings, especially in comparative settings.

Summary of the Confirmatory Factor Model

Matrix	Dimension	Mean	Covariance	Dimension	Description
ξ	(s x 1)	0	$\phi = E(\ \xi\ \xi\ )$	(s x s)	common factors
x	(q x 1)	0	$\Sigma = E(\ x\ x')$	(q x q)	observed variables
Λ	(q x s)	–	–	–	loadings of x on ξ
δ	(q x 1)	0	$\Theta = (\ \delta\ \delta')$	(q x q)	unique factors

Factor Equation: $x = \Lambda\ \xi + \delta$

Covariance Equation: $\Sigma = \Lambda\ \phi\ \Lambda' + \Theta$

APPENDIX: Self-report questionnaire (VA = vandalism; DA = Drug and alcohol abuses; PM = Person offenses; VO = Thefts; CO = official contacts; EF = Misconducts at school and family.

Il m'est arrivé durant cette derniere année ...

1. EF De m'absenter de l'école sans excuse valable.
2. VO De prendre des objets entre 100 frs et 1000 frs qui ne m'appartenaient pas.
3. CO D'avoir des ennuis avec la police ou des gendarmes.
4. VA De casser volontairement les glaces d'une automobile.
5. VO De prendre dans un magasin des objets de plus de 300 frs sans les payer.
6. VO D'arracher un sac à main à quelqu'un et me sauver.
7. VA D'abimer ou de casser l'une des choses suivantes: appareils automatiques de friandises, de cigarettes, cabine téléphonique, bancs publics, boites à lettres, matériel d'éclairage etc...
8. VO De derober un portefeuille, un sac à main ou des choses qu'ils contenaient.
9. EF De sortir le soir sans prévenir mes parents et de passer la nuit ailleurs.
10. PM De prendre part à une bagarre et de blesser quelqu'un.
11. DA D'avoir une sérieuse cuite.
12. VO De vendre des objets que j'avais volés.
13. VA D'aider à abimer chaises, bureaux et autres objets dans une école, une église, ou un autre lieu public.
14. VO De prendre un vélo ou un vélomoteur de quelqu'un avec l'intention de le garder pour moi.
15. DA De vendre des drogues à quelqu'un.
16. VA De mettre volontairement le feu à un local.
17. DA D'essayer l'un des produits: amphétamines, héroine, morphine, LSD, opium.
18. VO De rentrer dans un cinéma ou un stade sans payer le ticket d'entrée.
19. VO De prendre l'automobile de quelqu'un pour aller faire un tour sans son autorisation.
20. VA D'abimer des banquettes dans un bus ou dans une salle de spectacle.
21. CO D'être placé par un juge dans un centre d'éducation surveillée, une école spécialisée ou une autre institution.
22. DA De consommer: bière, vin, alcool + coca, alcool + orange.
23. EF D'être suspendu ou renvoyé d'une école.
24. VO De prendre des objets de moins de 100 frs qui ne m'appartenaient pas.
25. VO De prendre dans une magasin des objets de moins de 10 frs sans les payer.
26. VO De prendre des roues, la batterie ou d'autres pièces d'une automobile sans l'autorisation de son propriétaire.
27. DA D'essayer l'un de ces produits: Haschich, tranquillisants, marijuana, colle à rustines.

28. VA D'abimer volontairement des pneus, une antenne, la carrosserie
       d'une automobile, ou d'un vélomoteur, appartenant à quelqu'un
       d'autre.
29. PM De tirer avec une arme à feu sur une personne, des voitures
       qui passaient ou sur les vitres d'un local.
30. EF De repliquer à un professeur ou à un surveillant.

REFERENCES

Arnold, WR: Continuities in research: Scaling delinquent behavior.
    Social Problems, 13:59-65, 1965.
Canter, D (Ed.): Facet theory. Approaches to social research. New
    York: Springer, 1985.
Debuyst, C: Les nouveaux courants dans la criminologie contemporaine.
    La mise en cause de la psychologie et de son objet. Revue de droit
    pénal et de criminologie, 10:845-870, 1975.
Dentler, RA, & Monroe, LJ: Social correlates of early adolescent
    theft. American Sociological Review, 26:733-743, 1961.
Denzin, NK (Ed.): Sociological methods. A source book. Chicago:
    Aldine, 1970.
Dickes, P: Modele de Rasch pour items dichotomiques: Théorie, tech-
    nique et application à la mesure de la pauvreté. Cahiers
    Economiques de Nancy, 11:73-116, 1983.
Dickes, P. Prolégomenes pour l'étude psychologigue de la délinquance
    juvenile. Communication présentée au colloque "Handicap et Univer-
    sité." Université de Nanterre, juin, 18-21, 1985a (à paraître).
Dickes, P: Mise à l'épreuve d'un modele d'homogénéité pour conduites
    dérogatoires. Communication présentée aux 6 émes journeés de psy-
    chologie différentielle. Université de Grenoble, 3-4 octobre,
    1985b (à paraître).
Dickes, P, & Hausman, P: Définir et mesurer la délinquance juvénile.
    Bulletin de Psychologie, 359:441-455, 1983.
Dickes, P, & Hausman, P: New developments in the measurement of self-
    reported juvenile deliquency. Paper presented at the Inaugural
    European Conference of Developmental Psychology, Groningen, August
    1984.
Dickes, P, & Hausman, P: Régulation sociale du comportement délin-
    quant: Théorie et recherche. Communication présentée lors du
    quarantième anniversaire de l'école de criminologie. Université de
    Liège, 28 octobre 1986 (à paraître).
Ferdinand, TN, & Luchterhand, EG: Inner-city youths, the police, the
    juvenile court, and justice. Social Problems, 17:510-527, 1970.
Fischer, GH: Einführung in die Theorie psychologischer Tests. Grund-
    lagen und Anwendungen. Bern: Huber, 1974.
Fischer, GH, & Allerup, P: Rechentechnische Fragen zu Raschs eindimen-
    sionalen Modell. In Fischer, GH (Ed.), Psychologische Testtheorie.
    Bern: Huber, 1968.
Gold, M: Delinquent behavior in an American city. Belmont:
    Brooks/Cole, 1970.

266

Gustafsson, JE: The Rasch model for dichotomous items: Theory, applications and a computer program. Research Report No. 63, Institute of Education: University of Göteborg, 1977.

Hardt, RH, & Bodine, GE: Development of self-report instrument in delinquency research. Syracuse University: Youth Development Center, 1965.

Hausman, P: Régulation sociale du comportement dèlinquant. Thèse de doctorat non publièe. Universitè de Lìege, 1984.

Heise, DR: Norms and individual patterns of student deviancy. Social Problems, 19:78-92, 1968.

Hirschi, T: Causes of delinquency. Berkeley: University of California Press, 1969.

Hindelang, MJ, Hirschi, T, & Weis, J. Measuring delinquency. London: Sage, 1981.

Joreskog, KG: A general approach to confirmatory factor analysis. Pscyhometrica, 34:183-202, 1969.

Joreskog, KG: A general method for analysis of covariance structures. Biometrika, 57:239-251, 1970.

Joreskog, KG, & Sorbom, D. LISREL V. Chicago: International Educational Services, 1981.

LeBlanc, M, & Biron, L: Vers une théorie intégrative de la régulation de la conduite délinquante des garcons. Volume IV du rapport final. Montrèal: Universitè de Montrèal. Groupe de recherche sur l'inadaptation juvenile, 1980.

Levy, S. Lawful roles of facet in social theories. In Canter, D (Ed.), Facet theory. Approaches to social research. New York: Springer, 59-96: 1985.

Liska, AE: Causal structures underlying the relationship between delinquent involvement and delinquent peers. Sociology and Social Research, 58:23-36, 1973.

Nettler, G: Explaining crime. New York: McGraw Hill, 1974.

Nye, FI, & Short, JF: Scaling delinquent behavior. American Sociological Review, 22:326-331, 1957.

Quay, HC, & Blumen, L: Dimensions of delinquent behavior. Journal of Social Psychology, 61:273-277, 1963.

Rasch, G: Probabilistic models for some intelligence and attainment tests. Copenhagen: The Danish Institute for Educational Research, 1960.

Rasch, G: An item analysis which takes individual differences into account. British Journal of Mathematical and Statistical Psychology, 19:49-57, 1966.

Senna, J, Rathus, SA, & Siegel, L: Delinquent behavior and academic investment among suburban youth. Adolescence, 9:481-494, 1974.

Short, JF, & Strodtbeck, FL: Group process and gang delinquency. Chicago: University of Chicago Press, 1965.

Slocum, WL, & Stone, CL: Family culture patterns and delinquent-type behavior. Marriage and Family Living, 25:202-208, 1963.

Walberg, HJ, Yeh, EG, & Paton, SM: Family background, ethnicity, and urban delinquency. Journal of Research in Crime and Delinquency, 54:322-327, 1974.

West, DJ, & Farrington, FP: The delinquent way of life. London: Heinemann, 1977.

Winslow, RW: Anomie and its alternatives: A self-report study of delinquency. Sociological Quarterly, 8:468-480, 1967.

Woodcock, RW, & Dahl, MN: A common scale for the measurement of personality and test item difficulty. AGS Paper No. 10. Circle Pines, Minnesota: American Guidance Service, 1971.

Wright, BD: Sample-free calibration and person measurement. Proceedings of the 1967 Invitational Conference on Testing Problems. Princeton: Educational Testing Service, 1968.

Wright, BD, & Panchapakesan, N: A procedure for sample-free item analysis. Educational and Psychological Measurement, 29:23-48, 1969.

Part III. SELF-REPORT RESEARCH IN A LONGITUDINAL CONTEXT

The Office of Juvenile Justice and Delinquency Prevention in the U.S. Department of Justice provided augmented funding for the NATO Workshop in order to foster advances in self-report methods and also in order to expand the longitudinal component of the workshop. The U.S. is currently experiencing a renewed interest in prospective longitudinal studies. Major new projects have been initiated by O.J.J.D.P., and further developments are under way with the support of the National Institute of Justice and the MacArthur Foundation. These developments are not without controversy -- conceptual, methodological, and political -- so readers of Part III less familiar with the issues at hand may benefit from reading a series of attack and rebuttal articles in Criminology, volume 26 (1988).

In Part III, the Canadian and Dutch papers provide useful instances not of single studies, but programs of research which are affected by the use of self-report methods to assess criminal behavior over time. Weitekamp offers initial comments on some past self-report research as it affects longitudinal studies -- seriousness measurement and expanded age ranges are highlighted. Thornberry reports analyses of panel studies that suggest a major technical problem with panel effects of self-reported crime which must be resolved. The Le Blanc paper makes a strong case for taking a specifically developmental approach to longitudinal work, with attendant warnings for the methods employed, while Farrington ends this section with an illustration of the empirical benefits of the melding of self-report methods and the longitudinal design. In considering these six papers, the more dedicated reader might wish to return to the issues raised in Parts I and II to determine how materially they apply to the concerns of the longitudinal researchers.

METHODOLOGICAL ISSUES WITH SELF-REPORTED CRIME AND DELINQUENCY: AN ANALYSIS FROM A CANADIAN STUDY OF THE TRANSITION FROM SCHOOL TO WORK

Timothy F. Hartnagel and Harvey Krahn
Department of Sociology
University of Alberta
Edmonton, Alberta, Canada

1. INTRODUCTION

The self-reported delinquency/crime methodology discussed in this paper is only one part of a much larger longitudinal panel study that examines the transition from school to work and, more specifically, the causes and consequences of youth employment, underemployment and unemployment. Self-report delinquency/crime measures were included in the study since we were interested in the possible effects of various labor market variables, including under- and unemployment, on criminal behavior. However, the overall focus of the project placed limitations on the extent to which delinquency/crime measures could be included in the data collection instruments. Thus the present paper should be read as a commentary on self-reported delinquency/crime methodology carried out as part of a broader research project rather than as a study of delinquency/crime per se.

We will begin the paper with a brief review of the overall design of the study, including a discussion of sampling and follow-up techniques as well as response rates. The next section will focus upon measurement issues, including instrument development and choice of items and changes in measurement over the course of the study. After the presentation of some brief descriptive results we will turn to an analysis of the reliability and validity of the measures, including reliability with the panel data. Finally, we will conclude with some data analysis that addresses anonymity/confidentiality issues in self-report research.

2. STUDY DESIGN

This research was designed to trace the experiences of high school and university graduates in three Canadian cities -- Edmonton, Toronto and Sudbury -- with distinct labor markets, as these graduates leave this stage of their schooling and attempt to enter the labor market or pursue additional education. Therefore, we employed a multi-sample longitudinal panel design, with initial baseline data collection in the

M. W. Klein (ed.), Cross-National Research in Self-Reported Crime and Delinquency, 271–307.
© 1989 by Kluwer Academic Publishers.

spring of 1985 and subsequent data collection in the spring of 1986 and 1987 for a two year follow-up. In addition, in Edmonton only a sample of high school dropouts was interviewed in late fall 1984 and the first few months of 1985. However, the often transient nature of this population led to the decision not to attempt to follow-up these respondents.

2.1. Sampling and Data Collection

2.1.1. Dropout interviews. For the dropout component of this study a total of 168 young Edmonton residents who had left school without completing grade twelve were contacted by means of a non-random sampling technique. The goal was to interview a wide range of early school leavers in order to capture the diversity of their experiences. An attempt was made to include in the sample both employed and unemployed dropouts, males and females, and individuals who had contact with social service agencies as well as those who did not. The respondents were reached through referrals from employers, other youth already in the sample, social service agencies (including a corrections center), school counsellors, employment centers, and government-sponsored "job clubs" (job search and on-the-job training programs). From the 168 dropouts initially interviewed, 162 useable interview transcripts and completed questionnaires were obtained.

Following a referral, the potential respondent was contacted and provided with a one-page summary of the project. The purpose of the study was explained, and she or he was invited to participate. Because relatively little is known about this segment of the youth population, semi-structured, tape-recorded interviews seemed the most appropriate method for undertaking exploratory research. Interviews were conducted in public places such as libraries, restaurants and malls, and ranged from 30 minutes to over an hour in length. The interview schedule addressed nine central sets of concerns, with lead questions and probes designed to allow respondents to document their situations fully. Following the interview, respondents were asked to complete a short questionnaire which contained a number of key demographic, labor market, social-psychological and self-report crime measures.

All interviews went smoothly, and respondents appeared to feel comfortable about answering questions, not responding to those questions they felt were too sensitive, and completing the short questionnaire. To ensure anonymity, all identifying information about respondents was destroyed after the interview was completed. Taped interviews were subsequently transcribed and, using content analysis, coding frames were developed to facilitate quantification. Quantified interview data and questionnaire data for each respondent were then combined into a computerized data base.

2.1.2. High school graduates. Because of difficulties in contacting a random sample of high school graduates, a strategic sampling design using the school as the primary sampling unit was employed. In Edmonton, the city from which the study was directed, six high schools were selected on the basis of their mix of academic, vocational, business, and trades and services programs, as well as the diversity of student

social class backgrounds. Pre-testing of the questionnaire was done in
one high school (n = 48). Because very few changes in the questionnaire were made following the pre-test, the graduating students from
this school were kept as part of the sample. An additional five
schools were surveyed during May and June, 1985. Total sample size was
983, based on students in 66 different classes in these six schools.
Since access to schools and classes had to be negotiated, it was impossible to select them randomly. An attempt was made to obtain a cross-
section of academic and vocational/trade classes, although relatively
fewer of these latter classes were surveyed in the two schools that
could be clearly designated as serving "middle class" neighborhoods.
The other four schools contained a greater diversity (in terms of socio-
economic background) of students.

With the cooperation of administrators and teachers in each of the
Edmonton schools, members of the research team visited classes, briefly
described the study, and requested that students under the age of 18
have their parents or guardian sign a consent form authorizing the
student's participation in the study. Questionnaires were administered
in class, usually one week after this initial visit (to allow for the
return of consent forms). Completion of the questionnaire required an
average of 30 minutes. Student participation was voluntary. The last
page of the questionnaire asked for names and addresses for follow-up
purposes. A large majority of the sample (all but 89 of 983) provided
this information which was later removed from the questionnaire and
stored in a separate location in order to ensure confidentiality of
responses.

Somewhat similar sampling strategies and data collection techniques were used to obtain information from graduating high school
students in the other two cities. However, in both sites some additional efforts were made to include sufficient numbers of classes likely to contain students terminating their education on completing high
school. In Toronto, the boards of education of Toronto and York allowed data collection in 12 high schools, chosen to provide a cross-
section of different sizes and types of schools in different parts of
this large urban center. A total of 754 questionnaires were completed
but, as in the case of Edmonton, a minority (n = 80) did not provide
names and addresses and so could not be included in follow-up surveys.
High school graduates from seven Sudbury high schools, again chosen to
emphasize diversity of programs, made up the remainder of the Year 1
sample. A somewhat smaller proportion (338 out of 492) provided names
and addresses, signifying their willingness to participate in the longitudinal study. Thus, while the Edmonton, Toronto and Sudbury samples
in Year 1 added to 2,229, only 1,906 (86%) of these high school graduates provided the information necessary to include them in the follow-
up surveys.

2.1.3. _University graduates_. In cooperation with officials at the
Registrar's Office at the University of Alberta, a systematic sample of
spring 1985 graduates was generated by choosing every third name on the
list of graduates from the five largest faculties: arts, business,
education, science, and engineering. Faculties such as law, medicine

and dentistry were omitted from the study because their graduates enter unique, specialized labor markets. Several other faculties were omitted because of small enrollments. Questionnaires quite similar to those completed by high school graduates were mailed to the home addresses of graduates early in April. This was followed over the next three weeks by a reminder letter, a second questionnaire and a final reminder letter. In addition, phone calls were made to about 200 individuals who had not responded to the mail appeals. A total of 628 of the 980 mailed questionnaires were returned, yielding a total response rate of 64%; response rates across faculties varied from a low of 59% in science to a high of 70% in the engineering faculty. Some of those responding were mature students who had returned to the university. Since the study was targetted at youth, those born before 1955 were excluded from the analysis (and from subsequent follow-ups), leaving a Year 1 sample of 589 Edmonton university graduates.

University of Toronto graduates from the same five faculties were surveyed by mail at the same time as the Edmonton survey was being completed. A systematic sampling approach (every third graduate) produced an initial sample of 1,563. In this case, university officials did not provide the local research team with direct access to their mailing lists, so follow-up efforts were less extensive (only one blanket second mailing). A total of 537 graduates completed and returned their questionnaire, producing an initial response rate of 33%. At Laurentian University in Sudbury, one-half of the graduating class in the same five faculties (plus the faculties of social work and physical education) were sent questionnaires at the same time. The more extensive follow-up techniques used in Edmonton were replicated in this city, producing an initial response rate of 50% (n = 240). As in Edmonton, some of the university graduates who completed questionnaires in Toronto and Sudbury were mature students. The university sample sizes in these two cities after these few respondents were omitted were 519 and 227 respectively. Thus, the total Year 1 university sample size added to 1335, although only 1187 (89%) of these individuals provided their names and addresses for follow-up purposes. In combination with the three-city Year 1 high school sample, the first round of data collection in this panel study drew responses from 3564 Canadian youth.

2.2. Year 2 and Year 3 Follow-ups

Year 2 and Year 3 surveys were completed by mail for both the high school and university graduate members of the total sample. A number of techniques were used to remain in contact with or to trace sample members who had moved between data collection points (May 1986 and May 1987). At initial contact, sample members had been asked for the names, addresses and phone numbers of family members and friends who might be contacted if efforts to reach the respondent failed. These contacts, along with the use of telephone directories, drivers' license registries and other sources ensured that few sample members totally disappeared (although a very small number were completely impossible to trace). Tracing efforts prior to data collection months were assisted through the mailing of a newsletter several months earlier.

Newsletters returned through the postal system identified respondents who had moved from the address listed in our mailing lists and for whom tracing efforts should be instigated.

TABLE 1. Canadian youth employment and unemployment study: sample sizes and response rates.

	{May 1985} TIME 1		{May 1986} TIME 2		{May 1987} TIME 3	
	H.S.	Univ.	H.S.	Univ.	H.S.	Univ.
Edmonton	983	589	665	458	547	421
	{894}	{533}*	(68%)#	(78%)	(56%)#	(71%)
					{61%}@	{79%}
Toronto	754	519	412	358	296	326
	{674}	{433}	(55%)	(69%)	(39%)	(63%)
					{44%}	{75%}
Sudbury	492	227	240	156	187	128
	{338}	{221}	(49%)	(69%)	(38%)	(56%)
					{55%}	{58%}
Total	2229	1335	1317	973	1030	875
	{1906}	{1187}	(59%)	(73%)	(46%)	(66%)
					{54%}	{74%}
TOTAL	3564		2289		1905	
	(3093)		(64%)		(53%)	
					{62%}	

* Number of Year 1 respondents who provided their name and address for follow-up purposes.
# Percent of total Year 1 sample that we have been able to trace and re-interview (high school rates are lower because they were a 'captive' audience at Time 1; university response rates would also be lower if calculated on the basis of the Year 1 MAILING sample rather than the RETURN sample).
@ Percent of those Year 1 respondents who gave us their name and address signifying their willingness to participate in the panel study.

3. MEASUREMENT

A decision to select measures utilized in previous research on the topics of the overall project was made early in the study. This decision reflected a desire to maximize the comparability of this with previous research, as well as the reliability and validity of the measurement. Consequently, most of the self-report delinquency/crime

measures were selected and/or adapted from published sources (Hindelang, et al., 1981; Johnson, 1979). In selecting items from these
sources we were sensitive to the evidence concerning the relative frequency of different types of delinquent/criminal acts and the anticipated sizes of our several samples. Therefore, relatively infrequent
(in this age group) offenses were excluded. As a result some of the
most serious acts, such as murder and rape, were not included in the
list of self-report items; but items intended to measure the serious
crimes of robbery, assault with bodily harm, break and enter, and serious theft were included. However, since the total number of items had
to be limited by the demands of the overall study, the scope of illegal
acts covered by the items is considerably more limited than that found
in some of the recent research focused specifically upon the measurement of delinquency (Elliott & Ageton, 1980; Hindelang, et al., 1981).

Since, as will shortly be seen, the specific measurement varied
somewhat for the different samples at the several data points, the
discussion of specific measures can best proceed by examining separately the three different samples -- dropouts, high school graduates and
university graduates -- at the different time points.[1] Turning first
to the dropouts, self-report measures of crime were used in a self-
-administered questionnaire. Respondents were asked whether, in the
past year, they had been questioned by the police as a suspect about
some crime and whether they had been convicted of some crime, other
than traffic violations. In addition, self-reports on a range of specific violent and property crimes were included. Specifically, the
dropouts were asked how many times in the past year they had:

1. broken into a building or a car?
2. taken something from a store without paying for it?
3. sold marijuana or other nonprescription drugs?
4. used physical force (like twisting an arm or choking) to get
money or things from another person?
5. attacked someone with a weapon or fists, injuring them so
badly they probably needed a doctor?
6. got into a fight with someone just for the hell of it?
7. damaged or destroyed on purpose property that did not belong
to you?
8. other than from a store, taken something worth less than $50
which did not belong to you?
9. other than from a store, taken something worth more than $50
which did not belong to you?

Dropout respondents were also asked to report how frequently they
drank beer, wine or other alcohol, smoked marijuana or hash, and used
other nonprescription drugs. The original response categories for
these questions were: every day, several times a week, once a week,
once or twice a month, less than once a month and never.

In addition, the interviewers were provided with a set of optional
questions dealing with criminal behavior which they could ask at the
end of the semi-structured interview. These questions focused upon
types of criminal activity, on how the respondent had become involved,

----
1. All of the specific items appear in Appendix 1.

and specifically on his or her opinion about whether unemployment had been part of the process. Given the potential sensitivity of the subject and the fact that the interviews were recorded, interviewers were instructed to ask about crime only if they felt that enough rapport had been developed. In some cases, however, the topic had already come up earlier in the interview. These optional questions were introduced with 80% of the dropout sample and over two dozen of them went on to discuss this subject at length.

For the graduating high school students at Year 1 the self-report was part of a self-administered questionnaire filled out in a regular classroom setting. Our original intent was to include the same items as found in the dropout questionnaire. However, when the draft high school questionnaire was submitted to the central administration of the school system in Edmonton prior to pre-testing, they objected to the specific delinquency items and the request for students to state the specific number of times in the previous year they had engaged in any of these acts. These school administrators were particularly sensitive to the fact that at the end of the questionnaire respondents were asked to provide their name and address for follow-up purposes. They also insisted that parental permission be obtained in advance (although some individual school principals chose to modify this) and that students be told that any question they considered to be an invasion of personal or family privacy could be left blank. We should point out that the draft questionnaire and study design had previously received the ethics review approval required by the University and the Social Sciences and Humanities Research Council of Canada.

Since we had no practical alternative to data collection within the schools, given the funding available, and since we had to ask for names and addresses to initiate the follow-up aspect of the study, we reluctantly agreed to modify our draft measures. Consequently, at Year 1 the high school sample was only asked a few fairly broad delinquency questions. Specifically, they were asked how often in the past year they had been involved in any illegal activities, excluding traffic violations, with response categories of never, seldom, sometimes, often, and very often. With yes or no response categories, they were also asked whether they had been questioned by the police as a suspect about some crime or convicted in court of some crime (excluding traffic) in the past year. Finally, high school respondents were asked to report how frequently they drank beer, wine, or other alcohol; smoked marijuana or hash; and used other illegal drugs, with response categories of every day, several times a week, once a week, once or twice a month, less than once a month, and never.

For the first follow-up of the high school sample approximately one year after the baseline data collection, this identical set of measures was included. But in addition, we were now free to include a set of more specific offenses as well.[2] Three of these were identical to the self-report questions asked of the dropouts; two involved slight changes in wording (sold marijuana and beat up someone) to improve the specificity of the question; two represented a reworking of the break

----

2. See Appendix 1.

and enter and theft questions in order to eliminate one of the dropout
questions on theft; and the final question in the list was an addition
to cover fraud, which was not asked of the dropouts. In addition, the
question asked of the dropouts concerning fighting for the hell of it
was eliminated. These decisions were informed by the frequency of crime
data obtained from the school dropouts.

At the second follow-up of the high school sample in the spring of
1987, no wording changes were made or additional questions added.
However, we did decide to eliminate several questions in light of their
quite low frequencies in the previous time period, along with the
desire to make room for additional questions for the overall study.

Data from the university sample were collected at all three time
points through a mailed questionnaire. At Year 1 the self-report crime
questions were identical to those asked of the high school sample at
Year 1; that is, no specific offenses were included. This was partly
the result of a desire for comparability at the baseline and partly the
result of some skepticism concerning the feasibility of collecting such
specific data in a mailed questionnaire. We also anticipated a
relatively low frequency of self-reported crime from this sample, a
problem that would be exaggerated for any specific offenses listed.
But most importantly, we were concerned about the potential effect on
response rates, as well as the respondents' provision of names and
addresses for follow-up purposes, of including items measuring specific
offenses. These same general items were asked of the university students at Years 2 and 3 (except that the questions concerning the police
and court conviction were dropped at Year 3 due to extremely low frequencies admitting to this involvement with the criminal justice
system).

4. DESCRIPTIVE RESULTS

4.1. High School and University Graduates

Approximately 64% of respondents from the three cities (excluding
dropouts) reported not having engaged in any illegal activities in the
year prior to the initial data collection. Of the 36% who did report
some illegal activity, only 8% were frequently involved. But the graduating high school students were more likely than the university students to report illegal acts (43% compared to 26%) and more frequent
illegal activity (12% compared to only 2%). Only 6% overall reported
being questioned by the police and only 2% said they had been convicted
of a non-traffic crime in the previous year. These figures were slightly higher for the high school (10% and 3%) than the university (1% and
.1%) respondents.

Table 2 presents the frequency of alcohol and drug use generally
and for the high school and university sub-samples. Alcohol is clearly
the drug of choice with, as expected, more frequent consumption by the
university students. A quarter of the respondents admitted using marijuana in the previous year but weekly or more frequent use was low
(8%). However, the high school students reported slightly more use of

marijuana overall, as well as more frequent use, than the university
sample. The use of other illegal drugs is much more infrequent, particularly for the university sample.

TABLE 2. Alcohol and drug use for total sample and high school and
university samples, Year 1.

	Never	< 1 per month	1-2 per month	1 per week	> 1 per week	Daily
				Percent		
Alcohol Use						
Total Sample	13	17	23	28	17	2
High School	17	19	21	26	15	3
University	8	14	26	31	20	1
Marijuana Use						
Total Sample	75	13	5	3	4	1
High School	73	11	5	3	5	2
University	77	16	3	2	1	0
Other Illegal Drugs						
Total Sample	93	4	1	1	0	1
High School	90	5	2	1	1	1
University	96	3	1	0	0	0

Self-reported involvement in illegal activity in the year between
the baseline data collection and the first follow-up declined to 24% of
the total sample at Year 2. Again, such activity was more frequent in
the high school graduates' sample (27%) than among the university sample (19%). But even among the high school graduates only 3% reported
frequent (often-very often) illegal activity. Self-reported involvement with the criminal justice system similarly declined; for example,
only 4% and 1% of the high school graduates said they had been questioned by the police or convicted of a crime, respectively.

The frequency of alcohol use remained approximately the same during this first year of the follow-up, with the university graduates
continuing to report somewhat more frequent drinking. Marijuana use
dropped slightly (to 21%) and was approximately at the same level for
both samples. The use of other illegal drugs also declined from 7% to
5%, with the high school sample only slightly more likely to report
some use.

Seven specific crimes were included in the first follow-up questionnaire for the high school sample and Table 3 displays the frequency
data for these offenses.

From 1% to 17% of these respondents reported some involvement over the previous year, depending upon the specific type of crime. Generally, as would be expected, frequency of involvement varied inversely with the seriousness of the offense. For example, while 17% admitted to theft, only 1% admitted to having committed break and enter, robbery, serious assault, or fraud. Five percent reported shoplifting, 3% sold marijuana or other drugs and 5% admitted to vandalism. But even for simple theft few were repetitively delinquent; only 8% reported stealing more than once in the previous year.

TABLE 3. Self-reported crimes, high school sample, Year 2.

	None	1	2	3 or more
		NUMBER OF CRIMES		
			%	
Break and Enter	99	.3	.2	.4
Shoplifting	95	3	2	1
Sold Drugs	97	.4	1	1
Robbery	99	.3	.1	.6
Assault	99	1	.2	.1
Vandalism	95	3	1	1
Theft	83	10	4	3
Fraud	99	.3	.1	.2

By the second follow-up, overall reported involvement in illegal activity for the intervening year had declined further to 18%, with the high school sample continuing to exhibit higher levels of involvement (21% compared to 14% for the university sample). But frequent illegal activity continued to be at a very low level (2%). Alcohol use increased only slightly over the previous year, but the university sample continued to report more frequent drinking. Marijuana use dropped a further 3% (to 18%) but was by now again more frequent among the high school sample. The frequency of use of other illegal drugs remained low at 4% overall, with the high school sample again slightly more likely to report at least some such use.

Given the low frequency on several of the specific criminal offenses at Year 1, only four of these items were included at the second follow-up of the high school sample. Simple theft remained the most

frequently admitted of these offenses and at 16% was at approximately
the same level as at Year 2. Also, 8% of this sample continued to
report stealing more than once in the previous year. Six percent admitted damaging or destroying property during the previous year; 4% reported some shoplifting, and 3% said they sold drugs during the last year.

4.2. Dropouts

Finally, we can also report descriptive results for the sample of
dropouts studied in Edmonton only. Thirty-one percent of the high
school dropouts reported having been questioned by the police and 23%
said they had been convicted in court of a non-traffic crime in the
past year.[3] These figures are substantially higher than those for
graduating high school and university students. Clearly, these dropouts are a more deviant group. On the specific self-report crime
items, from 7% to 26% of the dropouts reported some involvement over
the past year, depending upon the type of crime in question.[4] Generally, frequency of involvement varied inversely with the seriousness of
the crime. For example, 26% reported having taken something from a
store without paying for it. Excluding shoplifting, a total of 15% had
stolen something worth more than $50, and slightly more (19%) had taken
something worth less than $50. But only 7% said they used physical
force to get money. Twelve percent admitted breaking into a building
or a car and 16% had damaged or destroyed property. While 13% said
they had attacked someone with a weapon, 21% admitted getting into a
fight just for fun. Finally, 24% of the sample reported having sold
marijuana or other drugs.

Consistent with what we know from previous self-report research,
few dropouts were repeatedly delinquent. For most offenses, less than
8% of them reported three or more illegal acts. The two exceptions to
this generalization were shoplifting, a fairly common offense among
young people, and selling marijuana or other drugs. Twelve percent
admitted having taken something from a store three or more times and 6%
said they had done so ten or more times. A total of 17% said they had
sold drugs three or more times and 11% reported engaging in this crime
ten or more times. This high frequency of selling drugs is a bit more
surprising, and may be related to the relatively poor economic status
of these dropouts.

Sixty-four percent of the dropouts said they drank at least once a
week. Clearly, alcohol is the drug of choice since the frequency of
smoking marijuana or hash and, particularly, using other illegal drugs

----

3. With the ten dropout respondents from the correctional institution
excluded, the frequency of involvement in the criminal justice system
dropped slightly to 28% for police suspect and 18% for court conviction.
But it should also be noted that these respondents are less at risk for
crime during their time in incarceration.

4. The frequencies for all of the crime questions were examined with the
ten dropouts from the correctional institution excluded, with only minor
variation in the results.

is much lower. Thirty-eight percent of the dropouts said they smoked dope at least once a week. Use of other non-prescription drugs is much less frequent, with about 13% of the dropouts reporting such use at least once or twice per month during the past year.

5. RELIABILITY AND VALIDITY OF MEASURES

In order to provide some assessment of the inter-item reliability of our measures, we can examine the correlations among the different items. This should provide some evidence concerning the relative utility of the different measures of criminal behavior, particularly the general measures, and may prove useful to other researchers forced to rely upon similar self-report items. We will present these reliability data separately for the high school and university samples at the three different time points.

5.1. High School Graduates, Year 1

Table 4 shows the intercorrelations among self-report delinquency items for the high school sample at Year 1.

TABLE 4. Correlations among crime measures, high school sample, Year 1.

		1	2	3	4	5	6
1.	Any Crime	---	.212	.146	.442	.529	.372
2.	Police Suspect		---	.328	.181	.194	.172
3.	Conviction			---	.112	.177	.243
4.	Alcohol				---	.435	.282
5.	Marijuana					---	.596
6.	Drugs						---

As would be expected, there is a weak but positive realtionship between self-reported involvement in illegal activities and both measures of self-reported involvement with the criminal justice system. This weak positive correlation reflects the well known fact that many offenses go undetected or are not proceeded against, particularly for juveniles. When these three measures were cross tabulated, only 4% of the graduates claiming not to have committed any illegal act in the previous year said that they had been stopped by the police as a suspect; and, of course, these two responses are not incompatible. Also, only eight of 1,189 graduates who said they did not commit any illegal acts last year reported a court conviction in the same time period;

this is quite conceivable given court scheduling and delays. Self-reported involvement in illegal activity is also positively correlated with alcohol and drug use. Only 10% of those claiming not to have committed any illegal act reported any marijuana use and only 2% any other illegal drug use. It's quite possible that some in this age group may not define marijuana use as illegal. The pattern of the remaining intercorrelations in this table is as would be expected. For example, being stopped by the police and conviction in court are moderately correlated and both exhibit only a small correlation with drug use; but marijuana and other drug use are fairly strongly (.596) correlated.

5.2. High School Graduates, Year 2

When we examine the intercorrelations among the same items for the high school sample at Year 2 in Table 5, the results are quite similar to those above. Self-reported marijuana use increased its correlation with admitted involvement in illegal activities from .529 at Year 1 to .649 here. The correlation between use of marijuana and other drugs declined slightly to .478. But the remaining correlations in Table 5 are very similar to those found at Year 1.

TABLE 5. Correlations among crime measures, high school sample, Year 2.

		1	2	3	4	5	6
1.	Any Crime	---	.206	.123	.346	.649	.342
2.	Police Suspect		---	.325	.125	.092	.024
3.	Conviction			---	.058	.120	-.009
4.	Alcohol				---	.360	.206
5.	Marijuana					---	.478
6.	Drugs						---

We next turn to the specific offenses introduced for the first time at Year 2. Table 6 shows the matrix of correlations among these items. Before commenting upon these correlations we should be reminded of the quite skewed distributions of these variables and the generally small degree of variation in each, both of which will affect the correlation coefficients. None of these correlations are strong. But the measures of break and enter and assault are moderately correlated at .278, as are shoplifting and theft at .326. There are several other weak, positive relationships but these correlations are no doubt strongly affected by the shape and distribution of these measures. However, when we dichotomized each of these specific crime measures (never vs.

one or more times), the resulting matrix of intercorrelations is more predictable. Table 7 gives these results. First of all, selling drugs and fraud are both clearly independent of any of the other crimes. The three property offenses of shoplifting, vandalism and theft all show moderate, positive correlations with each other. Since vandalism has an element of violence associated with its occurrence, it's perhaps not surprising to discover that it is also positively correlated with the violent crimes of break and enter, robbery and assault. Robbery and assault have a weak but positive relation; and assault is similarly related to break and enter and, more surprisingly, shoplifting. So the pattern of these correlations is generally consistent with what we would expect. Furthermore, we would not expect the correlations among these specific crime measures to be very high since each item measures a different type of crime.

TABLE 6. Correlations among specific crime measures, high school sample, Year 2.

	1	2	3	4	5	6	7	8	9
1. B & E	---	.003	-.005	-.005	.278	.010	.011	.175	.163
2. Shop		---	.004	.046	.151	.036	.326	-.001	.042
3. Sold			---	.004	-.006	.017	.021	-.003	.137
4. Rob				---	.165	.098	.114	-.003	.072
5. Assault					---	.195	.038	-.005	.167
6. Vandal						---	.077	-.004	.089
7. Theft							---	-.002	.038
8. Fraud								---	.137
9. Any Crime									---

Table 6 also includes the correlations between the general question concerning the commission of any illegal acts during the previous year and each of the specific offenses. Given the shape and distribution of these variables, it's again not surprising that these correlations are positive but small in magnitude. But when these specific and the general crime measures were all dichotomized as above, many of the correlations increased somewhat in magnitude. So, for example, the correlation between general crime and shoplifting is now .258; selling drugs is .225; vandalism is .221; and theft is up to .242. These are exactly the offenses that should be correlated with the general measure of crime since they are the most frequently (but still relatively

rarely) occurring offenses in our sample. It should be kept in mind
that there is a limitation on the absolute size of these intercorrelations since it is possible for respondents to be categorized as yes on
the general measure but no on any one of the specific items, or to be
categorized as no on a specific offense but yes on the general measure.

TABLE 7. Correlations among dichotomized specific crime measures, high
school sample, Year 2.

		1	2	3	4	5	6	7	8
1.	B & E	---	.168	-.016	-.009	.193	.246	.134	.108
2.	Shop		---	.068	.050	.197	.200	.250	.030
3.	Sold			---	-.016	.019	.047	.095	-.012
4.	Rob				---	.184	.198	.104	-.007
5.	Assault					---	.199	.124	-.009
6.	Vandal						---	.272	-.017
7.	Theft							---	.049
8.	Fraud								---

There are some interesting results when we cross tabulated the
dichotomized measures of specific offenses with the more general question as to whether the respondent had engaged in any illegal activity
during the previous year (also now dichotomized into never versus one
or more times). A considerable number who admit to committing specific
offenses also state, on the general question, that they had not committed any illegal acts during the previous year. The greatest discrepancy occurs for personal theft where fully half of those admitting to
this specific offense claim not to have engaged in any illegal act in
the same time period. The offense with the least discrepancy is break
and enter (9% -- 1 of 11 respondents); the remainder are between 20 and
30%. However, since the overall frequency of all of these selfreported
behaviors is low, we still find that the vast majority (98% or more) of
those reporting no illegal behavior (general question) also admit to no
specific offenses. Personal theft is the exception -- 12% of those
claiming not to have engaged in any illegal acts subsequently admitted
to this crime.

At this point the sequence of these measures in the questionnaire
should be noted. The general report of any illegal behavior was placed
first, followed by the self-reports of involvement with the criminal
justice system. These were followed by a question concerning the illegal behavior of one's friends and then the reported use of alcohol

and drugs. Finally, the set of specific crime items was listed. This question ordering probably explains most of the above-noted discrepancies in reported general and specific crime. That is, when first asked a very general question concerning involvement in any illegal behavior, a number of respondents appear to answer in the negative; but when later presented with a list of specific crimes, their memories are jarred and they now recall specific illegal acts they have committed. As expected, the more serious and infrequent the crime, the less likely the discrepancy between the general and specific measures, also suggesting that more serious and "dramatic" crimes are more likely not to be forgotten. Some of the discrepancy between specific and general measures probably also has to do with definitional issues regarding illegal behavior. In the case of personal theft, for example, many may not recognize and define the taking of something from work, school or another person that did not belong to them as an illegal act until confronted with that specific question. So most probably a combination of memory lapses and definitional problems account for most of the discrepant results when specific crime measures are compared with the general measure. This results in a good deal of underreporting of illegal behavior on the general crime item; and since this was the only report of criminal behavior asked at Year 1, we are likely underestimating the baseline criminality of our students. It does not appear, however, that they were particularly fearful of revealing potentially incriminating information about themselves since they were more likely to report the commission of specific criminal acts than they were general involvement in illegal activity.

TABLE 8. Correlations among crime measures, high school sample, Year 3.

	1	2	3	4	5	6	7	8
1. Any Crime	---	.318	.660	.380	.105	.303	.081	.086
2. Alcohol		---	.293	.188	.009	.057	.081	.048
3. Marijuana			---	.525	.098	.309	.007	.036
4. Drugs				---	.056	.201	.013	-.006
5. Shop					---	.383	.030	.272
6. Sold						---	.018	.003
7. Vandal							---	.355
8. Theft								---

5.3. High School Graduates, Year 3

We can now turn to an examination of the self-reported crime measures for the high school sample at Year 3. Table 8 contains the relevant correlations. Self-reported involvement in illegal activity is
fairly strongly and positively correlated with marijuana use and it
also exhibits a moderately strong positive correlation with use of
other illegal drugs (.380) and the specific offense type of selling
drugs (.303). Marijuana and other drug use remain correlated at approximately the same level as at Year 1 and Year 2 (.525, compared to .596
and .478 respectively). Use of marijuana is also moderately positively
correlated with selling drugs and alcohol use. Theft, vandalism and
shoplifting again are all moderately positively intercorrelated. The
major difference from the Year 2 data concerns the relationship between
shoplifting and selling drugs (.383).

TABLE 9. Correlations among dichotomized crime measures, high school
sample, Year 3.

	1	2	3	4	5	6	7	8
1. Any Crime	---	.176	.566	.372	.233	.302	.324	.249
2. Alcohol		---	.192	.100	.061	.068	.065	.062
3. Marijuana			---	.453	.139	.328	.156	.124
4. Drugs				---	.087	.366	.107	.127
5. Shop					---	.156	.236	.159
6. Sold						---	.105	.087
7. Vandal							---	.299
8. Theft								---

Again we dichotomized all of these crime measures, given their
shape and distribution, and then reexamined the matrix of intercorrelations which is presented in Table 9. First of all, it is noteworthy
that the correlations between the general crime item and the four specific offenses are now all in the same range of magnitude while previously only selling drugs showed any significant correlation with
general crime. Selling drugs is correlated with both marijuana and
other drug use and the three property crimes of shoplifting, vandalism,
and theft are all positively related. However, the correlation between
shoplifting and selling drugs drops from .383 to .156. When the general measure was cross tabulated with each of the specific crime measures, the results were very similar to those reported above for Year

2, again raising questions concerning the validity of the general measure of illegal behavior. However, the intercorrelations among the various specific measures of crime for the high school sample exhibit similar patterns at the three time points and provide some evidence for the reliability of these measures.

5.4. High School Panel

The panel data from this study offer another opportunity for assessing the reliability of the various measures of self-reported criminal behavior. In a sense, the follow-up data provide evidence concerning the "test-retest" reliability of these measures at one year time intervals. However, before presenting these data, some potentially confounding factors should be noted. The first of these concerns the effect of age. There is ample evidence (Hirschi & Gottfredson, 1983; Rowe & Tittle, 1977) for a relationship: crime declines with increasing age. So simply on this basis we would expect something less than a perfect test-retest correlation between individual measures of crime. Furthermore, there are a number of other variables in the intervening time period that could potentially affect these test-retest correlations. In fact, one of the major objectives of the overall project is to examine the effect of a variety of labor market experiences on criminal behavior. So we would expect the relationship between reported crime at Year 1 and Year 3 to be affected, for example, by the amount of under/unemployment and job satisfaction experienced by respondents

TABLE 10. Correlations between identical crime measures, high school sample, Years 1 & 2.

	YEARS 1 & 2
Any Crime	.507
Police Suspect	.262
Court Conviction	.084
Alcohol	.726
Marijuana	.719
Other Drug	.364

over that time period. However, the investigation of these potential effects is reserved for a subsequent paper. A third potentially confounding factor concerns attrition. Those most likely to report criminal behavior at all three time points (i.e., high test-retest reliability) may also be most likely to drop out of the sample. Should this be the case, the correlations among the crime measures over time might be

affected by this systematic bias. We will analyze data later in this
paper which should shed some light on this question. Here we will
simply report the correlations among the crime measures, while recognizing that their interpretation in terms of reliability is clouded by
these other considerations.

Still focusing upon the high school sample, we first examine the
correlation between the crime measures at Year 1 and Year 2 for those
students from whom data were obtained at both of these time points.
Table 10 presents the relevant matrix of correlations. All of these
are positive and several are moderate to strong in magnitude. The
exceptions are for self-reported involvement with the police and
courts, where the relationships are much weaker (.262 and .084,
respectively). These latter, however, should be interpreted in light
of the relatively small amount of variability observed for these measures at both time points.

We can also examine the correlations among crime measures at Years
1, 2 and 3 for respondents still in the sample at the second follow-up.
The correlations in Table 11 between the general measure of crime at
Year 1 and each of the subsequent follow-ups are again moderately
strong and positive (.503 and .482, respectively). The correlation
between this measure at Years 2 and 3 is even stronger at .599. The
correlations among the alcohol and drug use items across the three time
periods remain in the moderate to strong range, although the correlation between the other illegal drug use item at Years 1 and 3 did
decline to .243.

TABLE 11. Correlations between identical crime measures, high school
sample, Years 1, 2, & 3.

	YEARS 1 & 2	YEARS 2 & 3	YEARS 1 & 3
Any Crime	.503	.599	.482
Police Suspect	.226	---	---
Court Conviction	.052	---	---
Alcohol	.724	.758	.630
Marijuana	.739	.749	.657
Other Drug	.341	.476	.243

Finally for this examination of test-retest reliability among the
high school sample, we can examine the relationship between the dichotomized specific crime measures at Year 2 and the comparable items at
Year 3 in Table 12. All four specific crimes are moderately postively
related for this two year comparison, suggesting that those who admit
to a given specific offense during the first followup time period are
at least moderately more likely to admit to the same specific offense

during the second follow-up item period.

Thus from this examination of test-retest correlations among crime measures in the panel data, there is evidence for reasonably high reliability in these measures. This is particularly so in view of our initial comments concerning the potential impact on these correlations of other variables operating over these same time periods. However, this conclusion concerning test-retest reliability should be qualified by the possibility that correlations between identical crime measures at different time points could result from their joint dependence upon a common cause, a possibility to be explored in later modeling.

TABLE 12. Correlations between identical specific crime measures, high school sample, Years 2 & 3.

	YEARS 2 & 3
Shop	.367
Sold	.404
Vandal	.345
Theft	.315

5.5. University Graduates, Year 1

Turning to the university sample, Table 13 contains the intercorrelations among the self-reported crime measures at Year 1. The results are similar to those previously observed for the high school sample, although some of the correlations are not as strong in magnitude. In fact, here there is virtually no correlation between the general crime measure and reported court conviction; however, this figure is meaningless since there is only one reported court conviction in the university sample. Also, only 18 university students reported being questioned by the police; this lack of variability certainly limits the magnitude of possible correlations. It is worth noting, though, that the correlations between the general crime measure and both reported marijuana and other drug use are a bit stronger here than in the high school sample. But generally, the results for the two groups are similar.

When the cross tabulations between general crime and each of marijuana and drug use were examined, additional doubt was cast on the validity of the general crime measure. For marijuana use, 30% of those who reported such use had already claimed not to have engaged in any illegal behavior during the previous year. But only 11% of those who reported at least some use of other illegal drugs also had claimed not to have engaged in any illegal behavior. These results suggest that definitional problems cloud the validity of the general measure of illegal behavior; that is, many respondents appear not to think of

marijuana use as illegal when responding to the general question. The
fact that this is much less likely to occur in the case of other illegal drug use gives added weight to this interpretation. In any event,
these results suggest some consistent under-reporting on the general
question due to definitional problems and therefore again raise some
question concerning the validity of the general measure of criminal
behavior.

TABLE 13. Correlations among crime measures, university sample, Year 1.

	1	2	3	4	5	6
1. Any Crime	---	.150	.063	.302	.697	.366
2. Police Suspect		---	.234	.049	.050	.025
3. Conviction			---	.013	-.012	-.005
4. Alcohol				---	.299	.106
5. Marijuana					---	.338
6. Drugs						---

5.6. University Graduates, Year 2

At Year 2 in the university sample, only a handful reported being
stopped by the police as a suspect (8) or convicted in court (2) during
the first follow-up year. Therefore, it is meaningless to correlate

TABLE 14. Correlations among crime measures, university sample, Year 2.

	1	2	3	4
1. Any Crime	---	.238	.734	.402
2. Alcohol		---	.273	.106
3. Marijuana			---	.361
4. Drugs				---

these two measures with any of the remaining measures of criminal behavior. The correlations among the remaining items in Table 14 are very
similar to those noted above at Year 1, with the correlations between

292

the general crime measure and both reported marijuana use (.734) and use of other drugs (.402) slightly stronger than previously. However, the same results as at Year 1 appear when the measures are cross tabulated.

5.7. University Graduates, Year 3

As was previously indicated, only the general self-report of illegal behavior and the alcohol/drug use questions were asked of the university sample at the time of the second follow-up. The correlations between general crime and marijuana use and use of other illegal drugs remained at a modestly strong level (.640 and .472, respectively). When each of these measures was dichotomized (never versus one or more times) and the cross tabulations were inspected, an interesting difference appeared. For the cross tabulation of general illegal behavior and marijuana use, 7% of those who answered never to illegal behavior later admitted to using marijuana at least on one occasion; but, reading the table in the opposite direction, 39% of those admitting to marijuana use previously stated they had not engaged in illegal behavior. When the similar table for other illegal drug use was examined, there was only one case of such discrepant information. These findings would suggest that a number of respondents don't consider marijuana use to be illegal when asked the general question since no such discrepancy occurred for other illegal drug use. So even though the correlation between general illegal behavior and marijuana use is moderately strong, these latter data cast some further doubt on the validity of the general crime measure.

5.8. University Panel

We also have some limited panel data from the university sample to assess the "test-retest" reliability of the few repeated measures. Table 15 presents the correlations between the general measure of

TABLE 15. Correlations among identical crime measures, university sample, Years 1, 2, & 3.

	YEARS 1 & 2	YEARS 2 & 3	YEARS 1,2, & 3
Any Crime	.698	.650	.614
Alcohol	.803	.757	.717
Marijuana	.834	.778	.717
Other Drug	.533	.527	.630

involvement in any illegal behavior at each of the three time points as well as the measures of drug use at these same points in time. These

correlations are all fairly positive and strong: university graduates
who report involvement in general illegal behavior at a given level of
frequency at Year 1 are fairly likely to report a similar level of
involvement at both of the subsequent time periods. The same relationship holds for the comparison of those at Years 2 and 3. And frequency
of drug use is similarly related at the various time periods. These
data provide additional evidence for reasonably good test- retest
reliability for these measures, subject to the same qualifications as
noted for the high school sample.

5.9. Predictive Validity

Additional evidence on the validity of our self-report measures of
crime derives from their correlations with some measures of closely
related phenomena. In the present study, respondents at each data
collection were asked to report on the level of illegal behavior of
their friends. Table 16 shows the correlation between this measure and
the respondents own reported involvement in illegal behavior (general
measure) for the same time period. We would expect respondents' and
best friends' involvement in crime to be related and, indeed, all of
these correlations, for both the high school and university samples,
are fairly strong, offering some evidence in support of the validity of
the measure of general illegal behavior. However, these results
should be considered in the context of our previously reported
results that cast some doubt on the validity of this same measure.
Since some respondents do not appear, on the general questions, to
consider personal theft and marijuana use as illegal, they probably
also are not thinking of these behaviors with respect to their friends'
criminality. Hence it is not surprising that the general measures of
respondents' and friends' criminal involvement are correlated.

TABLE 16. Correlations between friends' crime and respondents' crime,
high school and university samples, Years 1, 2, & 3.

High School Sample

YEAR 1   .712
YEAR 2   .650
YEAR 3   .671

University Sample

YEAR 1   .664
YEAR 2   .665
YEAR 3   .693

Another procedure for assessing the validity of the crime measures
is to examine their correlations with various predictor variables that

from previous research are known to be related to criminal behavior. We have already observed, as would be expected, that the Edmonton sample of high school dropouts were more likely to report involvement in illegal behavior than were the high school or university samples and that the latter sample was the least involved. We also examined the relationship between sex and self-reported criminal behavior among the high school sample, since males are found to be more criminal than females, at least for most types of crime. Our results are consistent with this expected relationship as the males reported more involvement in illegal activities at each of the three data collection points. In fact, this relationship strengthened over time such that by Year 3, 15% of females compared to 28% of males reported engaging in illegal activities during the previous year. However, this relationship is weaker in the case of drug use, particularly the use of illegal drugs other than marijuana.

6. ANONYMITY ISSUES

One of the issues that is sometimes discussed in the methodological literature of self-report research concerns the possible effect of the lack of anonymity on the reporting of criminal/delinquent behavior. The present study was not able to guarantee anonymity since the panel design required that we obtain the names and addresses of respondents. Although we did take pains to emphasize the confidentiality of the data and our procedures for ensuring this, it is possible that the lack of anonymity may have influenced the respondents.

We can compare the self-reported delinquency of high school students at Year 1 who did not provide us with their names -- thereby indicating their unwillingness to participate in the follow-up part of the study -- with the remainder of those who did provide their names, to determine if our follow-up sample is biased by an underrepresentation of the more delinquent students at Year 1. As previously reported, the vast majority of high school students did provide their names; however, it is possible for us to separate out those who did not and compare their self-reported delinquency for the year prior to the time of data collection with that of the remainder of the sample.[5]

When we cross-tabulated reported involvement in illegal behavior by whether names were provided, there was a very slight but insignificant tendency for those who did not provide their names to report more frequent involvement in illegal activity. However, the numbers are so few and the percentage difference so slight that we cannot conclude that those maintaining their anonymity by not providing their names were more delinquent. The same conclusion holds when we examine self-reported court convictions. But a somewhat larger (and statistically significant with N = 965) difference existed for self-reported involvement with the police. Seventeen percent of those who did not

----

5. We report these results for the Edmonton high school sample only since the necessary mailing list information is held separately at the three sites.

provide their names reported being questioned by the police compared to 8% of those who did provide their names. Differences in the same direction also occurred for self-reported alcohol and drug use: respondents not providing their names were a bit more likely to report more frequent use of alcohol, marijuana and other illegal drugs, though the differences in the latter case were quite small. Thus there is some evidence here that students who did not provide their names at Year 1 are slightly more deviant in their self-reports, although the differences are small. But it is certainly not the case that we lost an appreciable number of the most deviant students at Year 1 through refusal to supply a name.

We can use these same cross-tabulations to test the hypothesis that delinquents are less willing to reveal their identity by, in this case, providing their names for follow-up purposes. Reading the table in the opposite direction, we found that there was a small and statistically insignificant tendency for the more repetitively delinquent to provide their names less frequently. Similarly, there was a slightly greater chance that those convicted of a crime would not provide their names, but this also was not statistically significant. However, while only 8% of those not questioned by the police didn't provide their names, 18% of those who had been questioned failed to give their names. Similarly, there was a statistically significant tendency for those who use alcohol and drugs more frequently to be less likely to provide their names; however, none of these relationships is particularly strong. So although there is a tendency in these data for the more delinquent to be less likely to give their names, any effects of prior delinquency on anonymity are quite weak. Furthermore, any tendency for the more delinquent not to provide their names may not be the result of concerns about the possible ramifications of their loss of anonymity but rather because the more delinquent students may also be those who are less conventional generally and therefore less committed to school, work and social research.

A related check on the possible impact of lack of anonymity is to examine the previously reported deviance of respondents who initially gave us their names for follow-up but who did not participate in the follow-up. That is, we can compare the self-reports at Year 1 of those who returned questionnaires at Year 2 with those who were not part of the sample at Year 2. Again, people may drop out of a panel study for a variety of reasons unrelated to lack of anonymity; but this type of comparison does provide some evidence on possible sample bias arising at least in part due to fears associated with lack of anonymity.

These data show a very slight and insignificant tendency for those not in the sample at Year 2 to have reported more delinquency at Year 1, to have reported being questioned by the police, and to have been convicted at Year 1 than those still in the sample at Year 2. So there is no descriptive evidence here of sample bias. But those not in the sample at Year 2 were significantly more likely to report more alcohol and drug use at Year 1, though the relationship is weak (Contingency Coefficient of .18 for alcohol, .15 for marijuana, and .08 for other -llegal drugs). Similarly, when we test the hypothesis that the more delinquent respondents at Year 1 would be less willing to return

296

completed questionnaires at Year 2 by reading the table in the opposite
direction, the evidence is supportive, but again primarily for alcohol
and drug use. Those who were already heavy alcohol or drug users at
Year 1 were somewhat less likely to complete questionnaires at Year 2
even though they had provided their names and addresses at Year 1 for
follow-up purposes.

However, whatever relationship exists between sample attrition and
delinquency, it does not persist beyond Year 2. We compared those who
completed questionnaires at Year 3 with those that did not and found no
significant differences in their reported crime or alcohol/drug use at
Year 2, except for marijuana use. And even in the latter case, the
chi-square was barely significant (p = .04) and the relationship weak
(Contingency Coefficient of .10). So to the extent that lack of anonymity is an issue influencing the participation of delinquents in this
longitudinal study -- and it does not appear to be a major consideration -- it operates at earlier rather than later stages of the
research.

7. CONCLUSION

Several conclusions can be drawn from this methodological analysis
of self-reported delinquency/crime in a longitudinal panel study. As
expected, frequent and/or serious crime is rare while alcohol use is
much more frequent in this age group. Furthermore, the crime measures
ordered respondents with respect to frequency of involvement in the
predicted direction: school dropouts were most involved and university
graduates the least, with the high school graduates intermediate; males
were more involved than females; and those with more delinquent friends
were more involved in delinquency themselves. Thus these measures
behave in ways that would be expected based on previous research.

Similarly, the various crime measures generally exhibit the pattern of intercorrelations that would be expected. Self-reported illegal activity is only weakly correlated with self-reported involvement
with the criminal justice system, but more strongly correlated with
alcohol and drug use; marijuana and other drug use are fairly strongly
correlated; the correlations among specific crime measures generally
exhibit the expected pattern; and the correlations between identical
crime measures in the panel data are fairly strong, tentatively suggesting that those who admit to crime at one time period are more likely to
do so at others as well. Thus these data show a reasonably high degree
of consistency at the three different time periods as well as in the
panel data, suggesting that the crime measures are fairly reliable.

However, we did discover some evidence of underreporting of crime
on the general measure when it was compared with responses to the
specific crime measures. Consistent underreporting on the general
measure was revealed for some acts which may not be widely regarded as
illegal, at least in this age group. Evidence of such systematic under-
reporting was most apparent for personal theft and marijuana use, acts
which are less likely to be thought of as crimes than, for example,
robbery. Thus the general crime measure is probably reasonably valid

for a range of specific offenses widely regarded as criminal while not being a sufficiently valid measure of crime broadly defined.

Finally, we did not discover evidence for any systematic sample bias when we compared respondents who provided their names with those who did not, or respondents who participated in the study at Year 2 or 3 with those who did not in terms of self-reported crime. But we did discover some evidence to support the hypothesis that more delinquent respondents are more likely to drop out of the study, perhaps for fear of lack of anonymity. This is limited primarily to the more frequent users of alcohol and drugs; and even then the relationship is weak. Thus non-participation of the more delinquent respondents for fear of lack of anonymity does not appear to be a major problem.

AUTHOR NOTES

The assistance of Dave Odynak in data analysis is gratefully acknowledged. The Social Sciences and Humanities Research Council of Canada, Alberta Manpower, Solicitor General of Canada, the City of Edmonton, the University of Alberta, and the Centre for Criminological Research provided financial assistance for this study. Participation in the NATO Advanced Research Workshop was facilitated by a travel grant from the Central Research Fund, University of Alberta.

REFERENCES

Elliott, DS, & Ageton, S: Reconciling race and class differences in self-reported and official estimates of delinquency. American Sociological Review, 45:95-110, 1980.
Hindelang, M, Hirschi, T, & Weis, J: Measuring delinquency. Beverly Hills: Sage Publications, 1981.
Hirschi, T, & Gottfredson, M: Age and the explanation of crime. American Journal of Sociology, 89:552-84, 1983.
Johnson, RE: Juvenile delinquency and its origins. London: Cambridge University Press, 1979.
Rowe, AR, & Tittle, C: Life cycle changes and criminal propensity. Sociological Quarterly

APPENDIX: QUESTIONNAIRE ITEMS BY YEAR AND SAMPLE

HIGH SCHOOL YEAR 1

The next questions deal with a part of some young peoples' lives we
know very little about -- things they do which may be against the rules
or against the law. We hope you will answer all of these questions.
However, if you feel a question violates your personal or family privacy, or if there is a question which you cannot answer honestly, we
would prefer that you leave it blank. Remember, no one outside the
research team at the University will see your answers; they are completely confidential. Because of the way the information is coded,
your answers will not be traced back to you as an individual.

How often in the past year (since school ended last June) have you been
involved in any illegal activities (not counting traffic violations)?

   Never...............1

   Seldom..............2

   Sometimes...........3

   Often...............4

   Very Often..........5

In the past year (since school ended last June), have you been questioned by the police as a suspect about some crime?

   No..................1

   Yes................2

In the past year (since school ended last June), have you been convicted of some crime (other than traffic violations) in court?

   No..................1

   Yes................2

As far as you know, how often in the <u>past year</u> (since school ended last June) have your best friends been involved in any illegal activities (not counting traffic violations)?

        Never...............1

        Seldom.............2

        Sometimes..........3

        Often..............4

        Very Often.........5

How frequently do you:

	Every day	Several times a week	Once a week	Once or twice a month	Less than once a month	Never
a. drink beer, wine or other alcohol?	5	4	3	2	1	0
b. smoke marijuana or hash?	5	4	3	2	1	0
c. use other illegal drugs?	5	4	3	2	1	0

UNIVERSITY YEAR 1

The next questions deal with a part of some young peoples' lives we know very little about -- things they do which may be against the law. We hope that you will answer all of these questions. <u>However, if there is a question which you cannot answer honestly, we would prefer that you leave it blank</u>. Remember, no one outside the research team at the University will see your answers; they are <u>completely confidential</u>. Because of the way the information is coded, your answers will not be traced back to you as an individual.

How often in the <u>past year</u> (since university ended last spring) have
you been involved in any illegal activities (not counting traffic violations)?

      Never...............1

      Seldom..............2

      Sometimes...........3

      Often...............4

      Very Often..........5

In the <u>past year</u> (since university ended last spring), have you been
questioned by the police as a suspect about some crime (other than
traffic violations)?

      No..................1

      Yes.................2

In the <u>past year</u> (since university ended last spring), have you been
convicted of some crime (other than traffic violations) in court?

      No..................1

      Yes.................2

As far as you know, how often in the <u>past year</u> (since university ended
last spring), have your best friends been involved in any illegal
activities (not counting traffic violations)?

      Never...............1

      Seldom..............2

      Sometimes...........3

      Often...............4

      Very Often..........5

How frequently do you:

	Every day	Several times a week	Once a week	Once or twice a month	Less than once a month	Never
a. drink beer, wine or other alcohol?	5	4	3	2	1	0
b. smoke marijuana or hash?	5	4	3	2	1	0
c. use other illegal drugs?	5	4	3	2	1	0

HIGH SCHOOL YEAR 2

This last set of questions deals with a part of young peoples' lives we know very little about -- things which they do which may be against the law.

We hope you will answer all of these questions. However, if there is a question which you cannot answer honestly, we would prefer that you leave it blank.

Remember, no one outside the research team at the University will see your answers; they are completely confidential. Because of the way the information is coded, your answers will not be traced back to you as an individual.

How often in the past year (since May, 1985), have you been involved in any illegal activities (not counting traffic violations)?

> Never..............1
>
> Seldom.............2
>
> Sometimes..........3
>
> Often..............4
>
> Very Often.........5

In the past year, have you been questioned by the police as a suspect about some crime?

> No.................1
>
> Yes...............2

302

In the past year, have you been convicted of some crime (other than traffic violations) in court?

       No.................1

       Yes...............2

As far as you know, how often in the past year have your best friends been involved in any illegal activities (not counting traffic violations)?

       Never..............1

       Seldom.............2

       Sometimes..........3

       Often..............4

       Very Often.........5

How often do you think you drink beer, wine or other alcohol?

       Every day....................5

       Several times a week..........4

       Once a week..................3

       Once or twice a month.........2

       Less than once a month........1

       Never........................0

How often do you smoke marijuana or hash?

       Every day....................5

       Several times a week..........4

       Once a week..................3

       Once or twice a month.........2

       Less than once a month........1

       Never........................0

How often do you use <u>other illegal drugs</u>?

      Every day....................5

      Several times a week..........4

      Once a week..................3

      Once or twice a month.........2

      Less than once a month........1

      Never........................0

How many times <u>in the past year</u> (since May, 1985) have you:

<u>Number of times</u>

a. Broken into a house, store, school,   _____
other building or car and taken something you
wanted? (e.g. money, stereo, etc.)

b. Taken something from a store without paying   _____
for it?

c. Sold marijuana or other illegal drugs?   _____

d. Used physical force (like twisting an arm or   _____
choking) to get money or things from another
person?

e. Beaten someone up so badly they probably   _____
needed a doctor?

f. Damaged or destroyed on purpose, property   _____
that did not belong to you?

g. Taken something from work, school or another _____
person that did not belong to you?

h. Tried to pass a check by signing someone else's _____
name, or used someone else's credit card without
their permission?

UNIVERSITY YEAR 2

IDENTICAL TO YEAR 1

304

HIGH SCHOOL YEAR 3

These last questions deal with a part of peoples' lives we know very
little about -- things which they do which may be against the law.

We hope you will answer all of these questions. Only members of the
research team at the University will see your answers. Because of the
way we code the information, it will never be linked with your name.
It is kept <u>completely confidential</u>. <u>However, if for any reason there
is a question you do not want to answer, just leave it blank</u>.

How often <u>in the past 12 months</u> (May 1, 1986 to April 30, 1987), have
you been involved in any illegal activities (not counting traffic
violations)?

     Never...............1

     Seldom..............2

     Sometimes...........3

     Often...............4

     Very Often..........5

As far as you know, how often <u>in the past 12 months</u> (May 1, 1986 to
April 30, 1987), have your best friends been involved in any illegal
activities (not counting traffic violations)?

     Never...............1

     Seldom..............2

     Sometimes...........3

     Often...............4

     Very Often..........5

How often do you think you <u>drink beer, wine or other alcohol</u>?

     Every day....................5

     Several times a week..........4

     Once a week..................3

     Once or twice a month........2

     Less than once a month.......1

     Never........................0

How often do you <u>smoke marijuana or hash</u>?

     Every day....................5

     Several times a week..........4

     Once a week..................3

     Once or twice a month........2

     Less than once a month.......1

     Never........................0

How often do you use <u>other illegal drugs</u>?

     Every day....................5

     Several times a week..........4

     Once a week..................3

     Once or twice a month........2

     Less than once a month.......1

     Never........................0

How many times <u>in the past 12 months</u> (May 1, 1986 to April 30, 1987), have you:

Number of times

a. Taken something from a store without paying for it?   _____

b. Sold marijuana or other illegal drugs?   _____

c. Damaged or destroyed on purpose, property that did not belong to you?   _____

d. Taken something from work, school or another person that did not belong to you?   _____

UNIVERSITY YEAR 3

These last questions deal with a part of peoples' lives we know very little about -- things they do which may be against the law.

We hope you will answer all of these questions. Only members of the research team at the University will see your answers. Because of the way we code the information, it will never be linked with your name. It is kept <u>completely confidential</u>. <u>However, if for any reason there is a question you do not want to answer, just leave it blank</u>.

How often <u>in the past 12 months</u> (May 1, 1986 to April 30, 1987), have you been involved in any illegal activities (not counting traffic violations)?

Never..............1

Seldom.............2

Sometimes..........3

Often..............4

Very Often.........5

As far as you know, how often <u>in the past 12 months</u> (May 1, 1986 to April 30, 1987), have your best friends been involved in any illegal activities (not counting traffic violations)?

Never..............1

Seldom.............2

Sometimes..........3

Often..............4

Very Often.........5

How often do you think you <u>drink beer, wine or other alcohol</u>?

Every day....................5

Several times a week..........4

Once a week..................3

Once or twice a month.........2

Less than once a month........1

Never........................0

How often do you <u>smoke marijuana or hash</u>?

Every day....................5

Several times a week..........4

Once a week..................3

Once or twice a month.........2

Less than once a month........1

Never........................0

How often do you use <u>other illegal drugs</u>?

Every day....................5

Several times a week..........4

Once a week..................3

Once or twice a month.........2

Less than once a month........1

Never........................0

DESIGN OF AND SELF-REPORT IN A LONGITUDINAL STUDY ON THE RELATION
BETWEEN EDUCATION AND DELINQUENCY

Jan A. Nijboer and Fokke P. H. Dijksterhuis
Institute of Criminology
State University of Groningen
Groningen, The Netherlands

1. INTRODUCTION

Most of our research time is spent on the relation between
education and delinquency. In this paper we shall present a short
history of our research program and some of the most important results
acquired so far. Special attention will be given to our present longitudinal research project, and especially to its design, the selfreport
techniques used, and the results in terms of self-report.

2. HISTORY OF OUR RESEARCH ON "EDUCATION AND DELINQUENCY"

In 1977, Jan Nijboer was doing research on profession-oriented
education of juveniles in prison. Fokke Dijksterhuis had done research
on people convicted for robbery. During a discussion we discovered
that both of us were interested in the role of education with respect
to the later development of delinquency. We decided to start working
together on this subject, apart from the research we were doing at the
time.

First, a literature study on the subject of "School and Deviance"
was carried out by a student under our supervision [see Ploeg, 1977).
It intensified our interest in the relation between education and delinquency. In the next research project, the way teachers judged pupils
of different socio-economic classes was studied [Ploeg & Nijboer,
1980). The authors did not find the differences they had expected on
the basis of some of the literature.

It was then decided to do a larger, structured cross-sectional
study on a sample of about 1200 pupils in the different secondary
schools available in one local community in the northern half of the
Netherlands (Dijksterhuis & Nijboer, 1981, 1984a, 1984b, 1986a, 1986b,
1987a and 1987b); Nijboer & Dijksterhuis, 1981, 1983, 1984 and 1987).

In the next study, 40 pupils of one lower profession-oriented
school in a Dutch town were interviewed in-depth. The interviews were
recorded. Two years later most of these pupils were re-interviewed in
the same way (Dijksterhuis & Nijboer, 1986c; Ferwerda, 1986).

The next study was done by two graduate students under our

M. W. Klein (ed.), Cross-National Research in Self-Reported Crime and Delinquency, 309–328.
© 1989 by Kluwer Academic Publishers.

supervision. It concerned a structured cross-sectional study on a group of more than a thousand pupils in secondary schools in the northern part of the Netherlands (Janse & Schaefer, 1987).

In 1985, we started selecting a stratified panel of 400 boys and 100 girls for our structured longitudinal study on the development in delinquent behavior of pupils. This panel was to be interviewed each year over a period of five years. The pre-wave (Dijksterhuis, Ferwerda & Nijboer, 1987) and the first and second waves have been completed. The most at-risk subgroup of boys was also to be interviewed in more depth during the second, the third, and the fourth waves; of these three waves, the first wave has been completed.

3. SOME OF THE MAIN RESULTS

In this section we will describe some of the main results from the earlier research. In section 4 we will -- as promised -- pay attention to the design of and the self-report in the five-wave longitudinal study.

In 1983, we arrived at a tentative integrated model, combining elements of strain, labelling, control, and social class conflict perspectives (Nijboer & Dijksterhuis, 1983). This model [see Figure 1) describes the hypothesized relation between functioning at school and subsequent delinquency step by step.

Along general lines, the model can be described as follows. Within the system, pupils with poor performance are considered failures. This can result in a negative attitude towards school, in demotivation, and psychological tension. As a result of this cognitive assimilation of failure, some pupils rebel against school -- rebellion expressed in misbehavior at school and in truancy. The feedback from both cognitive assimilation and resulting rebellion affects school performance. The environment reacts to the pupil's rebellion or resistance, sometimes in the form of further negative labelling. This, in turn, influences the pupil's self-esteem. Moreover, negative labelling leads to isolation from conventional groups and to rejection of conventional roles. It increases the probability of the pupil seeking to ally himself with deviant subcultures which provide deviant or even delinquent models. The availability of delinquent models and the readiness to act according to them result in secondary delinquency.

It is evident that not all pupils who are malfunctioning at school will become delinquent. The process described above takes place only under certain conditions. Among the conditions are personality factors (e.g., disinhibition) and structural factors like school and background factors. One of the aims of our research program is to establish the relevant factors. At this time we also formulated seven points of departure for our research program on the relation between education and delinquency:

1. Becoming delinquent is a process;
2. In that process, different factors play a role;
3. One of the most important factors is the school as institution;

4. An integration or combination of different theoretical perspectives is needed in order to gain insight in the processes leading to delinquent behavior;

5. Quantitative and qualitative differences exist between the delinquency of boys and girls;

6. Structured survey studies and 'in-depth' interview studies should be combined or alternated;

7. Several pilot studies will be necessary to justify the costs of longitudinal research.

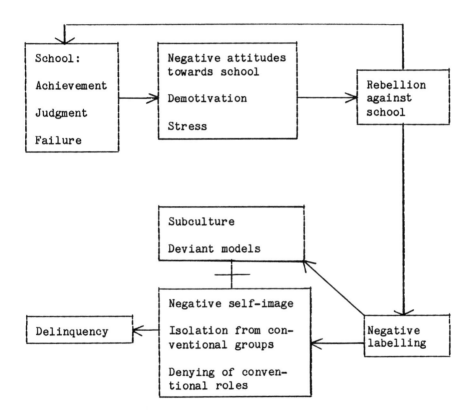

FIGURE 1. The tentative integrated model for the relation between functioning at school and delinquency.

Our model describes how some of the pupils become more and more deviant. It distinguishes two stages. The first stage leads to rebellion, which involves less serious rule breaking including less serious forms of delinquency such as petty theft and vandalism. The second stage deals with the implications of further negative labelling and,

312

especially, the acceptance of a delinquent way of life. In this way
the model suggests the more or less self-evident existence of different
levels of delinquency or types of delinquents. After reading Figueira-
McDonough (1983) we factor-analyzed the self-report offense data of
this study in a secondary analysis and found (Dijksterhuis & Nijboer,
1984a) four delinquency factors very similar to the factors she had
found (see Table 1).
    The four factors are:
    I. "Petty crime": this factor is determined by three of the less
    serious offenses, namely taking money from home, shoplifting, and
    vandalism. These are offenses which are neither unusual nor dis-
    turbing, considering age and youth culture. In Lemert's words
    (1967): primary delinquency.
    II. "Alcohol": driving a car or riding a bicycle or moped while
    under the influence of alcohol have the highest loading on this
    factor. This evidently would appear to be an alcohol factor,
    considering also that assault has a fairly high loading on this
    factor. It is well known that alcohol plays a disinhibiting role
    in aggressive behavior.
    III. "Aggression (especially against persons)": this factor is
    determined predominantly by extortion by means of violence and
    assault.
    IV. "Innovation" (Merton, 1968): joyriding, burglary, and "other
    kinds of theft" are predominant in this factor. More serious
    offenses, committed by young people whose aspirations exceed their
    legal opportunities. They find illegal means for achieving their
    goals. This criminal behavior seems to be utilitarian.
    Together, these four offense factors explain 61% of the variance.

TABLE 1. Rotated factor-matrix of eleven offenses.

| | Loading per factor | | | |
	I	II	III	IV
1. Taking money from home	77*	0	-13	1
2. Shoplifting	74*	12	25	20
3. Other theft	46	-1	42	49*
4. Burglary	37	-5	18	49*
5. Vandalism	56*	17	38	3
6. Extortion	-2	-6	84*	13
7. Assault	30	38	54*	-10
8. Joyriding	-7	16	-7	83*
9. "Borrowing" bicycle/moped	46*	40	20	37
10. Riding bicycle/moped while under influence	39	71*	5	8
11. Driving car while under influence	-15	84*	-1	6

* Variables not having a higher loading on any other factor: the
unique high-loading variables.

Classification by means of factor analysis clearly differs from a formal-legal classification. In other words, the legal classification differs from the preference of groups of young people for certain combinations of offenses.

Based on these factors we singled out seven types of delinquents and found rather clear differences in scholastic experience between the two less serious types (petty and aggressive) and the other more "hardcore" types of juvenile delinquents, and between the types mentioned last.

Because gender was one of the factors on which the seven types of juvenile delinquents differed, we factor analyzed the self-report data for boys and girls separately. This analysis showed that the main portion of the female self-report delinquency could be described by two factors, while four factors were needed to describe the main portion of male self-report delinquency (Dijksterhuis & Nijboer, 1986a). These female and male delinquency factors differed substantially in content (see Table 2).

TABLE 2. Rotated factor-matrix for girls and for boys.

	Girls		Boys			
	I	II	I	II	III	IV
1. Taking money from home	74*	-14	03	88*	-01	02
2. Shoplifting	74*	28	51	62*	08	18
3. Other theft	62*	19	70*	28	-01	28
4. Burglary			78*	-03	-05	06
5. Vandalism	32	70*	34	40*	16	32
6. Extortion	02	63*	10	00	-10	89*
7. Assault	04	72*	16	24	33	50*
8. "Borrowing" bicycle/moped			73*	17	28	03
9. Riding bicycle/moped while under influence			19	37	70*	01
10. Driving car while under influence			-03	-14	84*	06

* Variables not having a higher loading on any other factor: the unique high-loading variables.

The two female delinquency factors are called "Petty property crime" and "Aggression." Together, they explain 52% of the variance. The four male delinquency factors are called "Innovation," Petty crime," "Alcohol," and "Aggression (especially against persons)." Together, they explain 64% of the variance. In our opinion this means that girls and boys should be treated separately in etiological research.

The findings above are based on a structured cross-sectional study. With the next study, in which we used tape recordings of

in-depth interviews of 40 pupils of one lower profession-oriented
school, we wanted to check our findings, as far as was possible with
such a small and special selection of pupils, by analyzing the life
histories of these pupils. We purposively selected categories of pupils likely to be delinquent, using data with predictive value with
regard to delinquency, namely truancy, poor school performance, and
misbehavior at school. We asked the school the names of ten "normal"
pupils from their records, and of ten truants, ten pupils who got more
than normal attention from the pupil counseling service, and ten potential dropouts. The analysis of the interviews made it clear that the
classification of the pupils based on school records was not entirely
exact(Dijksterhuis & Nijboer, 1986c). The difference between the coun-
selled pupils and the truants could not be maintained. Furthermore,
the other categories were slightly over-represented. In the final
school classifica- tion we had eleven "normal" pupils, seventeen truants, and twelve potential dropouts. Moreover, it is remarkable that
no high-performance male pupils were found in our sample of normal
pupils. We do not know the reason for this, but the school management
did not put them forward as normal pupils.

Due to the sample being rather small and non-representative, we
limited the classification of types of delinquents -- based on their
self-report -- to "conformists" (N=16), "petty delinquents" (N=15), and
"serious offenders" (N=9). The last group contains a number of sub-
groups, namely "innovative delinquents" (N=5), "aggressive delinquents"
(N=2), and hard core delinquents or "bad guys" (N=2).

Recall that we distinguished two stages in our simplified model,
the first leading to rebellion and the second, via further labelling
processes, to secondary rebellion. The serious offenders seem to be on
the way to secondary delinquency, to a delinquent way of life. By
considering the differences between conformists and petty delinquents,
we can therefore form an impression of the empirical validity of the
first part of our model. An analysis of the points on which serious
offenders differ gives us some idea of the validity of the second part.
For Dutch girls, only the first comparison is possible because the
sample contains no female serious offenders. The subgroup of non-Dutch
descendants, due to their small number and their heterogeneity, was
left out of these comparisons.

3.1. The First Part of the Model.

On the whole, conformists do not have better school achievements
than petty delinquents. In fact, both groups fail at school to a similar extent. This may be an artifact of our selection procedures.
Nonetheless, the results of our first comparison make it clear that
failure at school does not necessarily lead to rebellion. Failure at
school may be a necessary, but is surely not a sufficient condition for
rebellion against school. Obviously there are other factors impeding
or furthering the development of primary delinquency. Other differences found between conformists and petty delinquents might shed a
light on this matter. For the girls, membership in a group of friends
seems to be important. The conformist girls have fewer friends among

their peers and their activities are mainly at home. Petty delinquent girls undertake more outdoor activities in peer groups in which delinquent behavior is not unusual. Moreover, they are more inclined to deal with their problems immediately and they are less law-abiding. The petty delinquent girls seem to have more "style" or to be more assertive. Maybe these traits make petty delinquent girls less inclined to accept the situation at school.

For the boys, the results are as follows. The conformist boys play truant and drink alcohol less often, they have a more pessimistic view of the future, and they are more oriented towards a future family life. The petty delinquent boys feel more able to cope with their situation in one way or another. They too seem to have more "style." Conformists -- girls as well as boys -- seem to resemble the ritualists described by Merton (1968).

We conclude that the first step in our hypothetical theoretical model -- from failure at school to rebellion -- is not supported by these results. Not everyone who is achieving badly at school displays delinquent behavior. Predictions based on the school history tend to overestimate delinquency. There must be other contributing factors at work which foster delinquency and/or inhibiting factors not at work to prevent delinquency. As contributing factors one can think of specific personality traits like impulsivity and assertiveness, and inhibiting factors such as the bond with the parents and/or other members of the family.

3.2. The Second Part of the Model.

The next step in our model goes from rebellion to secondary delinquency. To verify that step we compared the serious offenders with the petty delinquents. In the model, negative labelling -- by teachers, among others -- plays a part. Clear labelling cues were found in the histories of most serious offenders. Moreover, serious offenders had a clearly more negative self-image and worse relations with their parents and their teachers than other pupils. In general, neither their parents nor their teachers were figures they identified with or put trust in. They have delinquent friends more often, they play truant and in general function worse at school than the other groups in our study.

It seems justified to conclude that the differences found between serious offenders and the other pupils in this study support the validity of the second step in our model.

At this point we started thinking about types of delinquents and/or phases of delinquency. Is it probable that for every youngster a path lies prepared from conformism via petty crime to serious offending and finally to specialization in crime? Some people will remain conformist all their lives, others will go a shorter or a longer distance on that path to crime and then return to conformity (or to nearly accepted forms of crime like tax evasion), and finally there is that minority that goes on and will be responsible for the main part of the crime problem. These developments need not be exactly correlated to age and, moreover, the problem of natural age versus developmental age rises as it did in psychological research on intelligence. How does one cope with this problem in criminological research?

Two years after the first interviews, the larger part of the group described above was located and interviewed in-depth again. We found that a polarization in delinquency had occurred (Ferwerda, 1986). The number of serious offenders had increased the most and next came the number of conformists. Petty delinquency seemed to be a phase in the development of boys. It seemed to have another meaning for girls: except for one case, it is their extreme point on the delinquency scale. It disappears as soon as they achieve statuses such as work or courtship. For boys, the relational and rational ties the serious offenders have with conventional society are so weak that they are no longer kept from committing delinquent behavior. This behavior has developed strongly in seriousness and number.

In the next study (Janse & Schaefer, 1987), we wanted to examine the relations between parental support for school, pupil's motivation, school experience, self-image, and attitude toward the law as independent variables and [mis]behavior at school as the dependent variable. We would also have liked to have self-report data on delinquency, but in this case the negotiations with the school management to get permission would have been too lengthy for both student researchers who were involved in this study. The fact that misbehavior at school is closely related to delinquency (Schaber et al., 1982) made this next-best solution sufficient for our research program.

We shall limit our presentation to a verbal description of the multivariate relations between the independent variables and the dependent variable. For the girls, motivation, self-image, and attitude toward the law explain 38% of the variance in misbehavior at school. For the boys, motivation, school experience and attitude toward the law explain 39% of the variance. Apparently for girls, self-image seems to be more important than for boys. For boys, school experience -- and especially the relationship with their teachers -- plays a more important role. Of the three theories used -- control theory, anomie theory, and labelling theory -- only all of the hypotheses from control theory were confirmed.

After these preliminary studies, we dared start with the longitudinal study and the next section will be devoted to a presentation of that study as far as is possible at this stage in its development.

4. THE PRESENT LONGITUDINAL STUDY

In the following section we will give an overview of the design of our longitudinal study on the relationship between functioning at school and delinquent behavior. We will also present some preliminary results, especially with regard to self-report delinquency data. The description of the research design will concentrate on two topics, i.e., the selection of the panel and the instruments used.

4.1. Panel

4.1.1. Location. The study is located in three selected communities.

The following considerations led us to this choice. For reasons of efficiency and cost reduction we wanted to restrict the study to a maximum of three communities within a reasonable travelling distance from Groningen. Furthermore we wanted to select communities of medium range. No big cities (at least by Dutch standards) and no small villages were included. The final selection was based on statistical data on, among other things, officially recorded crime. One community has a high crime rate, one has a comparatively low but rising rate and the last community is characterized by a comparatively low and stable rate. We expected that these three communities would give us a reliable picture of delinquency patterns. Although complete representativeness for Holland as a whole was not our first concern, we believe that we have a good approximation. For reasons of guaranteed anonymity, we cannot give the names of these three communities. We shall refer to them as X, Y and Z.

4.1.2. **Age of respondents when first contacted.** It is known that some children start committing delinquent acts at an early age (Loeber, Stouthamer-Loeber, van Kammen, & Farrington, in this volume). It is also known that the bulk of delinquency takes place between the ages of twelve and eighteen. These facts presented us with a dilemma. Should we start at as early an age as possible, or should we concentrate on the adolescents who commit most of the delinquency? We decided to start with a group of children in the highest class of primary educational schools. Pupils are then about eleven to twelve years old. In this way we could also include data on the very important transition from primary to secondary school.

4.1.3. **Selection of respondents.** We intended to interview all pupils from the highest class of public primary schools. The next step would be to select a purposive sample from these, because a follow-up of the total number of pupils would strain our budget too much. Moreover a large number of pupils is not very appropriate to our research because they are far too "respectable" to require a yearly interview. Therefore, we decided to drop a certain number of these "respectable" youngsters.

But how were we to do this? Delinquency is a delicate subject, especially with regard to primary school children. We did not want to spoil our relations with the school managers by stressing the necessity of asking pupils about their delinquency. Our experience in this field had taught us that too many schools would stop cooperating if we insisted on the completion of a self-report delinquency measure. So we fired a shot from a different angle.

It is known that prediction tables are not very reliable in individual cases. But by using group prediction, a better than chance result must be possible. Therefore we decided to shrink our original sample by leaving out some of the pupils with a fairly good prediction of "respectability." We aimed at a panel of about 400 boys and 100 girls. We will give a more detailed description below of the way in which this was done. For the moment, suffice it to say that part of the panel -- those with the most unfavorable prognoses -- was kept apart for qualitative interviewing. They also completed, as did the other members of the panel, a quantitative interview. The instruments used are briefly described in the next section.

4.2. Instruments

4.2.1. <u>Instruments for selection of the panel</u>. A number of instruments was used. For the sake of brevity we will only mention the crucial characteristics. A first questionnaire served to select the panel from the original sample. It contained, among other things, questions which were thought to have predictive value with regard to delinquency. It concerned questions about family background, child rearing practices of the parents, children's functioning at school, misbehavior at school, etc. In this questionnaire there were no items concerning self-report delinquency. It was filled in by all pupils in the sample in a classroom setting. The teachers of the pupils completed another list with questions about, among other things, personality traits of their pupils. In addition, a number of questions for future identification of the respondents (e.g., home address) was asked. Children's answers to these last questions were checked by their teachers. Gathering of this first group of data in what we call the "zero wave" took place between November 1985 and the Spring of 1986.

4.2.2. <u>Main research instrument</u>. The main research instrument, which will be used in the continuation of the study, is a structured questionnaire with standard questions and standard categories for answering. Trained interviewers read the questions to the respondents and note down the answers in lists (first wave, November 1986) or in forms which are optically readable by machine (second wave, November 1987). Completion of this questionnaire takes about one hour, although for some respondents more time is needed. The interviewers only give illustrating remarks if the question is not fully understood. Interviewers are selected students (boys for interviewing boys and girls for interviewing girls) with enough social skills to establish an empathic relationship with the respondents. They have been trained to react as neutrally as possible to delinquency reports, in order to compensate for the non-anonymous interview setting.

As noted, part of the panel (boys with the most unfavorable prognosis) was selected for qualitative interviewing. The interview is done by using a checklist with topics that are considered to be potentially interesting. This qualitative interview, which is tape-recorded, is held after the completion of the standard questionnaire. In the qualitative interview the interviewer also has the opportunity to pose more in-depth questions about points of special interest emerging in the standard questionnaire.

A complete description of the contents of the questionnaire will not be given here. To mention a few topics, we asked about family background, parental attitudes towards child-rearing, respondents' opinions about breaking the law, attitudes towards school, functioning at school, relation with teachers, relation with peers, etc. Furthermore, repondents filled in a personality inventory, the "adolescents temperament list," constructed by Fey and Kuiper, which is fairly commonly used in Holland. The most relevant point for this paper, however, is the self-report measure we used. Therefore a more extensive description of this will be given.

4.2.3. Self-report instrument. Self-report delinquency was measured by using a list of fourteen delinquent acts. For each item on the list, the respondents were asked how many times within a certain period they had committed that act. Moreover, respondents were asked whether they had done each act alone or with others and, where economic goods were involved, the mean monetary value of the goods.

The items we selected were the same as we had used in our pilot studies. We consider acts as delinquency only if they can lead to penal prosecution. This means that acts like truancy, use of soft drugs, and drinking alcohol are not included in the self-report delinquency list, although we asked about matters like these in other parts of the questionnaire.

From a pool of possible items, we selected those we thought to be of relevance for the age categories we were dealing with. Very uncommon acts, for instance murder, were not included. We took great care in wording the items to avoid ambiguities and to make sure that the questions were properly understood. The items involved were stealing at home, shoplifting, other kinds of theft, burglary, vandalism, extortion, manhandling, joyriding, "borrowing" bicycle or moped, drunken driving (car or bicycle), forcing somebody to commit sexual acts, dealing in soft drugs, and dealing in hard drugs. We are aware of the fact that other delinquent acts might be included as well but one of our considerations was that the list should not be too long. In our conclusion, however, we will reconsider the selection of items in the light of our experiences up to now.

4.3. Some Preliminary Results

At the moment, we have completed two waves (and of course the zero wave) of the planned five. This means we can only give some early results. This is especially true for the results on self-report delinquency. In the zero wave no self-report items were included and in the first wave respondents were asked about their delinquency up to that moment, in order to establish the delinquent starting point. In the second wave the period was narrowed down to the past year. So, strictly speaking, the first- and second-wave delinquency reports may not be compared. The first wave concerns a period which cannot exactly be determined (at what age can a child be considered to be capable of committing certain delinquent acts?) and the second wave concerns a fixed period of a year. Nonetheless, we can offer some useful comments on the longitudinal design we used, and then on two self-report delinquency topics. We will present so-called turnover tables for delinquency in the first and second wave, followed by a comparison between quantitative and qualitative self-report data.

4.3.1. Data on the panel. From the total of 86 public primary schools

in the three selected communities, 71 (83%) took part in the research
project. The highest classes of these schools contained 1483 pupils.
Of them, 71 (4.8%) were absent when we visited the schools and in 82
cases (5.5%) pupils or their parents refused to cooperate in the research. The resulting 1330 pupils (89.7%) were interviewed. Because
of the special position of foreign-born children, these pupils were
discarded from the sample. This left us with a sample of 1252 pupils,
659 of which were boys and 593, girls.

A selection of predictor items was used to make a distribution of
the pupils into categories. We followed a very simple procedure. Our
concern was not to make the most efficient predictions but to exclude
some of the "respectables." Certain items, especially family background factors, school factors, and parental attitudes towards upbringing (as seen by the children) were scored as favorable or unfavorable,
based on the criminological literature. Favorable answers got a zero
score, unfavorable a score of one or two. "Bad marks" were summed up
and the correlation between each item and the total score was established. Only those items that correlated statistically significantly
with the total score were retained. The resulting distribution of
prediction scores for each of the three communities and for boys and
girls separately is given in Table 3. We are aware that this is a
rather clumsy procedure, but as we had no way of validating our instrument in advance (it can be done afterwards, of course), we consider it
the best possible alternative.

TABLE 3. Distribution of prediction scores according to sex and
community

Score	BOYS				GIRLS				TOTAL
	X	Y	Z	t	X	Y	Z	t	
0	8	3	3	14	8	–	2	10	24
1	25	23	8	56	23	16	5	44	100
2	51	34	22	107	56	30	16	102	209
3	53	28	30	111	61	61	32	154	265
4	61	37	35	133	59	29	26	114	247
5	33	29	18	80	33	20	20	73	153
6	27	21	14	62	18	11	17	46	108
7	24	13	6	43	4	9	9	22	65
8	6	10	6	22	5	3	3	11	33
9	4	9	6	19	4	3	2	9	28
10	2	1	6	9	2	3	–	5	14
11	–	1	1	2	1	–	1	2	4
12	–	–	–	–	–	–	1	1	1
13	–	1	–	1	–	–	–	–	1
M =	3.84	4.19	4.33	4.07	3.51	3.70	4.23	3.73	3.91
Total	294	210	155	659	274	185	134	593	1252

We planned to select a panel of 400 boys and 100 girls for follow-up purposes. Partly because of the different numbers, we followed different procedures for boys and girls. With boys, all pupils who had a total prediction score of five or more were included. From the category of three to four "bad marks" we randomly selected half of the boys and from those with scores zero, one, or two a quarter were randomly chosen. In that way a first selection of 405 boys was made. With girls, all who had a score of seven or more were taken, from scores five and six we took a fifth of the girls and from scores zero, one, or two, a sixth. This resulted in a group of 100 girls. The above procedure is certainly arbitrary in some respects, but we think it is defensible in the light of the purpose we had with our longitudinal research, to follow up as large a panel as we can handle within our budget, with an over-representation of criminologically interesting cases.

It would be much too optimistic to expect every selected pupil to participate in our study. Therefore a number of reserves (about 15 percent) was selected, so that a missing case could be replaced by someone of the same sex, and, as far as possible, in the same prediction category or else the nearest prediction score. In the first wave, 36 (8%) boys and 11 (9%) girls refused to be interviewed or their parents did not want their child to cooperate. Another 24 (5%) boys and 8 (7%) girls could not participate for other reasons (wrong address, moved, never at home). These non-participants were replaced. Tables 4, 5, 6 and 7 show the results of the first wave.

TABLE 4. <u>Boys</u>: non-response in the first wave (numbers and percentages).

Prediction Score	Selected	Refused N	%	Other non-response N	%	Result N	%
0 to 2	62	7	11	2	3	53	85
3 and 4	156	7	4	3	2	146	94
5 and 6	142	12	8	10	7	120	85
7 to 13	96	10	10	9	9	77	80
Total	456	36	8	24	5	396	87

In this first wave, 396 boys and 104 girls were interviewed. We consider the results of the first wave satisfactory. The total non-response was 14%.

In the second wave, we lost 36 respondents, of whom 27 were boys and 9 were girls. Although a figure of 7.2% non-response is very low, the fact that loss of respondents cumulates over the years makes so-called panel attrition a matter of concern. A yearly loss of 10%, for instance, will reduce an original panel of 500 members in the first

322

wave to 328 members in wave five, a total loss of about 35%. It is clear that we had rather stay on the safe side of that 10%.

TABLE 5. Girls: non-response in the first wave (numbers and percentages).

Prediction Score	Selected	Refused		Other non-response		Result	
		N	%	N	%	N	%
0 to 2	26	0	0	2	8	24	92
3 and 4	6	0	0	0	0	6	100
5 and 6	41	6	15	2	5	33	80
7 to 13	50	5	10	4	8	41	82
Total	123	11	9	8	7	104	85

TABLE 6. Total: non-response (numbers and percentages).

Prediction Score	Selected	Refused		Other non-response		Result	
		N	%	N	%	N	%
0 to 2	88	7	8	4	5	77	88
3 and 4	162	7	4	3	2	152	94
5 and 6	183	18	10	12	7	153	84
7 to 13	146	15	10	13	9	118	81
Total	579	47	8	32	6	500	86

4.3.2. Self-report data. To start with, we present a comparison of self-report data from the first and the second wave, for boys and girls separately. We used a simple summation of all reported delinquent acts. Next, three categories were made: those who reported no delinquency; those who reported one, two, or three delinquent acts; and those who reported four or more delinquent acts. By cross tabulating the data from the first wave and the data from the second wave, we get a so-called "turnover table." From such a table we can see how the different categories from the first wave are spread across the categories from the second wave. Table 8 gives the results for girls.

TABLE 7. Prediction score categories: panel and sample for boys and girls (numbers and percentages).

Prediction Score	Boys			Girls		
	Sample	Panel N	%	Sample	Panel N	%
0 to 2	177	53	30	156	24	15
3 and 4	244	146	60	268	6	2
5 and 6	142	120	85	119	33	28
7 to 13	96	77	80	50	41	82
Total	659	396	60	593	104	18

We can read Table 8 as follows. In the left top corner we find the number of girls (59) who reported no delinquency in both waves. In the same row we see how many of the girls who were conformistic in the first wave, reported respectively one to three (7) or four or more (3) delinquent acts. It is clear from Table 8 that there is some correspondence between the first and the second wave. The correlation (based on dichotomized data) however is not very high. We found a phi of .44.

TABLE 8. Self-report data for girls from the first and second waves.

Self-report first wave	Self-report second wave			
	No del. acts	1-3 del. acts	>3 del. acts	Total
No del. acts	59 (62%)	7 (7%)	3 (3%)	69 (73%)
1-3 del. acts	8 (8%)	5 (5%)	4 (4%)	17 (18%)
>3 del. acts	3 (3%)	5 (5%)	1 (1%)	9 (9%)
Total	70 (74%)	17 (18%)	8 (8%)	95 (100%)

Chi-square = 21.69 df=4 p<.001. Small expected cell entries make interpretation very problematic.

The same analysis was performed with respect to the boys. The results are shown in Table 9.

For boys as well, we see a correspondence between the data from the first wave and the data from the second wave. Phi (also computed on dichotomized data) amounted to .30, an even smaller value than we found among girls. These comparatively small correlations might be due

324

to the unequal time periods to which the self-report data are related. Another explanation would be that delinquency among younger children is qualitatively different from that of children at age 13 or 14. In a subanalysis within the group of boys who reported delinquency in the first wave, we compared those who also reported delinquency in the second wave with those who did not. We found no statistically significant differences between these groups regarding the self-report data from the first wave. The interpretation of this result is not easy, but the least we can say is that the predictive value of early delinquency with regard to later delinquency is, in our panel, not very high.

TABLE 9. Self-report data for boys from the first and second waves.

Self-report first wave	Self-report second wave			
	No del. acts	1-3 del. acts	>3 del. acts	Total
No del. acts	95 (26%)	21 (6%)	23 (6%)	139 (38%)
1-3 del. acts	40 (11%)	19 (5%)	25 (7%)	84 (23%)
>3 del. acts	97 (15%)	36 (10%)	53 (14%)	146 (40%)
Total	192 (52%)	76 (21%)	101 (27%)	369 (100%)

Chi-square = 25.91 df=4 $p<.001$.

4.3.3. <u>Quantitative and qualitative data</u>. Qualitative interviewing took place during the second wave. Therefore, we only have both quantitative and qualitative data at our disposal for that wave. In 74 cases, a comparison appeared to be possible. This was done by comparing the information given by the respondent in the qualitative interview with our standard self-report measure. A categorization of no delinquent acts, of one, two, or three delinquent acts, and of four or more delinquent acts was used because the exact number of delinquent acts could not be retrieved from the qualitative interview.
In 41 of the 74 cases (55%) there was a perfect match between the quantitative data and the scoring based on the qualitative interview. In another 16 cases (22%) we found small differences, but we could not conclude that the quantitative self-report figures were false. In some cases it was difficult to establish exactly whether a delinquent act had fallen within the relevant period.
That left us with 17 cases (23%) in which it was clear that the respondent had not given the correct information on the quantitative self-report measure. In 13 of these cases, delinquency had been exaggerated. This was especially the case with manhandling, vandalism and "other kinds of theft." It appeared that not all respondents were aware of the fact that only intentional acts counted and that

accidents, like breaking a window during a game of football, are not considered delinquent. Furthermore, reported other kinds of theft were in some cases obviously bagatelles. One case of burglary was discarded because the respondent had not broken anything and had no intention of stealing something. He just wanted to look around.

In only four cases (5%) did respondents fail to report acts which they had committed according to the qualitative interview. These involved stealing at home, shoplifting, and vandalism. One respondent evidently committed a lot more delinquency than he reported in the self-report measure. The other three respondents missed one or two acts.

On the whole, it can be said that over-reporting is more of a problem than under-reporting. This is especially a point of concern when somebody is regarded as delinquent while in fact he has not done anything worth mentioning. In this group of 74 respondents, 8 (11%) would have to be regarded as non-delinquents while on the basis of the self-report measure they would have to be considered delinquents. One could find such a result appeasing, but we certainly do not. We are stuck with a criterion variable which appears to be worrisome. An "easy" solution would be to drop the items giving most of the trouble, especially manhandling. However, we think that as the respondents grow older, their report will be more realistic and their tendency to exaggerate will decrease.

5. CONCLUDING REMARKS

5.1. Regarding the Panel

After two waves of interviewing, some evaluative remarks about the procedure we used for selecting our panel can be made. First of all, the loss of respondents in the two successive waves is within acceptable limits. This is of special importance for the group of respondents who had the most unfavorable prognosis and were also selected for qualitative interviewing. They are the ones of greatest importance to the research. Of the original 96 boys with a prediction score of seven or more, 19 were lost in the first wave (10 refused and nine were not included for other reasons) and only three in the second wave. This last figure of only three respondents who refused in the second wave gives hope that the total loss in this group can be kept down.

Especially for boys, a somewhat more extreme group might have been selected; that is, the original sample could have been larger and a more disproportionate panel could have been extracted from that sample. In that way the proportion of delinquent boys would be higher. Nonetheless, we are quite satisfied with the selected panel and the response of the panel members, and after the completion of two waves we do not see much reason to alter our original design.

5.2. Regarding the Instrument

Comparability of the results over the successive waves is an

326

important consideration for longitudinal research, meaning that only
small adaptations of the instrument are allowed in order to maintain
that comparability. For us, the NATO self-report workshop came a little too late, because we certainly would have changed our self-report
instrument in some respects. This is especially true for the selection
of items, the specificity of some items, and the possibilities of over-
reporting.

Our original selection of items was based on the expectation that
the most relevant delinquency (for this specific age category) was
covered. It appeared however that we overlooked arson and receiving
stolen goods. In some cases arson could be considered vandalism. In
our opinion there is no fundamental difference between burning or smashing the same object. However more serious forms of arson are not measured by our instrument. These serious forms may not be very common,
but still we should have taken them into account. Receiving stolen
goods is another delinquent act which is not covered by our instrument.
We should have included this item.

Some of the items in our list could be more specific. This is the
case with "other kinds of theft" and vandalism. After the first two
waves it appears that we should distinguish "thefts at school" from the
other kinds of theft. Our impression is that theft at school is not as
heavy as the other kinds of theft. Furthermore, vandalism could be
distinguished in destroying public goods and destroying private goods.
This distinction also appears to be of relevance for some sort of underlying scale of seriousness. At least in the eyes of the respondents,
destroying private goods is more objectionable.

We will consider a different wording of some items, especially
vandalism and assault, by further stressing the point of criminal intention. It is a little bit cynical that precisely the most conformist
children tend to report bagatelles. They do this just because they
think these acts to be very objectionable. Every respondent uses his
own yardstick of seriousness. Some consider an act as delinquent,
where others would not have second thoughts about it. One of the problems is that the frequency of committing delinquent acts and opinions
about the seriousness of those acts are not independent of each other
but are negatively correlated. In our research, the correlation between delinquency and opinions about the law is fairly high; for instance, in the second wave, we found a product moment correlation coefficient of -.38 for boys and -.50 for girls. It is possible that
conformist children have a tendency to over-report and delinquent children to under-report. Comparison of quantitative and qualitative self-
report data of the same respondents points in this direction.

REFERENCES

Dijksterhuis, F, & Nijboer, J: School en alcoholgebruik (Education and
use of alcohol). In G. Moor, Lodewijk e.a. (red.), Grenzen van de
Jeugd: actergronden van jeugdcriminaliteit. Nijmegen, 1981, p. 274-
284.

Dijksterhuis, F, & Nijboer, J: A typology of juvenile delinquents. Paper presented at the Tenth International Congress on Law and Psychiatry, Banff, Canada, 1984.

Dijksterhuis, F, & Nijboer, J. Spijbelen en delinquent gedrag: de signaalwaarde van spijbelen (Truancy and delinquent behavior: The predictive value of truancy). In TvC, 26/1, January 1984b, p. 32-46.

Dijksterhuis, F, & Nijboer, J: Delinquentiepatronen bij meisjes en jongens (Patterns of delinquency for girls and boys). In TvC, 28/1, January 1986a, p. 41-53.

Dijksterhuis, F, & Nijboer, J: Vandalisme: onderdeel van delinquent gedrag van jongeren (Vandalism: Part of delinquent behavior of juveniles). In Delikt en Delinkwent, 16/2, February 1986b, p. 110-125.

Dijksterhuis, F, & Nijboer, J: LBO-Onderwijs en Delinquentie (Lower profession-oriented education and delinquency). Criminologisch Instituut, Rijksuniversiteit Groningen, 1986c.

Dijksterhuis, F, & Nijboer, J: Meisjes- en jongensdelinquentie: dezelfde etiologische processen? (Delinquency of girls and boys: The same etiological processes?) In TvC, 29/4, May 1987a, p. 104-110.

Dijksterhuis, F, & Nijboer, J: Reproduktie van maatschappelijke kwetsbaarheid (Reproduction of societal vulnerability). In K. Doornbos & L Stevens (eds.), De groei van het speciaal ondewijs. Den Haag, 1987b, p. 198-222.

Dijksterhuis, F, Ferwerda, H, & Nijboer, J: Ontwikkelingen in delinquent gedrag van scholieren: voorronde (Developments in delinquent behavior of pupils: The pre-wave). Criminologisch Instituut, Rijksuniversiteit Groningen, 1987c.

Ferwerda, J: Leerlingen van het lager beroepsonderwijs: maatschappelijk perspectief en hun reacties (Pupils of the lower profession oriented education: Societal perspective and their reaction). Criminologisch Instituut, Rijksuniversiteit Groningen, 1986.

Figueira-McDonough, J: On the usefulness of Merton's anomie theory: Academic failure and deviance among high school students. In Youth and Society, 1983, nr. 3, p. 259-279.

Hirschi, T: Causes of delinquency. Berkeley, CA.: 1969.

Janse, N, & Schaefer, J: De relatie tussen enerzijds motivatie, schoolbeleving, wetsovertuiging en anderzijds wangedrag op school (The relation between motivation, school experience, and attitude regarding the law on the one hand, and on the other, misbehavior at school). Criminologisch Instituut, Rijkuniversiteit Groningen, 1987.

Lemert, E: Human deviance, social problems, and social control. New York, 1951.

Loeber, R, Stouthamer-Loeber, M, van Kammen, W, & Farrington, D: Development of a new measure for self-reported antisocial behavior for young children: Prevalence and reliability. Paper prepared for the NATO Advanced Research Workshop on Self-reported Methodology in Criminological Research, Noordwijkerhout, The Netherlands, June 26-July 1, 1988.

Merton, R: Social theory and social structure. New York, 1968.

Nijboer, J, & Dijksterhuis, F: School en delinquentie: een oriĕnter-
ende analyse (Education and delinquency: A pilot study). In G.
Moor, Lodewijk e.a. (Ed.): Grenzen van de jeugd: achtergronden van
jeugdcriminaliteit. Nijmegen, 1981, P. 148-163.

Nijboer, J, & Dijksterhuis, F: Onderwijs and delinquentie: de relatie
tussen het functioneren op school en delinquentie (Education and
delinquency: The relation between functioning at school and delinquency). Criminologisch Instituut, Rijksuniversiteit Groningen,
1983.

Nijboer, J, & Dijksterhuis, F: Differential scholastic experiences of
juvenile delinquents. Paper presented at the Tenth International
Congress on Law and Psychiatry, Banff, Canada, 1984.

Nijboer, J, & Dijksterhuis, F: De relaties tussen delinquentiepatronen
en school- en actergrondfactoren bij meisjes en jongens (The relations between patterns of delinquency and school and background
factors for girls and boys). In TvC, 29/5, September 1987, p.
156-173.

Ploeg, G: School en deviantie (School and deviance). Criminologisch
Instituut, Rijksuniversiteit Groningen, 1977.

Ploeg, G, & Nijboer, J: Door het oog van de leraar: een vooronderzoek
(In the eyes of the teacher: A pilot study). Criminologisch Instituut, Rijksuniversiteit Groningen, 1980.

Schaber, G, Hausman, P, Beaufils, M, Boniver, M. & Kerger, A: Le poids
de l'inadaptation au milieu scolaire dans le processus delinquan-
tiel. Centre Luxembourgeois de Recherches sociales et pĕdagogi-
gues, 1982.

SOME PROBLEMS WITH THE USE OF SELF-REPORTS IN LONGITUDINAL RESEARCH

Elmar Weitekamp
Sellin Center for Studies in Criminology and Criminal Law
University of Pennsylvania, Philadelphia, Pennsylvania, USA

1. INTRODUCTION

Since the publication of <u>Delinquency in a Birth Cohort</u> in 1972 (Wolfgang, Figlio, and Sellin), longitudinal research has become a major focus in criminological research. The term "longitudinal" is used somewhat ambiguously and appears to have a number of meanings. Spector stated that the longitudinal design is essentially a variation of correlational study "which involves two or more measurements of variables in a study taken on the same group of subjects" (1981, 35). Longitudinal research is also referred to as studies with experimental intervention and might cover research strategies including birth cohort studies, panel surveys, and time series experiments. Some of the several subcategories among longitudinal research are prospective studies and retrospective studies, following a group of individuals or examining a group's past experience by interviews, questionnaire or by existing records.

The recently published work by Farrington, Ohlin, and Wilson (1986), by Blumstein, Cohen, Roth, and Visher (1986), Blumstein, Cohen, and Farrington (1988a, 1988b), and by Gottfredson and Hirschi (1986, 1987, 1988) provide thorough reviews of longitudinal research and methodological discussions on contemporary issues in criminology. Farrington <u>et al</u>. (1986) and Blumstein <u>et al</u>. (1986, 1988a, 1988b) emphasize the importance of the power of the longitudinal research method whereas Gottfredson and Hirschi (1986, 1987, 1988) argue that results obtained by longitudinal research can be acquired in a more cost efficient way using cross-sectional studies, which collect information at one time only. We will not discuss the ongoing debate but will concentrate on the longitudinal research method which has produced to date a large number of studies (see Farrington, 1979, 1982, and Visher & Roth, 1986, to name but a few).

According to Weis (1986) we have five basic approaches to the measurement of crime: official crime records, self-reports of criminal behavior, reports of personal victimization, direct observations, and informant reports. Since the early work of Short and Nye (1957) which promoted interest in the self-report method in criminological research,

M. W. Klein (ed.), Cross-National Research in Self-Reported Crime and Delinquency, 329–346.
© 1989 by Kluwer Academic Publishers.

numerous studies have used either the self-report approach only or in combination with official data (Akers, 1964; Hirschi, 1969; Gold, 1970; Hindelang et al., 1981; Elliott & Huizinga, 1984; Wolfgang, Thornberry, & Figlio, 1987, for example). For extensive reviews of these studies, their advantages, disadvantages, and methodological problems, we refer to Hindelang, Hirschi and Weis (1981), Langan and Farrington (1983), and Weis (1986), and in the context of longitudinal research to Farrington (1979 and 1982).

The focus of the paper will be on three aspects of the use of self-reports in longitudinal research:

1. The use of self-reports during the life span of offenders. We will argue that research emphasizes the juvenile life span too heavily and neglects the childhood and the adult life span. As Farrington (1986) and Loeber (1987) rightly pointed out, more attention should be given to serious conduct problems in childhood. Consequently, different instruments should be used during that life span. One of the most neglected life spans is the adult one. We will discuss this period in detail and suggest that current self-reports are inadequate to capture the criminal involvement of adults.

2. The aforementioned problems are associated with item selection. It is a well known criticism that self-reports use more trivial items than "real" criminal acts. Hindelang et al. (1981), as well as Dunford and Elliott (1984), claim that they made important improvements in constructing their instruments. By using the National Crime Severity Survey we will show that only moderate improvements resulted and they failed to improve their instruments in a substantial way.

3. Longitudinal research focuses heavily on chronic or habitual offenders. We will argue that this category is often misleading and, as Cernkovich, Giordano, and Pugh (1985) pointed out, chronic offenders are the missing cases in self-report delinquency research. Another problem in the chronic offender classification is the reference to UCR Index Crimes which we consider problematic.

Before discussing these problems further we will review existing literature on longitudinal research and criminal behavior during the life course.

2. FROM CHILDHOOD DEVIANCE TO ADULT CRIMINAL BEHAVIOR: A REVIEW OF THE LITERATURE

Criminal behavior has been a major topic of investigation in the social and behavioral sciences, but it has rarely been examined at different phases of the life course. Because it is generally assumed that criminal behavior occurs more frequently during late adolescence and early adulthood (Cline, 1980), we find most studies focusing on these age periods; only a few studies provide data that span at least both phases in the lives of the subjects.

Society does not recognize criminality among children; therefore, this phase of life is grossly neglected. However, recent developments in sociobiological theory have paid more attention to early childhood and its impact on criminal behavior (Denno, 1982; Mednick, Mednick, Baker, & Gabrielli, 1983; Spivak, 1983; Farrington, 1986; Loeber, 1987). In addition, even those studies that cover adolescence and young adulthood usually end at age 30, with the exception of the work of Robins (1966), McCord (1978), and, most recently, Farrington, who is now interviewing his Cambridge sample at age 32. Even those studies have a common problem: the small sample size of their study populations restricts the development of subgroup-specific rates of offenses by offense type, for the purpose of deriving subgroup-specific career patterns. Furthermore, Robins and McCord drew their samples from "troubled" or "problem" youth rather than from a "delinquent" or criminal juvenile populations. But there is still little known about criminal behavior during the middle or older years despite the growing concern about corporate or organizational crime (see Wolfgang, Figlio, Tracy, & Singer, 1985). We know about professional criminals only from biographies, case histories, and anecdotes; and the view of criminal careers within the occupational orientation has been widely accepted (Akerstrom, 1983; Cameron, 1964; Irwin, 1970; Jackson, 1969; Klockars, 1974; Letkeman, 1973; Martin, 1952; Maurer, 1964; Miller, 1970; Polsky, 1969; Prus and Sharper, 1977; Sutherland, 1937; Waldo, 1983). Little is known about those who commit white-collar crimes in the middle years and the proportion of that group which was earlier adjudicated delinquent nor, for that matter, what happens to the majority of adolescents who become official offenders early in life and never again appear in official crime statistics.

The National Advisory Committee on Criminal Justice Standards and Goals (1976) reported that for years the national growth rate of juvenile arrests for all types of offenses had far outstripped that of adults. According to the Uniform Crime Report (hereinafter, UCR), the number of juveniles or persons arrested for serious index crimes increased 143% between 1963 and 1980. But the number of juvenile arrests for violent crimes increased by 300% during this same period (Wolfgang, 1983). Juveniles are more likely to be involved in property crimes. In 1984, they accounted for 38.2% of the arrests for burglary, 33.6% of the arrests for larceny, 36.3% of the arrests for motor vehicle theft, and 42.5% of the arrests for arson. Among the arrests for violent crimes, 7.3% were for homicide, 15.5% were for rape, 25.6% were for robbery, and 13.4% were for aggravated assault (U.S. Department of Justice, FBI, 1984). Despite the main involvement in property crimes, the UCR shows

> ...that from 1965 to 1980, youth aged 15, 16 and 17, who are responsible for the great majority of delinquencies, experienced dramatic increases in their rates (per 100,000 age-specific population) of each type of UCR violent index crime: Criminal homicide increased between 62 and 100%, forcible rape between 8 and 24%, robbery beween 138 and 172%, and aggravated assault between 90 and 144%. Between 1980 and 1983, forcible rape continued to incline for fifteen- and

sixteen-year olds (by 25 and 13%) but declined modestly for
seventeen-year olds (by 5%). Each other violent crime sub-
sided, however, for each age cohort: homicide by 5 to 14%,
robbery by 10 to 16%, and aggravated assault by 4 to 7% (Weiner, 1985:2).

Comparing the UCR data with the National Crime Survey (NCS) statistics, we find the NCS figures for rape and robbery are each 2.5 to 4
times higher, and those for aggravated assault are 3.5 to 5 times higher (Weiner & Wolfgang, 1985). Dunford and Elliott (1984) found in the
National Youth Survey that the ratio of self-reported to officially
recorded offenses was 40:1. According to their study, it appears that
the official data reflect only a small fraction of the illegal activity. Similar results are revealed by Tracy (1987) in the follow-up
study of the 1945 Philadelphia cohort in which a number of the subjects
with no arrest reported having committed fifty offenses on average.
Several studies have identified criminal involvement during adulthood by former juvenile offenders and adolescent juvenile delinquency
by young children who committed offenses. Although studies which com-
mence in the early childhood years are rare, there is some indication
that there exist transitional career patterns from childhood deviance
to delinquency to adult crime (Farrington, 1986; Loeber, 1987). Spivak
(1983), for instance, followed for fifteen years a group of 660 children in kindergarten who had interactional difficulties. These children in the early school years were unable to follow the standard in
their classes, displayed misbehavior, and collected -- as juveniles --
far more arrests than the children who were not identified in the high-
risk group.
One of a few studies identifying high-risk children at an early
age (identified by teachers on an aggressiveness scale) was that of
Magnusson, Stattin, and Duner (1983), who followed a sample of 412
school children from ages 10 to 26. They found a clear relationship
between expressed aggressiveness in early school age and later delinquency and adult criminal behavior. Not only did the aggressive children commit the majority of all offenses but they also committed the
most serious offenses.
Traulsen (1976), in following 223 delinquent children born in 1941
in Stuttgart up to age 26, found that 50% of the delinquent children
accumulated official offenses in their juvenile and adult years at a
rate 20% higher than the percentage of those who were not delinquent as
children, thus establishing a relationship between childhood, juvenile,
and adult criminal behavior. Similar results were reported by Spittler
(1986).
West and Farrington (1973, 1977) commenced their unique all-boy
sample when the latter were eight years old and are currently interviewing them at age 32. In the battery of interviews and tests undertaken over the years, they have found that those who start early are
more persistent.
Overall, only a few studies have researched early chldhood (Denno,
1982; Magnusson et al., 1983; Pongratz, Schaefer, Juergensen, & Weisze,
1977; Spittler, 1968; Spivak, 1983; Traulsen, 1976). Pongratz et al.

(1977) discovered early career children; Magnusson et al., (1983), West et al., (1973, 1977), Farrington (1986), and Loeber (1987) found early-identified troublemakers who later became persistent delinquents. But most of the studies begin around the tenth year in the lives of their subjects. Not only do we have almost no studies starting in early childhood but those we do have examine only small samples or exhibit sample problems (all of them), use just a delinquent group with no control group (Pongratz et al., 1977; Spittler, 1968; Traulsen, 1976), touch only one life phase, or follow the subjects through only two stages of their lives (all of them). There is certainly a need for more research, especially if we are to learn more about a group of "criminal career" children who later in their lives become career criminals as juveniles and adults.

A significant number of studies have suggested that there exists a transition pattern from juvenile delinquency to adult crime. Their findings have suggested a persistent career that continues into adulthood. Healy and Bronner ([1926], 1969) found that 43% of their institutionalized sample committed crimes as adults. Wikstrom (1985) showed that of the violent offenders in a Swedish birth cohort at age 23, more than half with a prior violent offense were recidivists in violent crimes. Magnusson et al. (1983) found that at age 26, 87% of all persons in their sample who committed four or more offenses had been given aggressiveness scores of five or higher (on a scale from one to eight) in their early school years. Traulsen (1976) showed that 50% of the delinquent children in her sample committed crimes as adolescents and adults. Robins (1966) found that 75% of her sample were arrested between ages 31 and 43, and 49% had at least three arrests as adults. Similar results were provided by Chaiken and Chaiken (1982), Chaikin and Dunham (1966), Feldhusen, Aversano, and Thurston (1976), Feldhusen, Thurston, and Benning (1973), Glueck and Glueck (1937, 1943), Hamparian et al. (1978, 1985), McCord and McCord (1959), Petersilia et al. (1978), Peterson, Braiker, and Polich (1980), Robins and Wish (1977), Rojek and Erickson (1982), Shannon (1982), Sinclair and Clarke (1982), Stott and Wilson (1977), and Wolfgang et al. (1987).

In studying the persistent offender, concern has emerged about whether the juveniles with the highest number of offenses would be most likely to become adult offenders, and, if so, would they have the highest number of offenses as adults? The chronic or habitual offender has received a great deal of attention in both research and policy matters. Most studies show that a small number of offenders commit a disproportionate number of offenses. Various results identify the number of chronic offenders as the 5 to 10% of the population group who commit at least 50% of all of that group's crimes.

Longitudinal studies in Philadelphia (Tracy, Wolfgang, & Figlio, in press; Wolfgang et al., 1972; Wolfgang et al., 1987); Cambridge (Farrington, 1982; Farrington et al., 1985; West, 1982; West et al., 1973, 1977); Stockholm (Janson, 1975, 1977); Copenhagen (Fry, 1985; Hogh, Strande-Soerenson, & Wolf, 1978); Berlin (Weschke & Krause, 1983) have shown that a small number of subjects in each birth cohort were responsible for a large number of the offenses committed by the members of those cohorts.

The best known results have been obtained by Wolfgang et al. (1972), Wolfgang et al. (1987), and Tracy et al. (in press). Having identified the chronic offender in two large-scale birth cohorts (1945 and 1958), they followed a fairly large subsample (the rest of the data were destroyed in a fire) of the 1945 cohort up to age 30. Six percent of the 1945 cohort were chronic offenders by age 18 and accumulated 51.9% of all of that cohort's offenses. These figures increased by age 30 to 14.8% who were responsible for three-fourths of the offenses (Collins, 1977).

Even though Shannon could identify the chronic offender in three Racine, Wisconsin, birth cohorts, he suffered a major problem in the area of criminal career research: most people do not commit serious offenses. As Petersilia pointed out, "Shannon had in his birth cohorts only about 8% of the 1942 cohort, 10% of the 1949 cohort, and 14% of the 1955 cohort who had a police contact for a felony" (1980:239). This leads us to a common problem in the study of the persistent and chronic or habitual offender. Even though there exists some evidence that there is an association between juvenile delinquency and adult crime and that chronic offenders are responsible for a disproportionate number of offenses, all of the studies have either too small a sample size or sample problems. If they begin with large birth cohorts, as did Hogh et al. (1978); Janson (1975); Tracy et al. (in press); Weschke et al. (1983); and Wolfgang et al. (1972), they take a long, long time to be completed and results are not available yet. Often they have no control group or cannot compare their offender cohorts with non-offender cohorts (Hamparian et al., 1978, 1985; Weschke et al., 1983), or the data were lost to fire and only a subsample could be saved (Wolfgang et al., 1987).

With the exception of the Scandinavian research, which in general has lower prevalence and incidence rates than comparable American research, there exist no up-to-date studies which have followed their subjects in sufficient numbers from their adolescence into their adult years. Most studies range between 100 and 500 persons, and the mortality rate usually diminishes the already small sample sizes.

One of the best-followed samples is that of Farrington and West, which consists of 411 subjects who were studied from ages eight to 33. Farrington, Gallagher, Morley, Ledger, and West (1985) reported that they could identify the chronic offenders, but they found only twenty-three habitual offenders who had accumulated 230 convictions by age 27.

The sample size of the third Rand inmate survey (Chaiken et al., 1982) was fairly large (N = 2,200) but suffered from recall lapses, did not use a validation sample, and was questionable in terms of the high numbers of offenses certain subjects reported. As Weis (1986) has pointed out, cognitive psychology tells us that it is impossible to recall the same event over and over in an accurate way. Chaiken and Chaiken's sample reported about 4,000 drug deals and 500 burglaries a year in addition to other offenses. Similarly, Elliott, Ageton, Huizinga, Knowles, and Canter (1983b) reported that their most serious offenders committed 261 offenses in 1976. These results are indicative of a high frequency pattern, but their validity remains to be determined.

Despite the results that a small number of persons are responsible for a large number of crimes, it is obvious that law-abiding behavior persists over the life span of most people (unless they shift to white-collar and occupation crimes) and that diminishing involvement in criminality occurs in conjunction with aging. The Gluecks (1968) found that "the original nondelinquents largely continued to be law-abiding with the passage of time and their growth into adulthood." Before age 17, 90.4% of the delinquents had become felons; this rated dropped to 59.6% by age 25 and then to 28.9% by age 30. This decline was described by Cline (1980) as a "burning out" process. J. McCord's (1978, 1979) data on her thirty-six year follow up revealed that one-third of the subjects followed the transition from nondelinquent status as adolescents to minor crimes as adults, and the second most common pattern was from nondelinquent to nondelinquent. Serious crimes in adulthood were committed by nearly as many adolescent nondelinquents (8.1%) as adolescent delinquents (9.9%).

Polk, Adler, Bazemore, Blake, Cardray, Coventry, Galvin, and Temple (1981) had no plausible explanation for their finding that of the ninety subjects they studied who committed offenses as adults, the majority (55 subjects) had no juvenile records. Guttridge, Gabrielli, Mednick, and Van Dusen (1983) noted that the rate of violence for their cohort was 2.5% by ages 15 and 16; it rose to over 8.0% by age 18, remained stable until reaching 9.0% by age 25, and then dropped to 1.0% by age 28. Seventy percent of the violent offenses were committed beween age 18 and 25.

Wolfgang et al. (1987) report:

Of the subjects who were nonoffenders during their juvenile years, 81.9% were classified as nonoffenders during adult-hood. Moreover, only 3% of the nondelinquents were arrested five or more times after age 18.

Of Langan and Greenfield's (1983) sample of 827 males who were age 40 or older when they entered prison, 46.6% had no record of incarceration during either adolescence or young adulthood. They found that over half of the sample members were first incarcerated for murder, man-slaughter, rape, or sexual assault, confirming that the most serious offenses were punished most severely regardless of the offenders' prior records.

The "burning out" process first introduced by the Gluecks is also described as a "maturation" effect (Fry, 1985; Janson, 1977; Polk et al., 1981). These concepts have since been accepted by many criminologists (Blumstein and Green, 1982; Blumstein, Cohen, & Hsieh, 1982; Blumstein, Farrington, & Moitra, 1985; Cline, 1980; Farrington, 1983; Fry, 1985; Guttridge et al., 1983; Hamparian et al., 1978; Hogh et al., 1978; and Janson, 1977).

As Reckless pointed out, "It is much easier to explain why an offender continues with his career rather than to understand why he stops the career" (1972:211). Similarly, Cline (1980) commented that little is known about the dynamics of the steeply declining rates after age 30; and Blumstein and Moitra (1980) found that individuals with

336

lengthy criminal records were found just as likely as the short-record "amateurs" to have made the current arrest their last. Wolfgang et al. (1987) report that in the 1945 cohort 62% of the one-time delinquents, 55% of the two-time delinquents, 45% of the three-time delinquents, 32% of the four-time delinquents, and 22% of the juvenile chronic offenders experienced no police arrest during adulthood. Similar results have been reported by Dinitz and Conrad (1984), Hamparian et al. (1978, 1975), and Shannon (1978). Polk et al. (1981) found that over half of their sample had been involved in crime during early childhood, but only 13% were so involved after age 27. Blumstein et al. (1982) reported that most of the people starting their careers relatively late (at age 18) drop out of crime by the time they reach age 30. The Scandinavian studies confirm a sharp decrease in delinquent behavior by age 25, when the number of arrests recorded dropped to less than half the peak volume (Fry, 1985; Hogh et al., 1978; Janson, 1977); their results to age 30 are not yet available to us.

As this review indicates, there is evidence that deviant, antisocial behavior starts in early childhood followed by delinquent behavior during the juvenile period and criminal behavior during adulthood.

3. THE USE OF SELF-REPORTS IN THE ADULT LIFE SPAN

By directing our attention to the use of self-reports during these life spans we find that, with a few exceptions, they focus on the juvenile period. Only a few studies use self-reports for more than one period and, if so, they use the same instruments. Since Loeber (1987) and Farrington (1986) pointed out already that it is necessary to focus more on the childhood life span, we will concentrate on the adult life span. As we have shown earlier, our knowledge about the transition of criminal behavior from juveniles to adults is limited and mostly established by official data. Exceptions are the studies by Wolfgang et al. (1987), Magnusson, et al. (1983), West et al. (1973, 1977), Robbins (1966), and McCord (1978, 1979) who use official data as well as self-reports. There is a clear need to conduct more research on the adult life span using self-reports. Despite the growing concern about corporate and organizational crime and the knowledge that large corporations are actually among the most persistent offenders (Sutherland, 1949), we do not know very much about the extent of adult criminal involvement to date. Self-report studies also allow for these offenses. Previous research has shown that juveniles are more likely to be involved in property crimes and that young adults are more involved in violent crimes, yet there is no evidence that these facts are considered in the development of self-report studies. It seems wrong (to us) to use the same instrument for different life spans since each life span represents certain attitudes and behavior, ergo different criminal behavior.

These problems indicate that there exist problems with the item selection of the self-reports. We will show, by using the National Crime Severity Study, that the best known instruments, despite their claim that they use all Index Offenses, are still using mostly trivial offenses. We will compare the instruments of Short and Nye,

Hindelang, Hirschi, Weis, and Elliott et al. and the Phildelphia Birth
Cohort II follow-up instrument which was recently developed.

TABLE 1. The items of the self-report questionnaires and interviews
ranked according to the National Crime Severity Scale.

Note: It was not possible to find an equivalent offense for every item
used in the self-report studies, especially for offenses dealing with
damaging property, since there is no equivalent in NCSS. In addition,
we had to adjust some of the offenses to the severity scale. In these
cases, we always used the more severe one of the National Crime Severity Study as the comparable offense.

Severity Scale	Elliott et al.	Short/Nye	Hindelang, Hirschi, & Weis	1958 Philadelphia Interview
1 - 10				1
11 - 20				1
21 - 30	1		1	1
31 - 40				
41 - 50				
51 - 60				
61 - 70			1	1
71 - 80	1			3
81 - 90				1
91 - 100	1			2
101 - 110				1
111 - 120	2			1
121 - 130				2
131 - 140			2	4
141 - 150	2	1	4	4
151 - 160	2	4	3	2
161 - 170	4	2	6	2
171 - 180	1	1	1	2
181 - 190	7		1	5
191 - 200	5	6		5
201 - 204	2	1		1

As Table 1 shows, there is a clear indication that the majority of
the offenses are above 141 on the severity scale. The scale is scored
so that low scores equal higher severity. In comparing the Short and

Nye questionnaire with Elliott et al. and the one by Hirschi, Hindelang, and Weis, we find Elliott et al. have only five questions ranked
higher and Hindelang et al. only four. This indicates that only moderate advancements have been made in attempting to improve self-report
instruments by taking more serious crimes into account.

The majority of the offenses are trivial offenses in all self-
reports. Only the Philadelphia interview takes into account white-
collar and occupational crimes: eighteen of the offenses score between
1 and 140 and twenty-one between 141 and 204. The most severe crime in
the Elliott et al. and Hindelang et al. questionnaires is rape, whereas
in the Philadelphia interview, murder was used. One notable exception
in the Hindelang et al. questionnaire is the inclusion of arson (no
other questionnaire or interview uses it) and could be justified by the
fact that according to the UCR juveniles committed about 40% of the
arson cases, indicating a severe problem. They also had included no
offenses ranked between 191 and 204 whereas Short and Nye had seven,
Elliott et al. seven, and the Philadelphia interview six in that category. This indicates a focus on too trivial offenses. Overall, the
claimed advances by Hindelang et al. and Elliott seem rather trivial
since their scales have only four and five offenses which score higher on the severity scale than the one by Short and Nye.

If we look at property offenses, we find that all of the instruments ask about minor amounts of money with a peak of one hundred dollars. Young adults and adults are clearly involved in burglaries and
larceny offenses of much greater value as well as in many more violent
offenses. The above-mentioned self-report instruments fail to take
these facts into account. The majority of the items deal with status
offenses or specific juvenile behavior and definitly should not be used
above the ages of sixteen or eighteen.

As we pointed out earlier, according to the UCR, between 1963 and
1980 the number of juveniles under age eighteen arrested for serious
index crimes increased 143% and the number of violent crimes increased
300%. This change or development is not reflected in the self-report
instruments. In looking at the item selection for self-reports from
various available results we have to conclude that, with the exception
of the Philadelphia interview, no attempts have been made to increase
our knowledge by including more serious offenses. If we consider the
ongoing three longitudinal projects by Thornberry et al., Loeber et
al., and Elliott et al. we find that they all use the instrument developed earlier by Elliott et al. Loeber is improving our state of knowledge by using a battery of interviews dealing with early serious conduct problems.

Recent developments are not taken into account, and researchers
prefer using a reliable and valid instrument rather than improving our
knowledge by including more serious offenses.

All this shows that, especially in longitudinal research, we have
to use different instruments during the various life spans of an individual. In addition, we should include more "realistic" crimes in our
self-report research. So far we do not have very encouraging evidence
for the latter.

4. THE CHRONIC OFFENDER IN SELF-REPORT STUDIES: A MISSING CASE?

One of the most publicized findings from longitudinal research is the report of chronic or habitual offenders who are also the most serious and dangerous ones. While the majority of the results were obtained by official data, the chronic offender was also found in self-report studies.

Wolfgang et al. (1972), by using official data, found that 6% of the 1945 cohort committed 51% of all the offenses by the age of eighteen. Tracy et al. (in press) showed that 7.5% of the 1958 cohort committed 61% of the offenses. The follow-up study by Wolfgang et al. identified 15% as chronic offenders who committed 74% of all offenses by the age of 30. In contrast to theses results obtained by official police records, Dunford et al. (1984) found that 75% of their chronic offenders had no official police record and only 7% of their chronic offenders would have been classified as habitual offenders in the Philadelphia birth cohort studies. They conclude therefore that official data capture only a small number of chronic offenders. These results suggest that self-reports are a better tool to find the chronic offender.

To confuse the picture a little more, Cernkovich et al. (1985), in contrast to Dunford and Elliott, point out that in self-report delinquency research the chronic offenders are the missing cases. Their study compared a sample of neighborhood youth with an institutional sample and found 13.6% of the former were chronic offenders versus 80.0% of the latter. Their results contradict the assumption that chronic offenders are represented in reasonable numbers in general youth samples -- a commonplace in self-report literature. In their conclusion they state

> ...that it is also important to locate the chronic delinquent
> offender, to compare the behavior of this youth with that of
> others along the behavioral continuum, and to identify those
> factors and processes that lead to this extreme level of
> delinquency involvement. We believe that such a focus will
> necessitate a return to the study of official delinquents,
> research subjects virtually abandoned with the advent of the
> self-report methodology some thirty years ago (731).

How can we have such contradicting results? One reasonable explanation is that the National Youth Survey which determines the chronic offender by frequency rather than severity of the crime does not capture the serious offender at all, as measured by seriousness. We argue that the offenders who commit a homicide, rape, robbery, or aggravated assault have a good chance of being taken out of circulation by putting them into juvenile facilities or a prison. Therefore the NYS only includes in its sample a small number of persons who commit a serious, violent crime and therefore underestimates the number of these criminals. In examining the research proposals of Thornberry et al., Loeber et al., and Elliott et al., we find that these researchers might run into the same problems. So is it reasonable to argue that official data identify the serious, violent chronic offender better? The answer is yes and no. While in the 1945 Philadelphia cohort the chronic offenders committed 71% of the homicides, 73% of the rapes, and 80% of the robberies, which indicate that the chronic offenders are not only the most frequent offenders but also the most threatening ones in terms of the severity of the crime, we can also look at the residuals of the percentages: 29% of the homicides, 17% of the rapes, and 20% of the robberies were not committed by chronic offenders. By arguing that these serious offenders were also incarcerated at an early stage and therefore prevented from becoming chronic offenders, we can conclude that official data as well underestimate the true number of chronic offenders. However, the majority of serious offenders get classified as chronic offenders by using official data; this cannot be said about self-report studies such as the NYS.

Let us examine now the use of the classifications of Wolfgang et al. and Elliott et al. and the role of the Index Crimes. Dunford et al. (1982, 1984) use the typology of the nondelinquents, exploratory delinquents, nonserious but patterned delinquents, and serious, patterned delinquents. A nondelinquent is a youth engaging in fewer than four self-reported offenses and no UCR Part I offenses during any given calendar year; an exploratory delinquent has engaged in four to seven self-reported delinquent behaviors and no more than one UCR Part I offense in any given calendar year; a nonserious, patterned delinquent has engaged in twelve or more self-reported delinquent behaviors and no more than two UCR Part I offenses in any given calendar year; a serious, patterned delinquent has committed at least three UCR Part I offenses in a given year of assessment irrespective of the frequency of involvement in any other delinquent offenses.

Even though the UCR Part I offenses are frequently used as an indicator for the seriousness of the crime, we think using them in these offender classifications is a fatal flaw. Using Dunford and Elliott's classification we can construct an exploratory delinquent -- and therefore by definition a less serious offender -- who committed a murder, rape, or robbery, and a serious, patterned delinquent -- therefore the most serious criminal -- who committed three auto thefts in any given calendar year. According to Dunford and Elliott's classification, the single murderer, rapist, or robber is not a serious criminal whereas the auto thief who steals three cars is. We think this is simply wrong since probably everybody would agree that the former is far more dangerous than the latter.

The absence of a weighting system among the UCR Part I offenses is a serious flaw in Dunford and Elliott's classification. If they would at least differentiate between offenses against the person and property one would get a better understanding of seriousness of the offenses. It seems clear that classifying a chronic offender just by frequency and the use of the UCR Part I offenses is not enough and is more confusing than clarifying. To give another example: we could construct a case using Dunford and Elliott's classification in which a person with twelve or more simple assaults in any given calendar year is considered a less serious delinquent than the above constructed three-time auto thief.

Similarly, we can argue that in the Wolfgang et al. classification, a one-time murderer, three-time rapist, or four-time robber is considered a less serious offender than a person with five arrests for auto theft or stealing property worth more than fifty dollars, since the former are not classified as chronic offenders, having fewer than at least five official arrests by the age of eighteen. Wolfgang et al., however, used the severity scale on an aggregate level to show the difference of the severity of the crime for one-time, repeat, and chronic offenders. The use of the UCR Part I offenses for establishing a classification as done by Dunford and Elliott seems therefore to be highly questionable because of its misleading character.

5. CONCLUSION

It is definitely desirable to use self-reports in longitudinal research, along with official data. One of the most neglected areas of self-reports is the adult life span. Previous research did not develop adequate instruments for that time period. Research focusing on the juvenile as well as the adult phase used inadequately constructed self-report instruments and paid more attention to the former life span.

By examining self-report items with the Crime Severity Scale we found that self-report items have at the most made modest progress since the development of the Short and Nye instrument. Improvement in that area is essential to developing a more comprehensive understanding of criminal behavior. By looking at the chronic offender problem we find that the serious, chronic offenders in self-report studies are the missing cases, especially in the NYS, and that official data also underestimate the true number of serious, chronic offenders. By further examining the classifications established to determine serious, patterned offenders we find that the use of UCR Part I offenses in combination with frequency as a main criterion is misleading. We should rather focus on the severity of offenses while taking into account the total number of offenses.

REFERENCES

Akers, R: Socio-economic status and delinquent behavior. A retest. Journal of Research in Crime and Delinquency, 1:38–46, 1964.
Akerstrom, MC: Crooks and squares. Stockholm: Studentlitterature Land, 1983.
Blumstein, A, Cohen, J, Roth, J, & Visher, C (Eds.): Criminal careers and "career criminals". Volumes I and II. Washington, DC: National Academy Press, 1986.
Blumstein, A, Cohen, J, & Farrington, D: Criminal career research: Its value for criminology. Criminology, 26:1-36, 1988a.
Blumstein, A, Cohen, J, & Farrington, D: Longitudinal and criminal research: Further clarification. Criminology, 26:57-74, 1988b.

Blumstein, A, & Moitra, S: The identification of "career criminals"
from "chronic offenders" in a cohort. Law and Policy Quarterly,
2:321-34, 1980.

Blumstein, A, Cohen, J, & Hsieh, P. The duration of adult criminal
careers. Final Report submitted to the National Institute of Justice. Pittsburgh: Urban Systems Institute, School of Urban and
Public Affairs, Carnegie-Mellon University, 1982.

Blumstein, A, Farrington, D, & Moitra, S: Delinquency careers:
Innocents, desisters, and persisters. In Morris, N, & Tonry, M,
(Eds.), Crime and justice: An annual review, vol. 6, 187-219.
Chicago: University of Chicago Press, 1985.

Blumstein, A, & Green, M: The length of criminal careers. Unpublished
paper. Pittsburgh, PA: Urban Systems Institute, Carnegie-Mellon
University, 1982.

Cameron, M: The booster and the snitch. New York: Free Press, 1964.

Cernkovich, S, Giordano, P, & Pugh, M: Chronic offenders: The missing
cases in self-report delinquency research. Journal of Criminal Law
and Criminology, 76:705-32, 1985.

Chaiken, J, & Chaiken, M: Varieties in Criminal Behavior. Santa
Monica, CA: The Rand Corporation, 1982.

Cline, H: Criminal behavior over the life span. In Brim, Jr., O, &
Kagan, J (Eds.), Constancy and change in human development. Cambridge: Harvard University Press, 1980, 641-74.

Collins Jr., J: Deterrence by restraint: Two models to estimate its
effect in a cohort of offenders. Ph.D. dissertation, University of
Pennsylvania, 1977.

Denno, D: Sex differences in cognition and crime: Developmental,
biological, and sociological correlates. Ph.D. dissertation, University of Pennsylvania, 1982.

Dinitz, S, & Conrad, J: Who's in that dark alley? In Mednick, S,
Harway, M, & Finello, K (Eds.), Handbook of Longitudinal Research,
vol. 2, 410-21. New York: Praeger Press, 1984.

Dunford, F, & Elliott, D: Identifying career offenders with self-
reported data. Journal of Research in Crime and Delinquency,
21:57-86, 1984.

Elliott, D: The identification and prediction of career offenders
utilizing self-reported and official data. Paper presented at the
Vermont Conference on the Primary Prevention of Psychopathology,
Bolten Valley, Vermont, 1983a.

Elliott, D, Ageton, S, Huizinga, D, Knowles, B, & Canter, R: The prevalence and incidence of delinquent behavior, 1978-1980. Boulder, CO:
Behavioral Research Institute, National Youth Survey Report No. 26,
1983b.

Elliott, D, Huizinga, D, & Ageton, S: Explaining delinquency and drug
use. Beverly Hills: Sage Publications, 1985.

Elliott , D, & Huizinga: The relationship between delinquent behavior
and DM problems. National Youth Survey Report No. 28. Boulder, CO:
1984.

Farrington, D: Longitudinal research on crime and delinquency. In
Morris, N, & Tonry, M (Eds.), Crime and justice: An annual review
of research, vol. 1, 289-348. Chicago: University of Chicago Press,
1979.
----------: Longitudinal analysis of criminal violence. In Wolfgang,
M, & Weiner, N (Eds.), Longitudinal analysis of criminal violence,
171-200. Beverly Hills: Sage Publications, 1982.
----------: Offending from 10 to 25 years of age. In Van Dusen, K, &
Mednick, S (Eds.), Prospective studies of crime and delinquency,
17-37. Boston: Kluwer-Nijhoff, 1983.
Farrington, D: Age and crime. In Tonry, M (Ed.), Crime and justice,
29-90. Chicago: University of Chicago Press, 1986.
Farrington, D, Ohlin, L, & Wilson, J: Understanding and controlling
crime. New York: Springer Verlag, 1986.
Farrington, D, & Tarling, R (Eds.): Prediction in criminology. Albany: State University of New York Press, 1985.
Farrington, D, Gallagher, B, Leger, R, & West, D: The Cambridge study
in delinquency development. Long term follow-up. First annual
report to the Home Office. London: Home Office, 1985.
Feldhusen, J, Aversano, F, & Thurston, J: Prediction of youth contacts
with law enforcement agencies. Criminal Justice and Behavior,
3:235-53, 1976.
Feldhusen, F, Thurston, J, & Benning, J: A longitudinal study of delin-
quency and other aspects of children's behavior. International
Journal of Criminology and Penology, 1:341-51, 1973.
Ferguson, T: The young delinquent in his social setting. London:
Oxford University Press, 1952.
Fry, L: Drug abuse and crime in a Swedish birth cohort. British Jour-
nal of Criminology, 25:46-59, 1985.
Glueck, S, & Glueck, E: Delinquents and nondelinquents in perspective.
Cambridge: Harvard University Press, 1968,
----------: Five hundred criminal careers. New York: Knopf, 1930.
Gold, M: Delinquent behavior in an American city. Belmont, CA: Brooks
Cole, 1970.
Gottfredson, M, & Hirschi, T: The true value would appear to be zero:
An essay on career criminals, criminal careers, selective incapacita-
tion, cohort studies, and related topics. Criminology, 24:213-34,
1986.
----------: The methodological adequacy of longitudinal research on
crime. Criminology, 25:581-614, 1987.
----------: Science, public policy, and the careers paradigm. Crimi-
nology, 26:37-56, 1988.
Guttridge, P, Gabrielli, W, Mednick, S, & Van Dusen, K: Criminal vio-
lence in a birth cohort. In Van Dusen, K, & Mednick, S (Eds.),
Prospective studies in crime and delinquency, 211-24. Boston:
KluwerNijhoff, 1983.
Hamparian, D, Davis, J, Jacobsen, J, & McGraw, R: The young criminal
years of the violent few. Report submitted to the U.S. Department
of Justice, 1985.

344

Hamparian, D, Schuster, R, Dinitz, S, & Conrad, J: The violent few: A study of dangerous juvenile offenders. Lexington, MA: Lexington Books, 1978.

Healy, W, & Bronner, A: Delinquents and criminals: Their making and unmaking. 1926. Reprint. Montclair, NJ: Patterson Smith, 1969.

Hindelang, M, Hirschi, T, & Weis, J: Measuring delinquency. Beverly Hills: Sage Publications, 1981.

Hirschi, T: Causes of delinquency. Berkeley: University of California Press, 1969.

Hogh, E, & Wolf, T: Registered delinquency in a birth cohort: A longitudinal study: Project Metropolitan. Copenhagen: Project Metropolitan Series No. 3, 1978.

Irwin, J: The felon. Englewood Cliffs, NJ: Prentice Hall, 1970.

Jackson, B: The thieves premier. New York: MacMillan, 1969.

Janson, C: Project Metropolitan: A longitudinal study of a Stockholm cohort. Stockholm: Project Metropolitan Research Report No. 1, 1975.

----------: Project Metropolitan: A longitudinal study of a Stockholm cohort: The handling of juvenile cases. Stockholm: Project Metropolitan Research Report No. 7, 1977.

Klockars, C: The professional fence. New York: The Free Press, 1974.

Langan, P, & Farrington, D: Two-track or one-track justice? Some evidence from an English longitudinal survey. Journal of Criminal Law and Criminology, 74:519-546, 1983.

Langan, P, & Greenfield, L: Career patterns in crime. Washington, DC: U.S. Department of Justice Statistics Special Report, June 1983.

Letkeman, P: Crime as work. Englewood Cliffs, NJ: Prentice Hall, 1973.

Loeber, R. The prevalence, correlates, and continuity of serious conduct problems in elementary school children. Criminology, 25:615-42, 1987.

McCord, J: Some child-rearing antecedents of criminal behavior in adult men. Journal of Personality and Social Psychology, 37:1477-86, 1979.

----------: A thirty-year follow up of treatment effects. American Psychologist, 33:284-89, 1978.

Magnusson, D, Duner, A, & Zetterblom, G: Adjustment: A longitudinal study. Stockholm: Almquist & Wiksell, 1975.

Magnusson, D, Stattin, H, & Duner, A: Aggression and criminality in a longitudinal perspective. In Van Dusen, K, & Mednick, S (Eds.), Prospective studies of crime and delinquency, 277-301. Boston: Kluwer-Nijhoff, 1983.

Martin, J: My life in crime: The autobiography of a professional thief. New York: Knopf, 1952.

Maurer, D. The big con. Indianapolis: Bobbs-Merrill, 1940.

----------: Whiz mob. New Haven, CN: College and University Press, 1964.

Mednick, B., Mednick, S, Baker, R, & Gabrielli, W: Longitudinal study of social and biological factors in crime; Executive summary. Los Angeles: University of Southern California, 1983.

Miller, G: Factors in school achievement and social class. _Journal of Educational Psychology_, 61:260-69, 1970.

Petersilia, J: Criminal career research. In Morris, N, & Tonry, M (Eds.), _Crime and justice: An annual review of research_, vol. 2, 321-79. Chicago: University of Chicago Press, 1980.

Petersilia, J, Greenwood, P, & Lavin, M: _Criminal careers of habitual felons_. Santa Monica: Rand Corporation, 1977.

Peterson, M, Braiker, H, & Polich, S: _Doing time: A survey of California prison inmates_. Santa Monica: The Rand Corporation, 1980.

Polk, K, Adler, C, Bazemore, G, Blake, G, Cardray, S, Coventry, G, Galvin, J, & Temple, M: _Becoming adult: An analysis of maturational development from ages 16 to 30; Final report_. Washington, DC: U.S. Department of Health, Education, and Welfare, National Institute of Mental Health, Center for Studies in Crime and Delinquency, 1981.

Polsky, N: _Hustlers, beats, and others_. Garden City: Anchor Books, 1969.

Pongratz, L, Schaefer, M, Juergensen, P, & Weisse, D: _Kinderdelinquenz: Daten, Hintergruende und Entwicklungen_. Muenchen: Juventa, 1977.

Prus, R, & Sharper, B: _Road hustler_. Lexington, MA: Lexington Books, 1977.

Reckless, W: _The prevention of juvenile delinquency_. Columbus: Ohio State University Press, 1972.

Robins, L: _Deviant children grown up: A sociological and psychiatric study of sociopathic personality_. Baltimore: Williams and Wilkins, 1966.

Robins, L, & Wish, E: Childhood deviance as a developmental process: A study of 233 urban black men from birth to 18. _Social Forces_, 56:448-73, 1977.

Rojek, D, & Erickson, M: Delinquent careers: A test of the career escalation model. _Criminology_, 20:5-28, 1982.

Shannon, L: Assessing the relationship of adult criminal careers to juvenile careers: A summary. Washington, DC: U.S. Department of Justice, 1982.

Short, J, & Nye, F: Reported behavior as a criterion of deviant behavior. _Social Problems_, 5:207-13, 1957.

Sinclair, I, & Clarke, R: Predicting, treating, and explaining delinquency: The lessons from research on institutions. In Feldman P (Ed.), _Development in the study of behavior: The prevention and control of behavior_. New York: Wiley, 1982.

Spector, P: _Research designs_. Beverly Hills: Sage Publications, 1981.

Spittler, E: Die Kriminalitaet Strafunmuendiger. Jur. dissertaion, Giesen, 1968.

Spivak, G: High risk early behaviors indicating vulnerability to delinquency in the community and school; Final report. Philadelphia: Hahneman University Hospital, 1983.

Stott, D, & Wilson, D: The adult criminals as juveniles. _British Journal of Criminology_, 17:47-57, 1977.

Sutherland, E: _The professional thief_. Chicago: University of Chicago Press, 1937.

346

----------: White collar crime. New York: Dryden, 1949.

Tracy, P., Jr. Race and class differences in official and self-reported delinquency. In Wolfgang, M, Thornberry, T, & Figlio, R (Eds.), From Boy to man -- From delinquency to crime. Chicago: University of Chicago Press, 1987.

Tracy, P, Jr., Wolfgang, M, & Figlio, R: Delinquency in a birth cohort II: A comparison of the 1945 and 1958 Philadelphia birth cohorts. New York: Plenum, in press.

Traulsen, M: Delinquente Kinder und ihre Legalbewaehrung. Frankfurt: Verlag Peter Lang, 1976.

Visher, C, & Roth, J: Participation in criminal careers. In Blumstein, A, Cohen, J, Roth, J, & Visher, C (Eds.), Criminal careers and "career criminals", vol. 1. Washington, DC: National Academy Press, 1986.

Waldo, G. Career criminals. Beverly Hills: Sage Publications, 1983.

Weiner, N: Violent recidivism among the 1958 Philadelphia birth cohort boys. Final report. Philadelphia, PA: University of Pennsylvania, 1985.

Weiner, N, & Wolfgang, M: The extent and character of violent crime in America, 1969-1982. In Curtis, L (Ed.), American violence and public policy, 17-39. New Haven: Yale University Press, 1985.

Weis, J: Issues in the measurement of criminal careers. In Blumstein, A, Cohen, J, Roth, J, & Visher, C (Eds.), Criminal careers and "career criminals", vol. 1. Washington, DC: National Academy Press, 1986.

Weschke, E, & Krause, W: Auswertung Polizeilicher Unterlagen in Berlin ueber Kiner, Jugendliche und Heranwachsende des Jahrgangs. Publikation der Fachhochschule fuer Verwaltung und Rechtspflege Berliner Kriminalwissenschaften. Berlin, 1983.

West, D: Delinquency: Its roots, careers, and prospects. London: Heineman, 1982.

----------: Present conduct and future delinquency. London: Heineman, 1969.

West, D, & Farrington, D: Who becomes delinquent? London: Heineman, 1973.

West, D, & Farrington, D: The delinquent way of life. London: Heineman, 1977.

Wikstrom, P: Everyday violence in contemporary Sweden. Stockholm: National Council for Crime Prevention, Report No. 15, 1985.

Wolfgang, M, Figlio, R, & Sellin, T: Delinquency in a birth cohort. Chicago: University of Chicago Press, 1972.

Wolfgang, M, Figlio, R, Tracy, P, & Singer, S: The National Survey of Crime Severity. Washington, DC: U.S. Government Printing Office, 1985.

Wolfgang, M, Thornberry, T, & Figlio, R (Eds.): From boy to man: From delinquency to crime. Chicago: University of Chicago Press, 1987.

PANEL EFFECTS AND THE USE OF SELF-REPORTED MEASURES OF DELINQUENCY IN LONGITUDINAL STUDIES

Terence P. Thornberry
School of Criminal Justice
The University at Albany
State University of New York, Albany, New York, USA

1. INTRODUCTION

Self-report techniques for measuring delinquent and criminal behavior have been developed, almost exclusively, in studies using cross-sectional designs. None of the formative self-report studies, such as those conducted by Short and Nye (1957), Reiss and Rhodes (1961), Clark and Wenninger (1962), or Empey and Erickson (1965) involved longitudinal designs and many early studies that applied self-report methods to substantive topics (e.g., Gold, 1966; Hirschi, 1969) were also cross-sectional. As a result, criminological research has paid relatively little attention to the particular problems that attend the repeated use of a self-report measure in panel studies.

Recently, however, there has been a substantial increase in the use of longitudinal designs, particularly in research on juvenile delinquency. Some of these studies (e.g., Wolfgang, Figlio & Sellin, 1972) have relied entirely on official information on criminal behavior, primarily because of the clear temporal ordering of criminal events provided by such data. Increasingly, however, longitudinal studies rely on a mixture of self-report and official sources of data to measure criminal involvement (see Thornberry & Farnworth, 1982; Elliott, Huizinga & Ageton, 1985; Wolfgang, Thornberry & Figlio, 1987). Yet these and other longitudinal investigations have generally adopted self-report scales developed in and for cross-sectional studies. They have not thoroughly examined the measurement problems that might arise with the use of these scales in longitudinal settings, nor have they tailored them to the specific needs of panel studies. The present paper addresses some of these issues, focusing attention on problems associated with testing effects.

2. DEVELOPMENT OF THE SELF-REPORT METHOD

2.1. History

Self-report measures of delinquent behavior have advanced

M. W. Klein (ed.), Cross-National Research in Self-Reported Crime and Delinquency, 347–369.
© *1989 by Kluwer Academic Publishers.*

remarkably in the thirty-odd years since their introduction to the field. The prototypical "early" self-reported delinquency scale was developed by Short and Nye (1957; Nye & Short, 1958) and can be discussed briefly. The inventory included twenty-one items, but the bulk of the analyses were limited to the nine, and in many cases seven, items that formed a Guttman scale of delinquency. The scale items refer to very trivial forms of delinquent behavior -- for example, there is no item measuring violent behavior and the most serious theft item concerns stealing things worth less than $2.00. Moreover, subjects were only afforded a four category response set -- "no," "once or twice," "several times," and "often," and the reference period for the instrument -- "since you began grade school" -- was both long and somewhat varied for these high school respondents.

Although the Short and Nye scale represents a very basic version of self-report measures, in essence a "stripped down" model, the impact it has had on criminological thought has been anything but simple. The introduction of the self-report method has had a greater impact on theory and research than any other single innovation and it has lead to fundamental shifts in how delinquent behavior is described and explained.

2.2. Development

Since its introduction, considerable attention has been paid to the development and improvement of the psychometric properties of the self-report method. The most sophisticated and influential work has been done by Elliott and his colleagues (Elliott & Ageton, 1980; Elliott, Huizinga & Ageton, 1985; Huizinga & Elliott, 1987) and by Hindelang, Hirschi and Weis (1979; 1981). From their work a set of characteristics for acceptable, i.e., reasonably valid and reliable, self-report scales has emerged. Four of the most salient of these characteristics are the inclusion of: 1) a wide array of offenses, 2) serious offenses, 3) frequency response sets, and 4) follow-up questions. Each can be discussed in turn.

2.2.1. <u>Inclusion of a wide array of delinquency items</u>. The domain of juvenile delinquency covers a wide range of behaviors, from truancy and running away from home to aggravated assault and homicide. If the general domain of delinquency is to be represented in a self-report scale, therefore, it is necessary for the scale to cover that same wide array of human activity. Simply asking about a handful of these behaviors does not accurately represent the theoretical construct of juvenile delinquency.

In addition, empirical evidence suggests that delinquency does not have a clear unidimensional structure that would facilitate the sampling of a small number of items from a theoretically large pool to represent adequately the entire domain. Hirschi <u>et al</u>., conclude that while " ... subsets of items are relatively highly correlated with each other [they are] relatively weakly correlated across subsets" (1981:72). Because of that it is necessary to include many individual items to represent both the general construct of delinquency as well as each of the subsets or sub-domains. Huizinga and Elliott arrive at much the same conclusion in their thorough assessment of the reliability of self-report measures of delinquency. They state:

> There is, in general, no a priori reason to assume that an individual engaging in a particular delinquent behavior is likely to engage in other delinquent behaviors ... or to engage in various delinquent behaviors at the same frequency. As a result, an SRD index is not likely to be unidimensional, nor will the items be homogeneous ... (1986:297).

In brief, these considerations suggest that an adequate selfreport scale for delinquency will be relatively lengthy. A large number of individual items are required to represent the entire domain of delinquent behavior, to represent each of its subdomains, and to insure that each subdomain, e.g., violence, drug use, etc., is itself adequately represented.

2.2.2. **Inclusion of serious offenses.** Early self-report scales tended to ignore serious criminal and delinquent events and concentrated almost exclusively on minor forms of delinquency. As a result, only certain sub-domains of delinquency, such as petty theft and status offenses, were measured, even though theoretical interest and conclusory statements focused on juvenile delinquency broadly construed. Because of the slippage between the domain of theoretical interest and the ones actually measured, the early studies produced as much confusion as enlightenment.

This confusion can be seen in the literature assessing the relative validity of self-report and official data and in the examination of the social correlates of delinquency based on these two data sources. Results from the two types of studies have been discordant since they measure, in large part, two different domains of criminal involvement. When explicit efforts are made to include serious forms of delinquency in the self-report measure and to bring the behavioral domains into alignment, however, the discordant results diminish considerably (Hindelang et al., 1979; Elliott & Ageton, 1980; Thornberry & Farnworth, 1982).

Based on these results, it is essential that a general self-reported delinquency scale tap serious as well as less serious behaviors. Failure to do so misrepresents the domain of delinquency and contaminates comparisons with other data sources. In addition, it misrepresents the dependent variable of many delinquency theories (e.g., Elliott et al., 1985; Thornberry, 1987) which set out to explain serious, repetitive delinquency.

2.2.3. **Inclusion of frequency response sets.** Many self-report studies rely on response sets with a relatively small number of categories; this tends to censor high frequency responses. For example, Short and Nye used a four point response with the most extreme category being "often." As a result, a respondent who committed a theft five times would be treated the same as a respondent who committed the act fifty times. Aggregated over items, the use of limited response sets had the consequence of lumping together occasional and high rate delinquents, rather than discriminating between these behaviorally different groups.

Elliott and Ageton have argued persuasively that the failure of self-report scales to identify high rate offenders has contributed greatly to the confusion that abounds in the literature with respect to the social correlates of delinquency. Indeed, when they use frequency rather than categorical response sets they demonstrate that discordant results between official and self-report data sets diminish considerably (1980:104). Both logically and empirically, therefore, it is appropriate to rely on specific frequency responses in the collection of self-report data.

2.2.4. <u>Inclusion of follow-up questions</u>. The self-report method seems to have an inherent tendency to elicit reports of trivial, non-actionable acts of delinquency or even acts that are not violations of the law. This occurs more frequently with the less serious offenses but also plagues responses to serious offenses. For example, respondents will include as theft such pranks as hiding a classmate's books in the respondent's locker between classes, or as serious assault events that are really rough-housing between siblings. My personal favorite involves the classification of an "official" delinquency that took place on a school playground. The events are as follows:

> One student asked another one for a dime and threatened
> to twist the kid's arm if he didn't get it. The victim said
> he only had a quarter, whereupon the offender took the quar-
> ter, went into the lunch room, got change and returned fif-
> teen cents to the victim. This humanitarian gesture notwith-
> standing, when the victim's mother learned of the incident
> and insisted that "something be done about it," the offender
> was charged with "highway robbery!"

Clearly these events, which are reported with some frequency in self-report scales, are not acts of delinquency. Some effort must be made to adjust or censor the data to remove them if the delinquency of the subject is to be reflected properly and if the rank order of subjects with respect to delinquency is to be portrayed properly.

Two strategies are generally available. First, one can ask a series of follow-up questions designed to elicit more information about the event, such as the value of property stolen, the extent of injury to the victim, and the like. Second, one can use an open-ended question asking the respondent to describe the event and then probe to obtain information necessary to classify the act. Both strategies have been used with some success.

2.3. Summary

Recent examinations of the self-report method have identified a number of shortcomings of earlier scales and suggested ways of improving the psychometric properties of this technique. The more salient suggestions include the following. Self-report scales should include a wide range of delinquent acts so that the general domain of delinquency, as well as its various sub-domains, is adequately represented. The scale should include serious as well as minor acts. A frequency scale should be used to record responses so that high-rate offenders can be isolated from low-rate offenders. Finally, extremely trivial, non-actionable acts that are reported should be identified and eliminated from the data.

These procedures are likely to improve the validity, and to some extent the reliability, of self-report scales since they improve our ability to identify delinquents and to discriminate among different types of delinquents. These are clearly desirable qualities.

To gain these desirable qualities, however, requires a considerable expansion of the self-report schedule. This can be illustrated by describing the major components of the scale currently being used in the Rochester Youth Development Study. The inventory includes thirty-two acts tapping general delinquency and twelve tapping drug use, for a total of forty-four acts. For each of these, the subjects are asked if they ever committed the act and, if they had, their age the first time and if they had committed the act in the past six months. For the most serious of each type of delinquency reported in the past six months subjects are asked to describe the event by responding to the question: "Could you tell me what you did?" If that open-ended question does not elicit the information needed to describe the event adequately, a series of probe questions, which vary from two to fourteen probes depending on the offense, are asked.

Although most of these specific questions are skipped for most subjects, since delinquency remains a rare event, this approach to measuring self-reported delinquency is a far cry from the initial days of the method when subjects used a few categories to respond to a small number of trivial delinquencies with no follow-up items. Current self-report scales are usually lengthy and time consuming, both to the researcher and the respondent. Moreover, the length is generated not by the inventory itself, but by the follow-up questions that are asked only if the respondent answers positively to a screen question. It is to the potential consequences of this that attention now turns.

3. TESTING EFFECTS

Testing effects, as the term is used here, refers to any alterations of a subject's response to a particular item or scale caused by the prior administration of the same item or scale. Memory is one of the clearest examples of a testing effect. If test-retest periods are not separated by a sufficiently long period of time, a response at time two may be affected by recall of the same response at time one. Subjects may either repeat their earlier response to appear more consistent or they may change their earlier response to appear more dynamic. In either case, the response at time two is driven to some extent by recall of the response at time one.

While this type of testing effect may influence the collection of self-report data in panel studies of delinquency, a potentially more disruptive effect is produced, not by individual items, but by the structure of the self-report scale itself. The previous section demonstrated that recent developments in self-report techniques have had two rather direct consequences on their administration. First, they have become increasingly lengthy and second, the length is primarily a direct consequence of responding positively to screening items. The more often a respondent admits to committing a delinquent act, the more follow-up questions are asked and the longer the overall interview takes. This outcome is quite obvious to respondents, as suggested by even casual observations of interviews.

One possible consequence of this approach is to make respondents increasingly unwilling to respond affirmatively to screening items since those responses produce an increase in the overall length of the interview. This will not be a salient issue to all respondents, but if even a substantial minority of the respondents reduce their positive responses to screening questions, that would have a considerable impact on the results. Moreover, it is reasonable to assume that this effect is unequally distributed across respondents; those who have the most extensive involvement in delinquency would have the most time to lose by complete honesty and may therefore be more susceptible to censoring responses.

Obviously this is a potentially serious issue in the use of the self-report method in longitudinal designs. If it occurs to any substantial extent, then the data would systematically underestimate both prevalence and incidence rates. Moreover, the amount of underestimation would increase with each successive wave of data collection as respondents learn that positive responses lead to extended interview time.

Such an effect would obviously bias both correlational and causal analyses. The relationship between age and crime illustrates the point. Delinquent behavior would appear to increase more gradually than in fact it does prior to the peak age of delinquency and, following the point of inflection, it would appear to decrease more rapidly than in fact it does. Moreover, if this same effect is not present in official data on delinquency involvement, and there is no reason to assume it is, then comparisons between official and self-report data would suggest yet another "discrepancy" between the two data sources that is merely an artifact of the self-report method.

In brief, if a testing effect of this nature is present it poses serious problems for the validity and reliability of self-report data in panel studies. The data would underestimate the rate of delinquency, that underestimation would increase from wave to wave, and it is likely to be most pronounced for those who have the most to report, high rate offenders.

3.1. Empirical Evidence

Clearly, testing effects have the potential for being a serious problem. Is there any evidence that subjects respond in this manner and reduce affirmative answers to screening questions over the life of a panel? Unfortunately, this issue has not been systematically examined in the self-report literature, perhaps because of the cross-sectional design of most of the methodological studies in this area. Despite the absence of direct evidence on this point, two data sources can be used to inform this discussion. The first is a set of results from the U.S. National Crime Survey (NCS) that bear on the issue. The second are preliminary estimates of testing effects drawn from the National Youth Survey conducted by Elliott and Huizinga (Elliott et al., 1985; Huizinga & Elliott, 1986).

3.1.1. National Crime Survey.

At the outset, some similarities and differences between victim and self-report studies should be mentioned. Both approaches are concerned with the measurement of criminal behavior, both use panel designs, and both use screening questions with extensive follow-up items if the initial response is positive. On the other hand, there are considerable differences between the studies. Most notable, of course, is the fundamental difference between reporting being an offender and being a victim. Also, the follow-up questions tend to be somewhat longer and more detailed in the victim survey than in most self-report surveys.

The most important NCS data on testing effects, or what they call panel bias, are presented in a paper by Woltman and Bushery (1984). Their analyses start with the second wave of data collection since the NCS uses the initial interview only for bounding purposes. Although they analyze data for personal and for household offenses, only the personal offenses are examined here since there is no ready counterpart to household offenses in self-reported delinquency. Nevertheless, the pattern of results is quite similar for the two types of offenses.

Woltman and Bushery compare the victimization rates calculated from successive panels and, if testing effects are present, one would anticipate that the rates would decrease from a panel interviewed at time t to one interviewed at time t+1. And indeed, this is what they find. The victimization rate per 1,000 people aged twelve and over calculated from wave 2 data is 67.21 but the same rate caluclated from wave 3 data is 62.37, a statistically significant drop of 7.2% (Woltman & Bushery, 1984:98-99).

The other comparisons across adjacent waves of data collection, from the second and third waves out to the eighth and ninth waves, reveal similar decreases, although by and large the drops are not significant. Nevertheless, it appears that people are less willing to report being a victim of criminal events the longer they remained in the panel, and the wave to wave decreases, which average 5.2% over a six month interval, appear to be larger than one would expect for this type of behavior. That is, one would not expect general crime rates, especially those calculated from such a large sample, to decline by an average of 5% every six months. Population rates such as this tend to be much more stable phenomena.

The previous results may have underestimated the true testing effect since the point of comparison was always the previous data collection wave, rather than the initial wave, and therefore would be the one least effected by testing. Woltman and Bushery address this issue by presenting data out to the seventh wave, always using the second wave as the point of comparison. When this is done the evidence for a testing effect is even stronger. Compared to second wave results, rates calculated for the third wave are 7.2% lower, those from the fourth wave are 12.6% lower, those from the fifth wave are 12.7% lower, those from the sixth wave are 13.1% lower, and those from the seventh wave are 18.0% lower. As Woltman and Bushery conclude: "...fewer and fewer crimes are reported each time a panel is interviewed. There is no point in the 'aging' process at which panel bias reaches a maximum and tends to remain constant thereafter..." (1984:100).

Although the previous comparisons control for differential attrition from the panels, they do not control for history or period effects. That is, over the period of a number of years there could have been a secular decline in the actual victimization rates which is accurately reflected in the above data. To control for this possibility Woltman and Bushery restricted analyses to interviews conducted between January and June 1976. Using data from just these six months they calculate victimization rates for panels already interviewed between two and seven times. In other words, the observation period is constant, the first six months of 1976, but the number of prior interviews varies from two to seven (Woltman & Bushery, 1984:101).

These data also suggest a substantial drop in reported victimizations as a function of the number of times the person had been interviewed. The rate drops monotonically from 73.92 per 1,000 for those interviewed for only the second time during this six month period to 62.29 for those whose seventh interview occurred at that time. This represents an absolute drop of 11.63 victimizations per 1,000 people and a percentage decline of 16%.

A similar analysis of response effects in the NCS was carried out by Lehnen and Reiss (1978). They analyzed NCS data collected between July 1972 and December 1975 to see if victimization reports varied as a function of the number of prior interviews and also the number of prior reported victimizations. The number of prior interviews had the greatest effect and systematically reduced the number of current reports. They found "first timers" to be the most likely to report victimizations and that there was a general and significant decline in reporting associated with prior interviews (Lehnen & Reiss, 1978:120).

Results with respect to the effect of the number of prior victimization reports on current reporting are somewhat more complex:

> ... regardless of the number of prior interviews, there
> is an increase in reporting associated with previous incident
> reportings, and ... it is generally a constant (linear) in-
> crease. The rate of increase, however, varies with prior
> interview experience. The rate of increase in incident
> reporting is largest for respondents with the least number of
> prior interviews (Lehnen & Reiss, 1978:120).

Based on these results, it would appear that the methodological artifact may be more of a "panel effect," a general reaction to the entire interview rather than a "testing effect," a specific reaction to the screening questions themselves. The relative importance of panel versus testing effects is addressed in later sections of this chapter.

The observed drop in victimization rates across panels of the NCS may not be entirely due to either panel or testing effects. Alternate explanations have been offered. For example, since the NCS samples households, household composition may change over the course of the study, with more victim-prone teenagers leaving households, thereby driving down the overall rate across time. But it is also likely that mortality, which affects older, less crime-prone members of households, would also occur, thereby counterbalancing the effect just mentioned.

Household attrition might also produce the observed effect since families that stay in the NCS for the entire time period are more stable and therefore would be expected to have lower victimization rates than those who move and leave the panel. Unfortunately, these same families would also be expected to have lower victimization rates at the earlier interviews so this effect is largely controlled in the analysis.

In the end, it is hard to explain away the testing effect, or panel bias, observed in the NCS. The analysis was carefully done and competing explanations are simply not persuasive. It is unusual to observe such sizeable and systematic declines in population rates over such short time periods without a methodological effect. And the most likely effect to produce this outcome is the consequence of being re-interviewed.

3.1.2. **National Youth Survey**. Age-specific prevalence rates from the National Youth Survey (NYS) can be examined to offer a more direct estimation of testing effects in a longitudinal study of delinquent behavior. The NYS selected a nationally representative sample of 1725 youth between the ages of eleven and seventeen in 1976 and, between then and 1981, re-interveiwed the same subjects annually (Elliott et al., 1985). Because of this design it is possible to calculate age-specific delinquency rates that vary by the number of times the respondents were interviewed. That is, an age-specific delinquency rate, say for age fourteen, can be calculated from 1977 data but this represents the second wave of data collection for these subjects since they were also interviewed in 1976 when they were thirteen. A fourteen year old rate can also be calculated from 1978 data but this represents the third wave of data collection for these subjects, and so forth. Similar rates can be calculated for other ages and years.

If testing effects do not play a role in generating responses one would not expect these age-specific rates to vary systematically by data collection wave. Except for random fluctuations, the age-specific rates should be the same for subjects interviewed the first time and for subjects interviewed the Nth time. If there are testing effects, however, one would expect the age-specific rates to decline systematically by interview wave. The more frequently the respondents had been interviewed, the less willing they would be to report and the lower the age-specific delinquency rates would become.

To test this possibility seventeen items from the NYS self-report index are selected for analysis. They represent each of the major domains of delinquency measured in the NYS and, with the exception of some of the more serious items, the most frequently occurring items are selected since they provide more stable estimates of changes from wave to wave. For each of the selected items, age-specific prevalence rates are calculated for each wave of data collection. Table 1 presents the rates for four offenses -- gang fights, marijuana use, stealing something worth less than $5, and buying stolen goods. The matrices in Table 1 indicate that, in general, forty cells and a total of thirty comparisons between adjacent cells are available. Adjacent cell comparisons form the basis of this analysis, for if testing effects are present one would expect a downward trend as comparisons are made from cell to cell across the rows of these matrices.

TABLE 1. Age-specific prevalence rates by wave of data collection (percent reporting one or more offenses).*

Offense	Age	Data Collection Wave						Direction of Change				
		1	2	3	4	5	6	1-2	2-3	3-4	4-5	5-6
Gang	12	13	11					-				
Fights	13	13	11	7				-	-			
	14	10	10	8	8			=	-	=		
	15	16	10	10	11	7		-	=	+	-	
	16	9	14	9	8	5	3	+	-	-	-	-
	17	13	9	8	9	7	2	-	-	+	-	-
	18		6	8	8	6	4		+	=	-	-
	19			4	7	6	0			+	-	-
	20				2	4	1				+	-
	21					2	1					-
Used	12	2	4					+				
Marijuana	13	9	9	12				=	+			
	14	18	19	21	22			+	+	+		
	15	28	32	30	31	30		+	-	+	-	
	16	31	38	45	35	35	27	+	+	-	=	-
	17	39	43	49	46	42	34	+	+	-	-	-
	18	49	52	50	53	39		+	-	+	-	
	19	49	52	51	41			+	-	-		
	20	56	49	41				-	-			
	21	52	43					-				
Stole	12	15	10					-				
Something	13	16	16	15				=	-			
Under	14	21	18	17	11			-	-	-		
$5	15	25	21	11	12	12		-	-	+	=	
	16	18	25	19	12	13	10	+	-	-	+	-
	17	21	18	15	9	9	7	-	-	-	=	-
	18		17	15	10	10	8		-	-	=	-
	19			10	9	8	6			-	-	-
	20				7	9	7				+	-
	21					6	8					+

TABLE 1. (Continued) Age-specific prevalence rates by wave of data collection (percent reporting one or more offenses).*

Offense	Age	Data Collection Wave						Direction of Change				
		1	2	3	4	5	6	1-2	2-3	3-4	4-5	5-6
Bought	12	6	3					-				
Stolen	13	10	4	3				-	-			
Goods	14	11	7	6	4			-	-	-		
	15	14	11	11	5	5		-	=	-	=	
	16	9	14	11	8	7	3	+	-	-	-	-
	17	14	9	14	7	5	3	-	+	-	-	-
	18		11	11	10	9	5		=	-	-	-
	19			8	6	8	2			-	+	-
	20				7	3	3				-	=
	21					8	3					-

*All the NYS data in this paper were presented in Table B.9 of Elliott, et al., 1983

Data for gang fights indicate such a downward trend. For twelve year olds, 13% report engaging in gang fights at wave 1 but this drops to 11% at wave 2. For the thirteen year olds, 13% report being in gang fights at wave 1, 11% at wave 2 and only 7% at wave 3. In other words, as the frequency of interviewing increases, the rate of positive responses to the self-report item decreases.

The overall trend for gang fights can be seen more clearly in the matrix that simply represents the direction of change from wave to wave. In 67% of the comparisons there was a decrease in the prevalence rates, in 20% there was an increase, and in 13% there was no change. In other words, the number of comparisons in which the rates declined exceeded the number in which they increased by a factor of three.

The data for marijuana use presents a somewhat different picture. In this case there are an equal number of wave-to-wave increases and decreases, forty-seven percent, with six percent representing no change. The comparisons for the two property offenses, stealing something worth less than $5 and buying stolen goods, present patterns similar to those for gang fights. That is, they too suggest a reduction in the reporting of delinquent acts.

Table 2 presents summary data for all seventeen offenses selected for analysis. The total number of comparisons is less than thirty for some offenses; in some cases the data are not available from the NYS and in other cases, e.g., hitting a student, data collected after age eighteen are not used.

For all of the offenses, with the single exception of marijuana use, the number of negative changes exceed the number of positive changes, often by a considerable margin. The largest differential is for hitting a student, where prevalence rates decline in 90% of the comparisons and increase in only 10%. The smallest difference is observed for

TABLE 2. Direction of change in prevalence rates across adjacent waves of data collection.

Offense	Negative		Positive		None		Number of
	N	%	N	%	N	%	Comparisons
Felony assaults							
Aggravated assault	17	57	6	20	7	23	30
Gang fights	20	67	6	20	4	13	30
Minor assaults							
Hit teacher	13	65	3	15	4	20	20
Hit parent	13	65	6	30	1	5	20
Hit student	18	90	2	10	0	0	20
Felony theft							
Broke into building or vehicle	15	50	12	40	3	10	30
Bought stolen goods	23	77	3	10	4	13	30
Minor theft							
Stole something under $5	21	70	5	17	4	13	30
Stole something between $5 and $50	14	47	6	20	10	33	30
Damaged property							
Damaged family property	19	83	3	13	1	4	23
Damaged school property	8	57	5	36	1	7	14
Drugs							
Alcohol	11	69	4	25	1	6	16
Marijuana	14	47	14	47	2	6	30
Sold marijuana	17	57	8	27	5	17	30
Public disorder							
Disorderly conduct	23	77	5	17	2	7	30
Public drunkenness	16	70	6	27	1	4	23
Status offense							
Runaway	11	61	4	22	3	17	18

breaking into a building or vehicle where 50% of the changes are negative and 40% are positive. Overall, however, the trend in these
comparisons is quite clear -- as the number of prior interviews increases, the age-specific rates decline. Across the seventeen offenses
there are a total of 424 wave-to-wave comparisons and of these, 64% are
negative, 23% are positive, and 12% represent no change. In sum, the
number of negative changes exceeds the number of positive changes by
almost a three to one margin. These are rather substantial differences
and it should be kept in mind that comparisons are only for adjacent
waves where testing effects would be expected to be at a minimum.

To provide an estimate of the magnitude of the decline in these
rates, Table 3 presents data for fourteen, fifteen, sixteen and seventeen year olds, compared across the first four waves of data collection. These ages are selected since they are the only ones in the NYS
design for which four waves of data collection, beginning with 1976,
are available. (Results based on other portions of the data matrices,
such as the ones presented in Table 1, indicate that these findings are
not a function of this particular selection.)

Table 3 presents two summary statistics. The first is the percent
change in the age-specific prevalence rates from wave 1 to wave 4, not
the prevalence rates themselves. In other words, this statistic represents the percent change in the percent of respondents who report committing the offense. The second statistic is simply the difference
between the wave 1 prevalence rate and the wave 4 prevalence rate. In
combination these statistics provide an estimate of both the relative
and absolute magnitude of the change.

The directional results of comparisons across four waves are similar to those presented above for adjacent waves. In this case, there
are a total of 68 comparisons and seventy-six percent of these indicate
a decline in reporting, twenty-two percent an increase, and two percent
no change. However, half of the positive changes are for the marijuana
items, using or buying, and if these are removed it is clear that there
is a very substantial downward drift in reporting behavior across non-
adjacent waves.

When the simple differences between the prevalence rates are examined, the reductions from wave 1 to wave 5 are seen to vary considerably across types of offenses and also to be relatively small. The
absolute value of the difference between wave 1 and wave 4 rates is
generally less than ten percentage points and, for the more serious
offenses, is less than five percentage points. This is not unexpected,
however, given the relatively low base rates for most delinquent acts,
especially the more serious ones. For this reason it is appropriate to
examine the percent change statistics which tend to compensate for
the low base rates and which allow for a clearer understanding of the
amount of data that are potentially lost due to testing effects. The
magnitude of the decline in prevalence rates presented in Table 3 appears to be quite substantial when the percent change statistics are
examined. For aggravated assault the rate for fourteen year olds
drops by 33% from wave 1 to wave 4, for fifteen year olds it drops by
43%, for sixteen year olds it drops by 25%, and for seventeen year
olds it increases by 12%. With the exception of the marijuana items

TABLE 3. Magnitude of change for age-specific rates across four waves of data collection (percent change in prevalence rate).*

Offense	14		15		16		17	
	(a)	(b)	(a)	(b)	(a)	(b)	(a)	(b)
Felony assaults								
Aggravated assault	33	2	43	3	25	2	(12)	*(1)*
Gang fights	20	2	31	5	11	1	31	4
Minor assaults								
Hit teacher	60	6	20	2	(33)	(3)	10	1
Hit parent	43	3	50	3	0	0	12	1
Hit student	26	13	31	16	17	7	21	8
Felony theft								
Broke into building or vehicle	28	2	57	4	20	1	(33)	(1)
Bought stolen goods	63	7	64	9	11	1	50	7
Minor theft								
Stole something under $5	47	10	52	13	33	6	57	12
Stole something between $5 and $50	17	1	50	5	37	3	14	1
Damaged property								
Damaged family property	52	13	68	17	44	8	44	8
Damaged school property	6	1	54	13	25	4	62	8
Drugs								
Alcohol	7	4	3	2	(6)	(4)	4	3
Marijuana	(22)	(4)	(11)	(3)	(13)	(4)	(18)	(7)
Sold marijuana	(20)	(1)	(33)	(2)	(11)	(1)	(50)	(5)
Public disorder								
Disorderly conduct	27	9	38	16	11	7	38	16
Public drunkeness	20	2	(5)	(1)	6	2	(6)	(2)
Status offense								
Runaway	33	2	(50)	(3)	14	1	33	3

*Positive changes are in parentheses.
(a) = percent change; (b) = difference in prevalence.

the declines are of a similar magnitude for the other offense types. To take one other example, stealing something worth between $5 and $50, the rate for fourteen year olds drops by 17% from wave 1 to wave 4, for fifteen year olds it drops by 50%, for sixteen year olds it drops by 37%, and for seventeen year olds it drops by 14%.

In part the size of these percent changes reflects the fact that, for many items, the prevalence rates are small and even relatively small absolute changes appear to be proportionately large. Nevertheless, the consistency of these findings, for even the most frequently occurring offenses, suggest that they represent a real and substantial decline in the self-reporting of delinquent behavior.

In sum, preliminary analysis of data from the National Youth Survey suggests that there may indeed be a serious problem in the use of traditional self-report measures in panel studies of delinquency. Examining prevalence rates across waves suggests a general downward trend in reporting, and examining the magnitude of the declines suggests that the loss of information is not insubstantial.

4. TESTING VERSUS PANEL EFFECTS

The present chapter set out to examine the impact of "testing effects" on the accuracy of the self-reported delinquency data collected in panel studies. Specifically, attention focused on the effect of a particular structure -- using a screening inventory followed by detailed probe questions -- on the willingness of respondents to report behaviors in repeated interviews.

On the surface the results of this analysis would support the conclusion that testing effects exist. Two specific considerations, however, suggest that this conclusion would be too narrow.

First, the analysis of the NCS victimization data by Lehnen and Reiss (1978) indicates that the reduction in reporting is more a function of the number of prior interviews than it is of the number of victimizations reported in prior interviews. As a result they, as well as Woltman and Bushery (1984), conclude that a more generalized "panel effect" produced the reduction in reporting. That is, rather than a specific reaction to the structure of the screening inventory and the follow-up questions, it appears to be a more general reaction to being re-interveiwed that produces the outcome.

Second, after reviewing earlier versions of this chapter, both Elliott and Huizinga (personal communication) pointed out that only at wave 4 did the NYS adopt its current structure of asking a screening inventory followed by detailed questions if the response is positive. Prior to that time only the screening items were asked. Yet the data presented in this paper show that the decline in the reporting occurred across all waves of the NYS. Again such a finding is more consistent with a "panel effect" than with a "testing effect."

In combination, these two observations suggest that the initial hypothesis of this paper, that the structure of these inventories produced a reaction to the testing, may well be too narrow. It would appear that the panel design itself may create a generalized fatigue with being re-interviewed that alters the respondent's willingness to respond to these questions.

This interpretation is also somewhat more consistent with the pattern of changes observed in the NYS self-report data. While there is a very noticeable downward trend in these data, the decline in reporting from wave to wave is not monotonic for all items in the NYS data. The non-monotonicity may be due to basing the analysis on individual items rather than scales which are far more stable than items. But it may also be due to the nature of a panel effect. If the respondent's reaction is to being re-interviewed, rather than to being asked the same question again, then the respondent may be more interested in reducing overall reporting than in reducing the reporting of specific items. Thus, from wave to wave there would be a monotonic decline in overall reporting but not necessarily the reporting of all items. Such an interpretation is consistent with the NCS data which showed monotonic declines when summary victimization rates are observed.

5. PERIOD EFFECTS

Overall, the results presented here suggest that there may well be a substantial method effect, probably a panel effect, when self-report data are collected in a panel design. The major competing hypothesis to this conclusion is that the observed downward trend is produced by a secular period effect. If, during the time period in which these data were collected there was a real decline in delinquent behavior, then the declining age-specific delinquency rates observed in the NYS would be both accurate and appropriate. It is to a test of this rival hypothesis that attention now turns.

For the NCS victim data it should be noted that a period effect is not a viable, alternative explanation. One of the analyses conducted by Woltman and Bushery (1984:101) explicitly controlled for period effects, by only analyzing data from the first six months of 1976, and arrived at the same conclusion as their general analysis.

For the NYS data, some alternate measure of delinquent behavior, not collected in a panel design and covering the same time period as the NYS study, is required to estimate the impact of secular trends on these findings. Fortunately, the Monitoring the Future Study, conducted at the University of Michigan (Bachman et al., 1986), meets these requirements.

Each year, from 1975 until the present, Monitoring the Future collected data from a nationally representative sample of high school seniors. The study is conducted in between 125 and 140 public and private schools, with a total sample size each year of approximately 15,000 seniors. Since the senior year interview is the first interview for these subjects, these data cannot be effected by panel bias. Because of this the following hypotheses can be offered:

   a) If data on delinquency and drug use from Monitoring the Future show a marked downward trend during this time period, the major conclusion of this chapter -- that panel bias effects the self-report data collected in panel studies

-- would be called into question.

    b) If, on the other hand, Monitoring the Future data suggest no secular trend, or an increasing trend, the major rival hypothesis to that of panel bias would itself be called into question.

Trend data for the delinquency items and drug items contained in the Monitoring the Future data are presented in Tables 4 and 5, respectively. These data cover the period 1976-1981, the same period covered by the NYS data analyzed in this chapter. These tables also present the same types of analyses conducted for the NYS data.

Looking first at the delinquency data (Table 4), one is struck by the remarkable stability of these prevalence rates for this time period. For each of the types of delinquency covered in the Monitoring the Future data the percentage of high school seniors who report engaging in the behavior in the last twelve months simply does not vary much from year to year. This can be seen in both the simple prevalence rates and the summary statistics. Each of the summary statistics, which replicate the types of analyses conducted above for the NYS data, can be discussed in turn.

First, the direction of change from year to year is not marked by the general negative or downward trend noted for the age-specific NYS panel data. For the Monitoring the Future data, 24% percent of the comparisons are negative, 25% are positive and 50% represent no change. This is a much different pattern than the one presented in Table 2, where 64% of the adjacent wave comparisons were negative, 23% were positive and only 12% represented no change. Second, the difference in prevalence rates over the four-year period, 1976-1979, are much smaller than the differences presented in Table 3. Indeed, the largest absolute difference is only two percentage points, and only one difference, for the arson item, is negative. Finally, given the direction of the simple differences, the percent change in the prevalence rates, which tend to be smaller than those observed above, are also positive rather than negative.

When information on the drug items contained in Monitoring the Future is examined (Table 5), a very similar picture emerges. With the exception of the use of cocaine and stimulants, which show a slight positive trend, use of the other types of drugs is remarkably stable.

In sum, the trend data collected in the Monitoring the Future study simply do not support the contention that there is a sizeable negative trend in delinquency or drug use during this time period. Indeed, these data suggest that there is no pronounced secular trend in delinquency between 1976 and 1981. Because of this, it is difficult indeed to rule out the presence of a sizeable panel effect in the NYS data. In combination, the findings of the NCS victimization study and the NYS self-report study appear to be far more consistent with a "panel effect" or "panel bias" explanation than a "period effect" explanation.

TABLE 4. Prevalence rates for delinquency items: Monitoring the Future.

	Year						Direction of Change			Difference in Prevalence Rates 1976-1979	% Change 1976-1979
	1976	1977	1978	1979	1980	1981	-	+	=		
Argued or had a fight with either of your parents?	87	86	87	87	86	86	2	1	2	0	0
Hit an instructor or supervisor?	3	3	3	3	3	3	0	0	5	0	0
Gotten into a serious fight in school or at work?	14	14	14	15	16	15	1	2	2	(1)*	(7)*
Taken part in a fight where a group of your friends were against another group?	15	15	15	17	18	17	1	2	2	(2)	(13)
Hurt someone badly enough to need bandages or a doctor?	10	9	10	10	12	10	2	2	1	0	0
Used a knife or gun or some other thing (like a club) to get something from a person?	3	3	3	3	3	3	0	0	5	0	0
Taken something not belonging to you worth under $50?	31	31	31	33	33	31	1	1	3	(2)	(6)

TABLE 4. Prevalence rates for delinquency items: Monitoring the Future (continued)

Item											
Taken something not belonging to you worth over $50	6	5	6	7	7	7	1	2	2	(1)	(17)
Taken something from a store without paying for it?	32	30	30	32	31	29	3	1		0	0
Taken a car that didn't belong to someone in your family without permission of the owner?	4	4	4	4	5	4	1	1	3	(0)	0
Taken a part of a car without permission of the owner?	6	6	6	7	7	5	1	1	3	(1)	(17)
Gone into some house or building when you weren't supposed to be there?	23	22	24	24	25	23	2	2	1	(1)	(4)
Set fire to someone's property on purpose?	2	2	2	1	2	2	1	1	3	1	50
Damaged school property on purpose?	12	12	12	14	13	13	1	1	3	2	(17)
Damaged property?	6	6	6	8	7	6	2	1	2	(2)	(33)
TOTAL							18	19	38		
							24%	22%	50%		

*Positive changes are in parentheses.

Source: Flanagan and Jamieson, 1988:264-265.

TABLE 5. Prevalence rates for drug items: Monitoring the Future.

	Year						Direction of Change			Difference in Prevalence Rates 1976-1979	% Change 1976-1979
	1976	1977	1978	1979	1980	1981	-	+	=		
Alcohol	86	87	88	88	88	87	1	2	2	(3)*	(4)*
Marijuana/hashish	45	48	50	51	49	46	2	3	0	(6)	(13)
Cocaine/"crack"	6	7	9	12	12	12	0	3	2	(6)	(50)
Heroin	1	1	1	1	1	1	0	0	5	0	0
Other opiates	6	6	6	6	6	6	0	0	5	0	0
Stimulants	16	16	17	18	21	26	0	4	1	(2)	(12)
Sedatives	11	11	10	10	10	10	1	0	4	1	9
Tranquilizers	10	11	10	10	9	8	1	1	3	0	0
TOTAL							5	13	22		

*Positive changes are in parentheses.

Source: Flanagan and Jamieson, 1988:281.

6. DISCUSSION

Panel bias appears to be a potentially serious threat to the validity of self-reported delinquency data collected in longitudinal studies. Victimization data from the NCS strongly suggest that the number of times a person has been interviewed reduces his or her willingness to respond affirmatively to victimization questions. Further, prevalence data from the NYS suggest that respondents may also be less forthcoming in reporting their illegal behaviors across data collection waves. In light of these data, it is essential that this issue be investigated in much greater detail than is possible here. For if the reduction in reporting is as great as it appears, then the consequences to investigations of the causes and correlates of delinquency would be substantial.

Two methodological approaches for detailed empirical study seem useful. The first model requires a multi-age panel design such as that used in the National Youth Survey (Elliott et al., 1985) and would extend the analysis begun here. In doing so it would be important to examine incidence as well as prevalence rates and also to examine the presence and magnitude of panel effects for scales rather than individual items. Also, it is crucial to control the effects of attrition which was not done in this paper since the analysis relied on published data only. In brief, more sophisticated analyses of the NYS, and other multi-age panel studies, are needed to estimate better the magnitude of panel effects in self-report data.

The second model estimates the magnitude of testing effects more directly. In this model, an initial panel would be randomly divided into t groups and then interviewed a maximum of t times. Table 6 diagrams the design for t equal to four. The second group would not be interviewed at the first data collection point but would be interviewed at each subsequent stage. The third group would not be interviewed at either of the first two stages but would be at the last two and so forth.

TABLE 6. Design for estimating testing effects.

Randomly Assigned Group	Interview Times			
	1	2	3	4
A	Yes	Yes	Yes	Yes
B	No	Yes	Yes	Yes
C	No	No	Yes	Yes
D	No	No	No	Yes

Since subjects are randomly assigned to groups, delinquency rates should not differ across groups within any of the time periods unless there is an effect from the number of times the respondent had already been interviewed. Thus, this design allows for a rather direct examination of panel effects. The major threat to its validity is differential attrition across groups and that would have to be carefully controlled. Assuming that the issue of attrition is properly handled, this seems to be the most straightforward design for assessing the presence of method effects in panel designs.

7. CONCLUSION

This paper has examined the possibility of a method effect contaminating the validity of the self-report delinquency data collected in panel designs. In light of the evidence from the NCS and NYS data it would appear that this effect is more the product of a "panel bias" than it is of a "testing effect." This conclusion represents both good news and bad news for longitudinal research into the causes and correlates of delinquent behavior. On the positive side of the ledger it suggests that the recent improvements in the self-report method, improvements which are empirically based and psychometrically justified, do not produce the reduction in reporting that was initially hypothesized. On the negative side of the ledger, however, results of this analysis suggest that the method effect may be more general and more subtle in nature than a specific "testing effect." That is, if a "panel bias" indeed exists, it may effect a wide array of data collected in panel studies, not just data that have a particular structure such as those with screening inventories and follow-up items.

In light of these results it seems imperative to continue the investigation of this issue in future research. As a first step, the magnitude of the panel effect should be estimated more precisely. Second, if the effect is sizeable, it would then be necessary to estimate its generalizability to different types of subjects and to the measurement of different types of concepts. Finally, if the panel bias is in fact not produced by specific testing effects, it is important to identify its sources so that it can be corrected in future longitudinal studies of delinquent behavior.

AUTHOR NOTES

This research was supported in part by the Office of Juvenile Justice and Delinquency Prevention (86-JN-CX-0007). The views presented are not necessarily those of the OJJDP.

REFERENCES

Bachman, G, Johnston, LD, & O'Malley, PM: Monitoring the Future 1985. Ann Arbor, MI: Institute for Social Research, University of Michigan, 1986.

Clark, J, & Wenninger, E: Socio-economic class and area as correlates of illegal behavior among juveniles. American Sociological Review, 27:826-34, 1962.

Elliott, D, & Ageton, S: Reconciling differences in estimates of delinquency. American Sociological Review, 45:95-110, 1980.

Elliott, D, Ageton, S, Huizinga, D, Knowles, BA, & Canter, RJ: The prevalence and incidence of delinquent behavior: 1976-1980. National Youth Survey Project Report #26, Behavioral Research Institute, Boulder, Colorado, 1983.

Elliott, DS, Huizinga, D., & Ageton, S: Explaining Delinquency and Drug Use. Beverly Hills: Sage Publications, 1985.

Empey, LT, & Erickson, ML: Hidden delinquency and social status. Social Forces, 44:546-554, 1966.

Flanagan, TJ, & Jamieson, KM (Eds.): Sourcebook of Criminal Justice Statistics - 1987. U.S. Department of Justice, Bureau of Justice Statistics. Washington, DC: USPGO, 1980.

Gold, M: Undetected delinquent behavior. The Journal of Research on Crime and Delinquency, 3:27-46, 1966.

Hindelang, MJ, Hirschi, T, & Weis, JG: Correlates of delinquency. American Sociological Review 44: 995-1014, 1979.

Hirschi, T: Causes of Delinquency. Berkeley: University of California Press, 1969.

Huizinga, D, & Elliott, D: Reassessing the reliability and validity of self-report delinquency measures. Journal of Quantitative Criminology, 2:293-328, 1986.

Lehnen, RG, & Reiss, AJ: Response effects in the National Crime Survey. Victimology: An International Journal, 3:110-124, 1978.

Nye, FI, & Short, JF, Jr.: Scaling delinquent behavior. American Sociological Review, 22:326-331, 1957.

Reiss, AJ, Jr., & Rhodes, AL: The distribution of juvenile delinquency in the social class structure. American Sociological Review, 26:720-732, 1961.

Short, JF, & Nye, FI: Reported behavior as a criterion of deviant behavior. Social Problems, 5:207-213, 1957.

Thornberry, TP: Toward an interactional theory of delinquency. Criminology, 25:863-891, 1987.

Thornberry, TP, & Farnworth, M: Social correlates of criminal involvement: Further evidence on the relationship between social status and criminal behavior. American Sociological Review, 47:505-518, 1982.

Wolfgang, ME, Figlio, RM, & Sellin, T: Delinquency in a Birth Cohort. Chicago: University of Chicago Press, 1972.

Wolfgang, ME, Thornberry, TP, & Figlio, RM: From Boy to Man -- From Delinquency to Crime. Chicago: University of Chicago Press, 1987.

Woltman, Henry, & Bushery, J: Summary of results from the National Crime Survey panel bias study, pp. 98-101 in Lehnen, RG and Skogan, WG (Eds.), The National Crime Survey Working Papers, Volume II: Methodological Studies. Washington: U.S. Government Printing Office, 1984.

DESIGNING A SELF-REPORT INSTRUMENT FOR THE STUDY OF THE DEVELOPMENT OF
OFFENDING FROM CHILDHOOD TO ADULTHOOD: ISSUES AND PROBLEMS

Marc Le Blanc
School of Psycho-Education and International Center for
Comparative Criminology
University of Montreal, Montreal, Quebec, Canada

1. INTRODUCTION

   Self-report delinquency research has a few major landmarks. During the Second World War, two surveys of self-report delinquency were
conducted, one with college students (Porterfield, 1946) and one with
the subjects of the Cambridge-Sommerville experiment (Murphy, 1946).
In 1955, the first standardized instrument was applied to a representative sample of adolescents and a cumulative scale of delinquency was
constructed (Nye & Short, 1958). And, in the late 1970s, the most
comprehensive study of the metric properties of self-report delinquency
was realized with a complex research design which provided controls for
different methods of administration (Hindelang, Hirschi & Weis, 1981).
There is, however, another landmark which is often forgotten. At the
Syracuse University Conference of 1965 (Hardt & Bodine, 1965), many of
the methodological questions concerning self-report delinquency instruments and measures were thoroughly reviewed and recommendations were
formulated to improve the measurement of delinquency. One of these
recommendations has been forgotten by many authors in the published
literature -- to provide a detailed description of the data collection
procedure.
   The Elliott and Huizinga chapter in the present volume shows the
distance covered since then and, in particular, it demonstrates that we
have attained and have even gone beyond the prescriptions formulated by
the Syracuse Conference. However, we still need to push the frontiers
of research on self-report delinquency further. This will be done
through two new themes of discussion: the demands of cross-cultural
comparisons on a self-report instrument and the accommodations that a
longitudinal research design would impose on such an instrument. This
theme is the task that I have undertaken.
   In order to cover the theme of longitudinal accommodations, I ask
myself which ones, the technical accommodations that a specialist in
measurement, a methodologist, would recommend or the substantive accommodations that a theorist would propose? The first option would concentrate exclusively on recommendations in relation to the form of the
instrument in the context of longitudinal research. The second option

M. W. Klein (ed.), Cross-National Research in Self-Reported Crime and Delinquency, 371–398.
© 1989 by Kluwer Academic Publishers.

372

would deal with points of view in relation to theoretical questions to be resolved. For purposes of the present discussion, I will give priority to the advances in delinquency theory more than to longitudinal research per se.

The organization of this chapter derives directly from that option. In the first part of the chapter, I will list some of the major theoretical questions to be resolved. This will be done concerning the dependent variable, offending, and also in connection to the independent variables, the antecedent conditions, correlates and causes of delinquency. I will give more attention to the dependent variable because the _why_ questions cannot be addressed properly without an adequate conceptualization of the _what_ question. In the second part of the paper, I will illustrate the positions of an epidemiologist and of a developmentalist on the accommodations to be made in a longitudinal research design. I will be mainly defending the second position because the first one has been sufficiently covered in other chapters in this volume.

2. SOME MAJOR THEORETICAL QUESTIONS TO BE RESOLVED

Since our methodological axis is the longitudinal design, we must look at the actual debate on the usefulness of longitudinal surveys. We will address this principal theme in the next two sections. There are two distinct sets of theoretical questions to be resolved. The most fundamental one, how we should elaborate and study crime, involves our key dependent variable. The complementary one is how the explanatory questions should be asked, the questions concerning the correlates and the causes of crime.

2.1. Usefulness of Longitudinal Surveys

In criminology, a caustic debate is presently going on between the supporters of longitudinal surveys and the upholders of cross-sectional surveys. This debate is carried on in many settings: funding agencies, scientific meetings, and publications. The advocates are Blumstein et al., (1986) and Farrington et al., (1986), while the prosecutors are Hirschi and Gottfredson (1983), (also Gottfredson and Hirschi, 1986, 1987). The advocates of longitudinal research emphasize the numerous uses and advantages of designs with repeated measures on the same people. The prosecutors vigorously question the usefulness of such surveys. Since we must address the question of the necessary accommodations to a self-report delinquency instrument, particularly in a context of longitudinal research, it is necessary to review the points of view of the prosecutors.

The argument of the prosecutors is that "longitudinal research is not required for the study of crime" (Gottfredson & Hirschi, 1987, p. 581). The demonstration of this argument is fivefold: there is an age invariance in crime (Hirschi & Gottfredson, 1983); the concept of criminal career is inconsistent with evidence (Gottfredson & Hirschi, 1986); and, in their most recent article (1987), three new arguments are documented: the features of the longitudinal design are not superior to the properties of the cross-sectional design; its superiority for measuring the effects of intervention can be challenged; and, a comparison of empirical results obtained from the two types of studies show that longitudinal surveys have produced no really new knowledge concerning the causes and correlates of crime. While the first four points have been subject to much controversy, the last one, that the results of longitudinal surveys have been confirmatory rather than heuristic, is very devastating. The prosecutors present numerous examples and they are sound ones. That leads us to doubt the usefulness of the longitudinal surveys. They show that for standard causal variables such as sex, race, age, family variables, and peer group influences, the two sets of surveys are producing facts that are confirmed one by the other. A reading of the literature reviews by Farrington et al., (1986) and Blumstein et al. (1986) do not demonstrate clearly that longitudinal surveys are proposing new outstanding facts concerning the correlates of crimes.

Our position is that the debate over the usefulness of longitudinal surveys over cross-sectional surveys will prove as sterile as has the qualitative-quantitative methods debate that was so prominent during the 1970s in the social sciences. We will argue throughout this chapter, as we are doing more fully elsewhere (Loeber & Le Blanc, 1989), that cross-sectional surveys are sufficient to study the distribution and the correlates of crime but that only longitudinal surveys can potentially help us to sequence events, crimes, and causal factors. Even if we accept the conclusion of Gottfredson and Hirschi that longitudinal research did not habitually address that question of the sequence of events, we think that there are more urgent tasks for criminologists than debating research designs. It is particularly important to elaborate the notion of crime and open ourselves to the concepts and methods of developmental psychology before we could draw conclusions about the usefulness of specific research designs.

2.2. Concerning the Dependent Variable

This section will start in that direction. Two ways of completing that urgent task will be explored: how to elaborate the notion of crime and how to introduce a developmental perspective in the study of offending. Only when our key dependent variable is adequately conceptualized will it be possible to address properly the question of the causal factors.

2.2.1. Elaborating the notion of crime. In criminology there are many possible dependent variables: crimes, social reactions, enacting legislation, and others. One of the major weaknesses of our discipline is the absence of a clear consensus on the notion of crime, the key dependent variable in criminology as stated explicitly by some authors (Cohen, 1969; Farrington, 1973). However, the levels of interpretation of the phenomenon of crime are not sufficiently distinguished in most theories. The absence of a clear understanding of the different objects of interpretation in criminology is a strong barrier to the development of theories. The debate between the advocates and the prosecutors of longitudinal surveys reflects the confusion in the literature between two main levels of interpretation -- the crime and the criminal.

The French criminologist, Jean Pinatel (1963), in a masterly effort to define the bases of criminology, was one of the first to propose that criminologists should distinguish between three levels of interpretation of the criminal phenomenon, namely criminality, the criminal and the crime, each level having its own persepctives, its own rationales, and its own methods. He defines the first, criminality, as the sum of infractions committed at a given time and place, influenced by demographic, economic, political and other factors which occur on a societal scale. The second level, the criminal, is centered on the transgressor himself and proceeds to a study of his personal characteristics as well as of the factors that influence the formation and the evolution of his personality as well as his social roles. The third level of interpretation, that of the crime, the act, should be studied only as a small part of the life or criminal career of the subject, considering it an event that has a beginning, a development, and an end, ascertaining the factors or mechanisms that cause its appearance. This basic rule, that there are three levels of interpretation, was rediscovered by American criminolgoy recently, but the emphasis has been mainly on two levels, crime and criminality (Hirschi, 1979, 1987; Short, 1985, 1987) just as Sutherland had suggested much earlier (Sutherland & Cressey, 1968).

It should be pointed out that this basic rule was far from being followed in the discourse of criminologists, who often use the term delinquency when vaguely referring to all three levels of interpretation (Matza, 1964; Muchielli, 1965). Others formulated their theory without specifying the level they were addressing (Mailloux, 1971; Lemay, 1973), while others expressed a concept of delinquency that did not correspond to the level concerned in their analysis. Thus Cohen (1955) and Cloward and Ohlin (1960) used a definition of delinquency that referred to the conduct, but in fact they were formulating a theory of the delinquent career or of the delinquent role. However, a number of more recent authors, from Hirschi (1969) to Cusson (1981), Arnold and Brungardt (1983), Pearson and Weiner (1985) and Short (1987), to cite only these few, took into account the need to specify the level of interpretation when elaborating a theoretical proposition. But even recently, Gottfredson and Hirschi (1988) added to the confusion by proposing the use of the term criminality to refer to the propensity to commit criminal acts.

Not only is it convenient to opt explicitly for one specific level of interpretation of the phenomenon of crime -- in conformity with the subject of this volume we will limit ourselves to the level of crime -- but this notion of crime must be specified and operationalized adequately. Thus we have proposed to distinguish three hierarchical levels of analysis of crime: offense, offending, and patterns (Le Blanc & Fréchette, 1988). Each level of analysis demands different explanations, and only offending and patterns, when they are studied developmentally, require longitudinal surveys.

European criminology has a long tradition of studying the completion of crime, particularly in Germany (see Seelig, 1956; Göppinger,
1987) and in the Latin countries (Pinatel, 1963). There is a large
accumulation of studies on this subject in which are described the
cognitive, affective, moral, and material conditions that govern the
perpetration of the crime whether in general, or in the case of particular types of criminals (perverts, the mentally ill, the professional,
the emotionally inspired, and so on). More recently, the works of Erez
(1980, 1987) on planning, and Felson and Cohen (1979, 1980), Hough et
al. (1980), and Cusson (1986) on utilitarian delinquency, are also in
the same vein. The level of analysis of the completion of crime does
not imply longitudinal surveys because we are then studying a specific
episode that is restricted to a very limited time period.

The analysis of offending is predominant in North-American criminology. It has received its **lettre de noblesse** in the Blumstein et
al. (1986) report where it is called individual offending. This notion
has the advantage of clarifying one of the levels of analysis of crime
and putting aside all ambiguities in the definitions and operationalizations that are used in empirical research. But under that notion criminologists have proposed many concepts and measures of crime as an individual behavior. These concepts are numerous: prevalence, incidence,
specialization, escalation, seriousness, duration, onset, variety and
so on. They are often redundant. For example, variety, diversity, and
polymorphy refer to the heterogeneity of crime; intensity, aggravation,
and seriousness refer to the gravity of crime, and so on. But, worst
of all, the same concepts can be operationalized by very different
measures. At this level of analysis of crime, longitudinal surveys are
essential because, as we will show later, the major themes concern the
changes in offending as time passes.

To clarify the situation conceptually, we have proposed (Le Blanc
& Fréchette, 1989) to adopt the Blumstein et al. (1986) definitions of
the parameters of offending, to add some parameters to their list, and
to distinguish between descriptive and evolutive constructs of offending. Table 1 presents these parameters of offending and a short definition for each. The estimation of descriptive parameters does not neces-
sitate a prospective longitudinal survey; it requires only a cross-
sectional survey. But the estimation of the evolutive parameters demands at least a retrospective longitudinal survey of subjects who are
in their adult ages.

Recently many authors have proposed some other lists of constructs
that are helpful in specifying the notion of offending (Blumstein et
al., 1986; Farrington et al., 1986; Loeber, 1987). If theoreticians
and researchers could attain a consensus on the components of the notion of crime, it would probably be easier to advance criminological
knowledge and, particularly, theories. Consensus could be helpful not
only for theorizing but also for instrument development, the theme of
this volume. With a more precise list of constructs of offending to be
measured, it would be easier to design a common instrument of self-
report delinquency. Therefore, we have proposed that the dynamics of
offending should be measured by combining descriptive and evolutive
parameters. That conception is developed in the next section.

376

TABLE 1. Descriptive and evolutive parameters of offending.

DESCRIPTIVE PARAMETERS

participation
the number of criminally active individuals in a
population at a given time

frequency
the number of crimes committed by an individual within a
given period of time

variety
the number of crime categories in which an individual is
involved

seriousness
the degree of gravity of the crimes of an individual
(for example Sellin and Wolfgang definition)

crime mix
the mix of crimes, combinatory structures

EVOLUTIVE PARAMETERS

onset
the age of the first crime

duration
the interval between the first and the last crime

age of termination
the age of the last crime in an individual life

transition
the transfer from juvenile delinquency to adult
criminality

2.2.2. Considering the perspective of development. There is an approach that is absent in criminology that could help the understanding
of offending. This is the developmental perspective that is standard
in psychology. It concerns the qualitative and quantitative changes in
human activities. As we will show, this approach is better served by
longitudinal surveys.
Some criminologists will say that the developmental approach is
not necessary and not even pertinent for the study of crime (Gottfredson and Hirschi, 1987a). Their conclusion is supported by two sets of
data: a high stability coefficient between measures of delinquency and

studies that show that early antisocial behavior predicts antisocial behavior in adulthood. This type of argument is fallacious because it does not take into account a distinction well known in psychology, the difference between continuity and stability (see Lerner, 1986). An individual can persist in delinquency by displaying juvenile and adult delinquency but the nature of his offending can change in frequency, seriousness, variety and so on. An individual can maintain a status of delinquent but his offending can regress or progress, become more or less serious, more or less frequent and so on. Continuity is then very different from stability. The studies that these authors are citing are only concerned with the continuity of offending; they do not involve the stability or the instability in crime.

Their position cannot be sustained because numerous data exist in criminology to describe offending in terms of the evolutive parameters that we have defined earlier. Many studies propose a description of the limits of offending, duration, onset and offset -- see the reviews of Blumstein et al. (1986), Farrington et al. (1986), and Loeber and Le Blanc (1989). Another perspective, a developmental analysis, could also be used. It is not only conerned with the distribution of the crimes over the life-span of an individual; it is, rather, much more concerned with the processes that sustain continuity in offending. Changes in offending as time goes on is the major interest of the perspective. Attention is given to the within-individual changes and to the identification of processes underlying offending. This perspective is very different from the way the study of offending is usually done in criminology, the study of the between-persons or group differences. A developmental approach implies concentrating on the dynamic of offending, for example the processes of escalation, diversification, and so on. In the criminological literature, the developmental approach to the understanding of offending is generally simplistic because criminologists have not informed themselves of the concepts of the sociology of occupations or developmental psychology. One of our objectives in this chapter is to identify some of the consequences of this perspective for designing self-report delinquency instruments.

Lerner (1986), in his textbook on developmental psychology, proposes an analysis of continuity-discontinuity of behavior -- what is generally done in criminology -- but he also shows that it is equally important to study the qualitative changes. The specialists of development have uncovered some general principles that should be helpful for the study of offending. One of them, the orthogenetic principle proposed by Werner (1957), is worth mentioning. It states that whenever development occurs, it proceeds from a state of relative globality and lack of differentiation to a state of relative differentiation, articulation, and hierarchic integration. This general law governing development not only states the nature of the changes but is also a guide for the analysis of continuity in behavior.

While applying this principle to the analysis of the development of offending we uncovered three dynamic processes: activation, escalation, and desistance (Le Blanc & Frèchette, 1989). What we have illustrated is how the characteristics of criminal activities -- the descriptive and evolutive parameters -- combine to constitute processes

that support its development, processes that show that this development
is not a matter of chance. Over the past fifteen years, since the
research done by Wolfgang et al. (1972), longitudinal studies have
furnished data on the relationship between several of the parameters we
are using, while syntheses, such as those of Loeber (1982, 1987) and
Blumstein et al. (1986) have led to clarification of the conceptualization of certain processes. All this work, however, is intuitive because it is not based on a well defined procedure for reconstructing
the natural dynamics of the development of criminal activity.

Duncan (1984) proposes such a procedure: a list of fundamental
elements is compiled; then the variables are defined according to the
combinations of these basic elements. By way of analogy, we propose to
define the processes that encourage the development of offending as the
result of the relationship between two or more descriptive and evolutive parameters that are the basic elements of the criminal activity.
The advantage of this procedure is twofold. First, it affords clarity
about the elements in the operational definition of constructs such as
escalation and specialization. Second, it can be reproduced; that is,
it is possible for another researcher to reconstruct the same measurements and thus find out whether or not he can arrive at the same results.

By applying this procedure, activation, escalation, and desistance
can be studied. Table 2 gives a definition of the general processes
and of the subprocesses that constitute them. These three processes
are perhaps not the only ones, but they seem to be the most important.
Little is known about the first, activation; there are references to it
in the literature surveyed by Loeber and which he conceptualzies as the
variety hypothesis (1982) and rate of progression or innovation rate
(1987). The second, escalation, is the subject of numerous controver-
sies in the criminological literature, as shown in the surveys done by
Klein (1984) on the evidence for and against specialization in certain
forms of crime, and by Loeber (1985a, 1987) and Blumstein et al. (1986)
on the progression from one criminal activity to another. The last
process, desistance, is a subject whose importance is recognized by
criminologists, for example Farrington et al. (1986), although very few
have studied it.

The activation process refers to the way the development of criminal activities is stimulated as soon as it has begun and the way its
persistence is assured. Once this process has begun, the result is
delinquent activity marked by a high level of frequency, duration, and
variety as well as precocity. We find that the process of activation
is based on three separate but closely interrelated mechanisms: acceleration, stabilization, and diversification. This means that if delinquency starts early, it will more probably be abundant, lasting, and
varied. We have also shown that the fundamental process of activation
is the combined effect of acceleration, stabilization, and diversification; the second of these mechanisms, stabilization, seems to be the
main support of the other two.

Stabilization more directly refers to the way in which the
delinquent activity becomes persistent, resulting in its longevity.
This presumes an inverse relationship between precocity and duration,

so that the earlier the delinquent activities begin, the longer they will continue. To the best of our knowledge, this mechanism has never been adequately described in the criminological literature. The mechanism of acceleration is better known. Recent studies show that persons who are arrested early have a higher rate of frequency than those arrested later (Farrington, 1983; Cohen, 1986); on the other hand, those who start early commit more serious crimes later (Shannon, 1978). It has similarly been established that early starters are more likely to become chronic delinquents and recidivists, according to the results of Glueck (1968) in the first case, and Mannheim and Wilkins (1955) in the second; these findings having been confirmed many times.

TABLE 2. Processes sustaining persistant offending.

ACTIVATION

acceleration
impact of age of onset on frequency

stabilization
impact of age of onset on duration

diversification
impact of age of onset on variety

ESCALATION

stages in offending
relationship between types of crimes, seriousness, age of onset, duration, age of termination and time

progression
progessing from minor to more serious delinquency

DESISTANCE

deceleration
reduction of frequency before age of offset

specialization
diminution of variety before age of offset

reaching a ceiling
after progressing to a certain stage in offending, staying at that stage for the rest of the active criminal time

In addition, Fréchette and Le Blanc (1979) were the first to describe
the exact relationship between precocity and frequency on the basis of
self-report delinquency followed by Loeber (1982), based on the data on
the official delinquency reported by Farrington (1982) and Hamparian et
al. (1978). We called this relationship the early onset hypothesis.
Finally, for its part, the mechanism of diversification refers to the
way criminal activity quickly becomes heterogeneous in precise relation
to precocity, variety being all the more accentuated the earlier the
illicit activities began.

In describing the processes of escalation and specialization, we
propose to clarify two questions fiercely debated in criminological
circles. Blumstein et al. (1986) make a clear distinction between the
two: "escalation is the tendency for offenders to move to more serious
offense types as offending continues" (p. 84) and "specialization is
the tendency to repeat the same offense type on successive arrests" (p.
81). In terms of the descriptive and evolutive parameters we are using, we have proposed the following definition (Le Blanc & Fréchette,
1989): escalation refers to the appearance of a sequence of diverse
forms of delinquent activities that go from minor infractions to the
most serious crimes against the person as the subject increases in age.
This sequence represents a more or less standard pattern of development
among subjects who are heading for significant delinquency; the different parameters -- types of crimes, seriousness, age of onset -- duration, age of offset, are obviously contributing factors here.

We have shown (Le Blanc & Fréchette, 1989) that there are five
sequential stages in offending: emergence -- minor larcenies around
the age of ten; exploration -- shoplifting and vandalism between the
ages of eleven and fourteen; explosion -- many types of theft (common,
burglary, personal, automobile) between fourteen and sixteen; conflagra-
tion -- more serious types of crimes (personal attacks, robberies, drug
trafficking) between sixteen and nineteen; and extension -- astute, or
violent crimes after nineteen. Virtually all the subjects of our delinquent sample are progressing to a more serious type of delinquency
(92%) and the majority of them for one or two steps on that five-step
ladder (73%).

Specialization can be manifested in at least three ways: first,
as described by Chaiken and Rolph (1985), the person, during a limited
period of time, concentrates on a particular form of crime and produces
a string of offenses; second, the subject shows a certain degree of
specialization over a given period of time, and it is this degree of
specialization that should be evaluated, as has been done in numerous
studies, from that of Wolfgang et al. (1972) to that of Farrington et
al. (1988) and studies surveyed by Klein (1984) and Kempf (1987);
third, with the passage of time, the person concentrates more and more
on certain crimes or certain specific forms of criminal activity,
which, according to Blumstein et al. (1986), is sufficient to be called
specialization. Considering that specialization implies desisting from
a versatile criminal activity into a more homogeneous offending, we
have proposed to include that process as part of desistance. We did so
because it is not a string of offenses that we are referring to with
the notion of specialization, but to the major reduction in versatility

that we have observed before termination (Le Blanc & Fréchette, 1989).

The last process we want to study is desistance, which depends on variety, escalation, and frequency of the criminal activity. This means that the higher the frequency, the greater the variety and the seriousness, and the greater the chance of saturation, then desistance becomes possible. It goes without saying that the mechanism of desistance should be studied only among persons whose delinquency is recurrent; one cannot speak of desistance for the occasional delinquent. This process of desistance is composed of three sub-processes: specialization, as defined earlier; deceleration, which refers to the reduction of frequency before terminating criminal activities; and reaching a ceiling, which refers to the situation when a delinquent is blocked at a particular level of seriousness before stopping offending.

We have shown that offending could develop according to three basic processes -- activation, escalation, and desistance -- in conformity with the orthogenetic principle. The changes in the criminal activity of an individual are systematic, organized, successive, and specific. They are not random. However, one demonstration is not sufficient. Replications must be undertaken in other countries, in other cultures, with different samples and for varying periods. The theory of the development of offending that we have outlined is only a source of questions to be resolved. It is a guide for the studies to be done concerning the elaboration of the key dependent variable in criminology.

Such demonstrations on the nature of the development of offending cannot be done with cross-sectional surveys. These surveys are well adapted for the comparisons between individuals, but they are not appropriate for the description of the sequence of events. The questions that follow from a developmental perspective on offending necessarily imply longitudinal surveys. Only frequently repeated measures can permit the description of changes over time in the behavior of an individual. Until now, most of the longitudinal surveys were not primarily concentrated on the dynamic of behavior from a developmental perspective. Rather, they presented offending with the descriptive and evolutive parameters without much attention to the processes. And Gottfredson and Hirschi (1986, 1987a) were not right in claiming that longitudinal surveys have not produced facts that are of a different nature than the ones proposed by the cross-sectional surveys on offending. Only if criminology introduces the notion of development will it be possible to overcome the actual stagnant state of knowledge. The debate on the usefulness of longitudinal surveys will never move forward until some other studies confirm or refute the type of model of the development of offending that we have proposed.

2.3. Concerning the Independent Variables

Hirschi and Selvin (1967) have proposed three criteria of causality: A and B should be statistically associated, A should be prior to B, and the association between A and B should not disappear when the effects of other variables are removed. For the purpose of this paper let us define correlates as variables statistically associated with

crime, and causes as variables that match this criterion and for which
causal order can be established. Let us also define three categories
of variables: antecedent conditions, structural, and psychosocial
independent variables. This classification of independent variables is
illustrated in Table 3.

TABLE 3. Classification of correlates and causal variables.

	ANTECEDENT	STRUCTURAL	PSYCHOSOCIAL
	age	economic status	attachment
CORRELATES	sex	school status	commitment
	race	delinquent friends	personality
	temperament	type of family	etc.
	etc.	etc.	
		economic status	attachment
		school status	commitment
CAUSES		delinquent friends	personality
		type of family	etc.
		etc.	

   Antecedent variables can be age, sex, race, temperament, and so
on. These are variables that have to be controlled, as Hirschi and
Selvin (1967) have argued strongly. They cannot be thought of as causal variables because they reflect the length, age, and the nature of
exposure to causal variables, sex, race, and temperament. Structural
variables, or risk factors, refer to specific events or situations such
as studying or working, one or two parent family, having delinquent
friends or not, and criminality of parents. Psychosocial variables can
be such things as attachment, commitment, and personality; these refer
to the attitudinal dimension and they can vary on a short term basis.

2.3.1. The state of empirical research. With this classification in
mind let us discuss the usefulness of the longitudinal design and identify the major theoretical questions to be resolved concerning the
causes of offending. But before turning to this, let us comment on
these questions in relation to antecedents and correlates of crime. As
shown by recent reviews (Blumstein et al., 1986; Farrington et al.,

1986), the distinction between antecedents and correlates of crime is not made and even some of the proposers of this distinction have forgotten this important difference in the status of the variables; Gottfredson and Hirschi (1987a) in their review do not distinguish these two sets of variables when they comment on standard causal variables.

If we leave this methodological question aside and address the knowledge-building question, all these reviews point to a common conclusion. Longitudinal surveys have confirmed cross-sectional surveys when it comes to findings concerning the correlates of crime. This is a major argument of the Gottfredson and Hirschi (1987a) critique. And we find this argument impossible to reject because the reviews of Farrington et al. (1986) and Blumstein et al. (1986) do not propose new facts on correlates that were produced by longitudinal surveys.

Until recently, empirical criminology did not really progress much through longitudinal surveys because the researchers did not make full use of the characteristics of their design. They did not concentrate on analyzing the causal order, or at least of the sequencing of events. There are a few exceptions when it concerns the impact of transitional life events on subsequent delinquency -- leaving school, entering work, getting married, and so on (Elliott & Voss, 1974; Bachman et al., 1971, 1978; West & Farrington, 1977; Fréchette & Le Blanc, 1987; Rand, 1987). Studies that did look at the ordering of factors for a long life-span perspective are even more rare (Robbins, 1966; Farrington, 1986) as are studies confronting the parallel changes in delinquency and psychosocial variables (Jessor & Jessor, 1977; Fréchette & Le Blanc, 1987).

These few studies are starting to make use of the particular features of the longitudinal design and they are helping us to state more properly two sets of questions: are the causes of initiation the same as the causes of maintenance of offending and do all the causal factors operate in equal strength along the developmental time line? Longitudinal surveys should help us to verify the time ordering of factors: to check if some factors are operating particularly during the perinatal period or infancy, if some are apparent during childhood (parenting for example), while others could be active during adolescence (school, peers) and others during youth (entry into the work market). This implies that there could be fundamentally different factors that can explain the onset of offending in late childhood as compared to its onset in middle adolescence or early adulthood.

Not only should longitudinal research be the most powerful instrument to identify the period when certain factors are most active but it should help us to distinguish between causal factors of initiation and maintenance of offending. For example, school and parenting could be strong initiation factors while life style and peers could be maintenance factors. In our study (Fréchette & Le Blanc, 1987), it was shown that social circumstances explain the initiation of crime while personality variables were more significant for the maintenance of chronic offending. The distinction between initiation and maintenance factors has recently been proposed (Farrington et al., 1986) but this question has not been studied enough. Probably, the main reason this question of time ordering of factors and of distinguishing between initiation and maintenance factors has become so important is the insufficient development of the theories.

2.3.2. The absence of developmental theories. From a substantive point of view, longitudinal surveys have not made any outstanding contributions to theory. They have been used to verify standard non-sequential, time-bound theories and to exacerbate the debate on the pertinence of each of them. The recent fashion for integrative models (Matsueda, 1982; Agnew, 1985; Elliott et al., 1985; Le Blanc & Ouimet, 1986; Albany Conference, 1987) have not much enhanced our knowledge about the ordering of causal factors outside of showing that delinquency is the most powerful predictor of delinquency.

The relative absence of interest in longitudinal models reflects the fact that most of the criminological theories are not of a developmental nature, except for labeling theory and particularly, Lemert's (1951) theory of primary and secondary deviance. It could also be argued that differential association can easily be interpreted in a developmental way. Control, strain and cultural deviance theories have not been stated in a developmental way. There are now some arguments for that perspective (see Ferdinand, 1987) and some new models are clearly developmental because they propose a specific time ordering of causal factors (Le Blanc et al., 1985; Thornberry, 1987).

Over all, longitudinal surveys can be of much help in sequencing causal factors in relation to offending and they can contribute to theory development. But these aims cannot be attained without a more precise definintion of the status of the independent variables as antecedent, correlate or causal and without the formulation of the existing theories and models from a developmental point of view. With these guidelines, longitudinal surveys will be of much more help in the development of criminological knowledge.

3. A LONGITUDINAL INSTRUMENT

From the preceding comments on the questions to be resolved, a developmental approach stands as essential in criminology; this argument is developed further in a recent article by Loeber and Le Blanc (1989). As defined earlier, a developmental approach implies the study of the within-individuals changes over time rather than the between-individuals differences.

This approach imposes a fundamental prerequisite to any instrument to be used in research: a skill for sequencing events, not only crimes but causal factors as well. The instrument must be able, for specific periods of time, to tell us all about crimes (frequency, nature, duration, and so on; see the list of descriptive parameters proposed earlier) and it should give us the exact status of the subjects in reference to the pertinent causal factors. These data have to be available for more than one of these short periods of time. Having this prerequisite in mind, we will discuss, from a developmentalist point of view, the standard instrument that would be proposed if we would follow the existing literature in criminology.

This literature is dominated by the epidemiological perspective.

Criminologists have generally adopted a specific approach; they are interested in the prevalence and the incidence of crimes or the participation and the frequency of offending. These themes concern the between-individuals and between-groups differences, not the within-individual changes that are more important for psychologists. The sequencing of events is not of major importance for the epidemiologist while it is fundamental for the developmentalist. Following this distinction between the approaches of the epidemiologist and of the developmentalist we will present the standard self-report delinquency instrument and the design that the first type of researcher would propose, and we will discuss it from the perspective of the other type of researcher.

3.1. The Epidemiologist Instrument and Design

If we were to follow the most recent methodological study (Hindelang et al., 1981), the last review (Weis, 1986), what is currently done in practice by researchers as revealed by the instruments that are reported in published empirical articles, some of the recommendations proposed by Elliott and Huizinga in this volume, the self-report delinquency instrument would have the following characteristics. It would be a non-anonymous, self- administered questionnaire; the questions would concern salient crimes and they would be long enough to be specific; they would include a recall period of one year (ongoing research favors a six months' interval between data gatherings); the responses would be open-ended; the crime events would always be the same for the duration of the research; and, the questionnaire would be administered by any trained interviewer.

The ideal features of the design of an epidemiologist would be to repeat measurements of the type outlined above at six months, every year, or for some other extended period of time on a large representative sample. But, if we were to follow the more economical research strategy proposed by Farrington et al. (1986), it should be added that multiple cohorts of at least 1,000 subjects would be followed for six years: from birth to six, from six to 12, from 12 to 18, and from 18 to 24. The instrument should include multiple measures of misconduct (arrest report, self-reports, and reports of parents, teachers and/or peers) and comprehensive individual data concerning all the major causal factors that might be implicated in offending -- social circumstances and personal characteristics of medical and psychological nature. This strategy implies a representative cohort of the population and selected cohorts of arrested and imprisoned subjects.

3.2. A Developmentalist Point of View

Let us discuss some of the features of this design and of this instrument from a developmentalist point of view. This means the perspective of a researcher who is mainly interested in the processes constituting the development of offending from a life-span perspective, a researcher who is concerned with the verification of a developmental theory of offending and with the exploration of the ordering of causal

factors in relation to delinquency and between the causal factors themselves. We will concentrate our comments mainly on the measurement of
offending which is the theme of this chapter, leaving aside the measurement of causal factors because the same principles should normally
apply to the two sets of variables.

3.2.1. On the design. A developmentalist would agree easily on the use
of multiple measures of offending and comprehensive individual data and
he would have reservations about the necessity of a representative
cohort of the general population and with the four six-year studies. A
developmentalist is concerned with processes in offending -- for example, activation, escalation, and desistance. As we have shown earlier
(see also Le Blanc & Fréchette, 1989) these processes do not stand out
in a representative sample of the population because of the low base
rate for most crimes. For this reason a developmentalist would favor
an at-risk sample of the general population -- for example, males from
a lower socio-economic community -- because it is well known that these
individuals are much more at risk of chronic criminal behavior. This
could also be argued for other markers of an at-risk population. However, a developmentalist would not discuss the recommendation for the
use of cohorts of known delinquents. In fact, as shown by Cernkovich
et al. (1985), serious delinquents are too often absent from delinquency studies which are habitually based on representative samples of
the population.
    The design proposed by Farrington et al. (1986) would respond
adequately to epidemiological questions related to participation and
frequency of offending. It would permit the identification of the
factors of initiation of offending; it would be very helpful to the
understanding of the causes of occasional offending which is the dominant type of delinquency in a representative sample of the population,
or of a specific age cohort. But as acknowledged by these authors, the
number of repeaters would be very small in this type of sample and it
is our experience that it would not permit the study of processes or of
the factors of maintenance if the sample size is not raised from 1,000
to several thousands. The complexity and the diversity of the processes postulated by a developmental theory of offending imply the use of
a large sample of repeaters.
    The four cohort design (0 to 6, 6 to 12, 12 to 18, 18 to 24) has
two important defects. First, it does not take into account the transition periods from the family to school, from elementary to secondary
school, from school to work and so on, mainly because the cutting
points on the age continuum are exactly situated in the center of these
periods. The developmentalist is very much concerned with these transition periods because it is well known that they are sources of important turbulences; major textbooks insist on some of these transitions
(Conger and Peterson, 1984; Kagan and Moss, 1962; Offer, 1969). Some
of these transition periods are from four to eight (entry in school),
from 10 to 14 (puberty and transfer to secondary school), from 16 to 20
(leaving school and entering the work market). A longitudinal design
must make sure that the same individuals are followed during these
periods; it is necessary to check if these transitions are so important

for crime, since it is known that they are significant for physical and psychological development.

Second, such sequential strategy is incompatible with the existing knowledge base that shows that cohort effects are stronger than age effects (Nesselroade and Baltes, 1984) and even stronger than gender effects (Le Blanc & Coté, 1988) when personality is the object of study. It would mean that the results obtained with the older cohort could not be put end-to-end with the results of the other cohorts to infer the whole development, which is the major objective of longitudinal research from a life-span perspective. An alternative strategy would be to have overlapping cohorts that are studied for a longer period of time, for example, from 3 to 13, 10 to 20, from 16 to 26. The first cohort would help understand the development of conduct disorders, the second one would permit a description of the development of offending, and the third one would be helpful to understand desistance. A duration of ten years for the study is not much longer than what is proposed by Farrington et al. (1986), and it is the average length of the duration of offending for official delinquents. We must remember that replications in different cultures and for different generations is the only appropriate scientific solution to the problem of cohort effects and the only sufficient guarantee that a fact becomes a scientific law. All more economical strategies have important limits to generalization.

The ideal epidemiologist design would be to apply the self-report delinquency instrument every year from late infancy to the middle of the forties at least, if we are to have a life-span perspective. From a developmentalist point of view, data gathering at such frequent periods is not necessary for economical, empirical, and technical reasons.

Gathering data at such intervals of every six months or every year on large samples is very costly, and even more so if we are considering interviews of a few hours in length to gather comprehensive individual data. Not only is it too costly but it is also unnecessary. Looking at our data on participation and frequency -- a representative sample and a delinquent sample -- and on the developmental stages in offending (Le Blanc & Fréchette, 1989), it is evident that yearly changes are not very pronounced or regular before twelve. From there to the end of adolescence the changes over a two-year period are much more evident than on a yearly basis, and after adolescence the changes seem to happen at a slower pace. There are also no sound technical reasons to choose such a short recall period to counter-balance memory decay if we refer to Weis's (1986) discussion of empirical studies in cognitive psychology and survey methodology. It has also been shown, by Hindelang et al. (1981), that longer periods of recall are even more efficient than a one-year period in terms of reliability and validity of measures and in terms of association with correlates.

If there are no fundamental reasons not to have long intervals of time between data gatherings of self-report delinquency -- even three and four years -- it should be mentioned that the time lag must appreciate the causal factors. Since we know very little about the sequencing of causal factors themselves, and in relation to delinquency, it is appropriate to be very prudent and to test varying intervals. Looking

at the results of the London longitudinal study -- particularly West
and Farrington (1973, 1977) and Farrington (1986) -- we would be inclined to conclude that broad factors (low social class or parent's
criminal record, for example) could survive through long intervals
while other factors must be studied on short intervals because their
impact seems limited (labeling, leaving school, or getting married, for
example). A developmentalist would argue against a standard design
because even three month intervals may be too short to study the impacts of some factors. The intervals have to be adjusted to the nature
of the causal factors.

In sum, a developmentalist would gather multiple measures of offending and comprehensive individual data on a larger at-risk sample
for at least a ten-year period that covers life transitions adequately.
The spacing of data gatherings could be of more than one year, preferably two, but they could also be of longer intervals such as three or
four years since for salient events the respondents do not always make
a rigid distinction between the last year and a longer period of time
(see Weis, 1986). They also could be shorter because the impacts of
some causal factors can only be studied with very short intervals. For
example the impact of leaving school on delinquency may require a design with data gatherings every two months.

3.2.2. On the content. An epidemiologist would choose a set of criminal events which would be used at every data gathering and the response
categories would be open-ended for a fixed time period, usually one
year. This strategy is reasonable when the duration of the study is
relatively short -- for example if it covers only childhood or adolescence or youth or adulthood -- but it is a questionable strategy when
the duration of the study overlaps two or more phases of life. A
developmentalist would recommend some variability in criminal events
and in the response categories according to age and settings.

From the points of view of logical validity and of existing empirical data, a study that would cover more than one phase of life -- for
example childhood, adolescence, and youth -- should vary the content of
the instrument because the instrument would be too lengthy if every
category of crime were used at every age. It is also well known that
the crime mix changes with age (Blumstein et al., 1985; Le Blanc &
Fréchette, 1989). During childhood, it is composed of minor larceny
(minor thefts at home, in school), vandalism, and fights. During adolescence, all varieties of theft are committed, as well as personal
crimes more serious than fights, and some victimless crimes (drug trafficking for example). Finally, during youth, minor delinquency tends
to disappear and it is replaced by more serious personal crimes, more
sophisticated economic crimes, and occupational crimes. It follows
that it would be inappropriate to ask a child about his assaults,
frauds, thefts at work, or income tax evasions. In turn, it would be
inappropriate to ask an adult about minor larcenies, vandalisms, or
minor fights because the participation in these crimes approaches zero
for the members of that age group.

If we were to study offending from childhood to adulthood, it
would then be necessary to have at least three sets of criminal items

adapted to age, with some overlapping. From a strict comparative point of view a score of 20 during childhood would not mean the same thing as a score of 20 during adolescence. But what is important for a developmentalist is the relative level at each stage of life and knowing if a certain crime-mix during childhood is followed by a certain crime-mix during the first part of adolescence, and others later on. It is the processes in a life-span perspective that is of interest, not the absolute comparison between two or more adjacent measures of offending. A standard epidemiological instrument is strong on comparability because of the representativeness of the gamuts of crimes, but it could be inapprorpriate from a clinical point of view. Is it reasonable to ask a child of nine about automobile theft?

The variability of criminal events should not be extended to a point where there would be no overlapping of items or no adaptation to settings. For example, minor larceny at home could transform with age to minor larceny in school, and, later on to minor larceny at work. Fraud, which has an average age of onset of 20, could be introduced in the instrument at the end of adolescence. Other types of crime could be introduced when the subject changes setting; as soon as he enters the work market he should be asked about income tax evasion or other types of thefts at work. The adaptation to age should not go so far as taking the earliest age of onset as the moment of introducing a new item: it should be done earlier to avoid sampling biases.

This question of adaptation to setting is particularly important because it is basically a problem of comparability. An adolesent who is working tends to forget about thefts or vandalism at work when he is asked about his thefts and vandalism in general, and the same is true for an adolescent in school. Introducing the setting is a guarantee of precision, a reduction of communication errors as Weis (1986) calls them. It is also a question of comparability between subjects who do not have the same life style.

The necessity of adapting the instrument to ages and settings opens a discussion that is not common enough in the self-report delinquency literature: the question of the representativeness of the crime events chosen or of the sampling of crime events from the whole range of possible crimes. Every researcher constructs his own instrument using items from other research and introduces new items. In a survey of 30 questionnaires that were reported before 1973, we found 491 descriptions of behaviors and 142 items that were not equivalent in wording (Le Blanc et al., 1973). This diversity refers to a particularly fundamental question for the construction of a self-reported delinquency instrument, and even to a more complex question for an instrument that is adapted to ages and settings. Hindelang et al. (1981) proposed 10 to 15 items as a sufficient number of crimes, and Weis (1986) suggests salient events, but there is no agreement on which crime events should be present in an instrument. Since this question is being addressed by other chapters in this volume we will not discuss that major problem further.

The state of the art in self-report delinquency questionnaire construction states that the response categories should be open-ended. Weis (1986) notes the change from closed-ended to open-ended and finds no technical literature contrary to the use of frequencies. In a life-span perspective, this practice should be questioned. It is our exper-ience that with adolescents and adults it is relatively easy to obtain precise frequencies for low rate offenders and somewhat reliable esti-mates for high rate offenders. But it is also our experience that with children and some 12, 13, and 14 year old adolescents it is often diffi-cult to obtain frequencies. First, many do not count in time or years, but their reference is the first grade, the second grade, and so on, or something else. Second, when they are answering questionnaires with open-ended questions, it is very time consuming because they try to count all the events exhaustively. In an interview situation, it is not simpler to obtain frequencies but it is easier because the inter-viewer can help them. In our experience, it is much easier if we use a limited number of qualitative categories during childhood; the reports of parents or teachers are not necessarily a better alternative; they are much less accurate in regard to frequencies in relation to covert behaviors and to behaviors outside home.

On the other hand, even for adolescents and adults, frequencies can be misleading when they are reported by chronic offenders and if they concern crimes of high frequency. Weis (1986) also dicusses these questions. For example, the estimate of events of selling drugs is virtually impossible for individuals who are involved for relatively long periods of time. Even for offenses like breaking and entering by a chronic offender, it would be difficult to say if they occurred 150 or 200 times. Estimates can be highly unreliable in those two types of situations and in others. There are not enough systematic studies of the impacts of the types of response categories to adopt a standard strategy, and we cannot assume that frequencies can be appropriate for all types of respondents.

There is another marker that should be introduced in a self-report delinquency instrument, namely the age at which each type of crime started and stopped. Tables 1 and 2 state that this is an important element in the study of the development of offending. It should then be incorporated in the instrument for every crime. This type of infor-mation is necessary to deduce duration and to demonstrate the existence of some of the processes in the development of offending. This type of marker is absent from most of the existing self-report delinquency instruments.

In sum, a developmentalist would not use a standard instrument for all ages. He would prefer criminal event items that are adapted to age and settings and response categories adapted to the cognitive capacity of the respondent.

3.2.3. On the method of administration. If we accept the conclusions of previous sections that a developmentalist would gather multiple measures of offending and comprehensive individual data on a large at-risk sample for at least a ten-year period, that the spacing of data gathering on salient criminal events could be of more than one year and that they would probably be of longer intervals, and that a developmen-talist would not use a standard instrument for all ages, a developmen-talist would then choose a semi-structured interview where an epidemiologist would recommend a self-administered questionnaire, or a structured interview. Hindelang et al. (1981) showed that there is no difference between these two methods of administration. Two sets of arguments will be proposed to support that choice. The lack of solid knowledge on the within-individual changes and the complexity of the instrument to be used.

3.2.3.1. The lack of knowledge on processes. In the reviews of the criminological literature there is some basic agreement on the definition of some of the fundamental parameters of the develoment of offending: age of onset, duration, and age of termination (see Blumstein et al., 1986; Le Blanc & Fréchette, 1989). When it comes to the modeling of the development of offending there is only one model: Blumstein et al. (1986) propose a simplistic model of the criminal career using the individual crime rate and age, and distinguishing the career length, along with incapacitation, rehabilitation and criminogenic effects.

When it comes to the processes, the confusion is great and the facts are rare. Much of this confusion arises because the development of offending has been mainly studied through official records of crime. As we have been able to show, many processes do not stand out with this type of data, but their existence is confirmed by self-report data (Le Blanc & Fréchette, 1989). From a taxonomical perspective, some processes are clearly identified (see Cohen, 1986, review) -- for example, specialization and escalation -- but there is no agreement on the facts between researchers because of divergent operationalizations, or due to the use of transition matrices as the main procedure of analysis, or due to the reliance on cross-sectional data sets (see Le Blanc & Fréchette, 1989, for a discussion of these flaws). Some other processes are just being recognized, like activation and desistance (see Table 2, and Loeber & Le Blanc, 1989). The conceptualization is far from sufficient to be operationalized easily in a standard instrument.

For these reasons we can state that the study of the development of offending is just barely starting. We need to explore more thoroughly the evolution of offending, which means that it is premature to rely on a standard and relatively simple instrument; it is time to develop hypotheses rather than verify hypotheses. What is needed is an instrument that goes beyond information on participation and frequency for a specific set of crime events, like the one that is proposed by epidemiologists. As implied by the theoretical formulation set forth earlier, we need to know the frequency for each crime but also the sequence of offenses, when each started, its duration, and when it stopped; and we need to know this for short periods of time in relation to age. What we need to avance our knowledge of the development of offending is a list of crimes that are precisely situated in time for each individual in a sample. It is our position that only a semi-structured interview can produce such precise information.

3.2.3.2. A complex instrument. It is not our contention that a semi-structured interview is superior to a questionnaire. That question has been discussed at length by many authors without any clear recommendation (Hardt & Bodine, 1965; Gold, 1966; Belson & Beeson, 1974). It is superior at this time in the development of knowledge on offending because we do not know much about the dynamics of criminal activity.

Using a standard questionnaire would be too restrictive and the questionnaire would be too complex. Let us first present the advantages of a semi-structured interview in relation to the need for heuristic studies of the development of offending. Then we will outline the complex instrument a developmentalist would use to elicit delinquency.

The advantages of a semi-structured interview have been discussed at length by numerous authors (Hardt & Bodine, 1965; Robins, 1966; Belson & Beeson, 1969; Hood & Sparks, 1970; Nettler, 1974). A non-exhaustive list of some interesting features of that method of data gathering would be the following. The direct personal contact with the subjects may help eliminate general or specific resistance to reporting crimes and it may produce conditions that can encourage communication. It may control for cognitive problems, for example, reading capacity or the ability to concentrate, or motivational errors such as interest or fatigue. The interviewer can also prevent insufficient validity and reliability because he is able to probe, for a surprising frequency, or for something that may have been forgotten, or a misunderstanding. He can also verify if the crimes reported are real crimes by asking questions on the modus operandi.

There are two features of the semi-structured interview that are more important for the developmentalist -- the possibilities it offers in precision and in sequencing events. With the interview it is possible to explore, in detail, many aspects concerning the exact nature of the crime. But, other information is also available, such as the presence of a series of crimes, the number and characteristics of accomplices, the presence of planning and instruments, the nature of intimidation and intoxication, and so on. In fact, it is possible to construct a time chart of the offending of an individual. This is related to the most interesting feature of a semi-structured interview, the ordering of crime events, and of causal factors. In a semi-structured interview, the interviewer can situate more precisely the location of life transition events in the life of the individual -- when he left school, when his father left home, for example -- and inquire about psychosocial factors such as the supervision or sanctions at certain ages, occupational aspirations, etc. These types of information may be of much more importance when the knowledge base is lacking, as in the case of the development of offending and in relation to the causal ordering of factors.

The use of a semi-structured interview will raise the question of the characteristics of the interviewers. Even if interviewer characteristics such as age, sex, or race do not seem to play any important role in distorting answers to survey questions about crimes (Hindelang et al., 1981), it is important to note that this is true for adolescents but it may not be the case for children or adults. It is our experience, which has been shared by others, that with a child, mother-type interviewers have better rapport with subjects, and that with young adults an older adult seems to elicit more valid and reliable information. Not only should we control the importance of these structural characteristics, but interpersonal skills should also be questioned. In particular, with a semi-structured interview, it is our experience that more skilled persons produce more detailed data.

Such a defense of the semi-structured interview as the most appropriate tool to study the development of offending and the ordering of causal factors stand in relation to the state of existing criminological knowledge. Since it is definitely insufficient concerning the conceptualization and the data, a standard self-administered questionnaire, even adapted to age, would limit us too much in this exploratory phase. To illustrate the potentials of a semi-strucutred interview, let me present an outline of a protocol that we have used in Montreal (Le Blanc & Frèchette, 1989).

The interviewer starts the part of the interview on delinquency with the first crime and has a set of a dozen precisely defined categories of crimes to cover -- to these categories of crime can be added types of conduct disorders (use of drugs, fights, and so on). For each crime, or set of crimes, he has a list of questions to cover: When the crime was first and last performed, the period during which there was any series of this type of crime, the frequencies obtained, how the crime was committed (planning, instrument, violence, accomplices, and so on). The interviewer knows the coding to all these questions which helps him to cover all topics. During the interview a report sheet is completed which orders all crimes and series of crimes with the appropriate information on each. With this type of data, it is possible to study precisely the development of offending. Such a strategy can also be applied to causal factors.

In sum, we have argued in this section that the state of knowledge on the development of offending and the ordering of causal factors call for data gathering techniques that will produce more detailed information. The semi-structured interview is not superior **per se** to the self-administered questionnaire or the structured interview, but it is more appropriate because of the need for more qualitative data and because of its capacity to sequence data.

4. CONCLUSION

Studying self-report delinquency in a developmental perspective implies a certain number of accommodations to longitudinal surveys. In this paper, we have discussed some of them in relation to the design of such a study and to the content of the instrument to be developed. Over all, two options are available to the criminologist who is interested in the development of offending from childhood to adulthood. The criminologist can use a strategy of hypothesis testing, or he can favor a strategy of grounded theory.

The first type of researcher will take existing criminological theories -- mainly sociological if he were to follow American criminology -- and develop some sort of integrative model of causal factors and operationalize that model in a standard instrument. Population samples and a sequential multiple cohort design will be favored for the purpose of generalization. Self-report delinquency will be assessed with an extended sample of crimes but limited information will be available on each crime. These data will be gathered regularly, preferably every year. The data gathered will cover a large spectrum of causal

394

factors, superficially because of the time and cost constraints involved in these studies. The results will undoubtedly help to understand the sequence of criminal events and of causal factors and in
particular the initiation of delinquency.

The second type of researcher will be guided by a multidisciplinary list of causal factors that are highly plausible in the literature. He will use relatively large samples of at-risk subjects. Each
of them will be subjected to relatively long, semi-structured interviews because he would stress the need for psychological as well as
habitual socio-criminological data. The data would be gathered for
longer periods of time but at interals of at least a few years. This
researcher will want to sequence events and factors very precisely.
Undoubtedly the results would be important to develop a theoretical
formulation of the development of offending and of the factors in each
period of life that are highly significant for the maintenance of delinquency.

The two strategies are clearly needed to increase our understanding of delinquency because the first one will be synthesizing, moving
toward generalizations, and the second one more analytic, decomposing
the multiple aspects of offending. They are complementary from a methodological point of view because one relies on deduction and the other
on induction. From a substantive perspective, one will uncover the
mechanisms of initiation of offending while the other will give more
attention to the dynamics of chronic delinquency. To a certain extent
they can replicate each other concerning the sequence of causal factors
and certain aspects of offending. There is also no reason to think
that one strategy is more costly than the other because in one case
very large samples are substituted by long interviews in the other.
Neither of these two strategies is necessary and sufficient for the
development of criminological knowledge.

For all these reasons we will plead for tolerance. In funding and
publishing, everyone should have equal opportunity to propose his approach. Needless to say, tolerance should not be equated with naiveté
or as a support for studies that are of inferior caliber. Standardization, which means relying on one methodology and one specific instrument, is a possible threat to the development of criminology. It may
be a fashion or an ideology in certain circles, but it is certainly not
the only reasonable way to study an object and its causes that are far
from being explored thoroughly so far.

REFERENCES

Agnew, R: Social control theory and delinquency: A longitudinal test.
    Criminology, 23(1):47-61, 1985.
Albany Conference: Theoretical integration in the study of deviance and
    crime: Problems and prospects. Albany: State University of New York
    at Albany, 1987.
Arnold, WR, & Brungardt, T: Juvenile misconduct and delinquency. Boston: Houghton Mifflin, 1983.

Bachman, JG, Green, S, & Wirtanen, ID: <u>Youth in transition: Dropping out, problems or symptom</u>. Ann Arbor: Institute for Social Research, 1971.

Bachman, JG, O'Malley, PM, & Johnston, J. <u>Youth in transition: Adolescence to adulthood. Change and stability in the lives of young men</u>. Ann Arbor: Institute for Social Research, 1978.

Belson, W, & Beeson, M: <u>Identifying difficulties and facilitating factors in getting information from boys about their stealing and about associated matters: An exploratory study</u>. London: The Survey Research Center, London School of Economics, 1969.

Blumstein, A, Cohen, J, Roth, JA, & Visher, CA: <u>Criminal careers and "career criminals,"</u> Vol 1 and Vol 11. Washington, DC: National Academy Press, 1986.

Cernkovich, SA, Giordano, PC, & Pugh, MD: Chronic offenders: The missing cases in self-reported delinquency research. <u>The Journal of Criminal Law and Criminology</u>, 76:705-732, 1985.

Chaiken, J, & Rolph, JE: <u>Identifying high-rate serious criminal offenders</u>. Santa Monica: Rand Corporation, 1985.

Cloward, RA, & Ohlin, LE: <u>Delinquency and opportunity. A theory of delinquent gangs</u>. New York: The Free Press, 1960.

Cohen, AK: <u>Delinquent boys: The culture of the gang</u>. New York: Mac-Millan, 1955.

Conen, AK: The study of social disorganization and deviant behavior. In Merton, RK, Broom, L, & Cottrell, LS (Eds.), <u>Sociology today: Problems and prospects</u>. New York: Basic Books, 1969.

Cohen, J. Research on criminal careers: Individual frequency rates and offense seriousness. In Blumstein, A, Cohen, J, Roth, JA, & Visher, CA (Eds.), <u>Criminal careers and "career criminals."</u> Washington, DC: National Academy Press, Vol. 1:292-418, 1986.

Cohen, LE, & Felson, M: Property crime rates in the United States: A macrodynamic analysis, 1947-1977, with ex ante forecasts for the mid-1980s. <u>American Journal of Sociology</u>, 86:90-118, 1979.

Conger, JJ, & Petersen, AC: <u>Adolescence and youth: Psychological development in a changing world</u>. New York: Harper & Row, 1984.

Cusson, M. <u>Délinquant pourquoi?</u> Montréal: Hurtubise, H.M.H., 1981.

Cusson, M. L'analyse stratégigue et quelques développments récents en criminologie. <u>Criminologie</u>, XIX, 1:53-72, 1986.

Duncan, OD: <u>Notes on social measurement: Historical and critical</u>. New York: Russell Sage Foundation, 1984.

Elliott, D, & Voss, H: <u>Delinquency and dropout</u>. Lexington: Health, 1974.

Elliott, DS, Huizinga, D, & Ageton, SS: <u>Explaining delinquency and drug use</u>. Beverly Hills: Sage Publications, 1985.

Erez, E: Planning of crime and the criminal career: Official and hidden offenses. <u>The Journal of Criminal Law and Criminology</u>, 71(1):73-76, 1980.

Erez, E: Situational or planned crime and the criminal career. In Wolfgang, ME, Thornberry, TP, Figlio, RM (Eds.), <u>From boy to man, from delinquency to crime</u>, 122-133. Chicago: University of Chicago Press, 1987.

396

Farrington, DP: Self-reports of deviant behavior: Predictive and stable. *Journal of Criminal Law and Criminology*, 64:99-110, 1973.

Farrington, DP: Delinquency from 10 to 25. In Mednick, SA, (Eds.), *Antecedents of Aggression and Antisocial Behavior*. Boston: Hingham & Kluwer, 1982.

Farrington, DP: Offending from 10 to 25 years of age. In Teilmann-VanDusen, K, & Mednick, SA, (Eds.), *Prospective studies of crime and delinquency*. Boston: Kluwer Nijhof, 1983, 17-38.

Farrington, DP: Stepping stones to adult criminal careers. In Olweus, D, Block, J, & Radke-Yarrow, M (Eds.), *Development of antisocial and prosocial behavior*. London: Academic Press, Inc., 1986, 359-384.

Farrington, DP, Ohlin, LE, & Wilson, JQ: *Understanding and controlling crime: Toward a new research strategy*. New York: Springer-Verlag, 1986.

Farrington, DP, Snyder, HS, & Finnegan, TA: Specialization in juvenile court careers. *Criminology*, 26:461-485, 1988.

Felson, M, & Cohen, LE: Human ecology and crime: A routine activity approach. *Human Ecology*, 8:384-406, 1980.

Ferdinand, TN: The methods of delinquency theory. *Criminology*, 25(4):841-863, 1987.

Fréchette, M, & Le Blanc, M: *La délinquance cachée à l'adolescence*. Montreal: Université de Montréal, Groupe de Recherche sur I'lnadaptation Juvénile, 1979.

Fréchette, M, & Le Blanc, M: *Délinquances et délinquents*. Chicoutimi: Gaetan Morin.

Glueck, ET: *Delinquents and non-delinquents in perspective*. Cambridge: Harvard University Press, 1968.

Gold, M: Undetected delinquent behavior. *Journal of Research in Crime and Delinquency*, 3:27-46, 1966.

Gottfredson, M, & Hirschi, T: The true value of lambda would appear to be zero: An essay on career criminals, criminal careers, selective incapacitation, cohort studies and related topics. *Criminology*, 24(2):213-234, 1986.

Gottfredson, M, & Hirschi, T: The methodological adequacy of longitudinal research on crime. *Criminology*, 25(3):581-614, 1987a.

Gottfredson, M, & Hirschi, T: A propensity-event theory of crime. *Advances in Criminological Theory*, 1:57-67, 1988.

Göppinger, H: *Lifestyle and criminality*. New York: Springer-Verlag, 1987.

Hamparian, D, Schuster, R, Dinitz, S, & Conrad, J: *The violent few: A study of dangerous juvenile offenders*. Lexington, MA: Lexington Books, 1978.

Hardt, RN, & Bodine, GE: *Development of self-report instruments in delinquency research: A conference report*. Syracuse: Youth Development Center, 1965.

Hindelang, MJ, Hirschi, T, & Weis, JG: *Measuring delinquency*. Beverly Hills: Sage Publications, 1981.

Hirschi, T: *Causes of delinquency*. Berkeley: University of California Press, 1969.

Hirschi, T: Separate and unequal is better. *Journal of Research in Crime and Delinquency*, 16(1):34-38, 1979.

Hirschi, T: Exploring alternatives to integrated theory. In the Albany Conference, Theoretical integration in the study of deviance and crime: problems and prospects. Albany: Department of Sociology, State University of New York, 1987.

Hirschi, T, & Gottfredson, M: Age and the explanation of crime. American Journal of Sociology, 89:552-584, 1983.

Hirschi, T, & Selvin, HC: Delinquency research: An appraisal of analytic methods. New York, The Free Press, 1967.

Hough, JM, Clarke, RVG, & Mayhew, P: Introduction. In Clarke, RVG, & Mayhew, P, Designing out crime. London: Her Majesty's Stationary Office, 1980.

Kagan, J, & Moss, HA: Birth to maturity, a study in psychological development. NY: John Wiley and Sons, Inc., 1962.

Kempf, KL: Specialization and the crimnal career. Criminology, 25(2):399-420, 1987.

Klein, MM: Offense specialization and versatility among juveniles. British Journal of Criminology, 24(2):185-194, 1984.

Le Blanc, M, Caplan, L, & Biron, L: La délinquance juvénile commise, observée, subie: prolégomènes à une étude extensive. Montréal: Ecole de criminologie, Université de Montréal, 1973.

Le Blanc, M, & Ouimet, M: Validation d'une théorie intégrative de la régulation de la conduite délinquante. Montréal: Centre international de criminologie comparée, Université de Montréal, 1986.

Le Blanc, M, & Côté, G: Adolescent modal personality and cohort effects. Journal of Personality, (submitted), 1988.

Le Blanc, M, & Fréchette, M: Male criminal activity from childhood through youth: multilevel and developmental perspectives. New York: Springer-Verlag, 1989.

Lemay, M: Psychopathologie juvénile: Les désordes de la conduite chez l'enfant et l'adolescent. Paris: Fleurus (2 vol.), 1973.

Lemert, EM: Social pathology. New York: McGraw-Hill, 1951.

Lerner, RM: Concepts and theories of human development. New York: Random House, 1986.

Loeber, R: The stability of antisocial and delinquent child behavior: A review. Child Development, 53(6):1431-1446, 1982.

Loeber, R: Patterns and development of antisocial child behavior. In Whitehurst, GJ (Ed.), Annals of child development (Vol. 2). Greenwich: Jay Press, 1985.

Loeber, R: Natural histories of conduct problems, delinquency and associated substance use: Evidence for developmental progressions. In Lahey, BB, & Kazdin, E, Advances in clinical child psychology (Vol. 10). New York: Plenum, 1987.

Loeber, R, & Le Blanc, M: Toward a developmental criminology. In Tonry, M, & Morris, N (Eds.), Crime and justice: An annual review, Vol 11. Chicago: University of Chicago Press, 1989.

Mailloux, N: Jeunes sans dialogue. Paris: Fleurus, 1971.

Matsueda, R: Testing social control theory and differential association. American Sociological Review, 47:489-504, 1982.

Matza, D: Delinquency and drift. New York: John Wiley & Sons, Inc., 1964.

Muchielli, R: Comment ils deviennent délinquants: genèse et développement de la socialisation et de la dissocialité. Paris: Editions sociales francaises, 1965.

Murphy, FJ: The incidence of hidden delinquency. American Journal of Orthopsychiatry, 16:686-696, 1946.

Nesselroade, JR, & Baltes, PB: Sequential strategies and the role of cohort effects in behavioral development: Adolescent personality (1970-72) as a sample case. In Mednick, SA, Harway, M, & Finello, K, Handbook of longitudinal research: Birth and childhood. New York: Praeger, 55-87, 1984.

Nettler, G: Explaining crime. Toronto: McGraw-Hill, 1974.

Nye, FI, & Short, JF: Socio-economic status and delinquent behavior. American Journal of Sociology, 63:381-389, 1958.

Offer, DE: The psychological world of the teenager. New York: Basic Books, 1969.

Pearson, FS, & Weiner, NA: Toward an integration of criminological theories. The Journal of Criminal Law and Criminology, 76:116-150, 1985.

Pinatel, J: Traité de criminologie. Paris: Dalloz, 1963.

Porterfield, AL: Youth in trouble. Fort Worth: Leo Potishman Foundation, 1946.

Rand, A: Transitional life events and desistance from delinquency and crime. In Wolfgang, ME, Thornberry, TP, & Figlio, RM, From boy to man, from delinquency to crime. Chicago: University of Chicago Press, 134-162, 1987.

Robins, LN: Deviant children grown up. New York: Robert E. Krieger Publishing Company, 1966.

Seelig, E: Traité de criminologie. Paris: Presses Universitaire de France, 1956.

Short, JF: The level of explanation problem in criminology. In Meier, RF, Theoretical methods in criminology. Beverly Hills: Sage Publications, 1985.

Short, JF: Exploring integration of the theoretical levels of explanation: Notes on juvenile delinquency. In The Albany Conference, Theoretical integration in the study of deviance and crime: Problems and prospects. Albany: Department of Sociology, State University of New York, 1987.

Weis, JG: Issues in the measurement of criminal careers. In Blumstein, A, Cohen, J, Roth, JA, & Visher, CA (Eds.), Criminal careers and "career criminals", p. 1-51. Washington, D.C.: National Academy Press, 1986.

Werner, H: The concept of development from a comparative and organismic point of view. In Harris, DB, The concept of development. Minneapolis: University of Minnesota Press, 1957.

Wolfgang, ME, Figlio, RM, & Sellin, T: Delinquency in a birth cohort. Chicago: University of Chicago Press, 1972.

Wolfgang, ME, Thornberry, TP, & Figlio, RM: From boy to man, from delinquency to crime. Chicago: University of Chicago Press, 1987.

SELF-REPORTED AND OFFICIAL OFFENDING FROM ADOLESCENCE TO ADULTHOOD

David P. Farrington
Institute of Criminology, Cambridge University
Cambridge, United Kingdom

1. INTRODUCTION

The research reported in this chapter had three major objectives. The first was to study the prevalence of different types of offending, as measured by self-reports and official convictions, of the same sample at different ages from adolescence to adulthood. The second was to investigate the relationship between self-reported and official offending of the same sample at different ages, and hence to advance knowledge about the concurrent and predictive validity of self-reports in comparison with official records. The third was to study the relationship between offending at one age and offending at another, as measured by both self-reports and official convictions, and hence to advance knowledge about the issues of continuity or discontinuity and specialization or versatility in offending.

Very few research projects have collected self-reported offending data on the same sample at several different ages over a time interval of at least five years. In the Youth in Transition project, Bachman, O'Malley, and Johnston (1978) followed up a nationally representative sample of over 2000 American high school boys from age 15 to age 23, collecting self-reports on five occasions. However, they did not obtain any official record data on offending. In the National Youth Survey, Elliott, Huizinga, and Menard (1989) followed up a nationally representative sample of over 1700 American adolescents aged 11-17 in 1976 for 11 years, collecting self-reports on seven occasions. They were also able to obtain the arrest records of this sample up to 1983. In Montreal, Le Blanc and Frechette (1989) followed up nearly 500 male delinquents from age 15 to age 23, collecting self-reports on three occasions and also official criminal records.

This chapter reports results obtained in a survey of over 400 London boys, analyzing self-reported offending data collected on five occasions between ages 14 and 32. In addition, the official conviction records of these males were obtained from age 10 (the minimum age of criminal responsibility in England) to age 32. In describing changes in the prevalence of offending with age, this chapter is to some extent a continuation of the report by Farrington (1983). While there is some

M. W. Klein (ed.), Cross-National Research in Self-Reported Crime and Delinquency, 399–423.
© *1989 by Kluwer Academic Publishers.*

disagreement in the literature about how the frequency of offending changes with age (Blumstein, Cohen, & Farrington, 1988; Gottfredson & Hirschi, 1988), there is broad agreement that the prevalence of most types of offending increases to a peak in the teenage years and then declines in the twenties (Farrington, 1986).

The relationship between self-reported and official offending has rarely been studied at more than one age. In a pioneering project, Williams and Gold (1972) in their 1967 National Survey of Youth found that 88% of American 13-16 year olds admitted committing at least one chargeable offense in the previous three years, but only 9% of them had been caught by the police during this period. More recently, Dunford and Elliott (1984) found that only 8% of self-reported offenders (who comprised 63% of their sample) were arrested, in comparison with 2% of self-reported non-offenders.

While the probability of a self-reported offender becoming an officially recorded offender is often quite low, all studies show significant overlaps between self-reported and official offenders (e.g., Huizinga & Elliott, 1986). In other words, the self-reported offenders are more likely to be official offenders than are the self-reported non-offenders, and conversely the official offenders are more likely to be self-reported offenders than are the official non-offenders. These results have been taken to demonstrate the concurrent validity of the self-report method (e.g., Hindelang, Hirschi, & Weis, 1981). However, another possible interpretation is that those who are officially recorded become more willing to admit their delinquent acts as a result, and indeed there is some evidence in favor of this argument (Farrington, 1977). The most convincing demonstration of the validity of self-reports, at least in comparison with official records, is to show, as Farrington (1973) did, that self-reported offending predicts future convictions among those who are currently unconvicted.

Very few projects have investigated how self-reported offending at one age is related to self-reported offending at another, although Bachman et al. (1978) found that their first and fifth measures were significantly correlated, despite the eight-year gap between them. Using the same data, Rankin and Wells (1984) constructed transition matrices demonstrating how broad types of offending at one age predicted broad types of offending at another. Generally, there was surprising continuity in offending, since non-offenders, status offenders and delinquents tended to stay in the same categories over time.

Dynamic analyses, comparing specific types of offenses at one age with specific types at another, have only been carried out with official offending. Farrington, Snyder, and Finnegan (1988) concluded that these analyses showed that there was some specialization in offending superimposed on a great deal of versatility. Whether the same conclusions would be reached with self-reported offending measures is an important question. Static analyses, comparing different types of self-reported offenses at the same age, indicate that all types are positively correlated and hence that there is a considerable amount of versatility (e.g., Hindelang et al., 1981).

An important controversy in self-reported offending research centers on the most frequent, serious, or "chronic" offenders.

Cernkovich, Giordano, and Pugh (1985) have argued that the worst offenders according to official records are often missing from samples used
in self-report studies. The counter-argument, by Dunford and Elliott
(1984), is that the worst offenders identified by self-reports are
often missing from the official records. The implications of this
controversy are that, in order to draw valid conclusions about offending, it is essential to minimize attrition and to collect self-reports
and official records on as many of the target sample as possible.
Attrition was unusually low in the present project (Farrington, Gallagher, Morley, St Ledger, & West, 1989).

2. THE PRESENT RESEARCH

2.1. The Project

The present analyses were carried out as part of the Cambridge
Study in Delinquent Development, which is a prospective longitudinal
survey of 411 males. At the time they were first contacted in 1961-62,
all were living in a working-class area of London, England. The vast
majority of the sample was chosen by taking all the boys who were then
aged 8-9 years and on the registers of six state primary schools within
a one mile radius of the study research office. In addition to 399
boys from these six schools, 12 boys from a local school for the educa-
tionally subnormal were included in the sample, to make it more representative of the population of boys living in the area. The boys were
overwhelmingly white, working-class, and of British origin (see Farrington, 1989; Farrington & West, 1981; West, 1969, 1982; West & Farrington, 1973, 1977).
The major aim of the project was to document the natural history
and development of delinquency and crime. Many variables that were
alleged to be causes or correlates of offending were measured at several different ages. The sample males were interviewed and tested in
their schools when they were aged about 8, 10, and 14, and they were
interviewed in the project research office at about 16, 18, and 21.
They were then interviewed in their homes at about 25 and 32.
In addition to the interviews with the sample males, their parents
were interviewed about once a year from when the boy was 8 until when
he was 14-15 and in his last year of compulsory education. The primary
informant was the mother, although most fathers were also seen. The
boys' teachers also completed questionnaires about them, when the males
were aged about 8, 10, 12, and 14. Furthermore, ratings were obtained
from the boys' peers when they were in their primary schools. Hence,
information was obtained about the sample males from several different
sources.

2.2. Measures of Self-Reported and Official Offending

In order to obtain information about official convictions, repeated searches were made in the central Criminal Record Office in London
to try to locate findings of guilt sustained by the boys, by their

parents, by their brothers and sisters, and (in recent years) by their wives and cohabitees. Convictions were only counted if they were for offenses normally recorded in this Office. This rule led to the exclusion of all motoring offenses except driving while disqualified, together with other crimes regarded as minor, such as public drunkenness and common (simple) assault.

Over one-third of the sample males (153, or 37%) were convicted for offenses committed between ages 10 and 32 inclusive. Convictions in this study were similar to arrests, because the majority of arrests of sample males were followed by convictions. Because of delays between offenses and convictions that could sometimes exceed one year, the dates of offenses were used to define ages of offending, not the dates of convictions. Since one criminal event could occasionally lead to several officially recorded offenses, for example when a burglar was convicted both of burglary and of going equipped to steal, only one offense per offending day (the most serious) was counted. The 153 convicted males accumulated a total of 613 convictions, and committed a total of 683 officially recorded offenses on different days (an average of 4.5 offenses each). These figures show that in the majority of cases one conviction was for only one offense.

During the interviews at ages 14, 18, 21, 25, and 32, the sample males were asked to self-report offenses that they had committed. The numbers interviewed at the five ages were 405, 389, 218, 85, and 378, respectively. At ages 14, 18, and 32, the aim was to interview the whole sample, and attrition was low. For example, 95 percent of the 410 still alive at age 18 were interviewed, and 94 percent of the 403 still alive at age 32. At age 21, the aim was to interview only the convicted delinquents and a similar number of randomly chosen unconvicted males. At age 25, four small subgroups were interviewed: persisting recidivists, temporary recidivists, unconvicted males from deprived backgrounds, and randomly chosen unconvicted males.

The self-report offenses were presented on cards, and the males were initially asked to sort the cards according to whether or not they had committed the act during a specified reference period. More detailed questions were then asked about the offenses admitted, such as how many times the person had done it. The median ages at interview were 14 years 9 months, 18 years 7 months, 21 years 5 months, 24 years 11 months, and 32 years 3 months. The reference periods were: ever, the last three years, the last two years, the last two years, and the last five years, respectively. Hence, these self-reports covered almost all of the period between ages 10 and 32.

Ten types of offenses were enquired about on virtually every occasion: burglary, shoplifting, theft of motor vehicles, theft from motor vehicles, theft from slot machines, theft from work, assault, vandalism, drug use, and fraud. The exact wordings of the items at the different ages are shown in the Appendix. These ten types of self-reported offenses could be compared with the corresponding ten types of offenses leading to convictions, which accounted for about three-quarters of all conviction offenses (490 out of 683): 119 burglaries, 41 shopliftings, 108 thefts of motor vehicles (including taking and driving away), 38 thefts from motor vehicles, 17 thefts from slot machines, 18 thefts from work, 68 assaults (including wounding and threatening behavior), 22 offenses of vandalism, 19 drug offenses, and 40 frauds. The other 193 conviction offenses comprised 72 other types of thefts, 30 offenses of receiving stolen property, 30 offenses of suspicion (such as going equipped to steal), 21 disqualified driving offenses, 17 robberies, 17 offenses of possessing an offensive weapon, and 6 sex offenses. Conviction offenses at ages 10-14, 15-18, 19-21, 22-25, and 26-32 were reasonably comparable with self-reported offenses at the five ages.

It has to be admitted that comparisons of offense types and time periods are in some cases only rough approximations. For example, the self-reports at age 32 covered the last five years, but they are compared with official offenses between ages 26 and 32 inclusive, in the interests of including all convictions in the 10-32 year period. There are reasons to expect non-comparability between self-reported and official offenses. For example, as pointed out above, minor assaults would not be counted as official offenses but would be included as self--reported offenses. Conversely, unsuccessful attempts to commit crimes would be included as conviction offenses but probably would not be self-reported.

There are a number of problems involved in measuring self-reported offending at different ages, and there is a constant tension between the desire to repeat earlier questions and the need to ask questions that are more appropriate to a person's age. For example, in connection with theft from slot machines, one man at age 25 said that he "hadn't done nothing like that for years," and another thought that these were "strange questions to ask people of my age." Changes over the time period also cause problems. For example, the reference to juke boxes in the slot machines item at age 14 and to purple hearts and reefers in the drug item at age 14 now seem rather dated. Changing fashions in drug use virtually force changes in questions designed to measure this topic, whereas the same is not true for burglary or shoplifting, for example. There is also a tension between the desire to ask numerous specific questions, which are likely to elicit more admissions but run the risk of exhausting the interviewee's cooperativeness, and the more practical approach of asking a few more general questions. In this project, more specific questions were asked at age 14 than at later ages.

In some cases, acts which can be committed at one age cannot be committed at others. For example, the fraud questions at age 32 included tax fraud, credit card fraud, and fraudulently obtaining government benefits, none of which could be done at age 14. In retrospect, it is unfortunate that the main fraud question at age 14 referred to bus and rail fraud (traveling without a ticket), which is clearly in the legal category of fraud but is rather different from the other three types of fraud. Some of these problems are caused by heterogeneity within legal categories of offenses. An offense at one age could be behaviorally different from the same offense at another age. For example, Langan and Farrington (1983) found that burglaries and robberies committed by sample males during their adult years tended to be more serious than those committed during their juvenile years (age 10-16). As another example, the vehicles stolen at the youngest ages tended to be mopeds, motor scooters, and motorcycles, rather than the cars which were stolen once the males could drive.

Dwelling on the difficulties should not obscure the strengths of this research, which is unique in having self-report and official measures of offending for five age ranges covering a 22-year time period. In nearly all cases (the main exception being fraud), the self-reported offenses in one age range were reasonably comparable both to official offenses and to self-reported offenses in other age ranges.

2.3. The Prevalence of Offending

Table 1 shows the prevalence of offending in different age ranges according to self-reports, and Table 2 shows comparable figures based on official conviction records. Because of the fact that not all males were interviewed at all ages, the admission rates shown in Table 1 have been adjusted to apply to the 387 males interviewed at both 14 and 18. Working with these 387 rather than all 411 introduced a negligible error (less than 1%; see Farrington, 1983). The adjustment was very simple, and will be explained in the case of burglary, although the same principles apply in all cases.

TABLE 1. Prevalence of self-reported offending.

			Percent at Age			
Offense	10-14	15-18	19-21	22-25	26-32	10-32
Burglary	13.2	10.9	4.5	2.2	2.2	21.8
Shoplifting	39.3	15.5	6.7	4.8	5.5	48.2
Theft of vehicle	7.5	15.2	6.4	3.0	3.0	23.2
Theft from veh.	9.3	13.4	4.1	2.3	2.3	21.5
Theft from mach.	14.7	19.1	2.4	5.1	1.7	29.6
Theft from work	2.3	*	0.2	13.6	23.9	32.3
Assault	39.8	45.2	4.9	24.1	36.1	69.9
Vandalism	71.1	21.2	3.6	0.4	1.1	74.1
Drug Use	0.3	31.5	20.4	17.7	19.9	37.7
Fraud	73.4	*	8.1	16.8	52.8	82.4
Any Theft**	45.7	38.2	28.3	18.7	29.0	69.2
Any Offense***	88.6	67.4	58.0	46.4	71.4	95.6

Note: *   = Not asked
       ** = Any Theft (Any of the first six listed here)
       *** = Any Offense (of the ten listed here)

Of the 387 males interviewed at both 14 and 18, 13.2% admitted burglary at 14 and 10.9% at 18. Only 217 males were interviewed both at 18 and 21. Of these, 16.6% admitted burglary at 18 and 6.9% at 21. The admission rate of this subsample at age 18 was high because convicted males were over-represented among those interviewed at 21 (and indeed 25). The proportional reduction in burglary between 18 and 21 for this subsample was 0.584 (since 6.9 divided by 16.6 is 0.416). This reduction was then applied to the original figure of 10.9% of 387 to produce an estimated admission rate at 21 of 4.5% (10.9 x 0.416). The 367 males interviewed at both 18 and 32 had admission rates at 18 of 10.9% and at 32 of 2.2%, so no adjustment was needed in this case. The 82 males interviewed at both 25 and 32 had admission rates at 25 of 6.1% and at 32 of 6.1%, so the estimated rate at age 25 was set at the same level as at age 32 (2.2%). Because of the small number interviewed at age 25, the estimate at this age is the least accurate.

TABLE 2. Prevalence of official offending.

Offense			Percent at Age			
	10-14	15-18	19-21	22-25	26-32	10-32
Burglary	3.4	8.5	2.7	3.0	2.5	14.1
Shoplifting	3.2	1.7	0.5	1.5	1.7	7.4
Theft of vehicle	2.7	9.8	4.2	2.2	1.7	14.6
Theft from veh.	2.4	2.9	0.7	1.2	1.0	6.7
Theft from mach	1.0	1.2	0.0	0.2	0.5	2.7
Theft from work	0.0	1.0	2.4	0.2	0.2	3.7
Assault	0.7	3.2	3.4	2.2	4.7	10.9
Vandalism	0.0	2.2	0.7	0.7	1.5	5.0
Drug Use	0.0	0.5	1.5	0.7	1.0	2.7
Fraud	0.0	1.2	0.7	2.7	1.5	5.7
Any Theft*	10.2	16.6	8.6	6.9	6.0	27.5
Any Offense**	10.7	19.5	3.0	10.6	11.2	33.0

Note: * = Any Theft (Any of the first six listed here)
       ** = Any Offense (of the ten listed here)

The comparison of the prevalence of offending in different age ranges is complicated by the different lengths of the age ranges, of course. However, self-reports and convictions show that burglary, shoplifting, theft of and from vehicles, theft from slot machines, and vandalism all declined markedly from the teenage years to the twenties. The sharpest decline in the self-reports is for vandalism, which 71 % admitted at 14 but only 1% at 32. In contrast, theft from work, assault, drug use and fraud did not clearly decline with age (although, as mentioned above, the fraud figures at different ages are not very comparable). For example, 40% of the sample admitted assault at age 14, and 36% at age 32. Nearly 5% of the males were convicted of assault between ages 26 and 32, despite the exclusion of minor assaults from the conviction figures. The highest prevalences of conviction were for burglary (8.5%) and theft of vehicles (9.8%) at age 15-18.

The cumulative prevalence of self-reported offending was very high. Only 4% denied all 10 offenses at all ages, and nearly 70% admitted at least one of the six theft items (including burglary). Over 80% admitted fraud, three-quarters admitted vandalism, 70% admitted assault, and nearly 50% admitted shoplifting. No offense was admitted by less than 20% of the sample. The cumulative prevalence of official offending was lower, of course. One-third of the sample were convicted of one or more of these offenses at some stage, including 15% convicted of theft of vehicles, 14% convicted of burglary, and 11% convicted of assault.

2.4. The Relation Between Self-Reported and Official Offending

Table 3 shows the percentage of known offenders in each age range who were convicted of each type of offense. The known offenders are those identified by either self-reports or official convictions, although it was unusual for a person to be convicted of an offense without also admitting it. For example, 89 males admitted burglary at some stage, and 44 of them (49.4%) were convicted of burglary at some stage. In contrast, 320 males never admitted burglary, and only 8 of them (2.5%) were convicted of burglary. The relationship between self-reported and official burglary was highly significant ($X2 = 134.0$, 1 d.f., $p < 0.001$, phi = 0.58). In all, 52 out of 97 known burglars (53.6%) were convicted of burglary. Conviction data were only included for periods when self-report data were available, and two males were not interviewed at any of these five ages.

The percentages convicted among those who never admitted each offense were 3.8% for shoplifting, 2.5% for theft of vehicles, 1.9% for theft from vehicles and vandalism, 1.0% for theft from machines, 1.4% for theft from work, 1.6% for assault, and zero for drug use and fraud. These percentages do not necessarily indicate concealment in the self-reports, because of the problems of comparability mentioned earlier.

The phi correlations shown in Table 3 indicate that the relationship between self-reported and official offending was statistically significant for all offenses except theft from work, vandalism, and fraud. The phi correlation (the product-moment correlation between dichotomous variables) is used here as a measure of strength of association. It is simply related to chi-squared, since

$$\text{phi squared} = \text{chi-squared}/N.$$

However, unlike chi-squared, the phi correlation does not increase with the sample size. In general, a phi correlation of 0.10 or greater is statistically significant at 0.05 (two-tailed) in a sample of 400.

The main problem of interpretation with the phi correlation is that its maximum value is only 1.0 when the marginal totals of the two variables being compared are equal, and it falls increasingly below 1 as the two marginal totals differ. For example, in the case of

TABLE 3. PERCENTAGE OF OFFENDERS WHO WERE CONVICTED

Offense	Percent at Age (N)						Phi
	10-14	15-18	19-21	22-25	26-32	10-32	10-32
Burglary	26.4 (53)	66.0 (22)	45.5 (22)	87.5 (8)	64.3 (14)	53.6 (97)	0.58
Shoplifting	7.7 (168)	9.7 (62)	8.0 (25)	33.3 (9)	26.1 (23)	13.7 (205)	0.13
Theft of vehicle	30.3 (33)	54.3 (70)	51.9 (27)	85.7 (7)	40.0 (15)	53.4 (103)	0.58
Theft from vehicle	26.3 (38)	20.3 (59)	18.8 (16)	20.0 (5)	27.3 (11)	24.5 (94)	0.31
Theft from machine	6.5 (62)	6.7 (75)	0.0 (8)	0.0 (3)	28.6 (7)	7.3 (124)	0.12
Theft from work	0.0 (9)	*	14.5 (62)	0.0 (12)	1.1 (91)	7.4 (136)	0.09
Assault	1.9 (160)	7.3 (177)	12.4 (97)	20.0 (25)	11.9 (143)	12.8 (288)	0.17
Vandalism	0.0 (284)	10.7 (84)	18.2 (11)	66.7 (3)	66.7 (9)	5.9 (305)	0.07
Drug Use	0.0 (2)	1.6 (122)	10.5 (57)	18.8 (16)	5.5 (73)	7.1 (155)	0.21
Fraud	0.0 (291)	*	12.5 (24)	29.4 (17)	2.0 (200)	3.3 (337)	0.08
Any Theft**	21.2 (193)	44.7 (161)	40.6 (101)	56.7 (30)	21.7 (120)	36.8 (288)	0.33
Any Offense***	11.9 (360)	29.1 (265)	30.3 (152)	47.6 (42)	14.7 (278)	32.1 (392)	0.12

Note: * = No self-report data
** = Any Theft (Any of the first six listed here)
*** = Any Offense (of the ten listed here)

The number interviewed was 405 at age 14, 389 at age 18, 218 at age 21, 85 at age 25, and 378 at age 32.

burglary, with marginal totals of 89 admitting and 52 convicted, the maximum possible value of phi is 0.72. The actual phi value of 0.58 looks more impressive in comparison with this maximum possible value. Generally, in these analyses the maximum possible value of phi was about 0.500.60, suggesting that a phi correlation of 0.30 or greater indicated quite a strong relationship. As a rule of thumb, a phi correlation of 0.30 corresponds roughly to a 30% difference between the two percentages being compared.

More than half of those known for burglary and theft of vehicles were convicted of these offenses, in comparison with about a quarter of those known for theft from vehicles, and about one in eight of those known for shoplifting or assault. The lowest percentages convicted were for theft from machines, theft from work, drug use (all 7%), vandalism (6%), and fraud (3%). Consequently, it was not true in all cases that the self-reports identified far more offenders than the official records.

There was a clear tendency for the probability of conviction to be lowest at the youngest age, 10-14 (for eight out of ten offenses). This probability tended to be highest at age 22-25 (for seven out of ten offenses), but it has to be remembered that the subsample interviewed at this age included a high proportion of convicted recidivists (about half). Comparing only ages where the aim was to interview the whole sample, the probability of conviction was higher at age 15-18 than at age 10-14 (for seven out of eight offenses), and higher at age 26-32 than at age 15-18 (for six out of eight offenses). Therefore, it might be concluded that the probability of conviction increased with age, although another possible interpretation is that undetected offenders became increasingly less willing to self-report their offenses as they got older.

2.5. The Validity of Self-Reports

As indicated earlier, it is important to investigate how far the significant relationship (seen for most types of offenses) between self-reports and official convictions may be caused by the tendency of convictions to make people more willing to self-report. In order for this to happen, the first conviction for an offense would have to precede the first self-report of it. However, for all offenses showing significant phi correlations in Table 3, the first self-report was far more likely to precede the first conviction.

In the case of burglary, for example, 45 males were identified only by self-reports, 8 only by official convictions (during age ranges when self-reports were obtained), and 44 by both. Of the 44 identified by both, 26 were first identified in the same age range by both, 17 by self-reports first, and only one by official convictions first. This figure of 17 out of 18 identified first by self-reports for burglary can be compared with 8 out of 10 for shoplifting, 10 out of 14 for theft of vehicles, 5 out of 6 for theft from vehicles, 4 out of 5 for theft from machines, 26 out of 26 for assault, 9 out of 9 for drug use, 37 out of 46 for any theft, and 78 out of 81 for any offense. These results suggest that very little of the relationship between self-reports and official convictions can be attributable to any increased tendency to self-report following a conviction.

Perhaps the most important test of the validity of self-reports is the extent to which they predict future convictions among currently undetected people, as mentioned earlier. Table 4 shows the results obtained with 8 types of offenses self-reported at both ages 10-14 and 15-18. For example, among 357 males not convicted of burglary up to age 18, 20% of 40 who admitted burglary were subsequently convicted of it, in comparison with only 2% of 317 who denied burglary (X2 = 23.7, phi = 0.28, p < 0.001).

TABLE 4. Predictive validity of self-reports among unconvicted males.

Percent Convicted at 19-32

Offense	Self-Reported at 10-18	Denied at 10-18	Phi
Burglary	20.0 (40)	2.2 (317)	0.28
Shoplifting	3.5 (173)	2.9 (209)	0.02
Theft of Vehicle	9.8 (41)	2.9 (312)	0.12
Theft from Vehicle	9.7 (62)	1.3 (320)	0.19
Theft from Machines	0.9 (106)	0.7 (285)	0.01
Assault	9.8 (224)	5.0 (161)	0.09
Vandalism	3.4 (290)	1.0 (100)	0.06
Drug Use	7.6 (119)	0.0 (278)	0.23
Any Theft*	10.6 (170)	6.8 (147)	0.07
Any Offense**	14.1 (284)	0.0 (23)	0.11

Note: Based on those not convicted of the offense at 10-18.
** = Any Theft
*** = Any Offense

In addition to burglary, self-reports of theft of vehicles, theft from vehicles, and drug use significantly predicted future convictions for the same type of offense. However, the other offense types did not show the same specific predictive validity. The admission of any offense had some predictive validity; none of the 23 males who denied all offenses was subsequently convicted of any offense, suggesting that they were telling the truth. In general, none of the tests of the validity of self-reports carried out in this project indicated that they were seriously invalid or that there was any serious problem of deliberate distortion or concealment.

410

2.6. Inter-Relationships of Types of Offenses

Table 5 shows the extent to which different types of offending were inter-related, according to self-reports (in the top right-hand part of the table) and official convictions (in the bottom left-hand part). These figures are based on offenses committed between ages 10 and 32. For example, 61.8 percent of the 89 males who admitted burglary at some stage also admitted theft from vehicles, in comparison with 10.3 percent of the 320 males who never admitted burglary, a highly significant relationship ($X2 = 106.2$, $p < 0.001$, phi = 0.52). Again, 54.4% of the 57 males who were convicted of burglary at some stage were also convicted of theft of vehicles, in comparison with 8.1% of the 346 males who were never convicted of burglary, a highly significant relationship ($X2 = 80.3$, $p < 0.001$, phi = 0.46). The number of convicted burglars here is 57 rather than the previous figure of 52, because all convictions for burglary were included in Table 5, not just those occurring in age ranges for which there were self-reports.

Generally, inter-relationships were stronger in self-reports than in official convictions. The average phi correlation was 0.26 for self-reports and 0.18 for official convictions. This difference was not a function of maximum phi correlations, because the average maximum phi was lower for self-reports (0.53) than for official convictions (0.64). All the phi correlations for self-reports were positive and greater than 0.10 and hence statistically significant. However, 11 of the 45 phi correlations for official convictions were less than 0.10, and two of these were (slightly) negative. The average phi correlations show that there was considerable versatility in offending. The average may have been higher for self-reports because of a common response bias (e.g., willingness to admit) affecting all items.

In self-reports, the first five theft offenses (all except theft from work) were quite strongly inter-related. The only other phi correlations of 0.30 or greater were between assault and vandalism, assault and drug use, and burglary and drug use. The weakest relationships were those involving theft from work, drug use, and fraud. In official convictions, the strongest relationships were those involving burglary, theft of vehicles, and assault, while the weakest relationships were those involving shoplifting, theft from machines, theft from work, vandalism, and drug use. The phi values for self-reports were significantly correlated with those for official convictions ($r = 0.48$, $p < 0.001$), showing that offenses which were strongly inter-related in self-reports also tended to be strongly inter-related in official convictions (and vice versa for weak inter-relationships). This result supports the proposal that self-reports and official records both measure the same underlying theoretical constructs, although with different measurement biases.

2.7. Offending from One Age to Another

Table 5 essentially shows two static correlation matrices; that is, matrices in which all variables refer to the same age range. Longitudinal projects are useful in constructing dynamic correlation matri-

TABLE 5. Inter-relationships of self-reported and official offenses.

Offense	Burg-lary (89)	Shop-lifting (197)	Theft of Vehicle (95)	Theft from Vehicle (88)	Theft from Machine (121)	Theft from Work (132)	Assault (286)	Vandalism (303)	Drug Use (155)	Fraud (337)
Burglary (57)	X	27	51	52	39	21	27	27	33	20
Shoplifting(30)	24	X	22	38	27	26	25	28	22	24
Theft of Vehicle(59)	46	20	X	49	37	24	22	22	20	18
Theft from Vehicle(27)	35	15	28	X	35	27	27	23	20	18
Theft from Machine(11)	24	07	19	14	X	19	20	18	19	24
Theft from Work(15)	26	09	14	16	13	X	22	24	16	17
Assault(44)	34	26	37	19	09	27	X	31	30	23
Vandalism(20)	07	07	23	12	-04	08	14	X	14	27
Drug Use(11)	24	24	19	02	-03	05	23	17	X	22
Fraud(23)	21	17	26	15	16	06	22	09	22	X

Note: Figures show phi correlations x 100. Top right figures show intercorrelations of self-reported offenses. Bottom left figures show intercorrelations of official offenses. Numbers of offenders in parentheses.

ces, relating variables measured in one age range to variables measured in another. For example, Wolfang, Figlio, and Sellin (1972) published transition matrices showing how types of arrests at one age were related to types of arrests at the next age. In the present project, three transition matrices of phi correlations were constructed from self-reports, relating types of offenses at 10-14 and 15-18, types at 15-18 and 19-21, and types at 19-21 and 26-32. Matrices involving age 22-25 were not constructed because of the small number of males interviewed at this age (85).

Table 6 shows the average of the three transition matrices. It is noteworthy that all average phi correlations shown in this table are positive, and the majority (61 out of the 100 in the main 10 x 10 offense type matrix) are 0.10 or greater. Therefore, it can be concluded that there was significant continuity and versatility in self-reported offending.

The largest average phi correlation by far (0.48) was for the transition from drug use at one age to drug use at the next age. This average was based on only two phi correlations, because the number admitting drug use at age 14 was too small to calculate a phi correlation between 14 and 18. Of 88 admitting drug use at 18, 51.1% also admitted drug use at 21, in comparison with 9.3% of 129 who denied drug use at 18 (phi = 0.47, p < 0.001; based on 217 interviewed at both 18 and 21). Of 54 admitting drug use at 21, 66.7% also admitted drug use at 32, in comparison with 15.5% of 155 who denied drug use at 21 (phi = 0.50, p < 0.001; based on 209 interviewed at both 21 and 32).

In several cases, the phi correlation for the transition from one type of offense to the same type of offense at the next age was the highest or nearly the highest of all correlations in a row, indicating some degree of specialization in offending superimposed on the general versatility. This was particularly noticeable for drug use, as indicated above. It was also true for assault (phi = 0.29) theft from work (0.24), burglary (0.23), and theft from vehicles (0.21), and these five offenses were the most specialized. The best predictor of a future theft offense, surprisingly, was a current fraud offense (0.21), and the worst predictor was a current vandalism offense (0.08). The best predictor of any offense in the future was a current assault (0.23), closely followed by current drug use (0.21).

It is not possible to construct exactly comparable transition matrices for official convictions, because of the very small numbers of some types of offenses. Table 7 shows the matrix relating convictions at age 10-18 to convictions at age 19-32. Three offenses (theft from work, drug use, and fraud) have been deleted at age 10-18 because of small numbers, and one offense (theft from machines) at age 19-32 for the same reason. Most of the phi correlations in the main 7 x 9 offense type matrix are positive (53 out of 63), and about half (35) are 0.10 or greater. Therefore, this official conviction matrix also shows continuity and versatility in offending.

The largest phi correlation (0.34) was for the transition from burglary at age 10-18 to burglary at age 19-32. One-third of the 42 males convicted of burglary at 10-18 were also convicted of burglary at 19-32, in comparison with 4.2% of the 361 unconvicted males (X2 = 43.7,

TABLE 6. Average age to age transition matrix for self-reports.

Second Age

First Age Offense	Burglary	Shop-lifting	Theft of Vehicle	Theft from Vehicle	Theft from Machines	Theft from Work	Assault from	Vandalism	Drug Use	Fraud	Any Theft	Any Offense
Burglary	23	14	16	21	14	11	20	13	23	04	16	14
Shop-lifting	09	17	09	18	03	16	12	08	15	12	15	13
Theft of Vehicle	24	03	16	19	07	10	16	10	11	09	14	13
Theft from Vehicle	21	16	10	21	09	11	15	11	13	02	18	13
Theft from Machine	15	05	09	06	09	09	10	09	15	06	14	13
Theft from Work	10	03	07	17	10	24	09	13	11	19	13	12
Assault	10	10	15	14	09	15	29	08	16	09	16	23
Vandalism	09	05	03	02	04	07	10	09	14	09	08	12
Drug Use	17	22	13	12	22	02	08	03	48	17	11	21
Fraud	07	12	07	11	14	19	11	08	09	09	21	13

Note: Figures show phi correlations x 100.

413

TABLE 7. Transition matrix for official convictions.

Convictions 10-18	Convictions 19-32										
	Burglary	Shop-lifting	Theft of Vehicle	Theft from Vehicle	Theft from Work	Assault	Vandal-ism	Drug Use	Fraud	Any Theft	Any Offense
Burglary	34	16	31	23	08	21	-01	26	15	37	34
Shoplifting	17	09	09	10	10	23	-04	04	07	14	19
Theft of Vehicle	32	19	32	21	07	22	18	24	21	36	42
Theft from Vehicle	-01	03	10	11	11	06	-04	-03	13	11	11
Theft from Machine	17	-03	18	08	-01	08	-02	-02	05	13	13
Assault	31	26	23	13	05	23	05	14	15	29	27
Vandalism	09	06	03	17	07	13	-03	08	13	07	15

Note: Figures show phi correlations x 100.

p < 0.001, phi = 0.34; excluding eight dead males). Other large phi correlations were for theft of vehicles to theft of vehicles, theft of vehicles to burglary, burglary to theft of vehicles, and assault to burglary. Apart from burglary and theft of vehicles, there was little sign of any specialization in official offending. Burglary and theft of vehicles were the best predictors of a future theft conviction and of a future conviction for any offense. Of 46 males convicted of theft of vehicles at age 10-18, 73.9% were convicted of an offense at 19-32, in comparison with 17.6% of the remaining 357 males (X2 = 67.5, p < 0.001, phi = 0.42).

Remarkably, the average phi correlation in Table 7 for official convictions was the same as the average phi correlation in Table 6 for self-reports, at 0.12 (comparing the 63 transitions in the 7 x 9 matrix of Table 7). Furthermore, the official and self-report phi values were significantly correlated (r = 0.34, p < 0.004, one-tailed), showing that offense transitions that were very likely in official convictions also tended to be very likely in self-reports (and vice versa for unlikely transitions).

Self-reports at age 10-18 were almost as good as convictions at age 10-18 in predicting future convictions for the same type of offense at age 19-32. For six offenses that could be compared (burglary, shoplifting, theft of vehicles, theft from vehicles, assault, and vandalism), the average phi correlation was 0.18 for convictions at 10-18 and 0.17 for self-reports at 10-18. As was the case for convictions, burglary was the type of offense that was predicted best by self-reports. Of 73 males admitting burglary at 10-18, 27.4 % were convicted of it at 19-32, in comparison with 2.8% of 326 males denying burglary at 10-18 (X2 = 50.1, p < 0.001, phi = 0.37). Self-reports also showed specific predictability for theft from vehicles (phi = 0.22) and theft of vehicles (phi = 0.21).

2.8. The Validity of Long-Term Retrospective Self-Reports

All self-reports are retrospective to some extent, of course, in that they provide information about offending during a certain prior time period. However, the self-reports collected in this project generally referred to a relatively short time period. They are also prospective, in the sense that they were obtained before key outcomes of interest were known, such as later convictions. In principle, long-term self-reports of the whole offending career could have been obtained retrospectively in one interview at age 32, rather than in repeated interviews. This approach was adopted, for example, by Petersilia, Greenwood, and Lavin (1978) in their survey of prisoners. It is important to investigate whether long-term retrospective self-reports of offending could provide the same information as in a prospective longitudinal survey.

When the sample males were interviewed at age 32, they were asked not only whether they had committed each offense in the last five years but also (in the case of eight of the ten offenses) whether they had ever committed it. The left-hand side of Table 8 shows, for those who had previously admitted each offense at ages 14, 18, 21, or 25, the percentage who said at age 32 that they had <u>never</u> committed it. For example, of 81 males who had admitted burglary in at least one of the first four interviews, 7.4% at age 32 said that they had done it in the last five years, another 49.4% said that they had ever done it, and 43.2% said that they had never done it. Over all eight offenses, an average of 46% of previous admitters denied the offense at age 32. This is surprising, since most of these males knew that they had been asked these kinds of questions before, and hence might have been more willing to admit than participants in a one-off cross-sectional survey. It can be concluded that long-term retrospective self-reports fail to detect many offenders identified in prospective self-reports.

TABLE 8. Validity of retrospective self-reports.

Offense	Percent Admitting at 10-25 Who Say at 32:			Percent Convicted 10-32: At 32, Who say Not in Last 5 Years				
	Never	Ever	Last 5	NE,NC	NE,YC	YE,NC	YE,YC	Last 5
Burglary	43.2 (81)	49.4	7.4	2.5 (275)	31.4 (35)	11.8 (17)	70.0 (40)	66.7 (9)
Shop- lifting	33.2 (187)	56.7	10.2	1.7 (116)	6.5 (62)	5.6 (71)	9.4 (106)	28.6 (21)
Theft of vehicle	40.5 (84)	51.2	8.3	1.9 (266)	20.6 (34)	22.7 (22)	74.4 (43)	45.5 (11)
Theft from vehicle	53.8 (78)	41.0	5.1	2.2 (275)	14.3 (42)	15.8 (19)	34.4 (32)	0.0 (8)
Theft from machine	59.5 (111)	36.9	3.6	0.0 (235)	3.0 (66)	10.7 (28)	7.3 (41)	16.7 (6)
Theft from work	28.2 (71)	26.8	45.1	1.5 (201)	0.0 (20)	4.4 (45)	10.5 (19)	7.7 (91)
Vandalism	74.8 (286)	23.8	1.4	1.3 (76)	4.7 (214)	7.1 (14)	8.8 (68)	50.0 (4)
Fraud	32.3 (282)	10.6	57.1	0.0 (48)	6.6 (91)	0.0 (9)	3.3 (30)	6.6 (198)

Note:　Last 5　　= In last 5 years (at 32). Numbers in parentheses.
　　　　NE　　　 = No, Ever (32)
　　　　YE　　　 = Yes, Ever (32)
　　　　NC　　　 = No, Cumulative (10-25)
　　　　YC　　　 = Yes, Cumulative (10-25)

This does not, however, mean that long-term retrospective self-reports have no value. On the contrary, they can be a useful supplement to prospective self-reports, especially when (as in the present project) the prospective data includes some missing age ranges. The right-hand side of Table 8 divides the 376 males interviewed at age 32 and with previous self-report data into those who admitted committing the offense in the last five years and the remainder. The remainder are then divided into four categories:

    a) says he has never done it at 32, no previous admission (NE, NC);

    b) says he has never done it at 32, but previous admission (NE, YC);

    c) says he has ever done it at 32, but no previous admission (YE, NC); and

    d) says he has ever done it at 32, and previous admission (YE, YC).

For example, in the case of burglary, 275 males were in the (NE, NC) category, 35 in the (NE, YC) category, 17 in the (YE, NC) category, 40 in the (YE, YC) category, and 9 admitted burglary in the last five years.

If the "ever" admissions were truthful, the percentage convicted of the offense should be greater in the (YE, NC) category than in the (NE, NC) category. This expectation was indeed confirmed for seven out of eight offenses, and the comparison in the eighth case (fraud) was made unreliable by small numbers. The average percentage convicted was 9.8 in (YE, NC) and 1.4 in (NE, NC). Furthermore, since admissions from two sources should identify an offender more reliably than admissions from only one source, the percentage convicted of the offense should be greater in the (YE, YC) category than in the (NE, YC) category. This expectation was also confirmed in seven out of eight cases (again, all except fraud). The average percentage convicted was 27.3 in (YE, YC) and 10.9 in (NE, YC). Hence, while "ever" questions are not an adequate substitute for repeated prospective self-reports in investigating prevalence, they might be a useful supplement.

3. CONCLUSIONS

Self-reported offending and official convictions show that burglary, shoplifting, theft of and from vehicles, and theft from slot machines declined in prevalence from the teenage years into the twenties and thirties. Similar declines were not seen for theft from work, assault, drug use and fraud. These results suggest that the relationship between age and crime should be studied for specific types of offenses, since it is not the same for all types. The cumulative prevalence of self-reported offending was very high, showing that, at least in this sample of urban working-class males, many types of offending were not statistically very deviant. Even for official convictions, the cumulative prevalence of three types of offending exceeded 10%, and one-third of the males were convicted of at least one of the ten types of offenses studied.

The relationship between self-reported offending and official convictions was strongest for burglary and for theft of and from vehicles, but it was also significant for shoplifting, theft from machines, assault, and drug use. The two measures were not significantly related for theft from work, vandalism, and fraud. When data were cumulated over the whole period between ages 10 and 32, the probability of an offender being convicted was quite high for several types of offenses: over 50% for burglary and theft of vehicles, and 25% for theft from vehicles. The probability of conviction increased with age.

Generally, the first self-report of an offense preceded the first conviction for it, suggesting that very little of the relationship between self-reported and official offending could be attributed to any tendency for convictions to make people more willing to self-report. For burglary, theft of and from vehicles, and drug use, self-reports of offending among unconvicted males significantly predicted future convictions for these offenses, suggesting that self-reports provided valid information about offending.

Most types of offending were significantly inter-related, suggesting that all types reflected the same general underlying construct to some degree. This construct might variously be termed "delinquency potential" or "antisocial tendency." The relationships in self-reports were stronger than in official convictions, although the pattern of relationships was similar in both. This similar patterning again indicated that self-reports and official convictions both measured the same underlying constructs (although with different measurement biases).

Transition matrices showing the relationship between offending at one age and offending at a later age suggested that there was significant versatility and continuity in offending. However, there was also some degree of specialization, especially in drug use, assault, theft from work, burglary, and theft of and from vehicles. The relationships between one age and another were equally strong in self-reports and official records, and the pattern of relationships in both were similar. Again, these transition matrices indicated that self-reports and official convictions measured the same underlying constructs.

In developing and testing explanations of offending, it is important to have adequate measures of offending, and to document changes in offending with age. This chapter suggests that self-reports and official convictions produce comparable and complementary results on such important topics as prevalence, continuity, versatility, and specialization in different types of offenses. Both measures seem valuable in advancing knowledge about delinquency and crime.

APPENDIX

WORDINGS OF ACTS AT DIFFERENT AGES

Burglary

14:    (a)   Breaking into a big store, garage, warehouse, pavilion.

        (b)   Breaking into a small shop, whether or not anything was stolen.

        (c)   Getting into a house, flat (etc.) and stealing things.

18, 21, 25, 32: Breaking and entering and then stealing something.

Shoplifting

14:    (a)   Stealing things from big stores, supermarkets, multiple shops (while shop open).
        (b)   Stealing things from small shops or private tradesmen (while shop open).

18, 21, 25, 32:   Shoplifting from shops, market stalls, stores, supermarkets (etc.).

Theft of Vehicles

14:    Taking an unknown person's car or motorbike for joy-riding.

18, 21, 25, 32:   Driving a car, van, motorbike, scooter (etc.) that has   been taken without the owner's permission.

Theft from Vehicles

14:    Stealing things out of cars.
18, 21, 25, 32:   Stealing from parked cars, vans, trucks (etc.).

Theft from Machines

14:    Stealing goods or money from slot machines, juke boxes, telephones (etc.).

18, 21, 25, 32:   Stealing from slot machines, such as gas or electricity meters, parking meters, telephone boxes, cigarette machines.

Theft from Work

14: Stealing tools, materials or any other goods worth 50p or more from employers in working hours. (Do not count breaking in here.)

21, 25, 32: Stealing goods, money, tools, or any other things from work worth L5.00 or more altogether.

Assault

14: (a) Belonging to a group of 10 or more people who go around together, make a noise, and sometimes get into fights or cause a disturbance.

(b) Annoying, insulting, or fighting other people (strangers) in the street.

(c) Attacking an enemy or someone in a rival gang (without using a weapon) in a public place.

(d) Using any kind of weapon in a fight - knife, cosh, razor, broken bottle (etc.).

(e) Struggling or fighting to get away from a policeman.

(f) Attacking or fighting a policeman who is trying to arrest someone else.

18: (a) Started (i.e., struck the first blow) a fight (i.e., an aggressive incident in which at least one blow was deliberately aimed at and hit another person).

(b) Used a weapon (such as a knife, broken bottle, bicycle chain, belt, etc.) in a fight.

21, 25, 32: Involved in a fight (defined above, but excluding being a victim of mugging and fights in the course of work as police officers, prison officers, or security guards).

Vandalism

14: (a) Smashing, slashing, or damaging things in public places - in streets, cinemas, dance halls, railway carriages, buses.

(b) Breaking windows of empty houses.

18, 21, 25, 32: Deliberately damaging property, such as telephone boxes, cars, windows, etc. (without stealing anything).

Drug Use

14: Taking illegal drugs like purple hearts or smoking reefers.

18: Taking drugs such as pep pills, sleeping pills, marijuana, LSD, heroin (etc.).

21, 25: Taking drugs such as speed, marijuana, LSD, heroin, mandrax, methadone, barbiturates, poppers.

32: Taking drugs such as marijuana (dope), heroin (smack), cocaine (coke), amphetamine (speed, sulphate, uppers), barbiturates (downers), LSD (acid), magic mushrooms, amyl nitrite (poppers), solvents (glue), etc.

Fraud

14: (a) Deliberately traveling without a ticket or paying the wrong fare.

(b) Obtaining money by false pretenses.

21: Obtaining money from the government, such as unemployment or sickness benefit, by telling lies.

24: (a) Obtaining money from the government, such as unemployment or sickness benefit, by telling lies.
(b) Avoiding tax illegally.

32: (a) Obtaining money from the government, such as unemployment or sickness benefit, by telling lies.

(b) Not admitting some earnings on which tax should have been paid.

(c) Stealing someone else's check, giro, or credit card and obtaining money with it.

REFERENCES

Bachman, JG, O'Malley, PM, & Johnston, J: Youth in transition, vol.6. Ann Arbor, MI: University of Michigan Institute for Social Research, 1978.
Blumstein, A, Cohen, J, & Farrington, DP: Criminal career research: Its value for criminology. Criminology, 26:1-35, 1988.
Cernkovich, SA, Giordano, PC, & Pugh, MD: Chronic offenders: The missing cases in self-report delinquency research. Journal of Criminal Law and Criminology, 76:705-32, 1985.

422

Dunford, FW, & Elliott, DS: Identifying career offenders using self-reported data. _Journal of Research in Crime and Delinquency_, 21:57-86, 1984.

Elliott, DS, Huizinga, D, & Menard, S: _Multiple problem youth_. New York: Springer-Verlag, in press (1989).

Farrington, DP: Self-reports of deviant behavior: Predictive and stable? _Journal of Criminal Law and Criminology_, 64:99-110, 1973.

Farrington, DP: The effects of public labeling. _British Journal of Criminology_, 17:112-25, 1977.

Farrington, DP: Offending from 10 to 25 years of age. In Van Dusen, KT, & Mednick, SA (Eds.), _Prospective studies of crime and delinquency_ (pp.17-37). Boston: Kluwer-Nijhoff, 1983.

Farrington, DP: Age and crime. In Tonry, M, & Morris, N (Eds.), _Crime and justice, vol.7_ (pp. 189-250). Chicago: University of Chicago Press, 1986.

Farrington, DP: Later adult life outcomes of offenders and non-offenders. In Brambring, M, Losel, F, & Skowronek, H (Eds.), _Children at risk_. Berlin: De Gruyter, in press (1989).

Farrington, DP, Gallagher, B, Morley, L, St. Ledger, R, & West, DJ: Minimizing attrition in longitudinal research: Methods of tracing and securing cooperation in a 24-year longitudinal study. In Magnusson, D, & Bergman, L (Eds.), _Methodology of longitudinal research_. Cambridge, England: Cambridge University Press, in press (1989).

Farrington, DP, Snyder, HS, & Finnegan, TA: Specialization in juvenile court careers. _Criminology_, 26:461-87, 1988.

Farrington, DP, & West, DJ: The Cambridge study in delinquent development. In Mednick, SA, & Baert, AE, (Eds.), _Prospective longitudinal research_ (pp. 137-45). Oxford, England: Oxford University Press, 1981.

Gottfredson, M, & Hirschi, T: Science, public policy, and the career paradigm. _Criminology_, 25:37-55, 1988.

Hindelang, MJ, Hirschi, T, & Weis, JG: _Measuring delinquency_. Beverly Hills, CA: Sage Publications, 1981.

Huizinga, D, & Elliott, DS: Reassessing the reliability and validity of self-report delinquency measures. _Journal of Quantitative Criminology_, 2:293-327, 1986.

Langan, PA, & Farrington, DP: Two-track or one-track justice? Some evidence from an English longitudinal survey. _Journal of Criminal Law and Criminology_, 74, 519-46, 1983.

Le Blanc, M, & Frechette, M: _Male criminal activity from childhood through youth_. New York: Springer-Verlag, in press (1989).

Petersilia, J, Greenwood, PW, & Lavin, M: _Criminal careers of habitual felons_. Washington, DC: National Institute of Law Enforcement and Criminal Justice, 1978.

Rankin, JH, & Wells, LE: From status to delinquent offenses: Specialization? _Journal of Criminal Justice_, 13:171-80, 1985.

West, DJ: _Present conduct and future delinquency_. London: Heinemann, 1969.

West, DJ: Delinquency: Its roots, careers, and prospects. London:
     Heinemann, 1982.
West, DJ, & Farrington, DP: Who becomes delinquent? London: Heine-
     mann. 1973.
West, DJ, & Farrington, DP: The delinquent way of life. London:
     Heinemann, 1977.
Williams, JR, & Gold, M: From delinquent behavior to official delin-
     quency. Social Problems, 20:209-29, 1972.
Wolfgang, ME, Figlio, RM, & Sellin, T: Delinquency in a birth cohort.
     Chicago: University of Chicago Press, 1972.

EPILOGUE: WORKSHOP DISCUSSIONS AND FUTURE DIRECTIONS

Malcolm W. Klein
Center for Research in Crime and Social Control
University of Southern California

1. INTRODUCTION

The preceding papers were written in preparation for the workshop. For the purposes of a published volume like this, they can stand alone as contributions to the growing literature on self-report approaches to crime and delinquency, and particularly to the relatively sparse literature on comparative criminology. However, for the workshop participants these papers and others not included in this volume served another function. Distributed and read by all participants prior to the workshop, they were supplemented by first-day technical presentations on recent advances in self-report technology (Elliott), measurement issues (Olweus), issues of comparative legal codes (Albrecht), and longitudinal considerations (Le Blanc). Together, the papers and presentations made it possible to provide a common core of knowledge and concepts for a highly diverse set of scholars.

In plenary sessions, in work groups, and in informal gatherings over four days, this sharing of prior information yielded highly focussed discussions and a minimum of irrelevant comment. Further, there was a remarkable sharing of discussion and participation opportunities. A total of sixteen casette tapes with ninety minutes of material each attests to the value of the plenary sessions. Short of having the reader listen to each of these, I can only provide in the pages to follow a brief summary of some of the more salient of the points discussed. And since the workshop also appears to have initiated an unplanned follow-up process, this too will be described.

I find it both providential and comforting that the presidential address at the 1987 meeting of the American Sociological Association should have been on the topic, "Cross-National Research as an Analytic Strategy" (Kohn, 1987). In his remarks, President Kohn cited the comment from William Form that "probably no field has generated more methodological advice on a smaller data base with fewer results than has [cross-national] comparative sociology." Kohn then noted several costs and difficulties in doing such research:

. Obtaining financial support is very frustrating. The NATO workshop is certainly an example, although eventually we were successful.

425

M. W. Klein (ed.), Cross-National Research in Self-Reported Crime and Delinquency, 425–438.
© *1989 by Kluwer Academic Publishers.*

426

Nonetheless, workshop participants were to spend some time on this
problem.

. Establishing enduring collaborative relationships is even more
difficult. Again, the workshop was an opportunity to foster these, and
as will be described at the end of this chapter, unexpected but material steps in this direction have resulted.

. There are numerous methodological gaps and interferences of an
unusual sort -- a sort not normally encountered by non-comparative
researchers. Certainly the NATO workshop reviewed many instances of
these, and found them mostly challenging but not insurmountable.

Judging from these three problems above, workshop participants
found themselves in the midst of some common experiences of a host of
other scholars. In particular, three broad categories of impediments
to progress received major attention, and these will be covered below:
the low prevalence of past self-report studies, technical problems
exacerbated by cross-national research, and issues on which consensus
was difficult to reach.

2. SELF-REPORT STUDIES IN FIFTEEN NATIONS

Workshop participants from a number of nations reported a discour-
agingly low level of self-report work. These included Martin Killias
for Switzerland, Uberto Gatti for Italy, Anastasios Marcos for Greece,
Amelia Diaz Martinez for Spain, and Haluk Yavuzer for Turkey. Little
was reported for France, Denmark (but Fleming Balvig is a solid exception there), Norway (with the notable exception of Olweus), and Sweden
(with the exception of Sarnecki). In Stockholm, the directors of Project Metropolitan have eschewed self-report methods for that country,
and this seems to have discouraged others.

For Belgium, van Kerckwoorde reported the existence of several
small studies. Le Blanc reported for Canada some coordinated work in
French Canada, but nothing on a national scale. The Home Office study
reported by Shaw and Riley was said to be the first national study for
England, but of course, the longitudinal studies of Wadsworth and particularly of West and Farrington have been major contributions, even
though based on very restricted cohorts.

For Germany, workshop participants were in some disagreement as to
how much self-report work has been carried out. The ensuing discussion
revealed a number of small studies, but seemingly with little coordination. Unlike the work in most countries, the German examples were
cited as being particularly driven by theory-testing interests.

Of all the European countries, Holland has perhaps exhibited the
greatest level of activity. The roots for this seem to lie at least in
part in the influence of Professor Wouter Buikhuizen, currently at
Leiden University, and the staff of the Research and Documentation
Center (W.O.D.C.) of the Dutch Ministry of Justice. National studies,
longitudinal work, and methodological developments can all be found in
the Dutch work. Certainly it was fitting that the workshop was located
in Holland and co-hosted by the W.O.D.C.

The United States, not surprisingly, has reported by far the

largest number of self-report studies, for reasons noted in the introductory chapter to this volume. In addition to many relatively uncoor-
dinated regional studies and program evaluations, there have been major
focussed attempts to refine self-report procedures (Hindelang, Hirschi,
& Weis, 1981; Elliott and his colleagues in numerous papers -- see the
contributions in Part II). Finally, the U.S. has now seen the completion of three nationwide panel studies (Gold and Reimer, 1975; Bachman
et al., the Monitoring of the Future Project with reports on high
school seniors every year, e.g., 1978; and the National Youth Survey --
see e.g., Elliott & Huizinga, 1987).

        With the exceptions of the U.S., Holland, and perhaps Germany,
none of these countries (or any others of which we are aware) has a
solid history of self-report development or usage. Thus the workshop
suffered to some extent from a knowledge deficit, and 40-plus participants leaned heavily on the practical experience of perhaps a dozen of
their colleagues. Additionally, it must be noted in particular that
specifically cross-national experience was almost non-existent.[1] Any
developments in this direction by workshop participants would thus
represent a quantum leap, a revelation that led to a great deal of
enthusiasm and some trepidation among them.

3. TECHNICAL PROBLEMS FOR CROSS-NATIONAL STUDIES

3.1. Definitions

        Issues under this heading included the most fundamental: can a
common definition of a delinquent or criminal act be accepted for the
use of a self-report instrument applied to several countries? For
practical purposes, there emerged among the participants some consensus
on Elliott's usage of an act for which detection by the police would
likely lead to arrest. However, the loss of minor offenses and awareness of variability in police response were acknowledged as confounding
problems with this definition.

3.2. Legal Parallels

        Both Albrecht and Elliott stressed the importance of using items
on the self-report instrument that would, in their terminology and
referents, parallel as closely as possible their analogs in the penal
code. This is required to maximize comparison of self-report and official data. But differences between penal codes makes this process a
bit problematic for comparative researchers. One compromise suggestion
was offered by Moffitt, employing country-relevant seriousness weights
for each item to obtain comparability (see her paper in Part I).

----

1. Bondeson reported to the workshop an attempt by a number of
Scandinavian researchers to develop and use common self-report instruments
in the 1960s. She also reported the exercise to be an overall failure
because the studies ended up non-comparable (see Christie, Andanaes, &
Skirbekk, 1965; Antilla, 1966; Greve, 1974; Hauge, 1983).

3.3. Trivial Offenses

Trivial offenses are handled quite differently across countries. For example, juvenile status offenses such as runaway, alcohol use, incorrigibility, and habitual truancy are treated in effect as delinquencies justifying arrest and court disposition in many states in the U.S. In most European countries, they are not. In some countries they may be viewed simply as norm violations or minor deviance. In low-crime countries (cf. Moffitt), the minor offenses may be required on self-report instruments in order to obtain enough data; in high-crime countries, they may seem irrelevant. Olweus' "bullying" behavior in Scandinavia, or hitting one's sibling in the U.S., may be seen as assaultive behavior by one researcher, and mere childhood "testing" behavior by another. The first would be inclined to include such items, the second to exclude them, in a common instrument.

3.4. Common Appearance and Meaning

Bicycle theft is common in many nations, but in the U.S. it is a minor offense, while in China, Holland, and other countries it is treated seriously, for the bicycle is a major form of transportation in those countries. In the U.S., carrying knives as concealed weapons can land many a youth in trouble with the law. In Switzerland, Killias reported the Swiss army knife is ubiquitous; as a concealed weapon, it would flood the jails with juvenile "delinquents." These and other examples led the workshop participants to a consensus on an instrument with common (cross-national) "core items" to be supplemented by nation-specific items.

3.5. Non-Common Changes Over Time

Patterns of crime and delinquency change over time, as do their definitions and responses to them. Such changes that are slow to develop or common across countries present no problem. But rapid or uneven changes can easily disrupt comparative descriptions. A fine example can be found in drug use patterns -- also drug distribution patterns. Marcos reported to the workshop that norms for drug use also changed rapidly in Greece, affecting his comparisons of Greek and U.S. drug use patterns. The rapid explosion of cocaine "crack" in the U.S. endangers any comparisons with that country. The moral for comparative researchers is that they must first ascertain, prior to instrumentation, any rapidly developing offense pattern.

3.6. Non-Common Sanctions

Some nations are generally more punitive than others, and some clearly differ with respect to specific offenses (drug-dealing, again, being a good example). With the understanding that sanctions are conceptually linked to the meaning of offense behaviors, workshop participants agreed that follow-up questions to self-report admissions should include the official response to the admitted act.

3.7. The Age Variable

Age intervenes in the measurement process in more than one way. Some offense items are not appropriate to young respondents -- e.g., fraud, forcible rape -- and others are not appropriate to older respondents -- e.g., liquor violations, illicit sex. Cross-national studies that apply to different age groups will have to avoid nonage-comparable offense items. Another age problem has to do with response validity. Loeber reports on failure of younger respondents to understand the meaning of some offenses, and Junger-Tas among others noted a greater tendency to under-reporting among adult respondents. Olweus and Loeber both commented on the low base rates of many offenses for younger respondents. What is called for, in each case, is careful attention to age comparability in comparative research.

3.8. Research Goals

Early in the workshop, a distinction was made between ecological and descriptive research, theory-testing research, and program or policy evaluation research. The three goals have major implications for study design, sampling, interests in prevalence vs. individual offending rates, and so on. Workshop participants were not uniformly interested in the three goal orientations, so understandably there was concern for which kind of cross-national research might be undertaken. Consensus emerged that the first goal should be the descriptive one, bringing us to the point of being able to compare self-reported delinquency and crime across national borders. If this could be accomplished, then the application of the new instrumentation should represent a lesser problem.

3.9. The Funding Problem

Far more than studies employing officially recorded offenses, self-report studies can be quite costly. Most countries devote little public funding to criminological research. These two factors alone have restricted the amount of self-report measurement more than the technique would seem to warrant. Further, following the lead in the U.S., a number of countries such as England, Switzerland, and Holland are investing their meager research resources in victimization studies. Thus some workshop participants such as Martin Killias and Jan van Dijk warned their colleagues of the incipient competition that would face an attempt at major cross-national self-report research. Their suggestion was to combine the two approaches, using common samples. The victimization approach currently has more governmental support, so some forms of compromise might be to the benefit of self-report researchers. Also, approaches to multi-national funding were discussed.[2] What is needed,

----

2. Coincidentally, James K. Stewart, Director of the U.S. National Institute of Justice, included in his remarks to a 1988 working luncheon of invitees at the American Society of Criminology the willingness to entertain the funding of the American portion (only) of comparative research ventures.

as suggested by Margaret Shaw and endorsed by others, was the development of a convincing "sales pitch" to open the door in the justice ministries of the various nations involved. The advantages inherent in self-report methods, and the recent advances in methodology, are not immediately apparent to policy makers.

4. PROBLEMS OF CONSENSUS

Certainly it is not possible to bring together some 40 scholars from 15 nations, focus their attention on a common, complex problem, and expect full consensus on all issues. Thus while the workshop did indeed yield a great deal of consensus on a broad cafeteria of issues, some points remained unresolved. It seems useful at this point to enumerate the more obvious of these in order to keep the dialogue alive.

4.1. The State of the Art

I noted earlier that during the workshop a good deal of enthusiasm developed over the possibilities of initiating some genuine cross-national research in the near future. Indeed, participants soon divided into two friendly camps, the enthusiasts for immediate development of a major study and the cautious members who emphasized the need for a program of instrument development and pilot studies. Both groups favored the eventual goal of fostering comparative studies with a common instrument, but differed as to how much further preliminary work was required. As will be noted in the final section of this chapter, the enthusiasts seem for the time being to have won the day.

4.2. Comparative Samples

Depending in part on their preferences for descriptive versus theory-testing goals, workshop participants argued for different approaches to establishing the samples for cross-national comparisons. The four major alternatives were:
    a. Nationally-representative probability samples;
    b. Purposive or "typical" samples, such as might represent "comparable" cities across nations;
    c. Convenience samples, based for practical reasons in the areas at which the researchers were based;
    d. Comparable samples of "high-risk" populations whose principal gain would be to include an analytically-sufficient number of serious or chronic offenders.
    The best choice is far from obvious, being a function of both conceptual and practical considerations. The choice for the first venture will probably emerge from the concerns of the actual researchers involved.

4.3. Instrument Content

Although not necessarily mutually exclusive, three kinds of item domains were distinguished by the participants; core offense items that could be common across nations, items that reflected "problem" or "deviant" behaviors that also are common across nations but are treated differently with respect to their legal status, and nation-specific items reflecting specific emphases, peculiarities of legal focus, or unique opportunities of a given region. The issue here is not so much the inclusion of the three types, given the limits of instrument length, but the commonly acceptable determination of each and the weight to be given to each. Cross-national comparisons require a sufficient number of common, core items; national relevance requires sufficient numbers of non-core items both for relevance to a national body of knowledge and as part of the "sales pitch" for national funding.

4.4. One Domain or Many

The development of a single, common instrument necessarily raises questions about the construct(s) being measured. Whether there is a single or comprehensive construct underlying the items of the instrument (as implied by the construct of "criminality" or "proneness to offend") has implications for the number and breadth of items to be included. A multiple-construct assumption makes common instrumentation considerably more difficult. Further, participants were not agreed fully on the _fact_ of offense versatility (the evidence clearly favors it), or its implications for measuring different categories of offenses, or the unidimensionality of such measurement, or on the implications for the one-versus-multiple construct assumption of a unidimensional scale (i.e., isomorphism between construct and instrument).

The preceding sentence is a compact statement of a very complex set of measurement issues. The Dickes paper in this volume speaks very directly to them and is worthy of the reader's attention. Resolutions will probably come less from continuing statements of belief than from further empirical research.

4.5. Seriousness Measurement

Beyond the more technical issue of the _processes_ of measuring offense seriousness noted in some of the papers in this volume, participants were not of one mind about the relative weight which _should_ be given to the common minor legal infractions and the less common major crimes. Past self-report measures have been widely criticized for containing proportionately too many minor offense items, yet minor offenses are by far the most common. To omit or limit them could distort the reality of delinquent behavior.

On the other hand, some measures have been criticized for an overemphasis on serious offenses which are relatively uncommon. Yet to avoid the most serious offenses because of their low prevalence can yield non-relevance to criminal justice policy and practice as well as public concern, since these are oriented toward the major felony end of the distribution.

So far, researcher interest and measurement practicalities have had more influence on item inclusion than has a conceptual analysis of the issues at hand. Workshop participants noted the interrelationship of this concern with that of the underlying construct (see above) and incident versus offense-based measurement (see below). Further dialogue clearly is needed.

4.6. Incident and Offense-Based Measures

A common exercise in self-report research is to compare self-reported offending with official reports of the same behaviors, where available. Yet a court "case" or a police "investigation" may include as a single unit a single offense behavior, or multiple "counts" of that particular behavior in a single event (e.g., assault on several people), or several offense types in a single event (e.g., assault, carrying a concealed weapon, robbery), or several events tied by a single victim (e.g., a kidnapping episode) or tied by an offense pattern (e.g., serial murders with victims' bodies discovered together; monthly embezzlements from the same employer). Obviously, self-reported offenses recorded in patterns different from their counterparts in official records can cause analytic problems.

Workshop participants were concerned not only about this comparison problem, but also with the question of what is the conceptually "proper" unit of analysis -- offense counts, incidents, patterns. Discussion revolved around appropriate "counting rules," but consensus on measurement decisions was not achieved. The use of follow-up questions as described by Elliott was seen as one approach to dealing with the different units of analysis.

4.7. Follow-Up Questions

The early self-report studies contained simple items started by "Have you ever --?" and "How many times...?" Further information was not sought. Currently, the best measures have achieved greater validity by using a series of follow-up questions to each or to selected items. Typically, the follow-ups seek information on the content of the admitted offense such as the setting (home, school, street), co-offenders (their number, roles in the event), and their quality (monetary value of items stolen, damage to property, level of injury to victims), and so on. Just which categories of follow-up are of most value was disputed by the participants. There was also discussion of which offenses should receive the follow-up (the most recent, the last three, the first of admitted thefts, for example).

Finally, given the limited attention span of respondents, it was recognized that the number of follow-ups could reduce the number of offenses included in the measure (and vice versa). It was suggested, in addition, that in longitudinal studies the respondents will learn to anticipate follow-up questions and therefore under-report their offense behavior in order to avoid follow-ups. The Thornberry paper looks at this issue and finds the evidence equivocal at best.

4.8. Genders: One or Two

Criminological research typically omits concern for female offenders because they are far less common, commit less serious offenses on the average, and (reportedly) are of less interest to a research community made up predominantly of male researchers. There is as well the issue of efficiency; limited resources are best targetted at the higher risk group, male respondents.

Workshop participants were not in agreement on the importance of the inclusion of female respondents. Discussion of the issue was not so much conceptual as it was practical -- females constitute inefficient research targets. While it was pointed out that understanding differences in female offending illuminates the meaning of male offending, the fact is (at least as observed by this writer) that positions on this topic were principally related to participant gender. Female participants almost uniformly upheld the importance of including female respondents; male participants were predominantly (although not uniformly) among the skeptics.

4.9. Longitudinal vs. Cross-Sectional Paradigms

The structure of the workshop clearly favored the support of prospective longitudinal models of research. No apology for this structure is offered here. Nonetheless, some participants who were particularly oriented toward comparative descriptive goals were concerned that the complications and expense of longitudinal models of research could seriously interfere with the progress of cross-national projects. Such projects can be adequately served by cross-sectional designs, even repeated ones. Participants more interested in theory-testing and program or policy evaluation understandably favored the longitudinal paradigm. While the disagreement was quite mild, and in no way reflective of the vehemence to be found in the current criminological literature, it did represent a diversity of viewpoint that can affect future endeavors.

5. DISCUSSANTS' CONCERNS

Workshop participants were almost all adherents of the self-report approach to crime measurement. It seemed appropriate therefore to include scholars who might be skeptical about the process and the workshop discussions and papers. Albert J. Reiss, Jr. from the U.S. and Carl-Gunnar Janson from Sweden were invited to serve as critics because both were acknowledged senior scholars who had consistently expressed reservations in the past about the value of self-report methods. Some of the questions they raised were not raised by the participants and are therefore noted here as additional cautions to the reader.

Janson included several specific concerns. For instance, he noted that measurement validity is a function of the criterion used. In some countries -- most notably the Scandinavian group -- official records provide a more reliable criterion than in many others. Non-comparable

criteria will lead to non-comparable validity estimates of a common
instrument used in different settings.

Janson also expressed concern over the way the "open" or non-
truncated response frequencies are scored and interpreted. The meaning assigned to seemingly equal intervals such as 0 to 2 thefts and 10
to 12 thefts should not be assumed to be the same. Then, in response
to work group reports, he questioned as well the utility of biographical material from the respondents. Expanding on this latter point,
Janson reminded participants that delinquency or crime self-reports
constitute a memory retrieval process. There is an extant relevant
literature on this, and Janson offered a number of examples, suggesting
that the developers of the self-report method had paid too little attention to this literature.

Finally, Janson questioned the weight given to longitudinal problems in the workshop precedings. Variables are even more variable over
repeated waves of questioning in many cases, raising problems of fair
comparisons. In other cases they are so stable that repeated measures
seem redundant. The only major justification for the longitudinal
emphasis, Janson suggested, is to study causal relationships rather
than derive descriptive cross-national comparisons, yet the workshop
discussions seemed more geared toward the latter.

To complicate matters, Reiss followed this by questioning the
value of the cross-national description; how would one explain the
differences found? What national-level variables could be introduced,
such as moral values, and conformity levels? What would one make of
inter-individual variation across countries? What would one make of
within-country versus between-country variation? In short, Reiss questioned what he saw as an atheoretical bias in the concern with cross-
national comparisons.

In response to work group comments suggesting the technical superiority of requiring greater specificity of item content (e.g., theft of
guns, or knives, or bicycles or petrol), Reiss felt that the reported
higher number of responses obtained via specific items would be unequally comparable across nations. The reason is that nations are not equal
in their criminal opportunities (bicycles in Holland, TV sets in the
U.S., and so on). Other matters could similarly yield non-comparability, Reiss noted, because of cross-national differences, interview vs.
questionnaire methods, record checks prior to interviews for lead-in
questions, level of police activity, and so on.

Reiss added his own trepidation about longitudinal models to those
of Janson. An additional problem he noted was that "we can't ask the
world to stand still for us" as we add subsequent waves or attempt
experimental interventions. It takes a sooth-sayer researcher to build
in all the questions and variables needed to account for intervening
events such as population shifts, economic swings, or changes in arrest
practices and policies.

Finally, Reiss supported the Janson comments on the memory and
cognitive processes in self-report responses; he used the term, "the
social construction of the recalled event," using the example of the
"new" offense called date rape. The meanings attached by the respondent to his self-reports may, unknown to us, not correspond to the

meanings assigned by the researchers.

6. TOWARD FUTURE COMPARATIVE RESEARCH

I mentioned earlier the enthusiasm for cooperative research which developed rapidly during the workshop. This was a spontaneous movement which took the workshop leadership quite by surprise. By the third evening, it led to a separate caucus of participants from twelve countries who gathered to harness and find direction for the enthusiasm. Principal responsibility for the next steps was taken by staff of the W.O.D.C. (Research and Documentation Center, Dutch Ministry of Justice), and the following initial report was sent within a week to the participants:

> Follow-up: Advanced Research Workshop on Self-Report
> Methodology 27 - 30/6 1988

- Some participants were convinced that much more research has to be done before we can even think of conducting comparative studies among several countries. Comparative research methodology would have to be improved, and some essential problems mentioned in Delbert Elliott's presentation and by some of the work-groups would have to be solved first.
- Although this may be essentially the right thing to do, some of us felt that we should exploit the interest and enthusiasm of so many participants of this workshop and try to achieve progress in a somewhat quicker way. They felt as
- I think - Paul Dickes has said, that "cooperative efforts in this respect in different countries will accelerate scientific development." Moreover, there was a feeling that without some very concrete follow-up, everybody would return to his country, pick up all the work that has been piling up on one's desk and slowly forget about the workshop.
- All this led to a meeting on Wednesday evening, June 29, of representatives of 12 countries discussing the possibility of conducting some small-scale pilot studies, and this is what has been decided (or proposed) so far:

1) A Consortium for comparative self-report research would be formed. This Consortium could be joined by any interested country. Its first task would be to make a prospectus in which the rationale, justification and objectives of comparative self-report research is exposed and which will contain a global design of such a comparative study.

2) The coordination needed for the Consortium and the comparative study will -- for the time being -- be taken care of by the WODC.

3)   Every participating country should form a local commit-
        tee of researchers interested in the development of
        self-report research, who will consult each other and
        eventually collaborate. The committee will be organized
        by a local coordinator.

4)   In order to reduce costs, preparatory meetings will be
        attended only by the local coordinators. At some later
        date -- for example in a year or three, four, when we
        have some preliminary results -- we could consider organ-
        izing a similar workshop as the one we have attended
        just now.

5)   A preliminary meeting will be held in October/November
        1988. During this meeting a prospectus will be designed
        containing the justification, objectives and global
        design of the study. In this meeting, the research
        agenda will be set and major decisions will be made
        concerning such essentials as sampling, age-limits,
        administration procedures, scale of the study, costs,
        funding possibilities and institutes under- taking the
        study.
        In preparation of this meeting the local coordinators
        should prepare a working paper summarizing the main
        methodological aspects -- such as sampling, sampling
        method, administration procedures, age limits, validity
        and reliability tests, etc. -- of the self-report stud-
        ies in their respective countries. The propectus will
        be sent to possibly interested institutes all over the
        world and will be used to approach agencies and/or min-
        istries for funding the research.

6)   A second meeting will be necessary in spring 1989, to
        finalize the instrument and take last decisions before
        starting the study.

7)   Efforts will be made to start the study end 1989.

   The important organizational points in the above would seem to be
the following:
        1. lodging initial organizational responsibility in a single,
        stable organization (W.O.D.C.);
        2. acceptance of a voluntary coordinating role by one named indi-
        vidual in each participating country;
        3. specification of sequential steps, as in points 3, 4, and 5
        above;
        4. promise of future meetings as a further consolidation of the
        initial relationships established at the workshop;
        5. settling on the Consortium as a vehicle for coordination -- not
        a formal organization capable of dampening individual interest or
        employing too much centralization without formal allocation of

resources, yet more than a mere fellowship of like-minded individuals whose common interests would be dissipated by distance and national boundaries.

Obviously it is too early at this writing (late 1988) to know what will come of the Consortium. It is interesting to note, nonetheless, that a second round of activity has been initiated. The W.O.D.C. has distributed to the national coordinators a series of four documents:

1. a "concept proposal" for a brochure describing the need for a comparative self-report investigation. This would be the initial "sales pitch" to facilitate discussion with funding sources;

2. a brief proposal for a pilot study, using a set of self-report items that emerged with some consensus from the workshop. Agreements on the specifics of the study are to be obtained at a small meeting of the national coordinators tentatively scheduled for the end of 1988;

3. a four-page information sheet for use by national coordinators to describe specific recent self-report studies in their countries -- definitions, sampling procedures, psychometric properties of the instrument -- for up to ten studies in each country. This would constitute the beginnings of a carefully focussed archive of the most current work;

4. a preliminary set of 21 core items, with five follow-up questions, to serve as a point of departure of coordinators' discussions.

All of this, I hasten to repeat, has been undertaken independently by a number of the workshop participants. It seems to this writer to represent a good deal more than mere enthusiasm. There is in these materials a clear sense of organization and planning which at the time of organizing the workshop would have seemed like pure fantasy. The participants have created their own "master plan," and the mechanisms for its implementation. Thus this volume of papers may be the first product of several to emerge from the workshop; fantasy may become reality.

REFERENCES

Antilla, I: Recorded and unrecorded crime. In Antilla, I (ed.), Unrecorded criminality in Finland. Helsinki: Kriminologinene tutkimuslaitos, 1966.

Bachman, J.G., O'Malley, PM, & Johnston, J: Adolescence to adulthood: Change and stability in the lives of young men. In Youth in transition, Volume 6. Ann Arbor: Institute for Social Research, 1978.

Christie, N, Andenaes, J, & Skerbekk, S: A study of self-reported crime. In Scandinavian studies in criminology, Vol. 1, pp. 86ff. Oslo: Universitetforlaget, 1965.

Elliott, D, Huizinga, D, & Morse, B: Self-reported violent offending. Journal of Interpersonal Violence, 1987, 1:472-514.

Gold, M, & Reimer, DJ: Changing patterns of delinquent behavior among Americans 13-16 years old - 1972. Crime and Delinquency Literature, 1975, 7:483-517.

Greve, V: Our non-deviant criminals. In Scandinavian studies in criminology, Vol. 5, pp. 99-106. Oslo: Universitetforlaget, 1974.

438

Hauge, R: Definition and scope of comparative studies in crime trends, including a review of work carried out since 1945. In Council of Europe (Ed.), <u>Trends in crime: Comparative studies and technical problems</u>, pp. 25-49. Strasbourg: Council of Europe, 1983.

Hindelang, MJ, Hirschi, T, & Weiss, JG: <u>Measuring delinquency</u>. Beverly Hills: Sage Publications, 1981.

Kohn, ML: Cross-national research as an analytic strategy. <u>American Sociological Review</u>, 1987, 52:713-731.